Greg Rucka writer
Klaus Janson artist and original covers
Steve Buccellato colorist
Clem Robins letterer
Batman created by **Bob Kane**

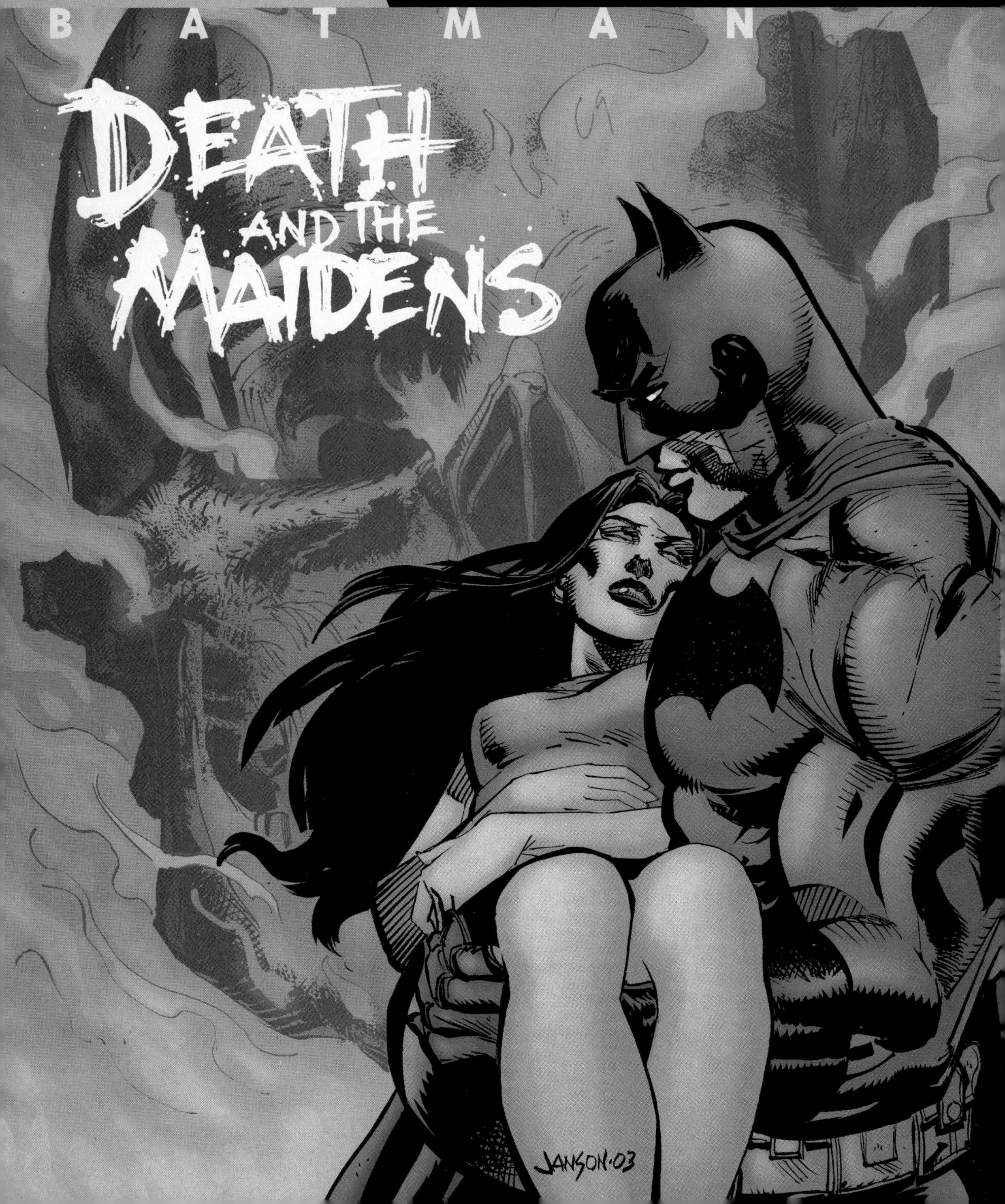
BATMAN
DEATH AND THE MAIDENS
JANSON·03

BATMAN: DEATH & THE MAIDENS

Published by DC Comics. Cover, introduction and compilation copyright © 2004
DC Comics. All Rights Reserved.

Originally published in single magazine form in BATMAN: DEATH & THE MAIDENS 1-9,
DETECTIVE COMICS 783. Copyright © 2003, 2004 DC Comics. All Rights Reserved.
All characters, their distinctive likenesses and related elements featured in this publication
are trademarks of DC Comics. The stories, characters and incidents featured in this publica-
tion are entirely fictional. DC Comics does not read or accept unsolicited submissions of
ideas, stories or artwork.
DC Comics, 1700 Broadway, New York, NY 10019. A Warner Bros. Entertainment
Company. Printed in Canada. First Printing. ISBN: 1-4012-0234-9

Cover illustration by Klaus Janson

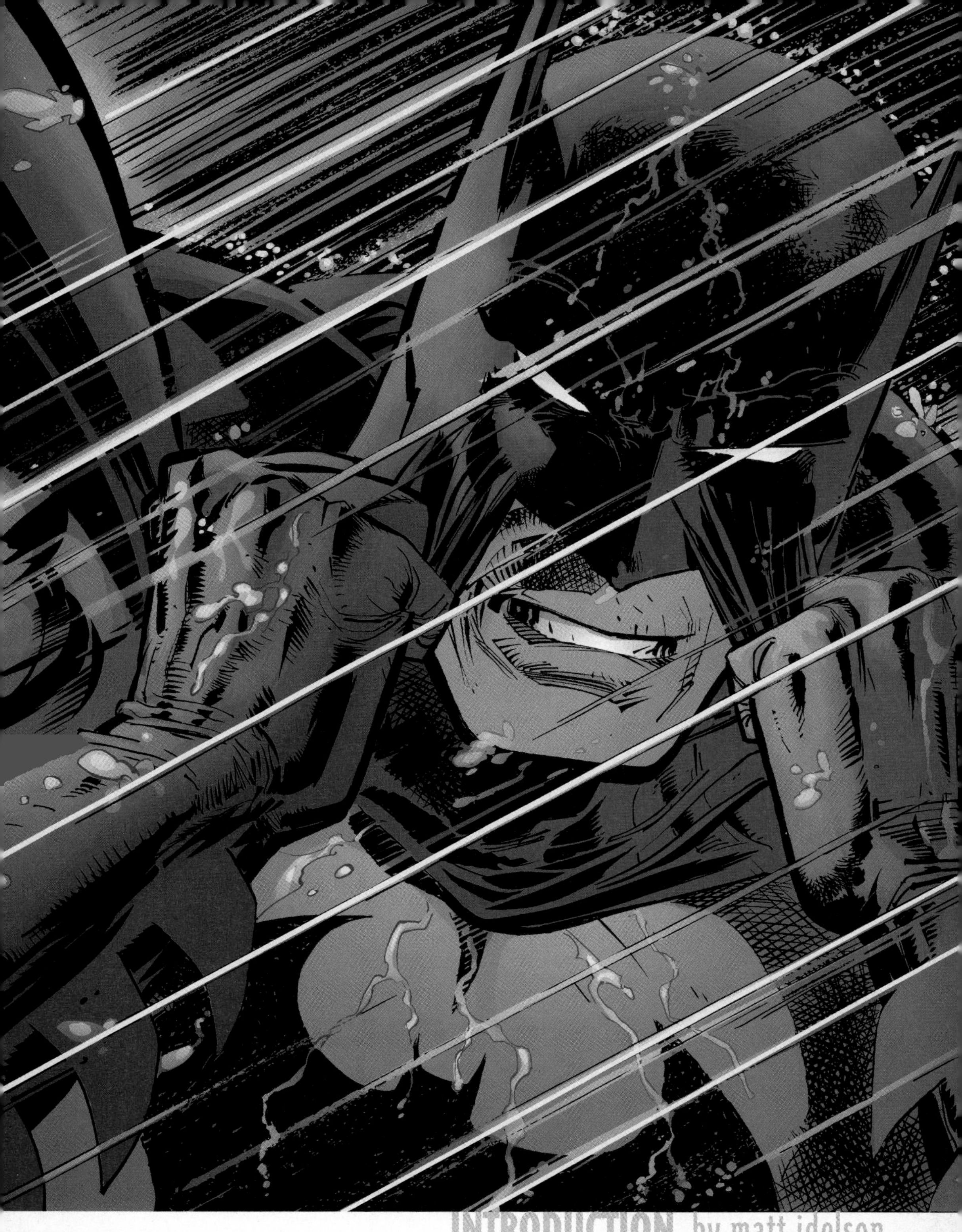

INTRODUCTION by matt idelson

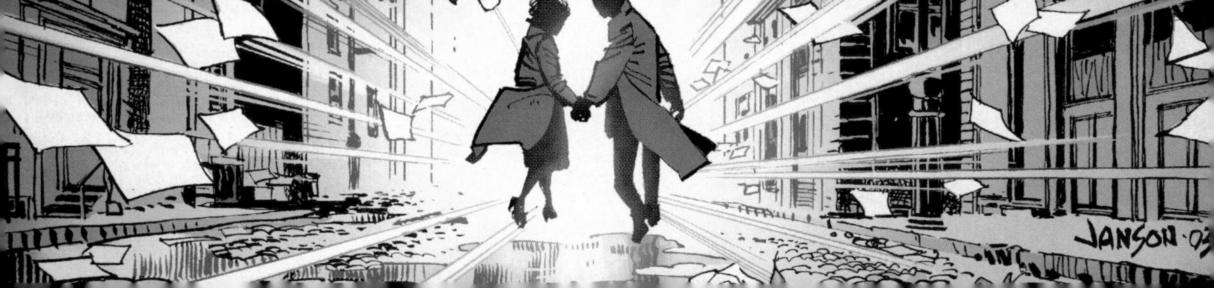
JANSON

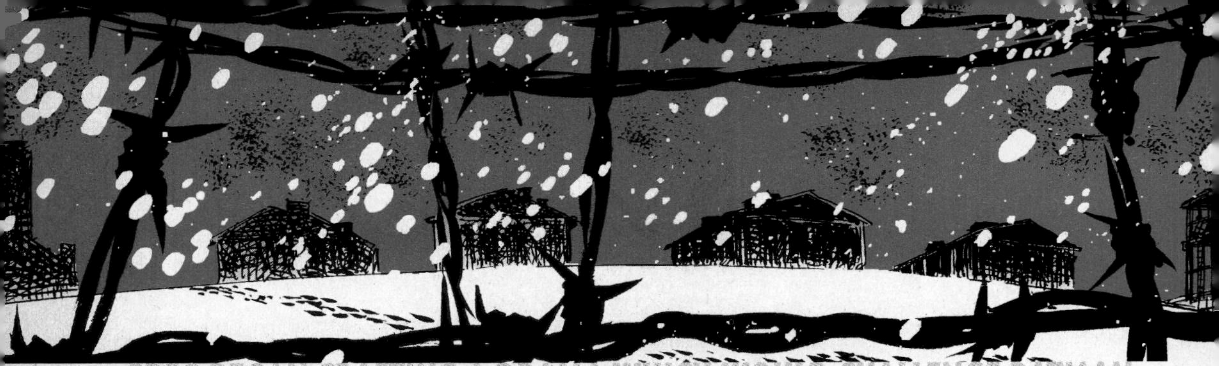

GREG BEGAN CRAFTING A DRAMA WHICH WOULD CHALLENGE BATMAN FIRST MENTALLY, THEN EMOTIONALLY, AND ULTIMATELY PHYSICALLY.

Back in the distant past of 1998, Klaus Janson and I were talking about a new project that he could possibly work on. "I want it to be about Batman," he said, "and I want it to be special! Oh, and I want Greg Rucka to write it!" And he said it exactly like that, too, with his little hands balled up into little fists. You should have seen it.

With no choice in the matter, I approached Greg (who also likes to ball his somewhat larger hands into fists). All we had to offer him was the idea that Bruce would be paid a visit by his mother, one of the most underdeveloped, yet idealized, characters in comics (aside from her killer, but that's another story). Mom would be most displeased with Bruce's career path and wouldn't make any bones about it. Add a little liquid Greg and, presto! Instant story, right? Wrong.

This was a tough one to crack, and I don't know how the heck Greg did it. But somewhere in that chaotic brain of his, Greg began crafting a drama which would challenge Batman first mentally, then emotionally, and ultimately physically. The story of Bruce's eternal-yet-vain quest for parental approval became a tale about heroism in the face of apathy. Now, if that sounds highfalutin', that's 'cause it is. Greg and Klaus wanted to do something important, something that would really get to the core of Batman and show us an element of him we'd never seen before in sixty years of publishing Batman stories. And I think they succeeded. Brilliantly.

Somewhere along the way, Ra's al Ghul became involved, much to the character's misfortune. But he made us pay for using him. Right up until the end. Ra's' role and machinations in this little morality play kept shifting. He's a shifty guy, even if his outfit *was* borrowed from Liberace.

Often regarded as Batman's ultimate foe, Ra's is one of those villains whose motivations aren't really all that terrible, it's just his methodology that could use some refining. Ra's recognized that the Earth was slowly dying under the burden of an oversized and uncaring population, and the only way to save it was to kill every person and start over. On the down side, Ra's was now hundreds of years old and starting to show his mileage. Since one of the themes of the story was about Bruce as the next generation of the Wayne line accepting his legacy for what it is instead of what he thought it should be, Greg felt that Ra's having an heir to his evil empire was in order. We could then present a contrast between Bruce's refusal to embrace his parents' intended legacy with Nyssa's inability to do the same, something that really hadn't been attempted before.

And so the pages began to roll in, and Klaus managed to do something I never thought possible: he topped himself. This was far and

KLAUS MANAGED TO DO SOMETHING I NEVER THOUGHT POSSIBLE: HE TOPPED HIMSELF.

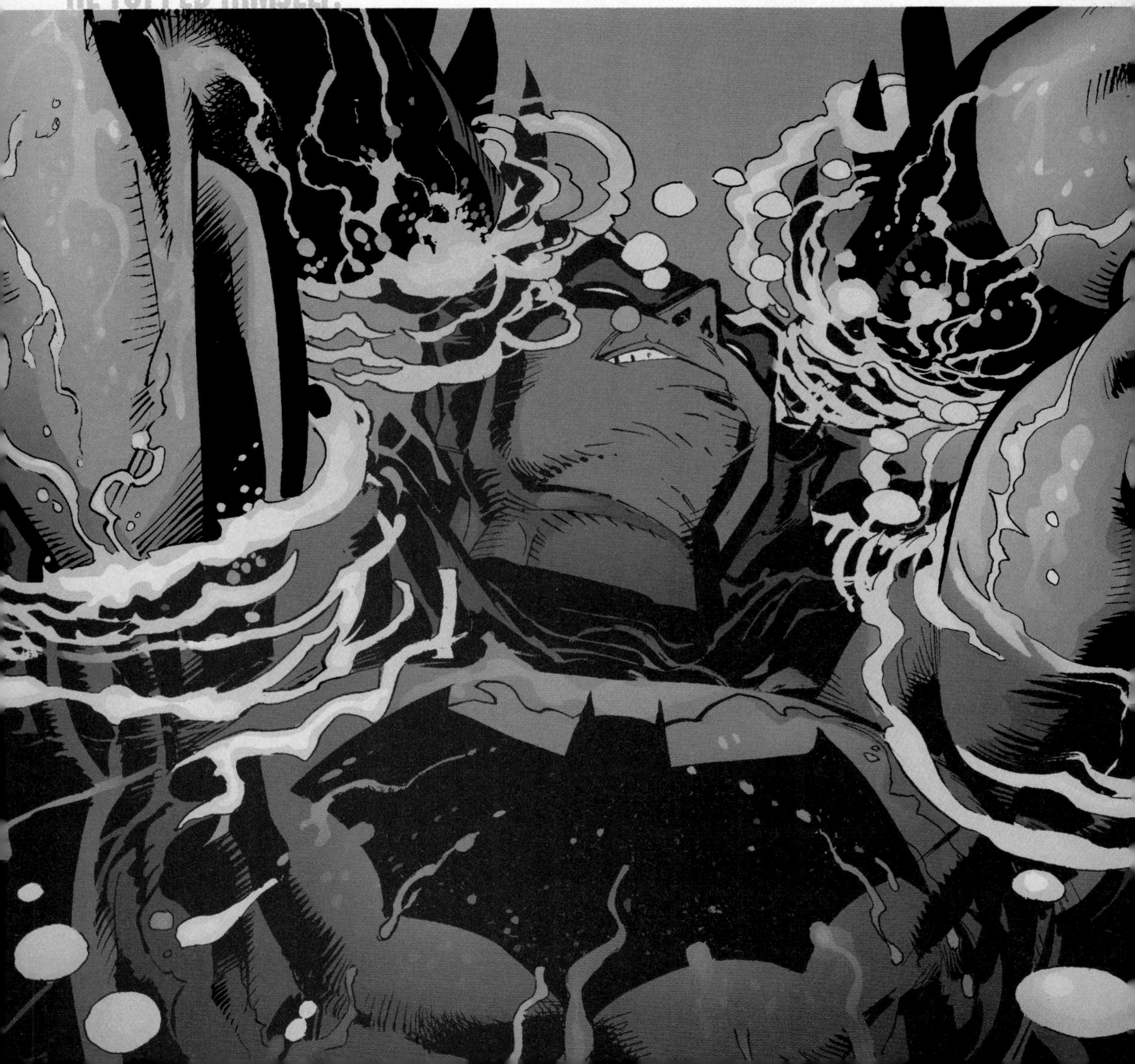

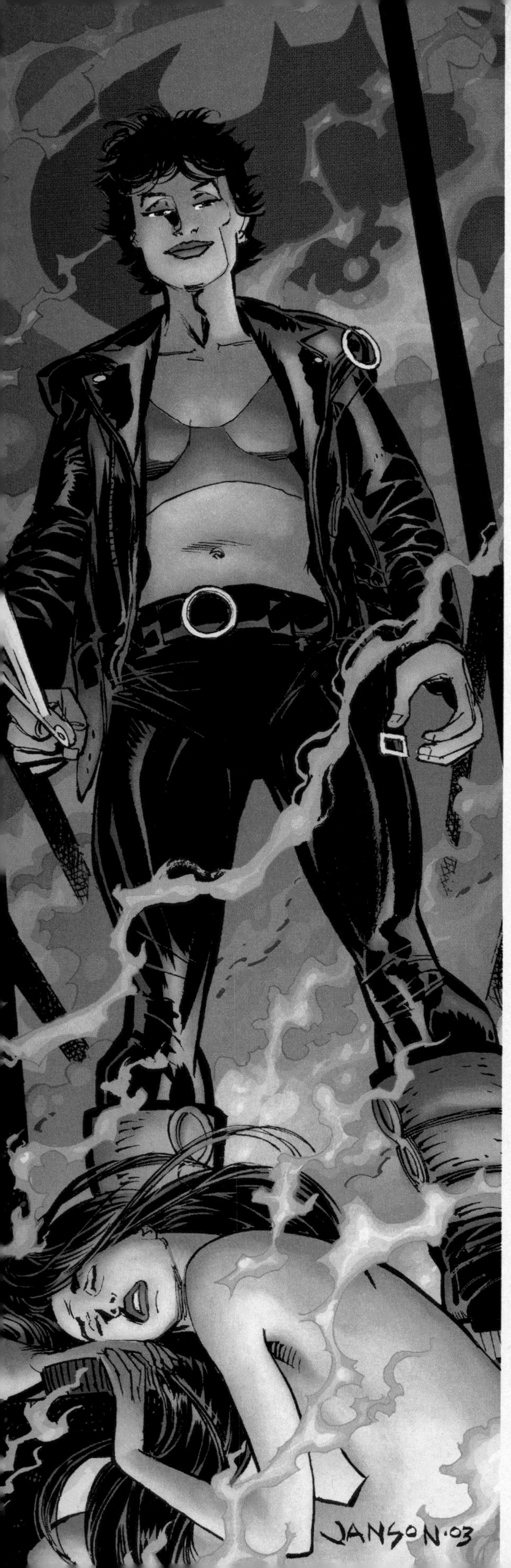
JANSON·03

away the best work I'd ever seen him do, and I'd seen him do a lot of amazing work. Klaus is a living legend in this industry, so for him to outdo himself was pretty incredible. This project was going to be the greatest! And then the "fun" began.

As the story continued to take shape, the very form of the project kept morphing. This story was quite different from anything we had tackled prior, and its nature demanded we change our format. From a hardcover, to a hardcover flip book, to a Prestige Format series until finally, a nine-part miniseries, we kept refocusing and refining how we wanted to present this story. We may even have toyed with printing the story on the side of a truck and driving it cross-country. It's hard to remember. While all this was happening, the book was actually being written and drawn, which led to one of the strangest story conferences I've ever attended.

Greg flew in from Portland, Klaus lumbered up from lower Manhattan, and my assistant Nachie Castro and I scurried over from our offices. And in a nicely furnished conference room, we laid out all the scenes that had been written and/or drawn thus far, mixing, matching, shuffling things around, while laying out the rest of the story. Usually our stories take us from point A to point B with lots of fun in the middle. This time we were jumping all over the place, taking a scene from issue three and

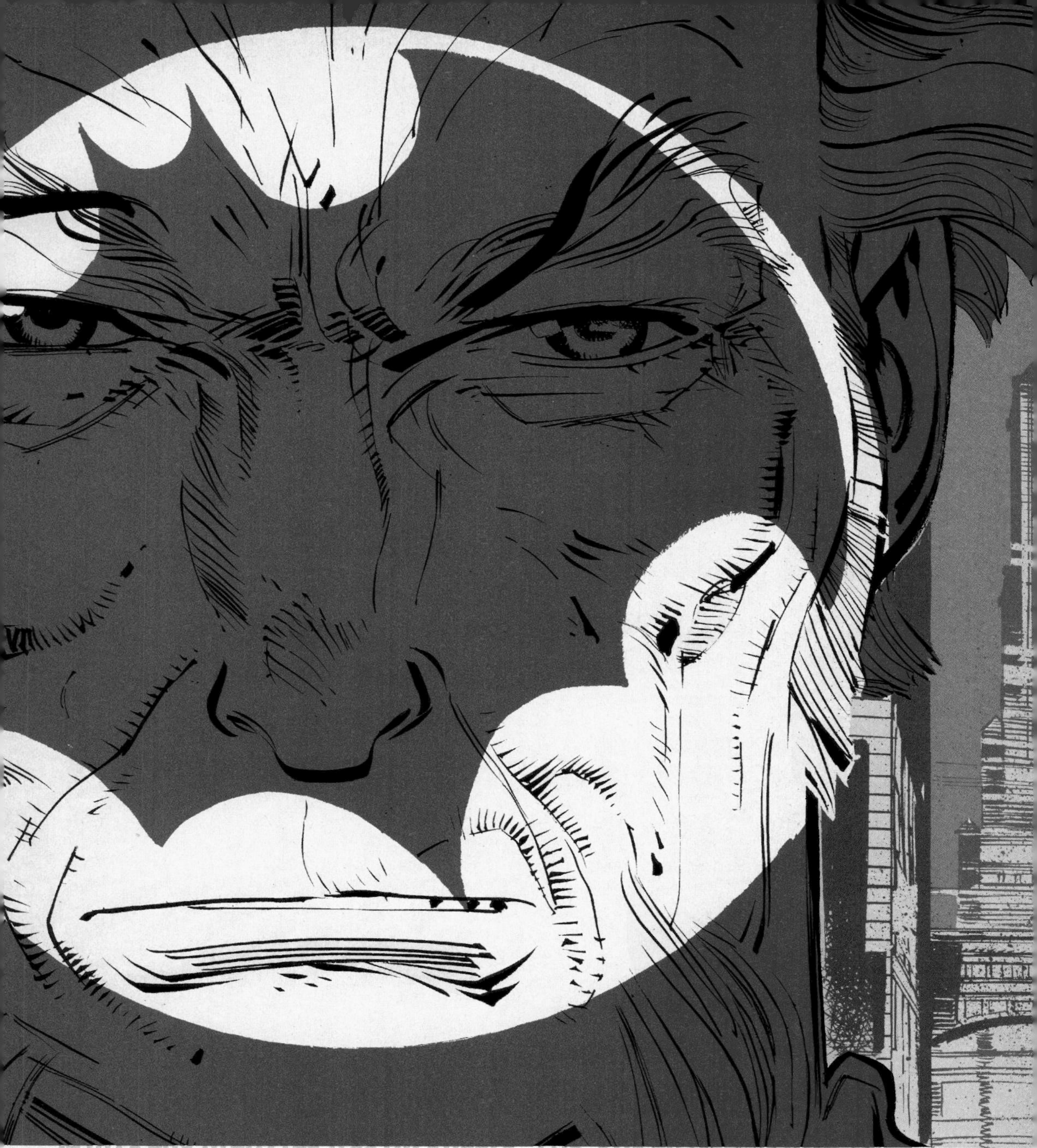

IT WAS THE ULTIMATE JIGSAW PUZZLE, AND ONE THAT, AGAINST ALL ODDS, CAME TOGETHER SEAMLESSLY.

moving it to issue one and so forth. It was the ultimate jigsaw puzzle, and one that, against all odds, came together seamlessly. In the process of this reconfiguring, certain scenes were rendered irrelevant or redundant, while the character of Nyssa changed so thoroughly that her rather dramatic introduction had to be totally changed. Thanks to the miracle of not throwing anything out, these excised scenes can be found at the back of this book.

As the light at the end of the tunnel began to come into view, two vital yet totally unherald-ed players came to the fore. Colorist Steve Buccellato brought a whole new dimension to Klaus's work, making it moodier when it was moody, more tense when it was tense. This wouldn't have been the same book without him. Or without Clem Robins, nice guy, terrific letterer, and dear, dear friend to the harried editor. And so a comic was born.

And all of that is a roundabout way of saying that you hold in your hands a story that is the product of great love, anxiety, indigestion, and more than a few moments of darkness and doubt. One that, hopefully, you'll find gives you new insight into Batman and his greatest foe, while also introducing a new villain who will vex Batman for the next sixty years of stories. Enjoy the ride!

— Matt Idelson

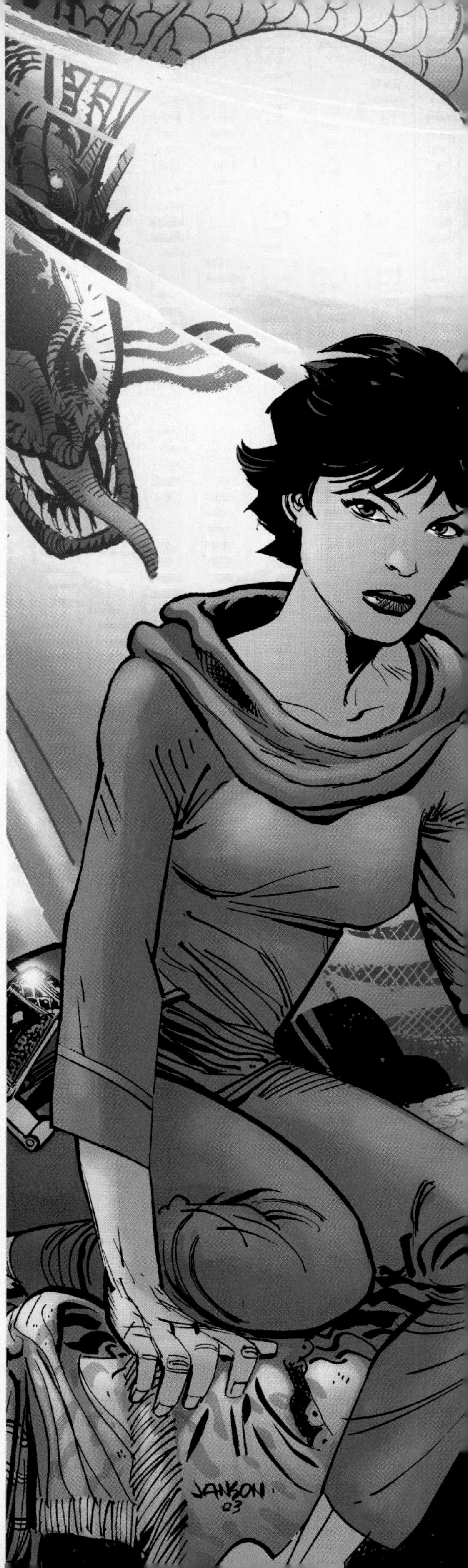
JANSON
03

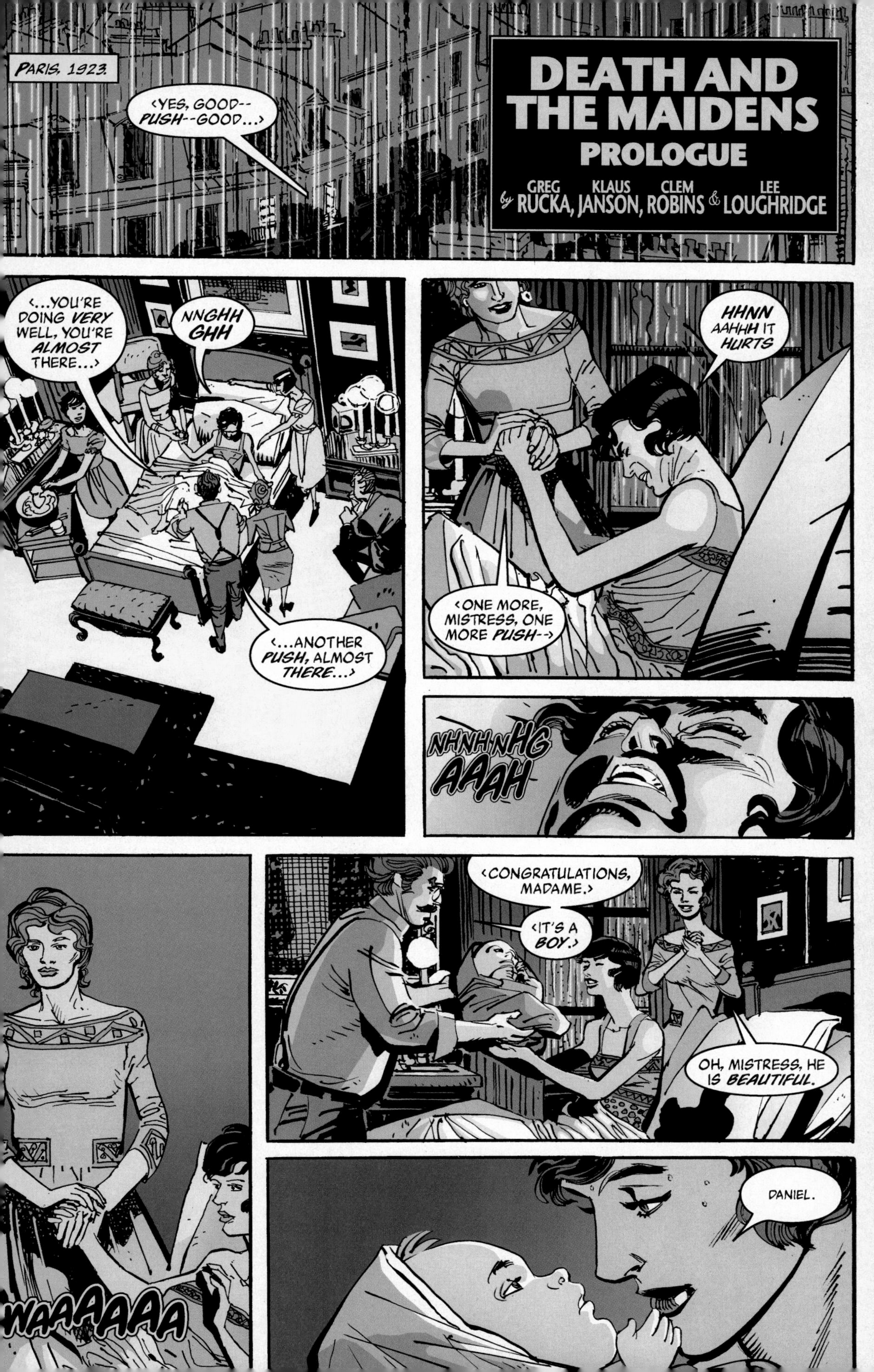
PARIS, 1923.
DEATH AND THE MAIDENS
PROLOGUE
by GREG RUCKA, KLAUS JANSON, CLEM ROBINS & LEE LOUGHRIDGE
‹YES, GOOD-- PUSH--GOOD...›
‹...YOU'RE DOING VERY WELL, YOU'RE ALMOST THERE...›
NNGHH GHH
‹...ANOTHER PUSH, ALMOST THERE...›
HHNN AAHHH IT HURTS
‹ONE MORE, MISTRESS, ONE MORE PUSH--›
NHNHNHG AAAH
WAAAAAAA
‹CONGRATULATIONS, MADAME.›
‹IT'S A BOY.›
OH, MISTRESS, HE IS BEAUTIFUL.
DANIEL.

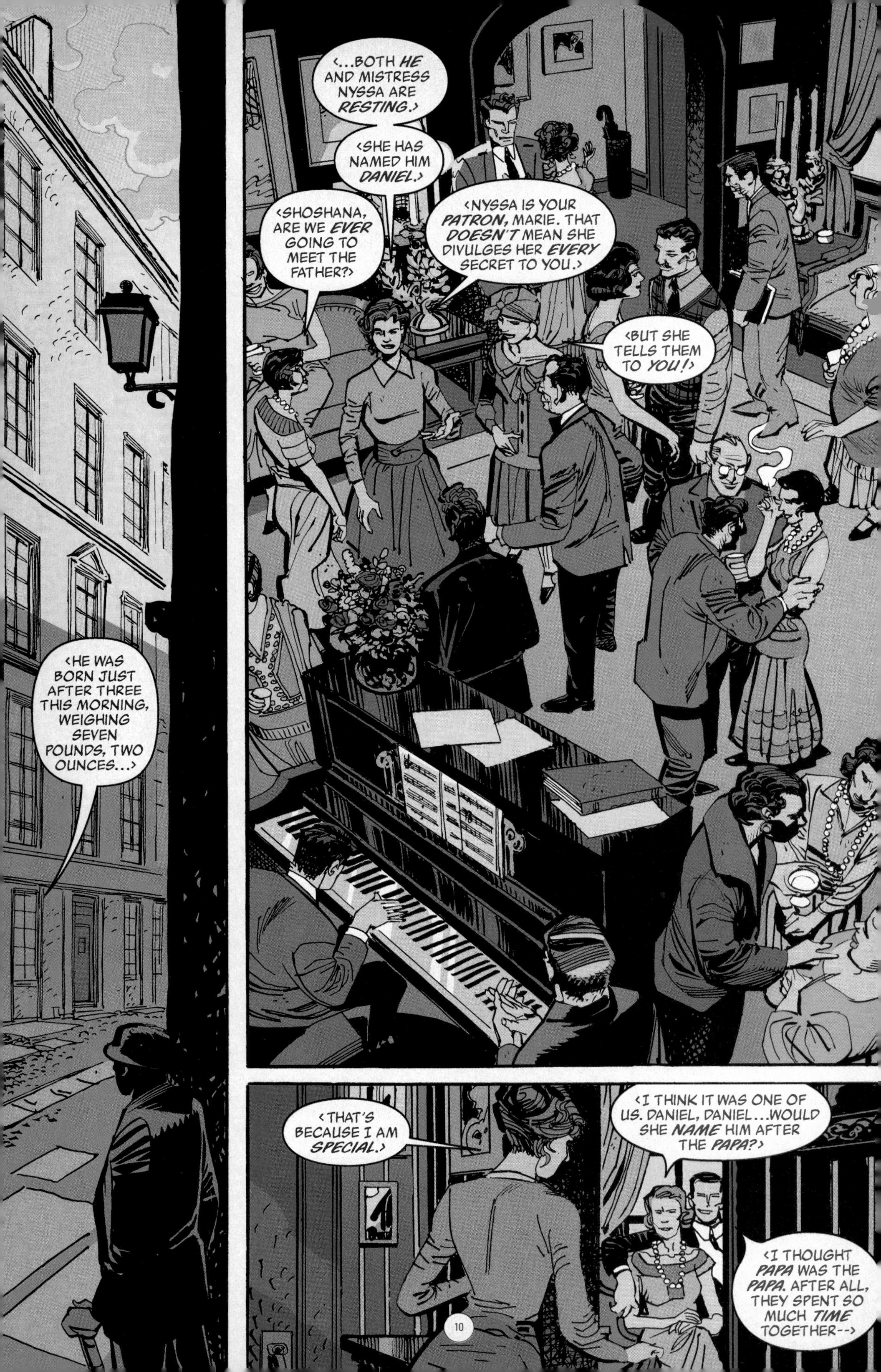

‹HE WAS BORN JUST AFTER THREE THIS MORNING, WEIGHING SEVEN POUNDS, TWO OUNCES...›
‹...BOTH HE AND MISTRESS NYSSA ARE RESTING.›
‹SHE HAS NAMED HIM DANIEL.›
‹SHOSHANA, ARE WE EVER GOING TO MEET THE FATHER?›
‹NYSSA IS YOUR PATRON, MARIE. THAT DOESN'T MEAN SHE DIVULGES HER EVERY SECRET TO YOU.›
‹BUT SHE TELLS THEM TO YOU!›
‹THAT'S BECAUSE I AM SPECIAL.›
‹I THINK IT WAS ONE OF US. DANIEL, DANIEL...WOULD SHE NAME HIM AFTER THE PAPA?›
‹I THOUGHT PAPA WAS THE PAPA. AFTER ALL, THEY SPENT SO MUCH TIME TOGETHER--›

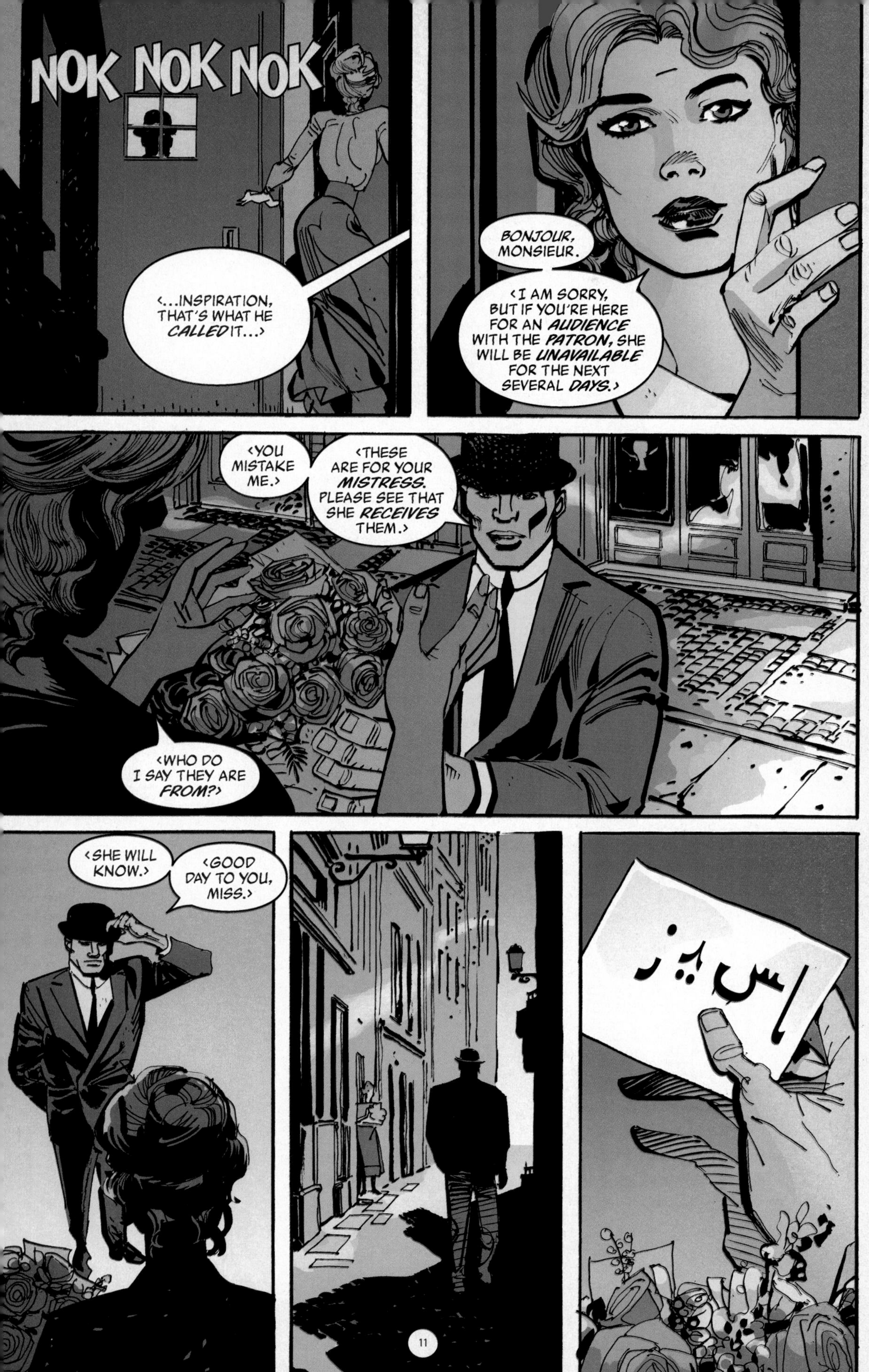
NOK NOK NOK
<...INSPIRATION, THAT'S WHAT HE CALLED IT...>
BONJOUR, MONSIEUR.
<I AM SORRY, BUT IF YOU'RE HERE FOR AN AUDIENCE WITH THE PATRON, SHE WILL BE UNAVAILABLE FOR THE NEXT SEVERAL DAYS.>
<YOU MISTAKE ME.>
<THESE ARE FOR YOUR MISTRESS. PLEASE SEE THAT SHE RECEIVES THEM.>
<WHO DO I SAY THEY ARE FROM?>
<SHE WILL KNOW.>
<GOOD DAY TO YOU, MISS.>

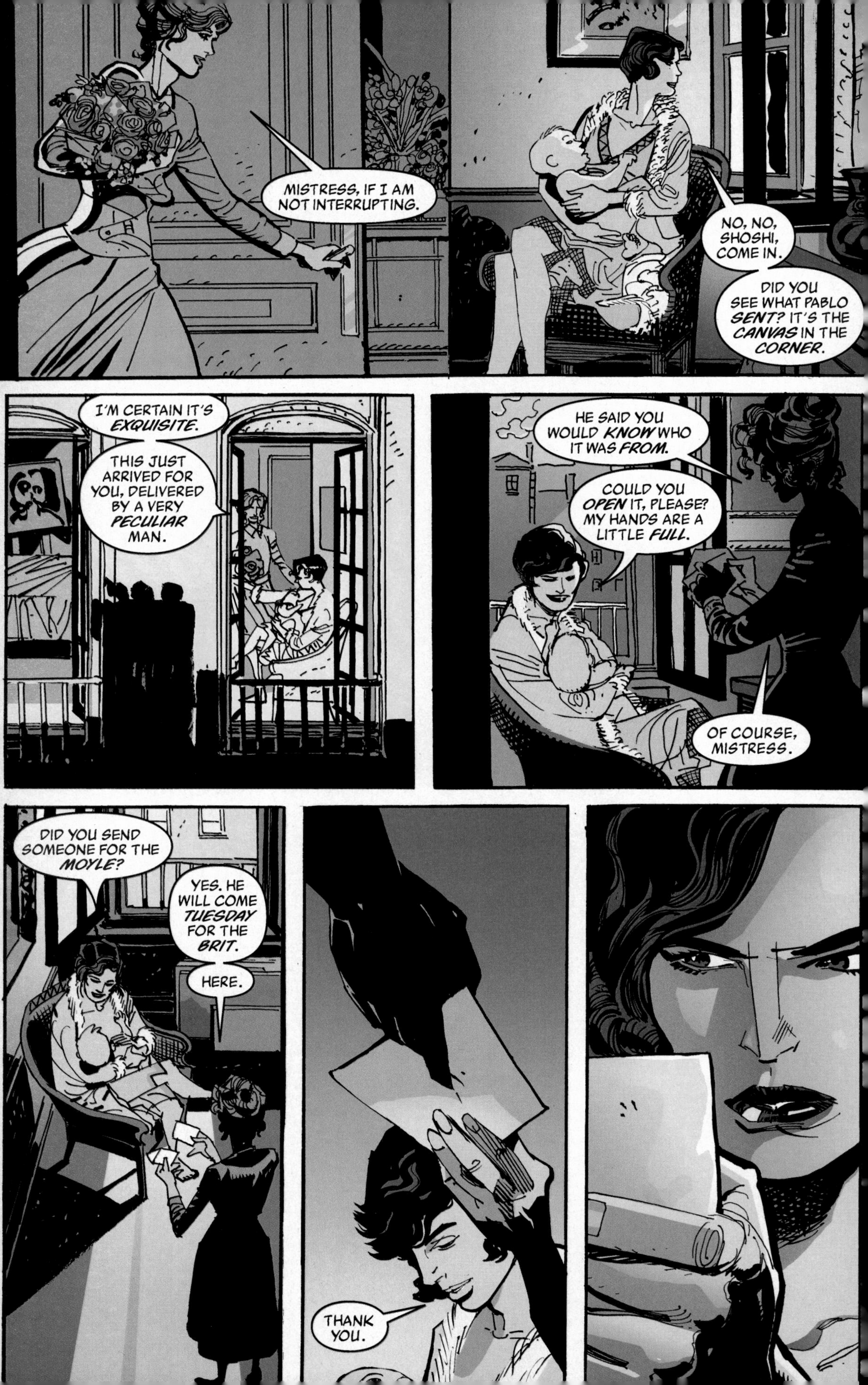
MISTRESS, IF I AM NOT INTERRUPTING.
NO, NO, SHOSHI, COME IN.
DID YOU SEE WHAT PABLO SENT? IT'S THE CANVAS IN THE CORNER.
I'M CERTAIN IT'S EXQUISITE.
THIS JUST ARRIVED FOR YOU, DELIVERED BY A VERY PECULIAR MAN.
HE SAID YOU WOULD KNOW WHO IT WAS FROM.
COULD YOU OPEN IT, PLEASE? MY HANDS ARE A LITTLE FULL.
OF COURSE, MISTRESS.
DID YOU SEND SOMEONE FOR THE MOYLE?
YES. HE WILL COME TUESDAY FOR THE BRIT.
HERE.
THANK YOU.

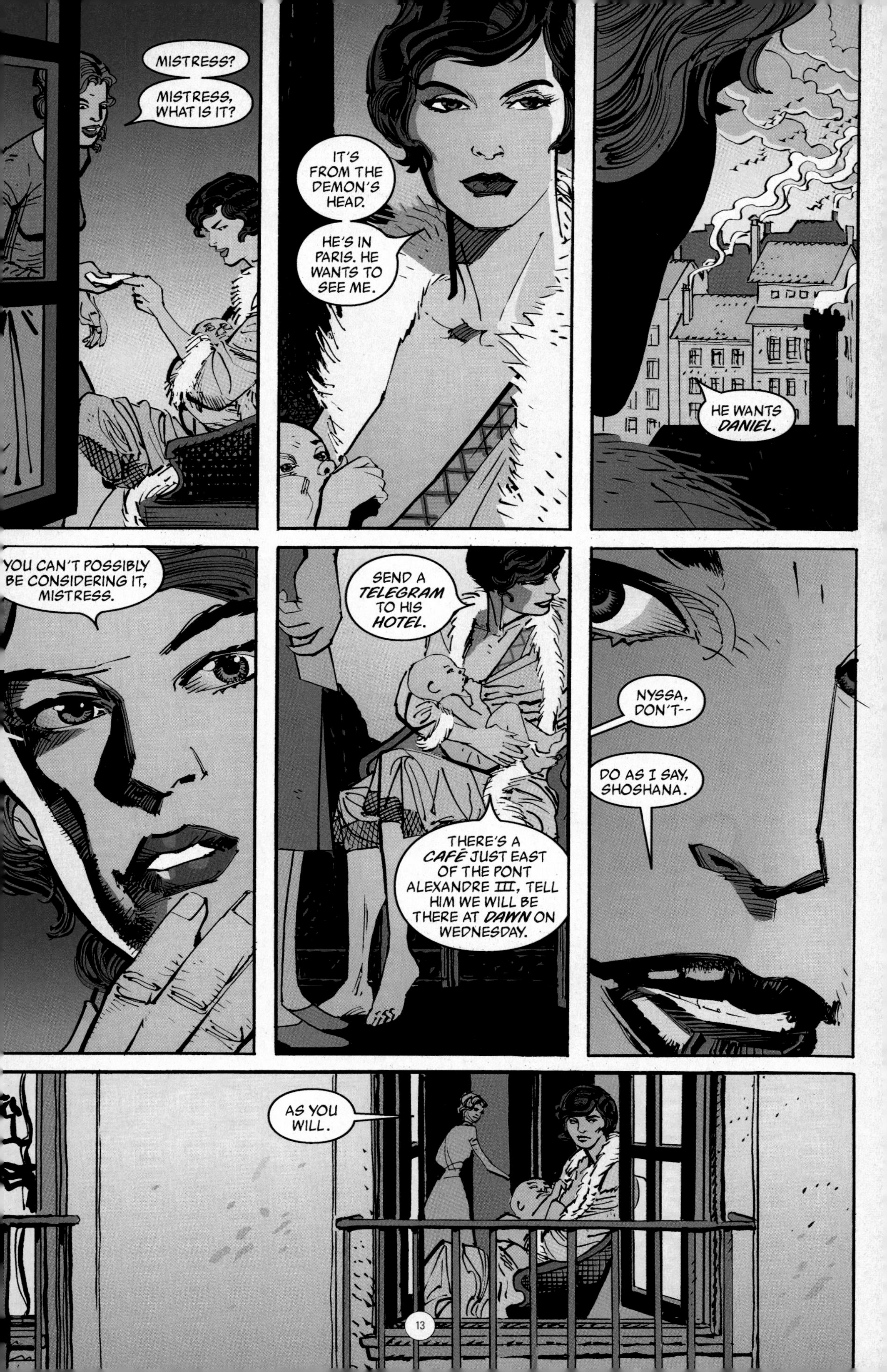
MISTRESS?
MISTRESS, WHAT IS IT?
IT'S FROM THE DEMON'S HEAD.
HE'S IN PARIS. HE WANTS TO SEE ME.
HE WANTS DANIEL.
YOU CAN'T POSSIBLY BE CONSIDERING IT, MISTRESS.
SEND A TELEGRAM TO HIS HOTEL.
THERE'S A CAFÉ JUST EAST OF THE PONT ALEXANDRE III, TELL HIM WE WILL BE THERE AT DAWN ON WEDNESDAY.
NYSSA, DON'T--
DO AS I SAY, SHOSHANA.
AS YOU WILL.

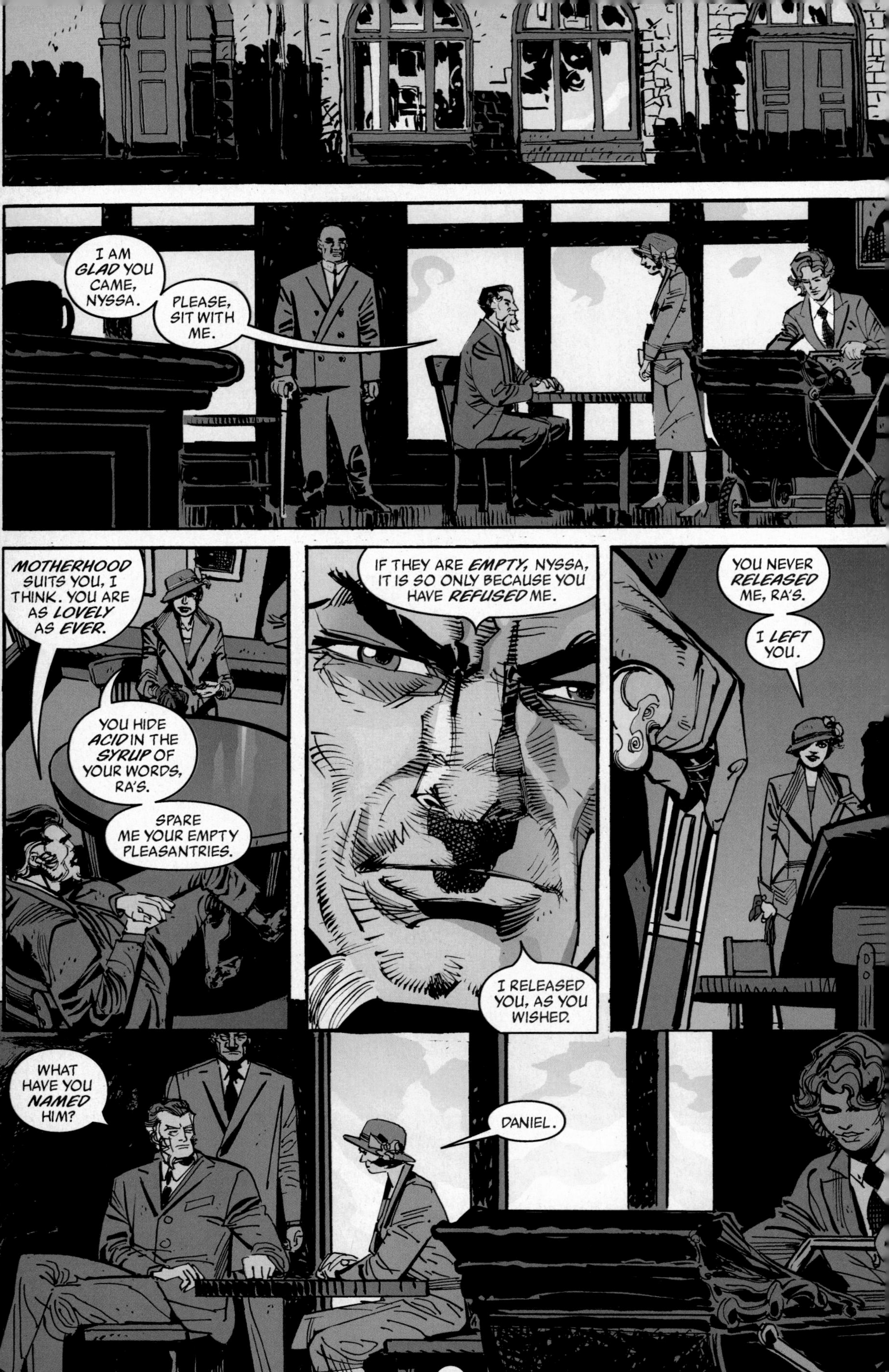
I AM GLAD YOU CAME, NYSSA.
PLEASE, SIT WITH ME.
MOTHERHOOD SUITS YOU, I THINK. YOU ARE AS LOVELY AS EVER.
YOU HIDE ACID IN THE SYRUP OF YOUR WORDS, RA'S.
SPARE ME YOUR EMPTY PLEASANTRIES.
IF THEY ARE EMPTY, NYSSA, IT IS SO ONLY BECAUSE YOU HAVE REFUSED ME.
I RELEASED YOU, AS YOU WISHED.
YOU NEVER RELEASED ME, RA'S.
I LEFT YOU.
WHAT HAVE YOU NAMED HIM?
DANIEL.

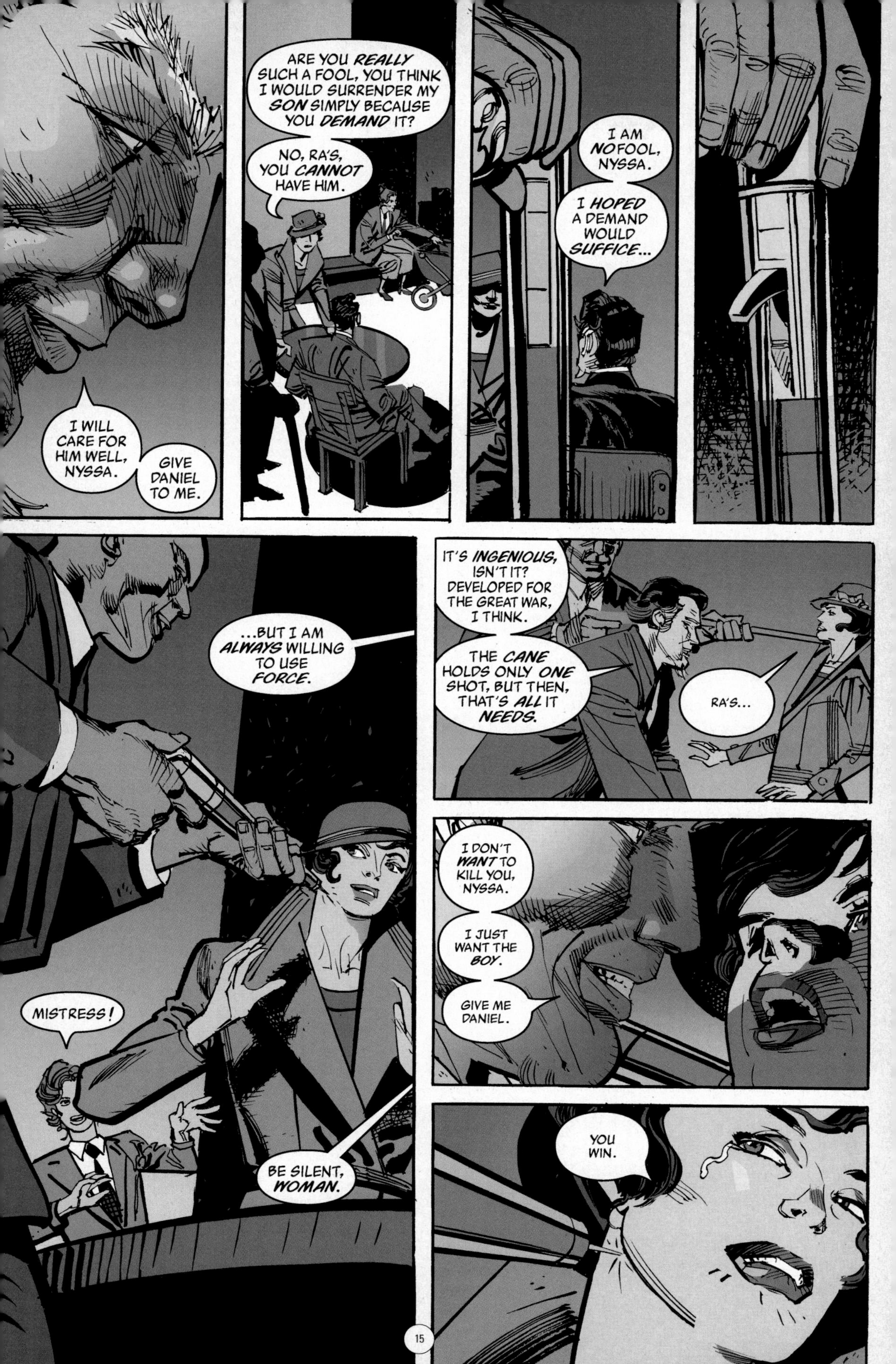
I WILL CARE FOR HIM WELL, NYSSA.
GIVE DANIEL TO ME.
ARE YOU REALLY SUCH A FOOL, YOU THINK I WOULD SURRENDER MY SON SIMPLY BECAUSE YOU DEMAND IT?
NO, RA'S, YOU CANNOT HAVE HIM.
I AM NO FOOL, NYSSA.
I HOPED A DEMAND WOULD SUFFICE...
...BUT I AM ALWAYS WILLING TO USE FORCE.
MISTRESS!
BE SILENT, WOMAN.
IT'S INGENIOUS, ISN'T IT? DEVELOPED FOR THE GREAT WAR, I THINK.
THE CANE HOLDS ONLY ONE SHOT, BUT THEN, THAT'S ALL IT NEEDS.
RA'S...
I DON'T WANT TO KILL YOU, NYSSA.
I JUST WANT THE BOY.
GIVE ME DANIEL.
YOU WIN.

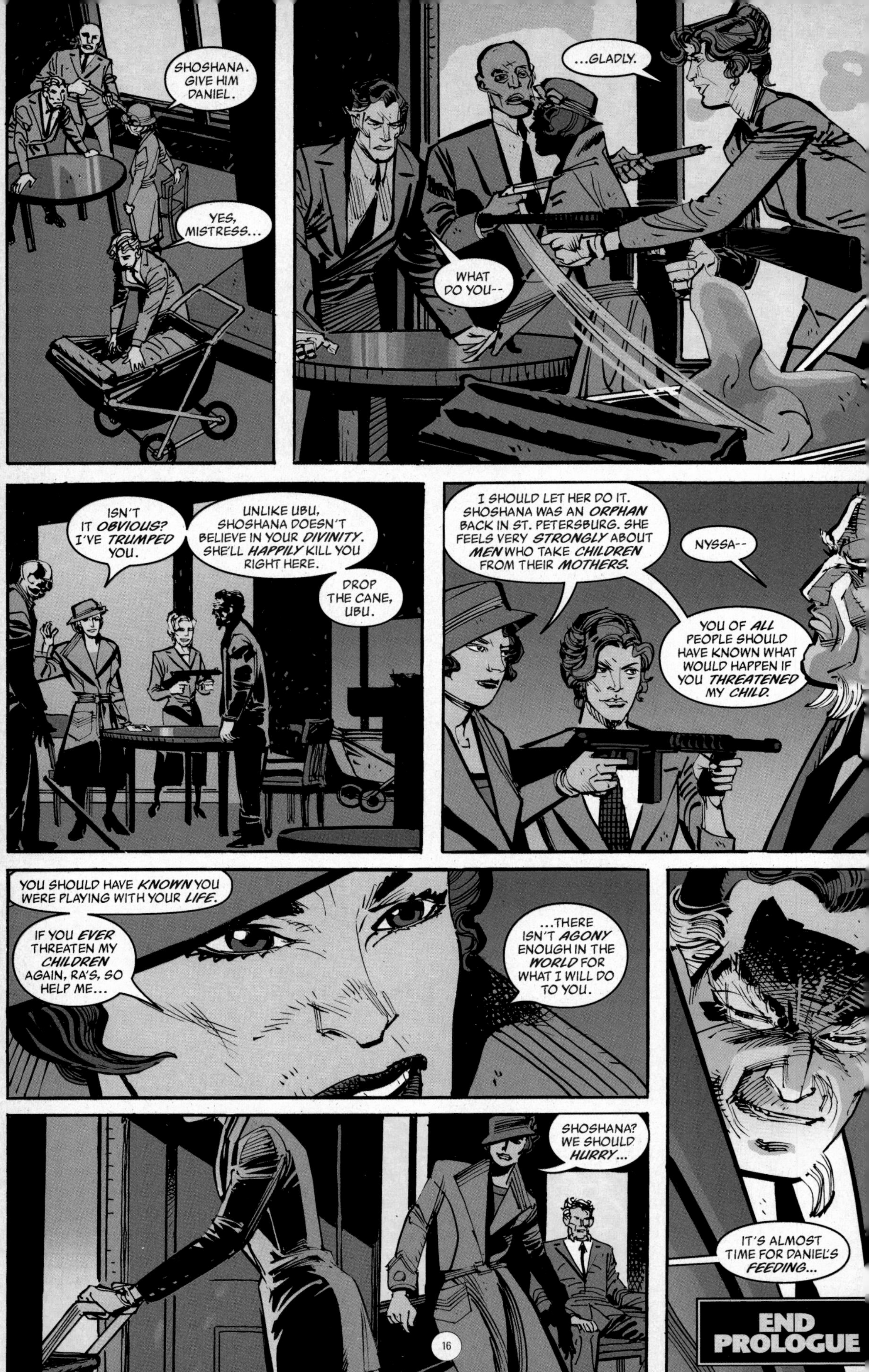
SHOSHANA. GIVE HIM DANIEL.
YES, MISTRESS...
...GLADLY.
WHAT DO YOU--
ISN'T IT OBVIOUS? I'VE TRUMPED YOU.
UNLIKE UBU, SHOSHANA DOESN'T BELIEVE IN YOUR DIVINITY. SHE'LL HAPPILY KILL YOU RIGHT HERE.
DROP THE CANE, UBU.
I SHOULD LET HER DO IT. SHOSHANA WAS AN ORPHAN BACK IN ST. PETERSBURG. SHE FEELS VERY STRONGLY ABOUT MEN WHO TAKE CHILDREN FROM THEIR MOTHERS.
NYSSA--
YOU OF ALL PEOPLE SHOULD HAVE KNOWN WHAT WOULD HAPPEN IF YOU THREATENED MY CHILD.
YOU SHOULD HAVE KNOWN YOU WERE PLAYING WITH YOUR LIFE.
IF YOU EVER THREATEN MY CHILDREN AGAIN, RA'S, SO HELP ME...
...THERE ISN'T AGONY ENOUGH IN THE WORLD FOR WHAT I WILL DO TO YOU.
SHOSHANA? WE SHOULD HURRY...
IT'S ALMOST TIME FOR DANIEL'S FEEDING...
END PROLOGUE

‹...SOURCE OF THE *EXPLOSION* THAT CLAIMED LIEUTENANT CAPTAIN ARKETOV, BUT WE KNOW VERY *LITTLE* RIGHT NOW, I AM AFRAID.›

‹WE ARE MAKING *EVERY* EFFORT TO RECOVER THE *BODIES,* OF COURSE.›

‹OF COURSE.›

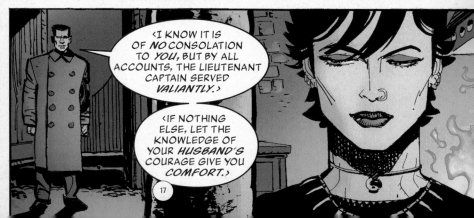

‹I KNOW IT IS OF *NO* CONSOLATION TO *YOU,* BUT BY ALL ACCOUNTS, THE LIEUTENANT CAPTAIN SERVED *VALIANTLY.*›

‹IF NOTHING ELSE, LET THE KNOWLEDGE OF YOUR *HUSBAND'S* COURAGE GIVE YOU *COMFORT.*›

17

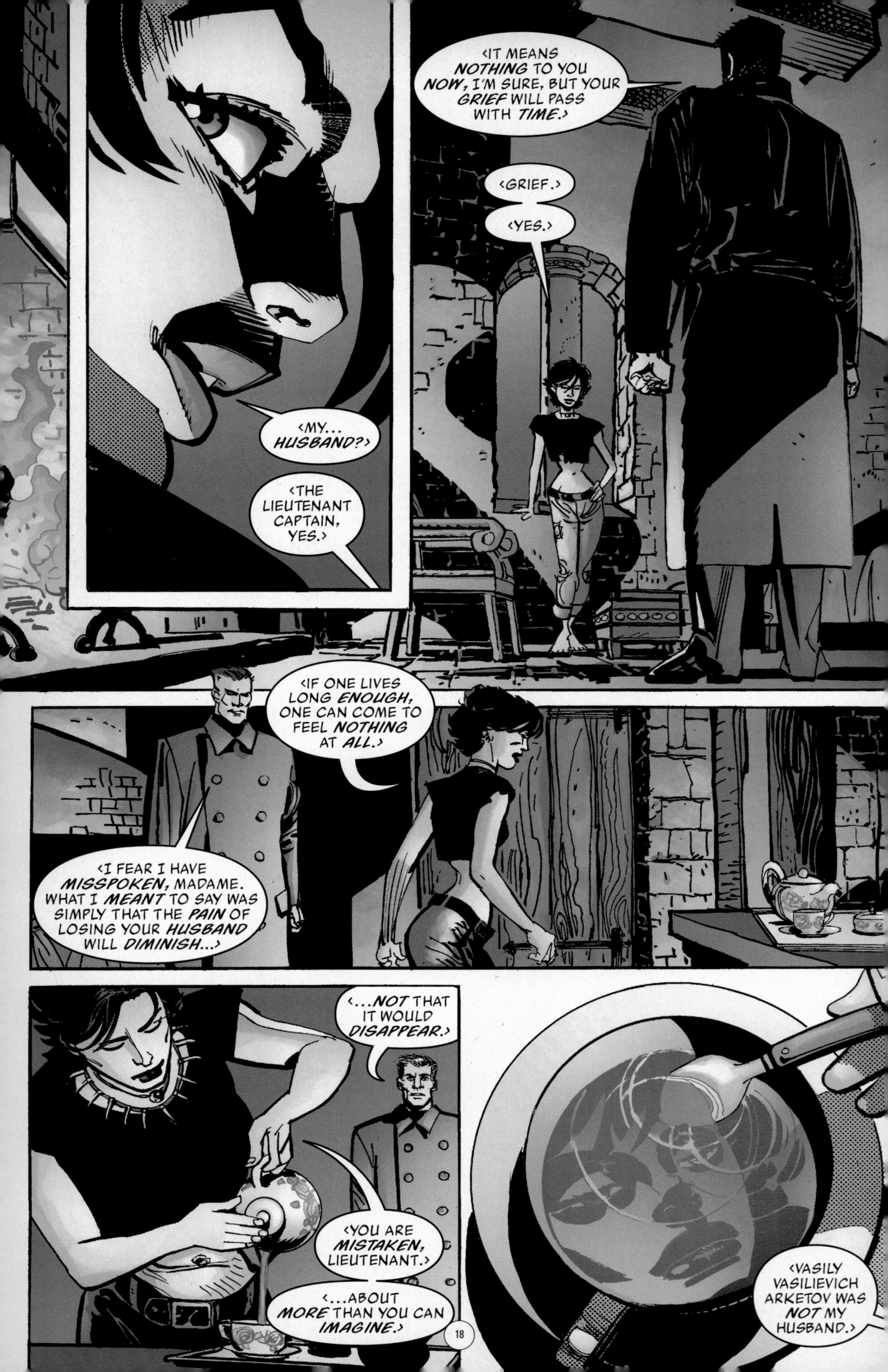

<MY... HUSBAND?>
<THE LIEUTENANT CAPTAIN, YES.>
<IT MEANS NOTHING TO YOU NOW, I'M SURE, BUT YOUR GRIEF WILL PASS WITH TIME.>
<GRIEF.>
<YES.>
<I FEAR I HAVE MISSPOKEN, MADAME. WHAT I MEANT TO SAY WAS SIMPLY THAT THE PAIN OF LOSING YOUR HUSBAND WILL DIMINISH...>
<IF ONE LIVES LONG ENOUGH, ONE CAN COME TO FEEL NOTHING AT ALL.>
<...NOT THAT IT WOULD DISAPPEAR.>
<YOU ARE MISTAKEN, LIEUTENANT.>
<...ABOUT MORE THAN YOU CAN IMAGINE.>
<VASILY VASILIEVICH ARKETOV WAS NOT MY HUSBAND.>

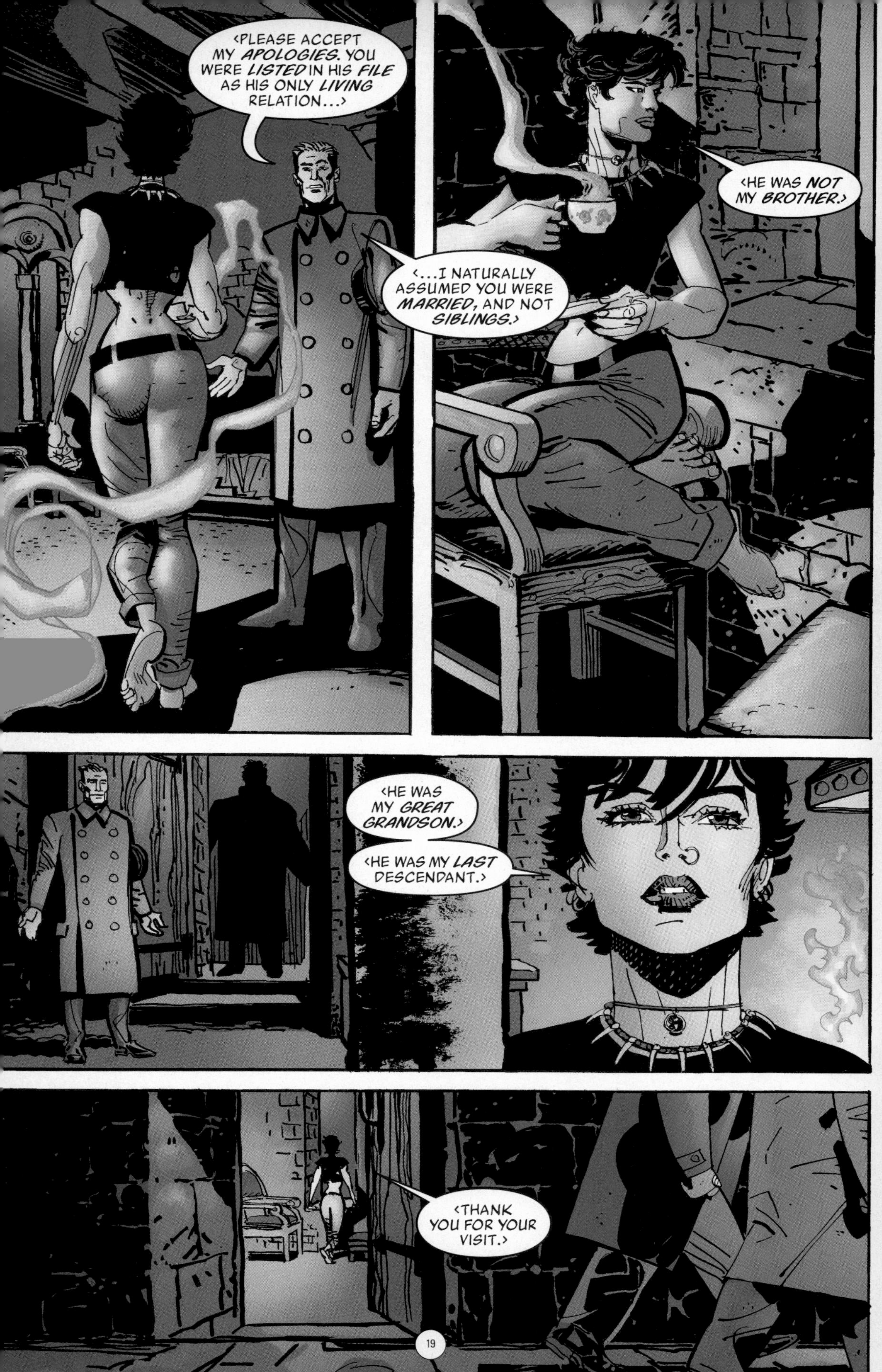
‹PLEASE ACCEPT MY APOLOGIES. YOU WERE LISTED IN HIS FILE AS HIS ONLY LIVING RELATION...›
‹...I NATURALLY ASSUMED YOU WERE MARRIED, AND NOT SIBLINGS.›
‹HE WAS NOT MY BROTHER.›
‹HE WAS MY GREAT GRANDSON.›
‹HE WAS MY LAST DESCENDANT.›
‹THANK YOU FOR YOUR VISIT.›

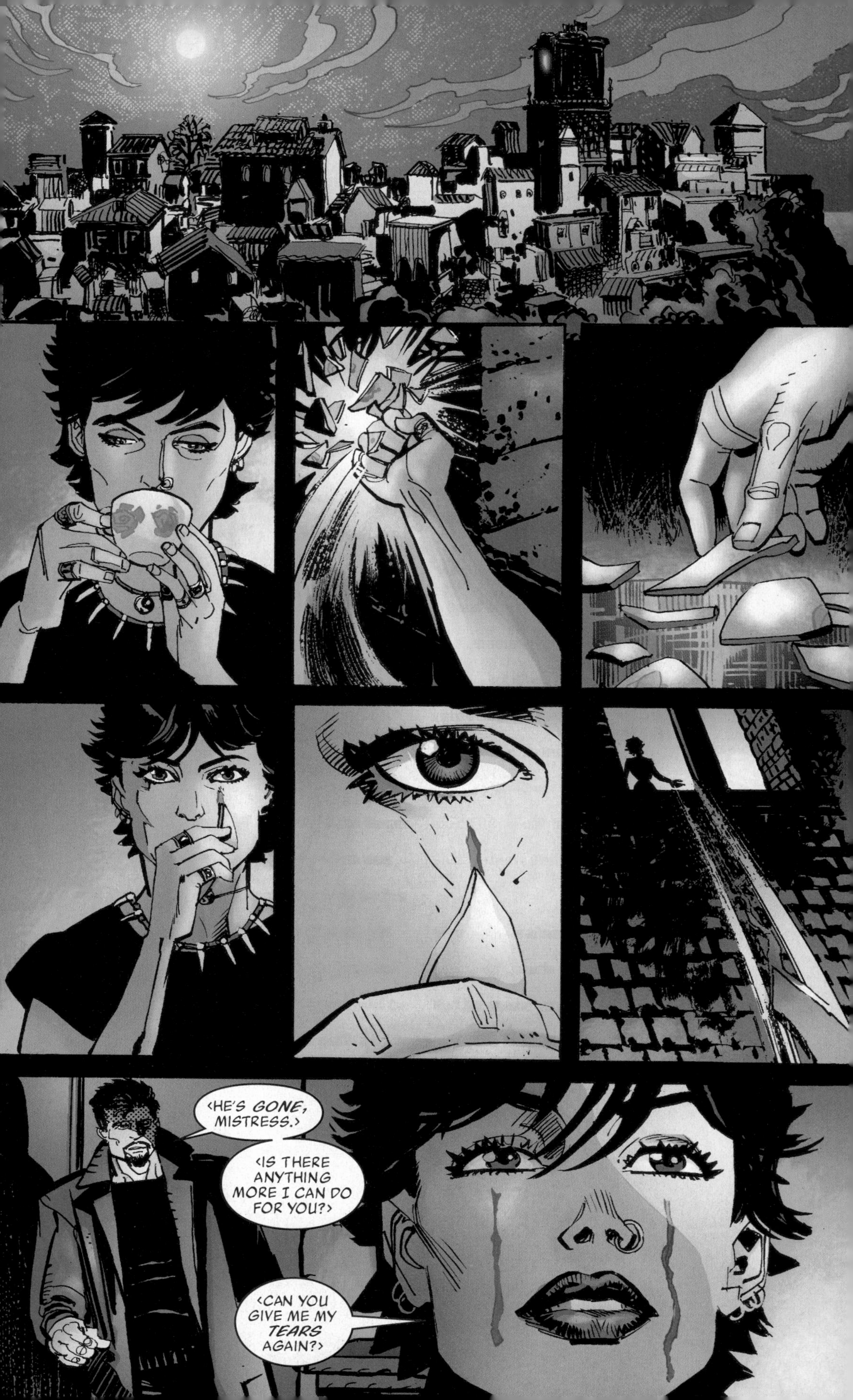

‹HE'S *GONE*, MISTRESS.›
‹IS THERE ANYTHING MORE I CAN DO FOR YOU?›
‹CAN YOU GIVE ME MY *TEARS* AGAIN?›

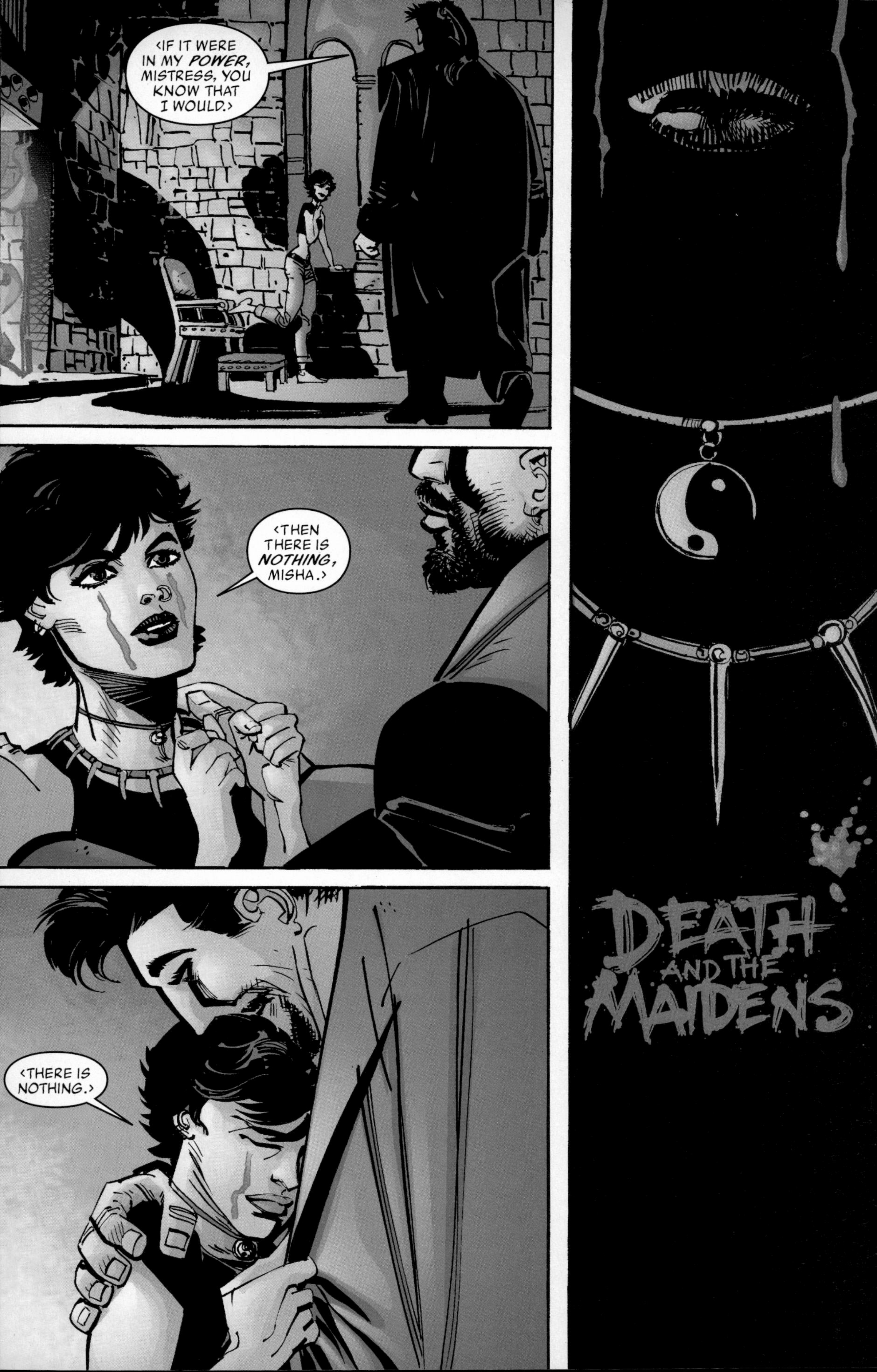
<IF IT WERE IN MY POWER, MISTRESS, YOU KNOW THAT I WOULD.>
<THEN THERE IS NOTHING, MISHA.>
<THERE IS NOTHING.>
DEATH AND THE MAIDENS

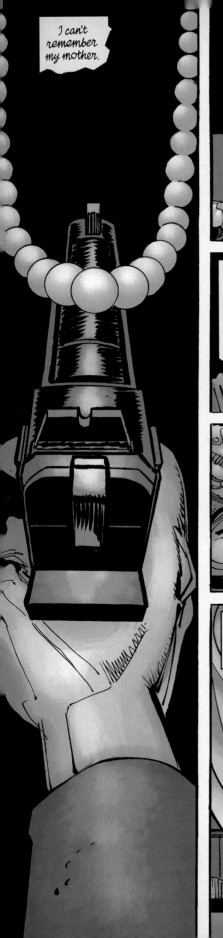

I can't remember my mother.

The mind betrays emotion. What the head knows, the heart forgets.

I live surrounded by the artifacts of tragedy, the idolatry of my worship.

I sleep in a replica of my parents' bed, on fine linen purchased before I was born...

...their eyes follow me wherever I step in this old house, observing me from salvaged paintings and recovered photographs.

But it is only intellect keeping them alive, now.

I can't remember them anymore. Not really. Not honestly.

And I am afraid...

...I don't feel it anymore...

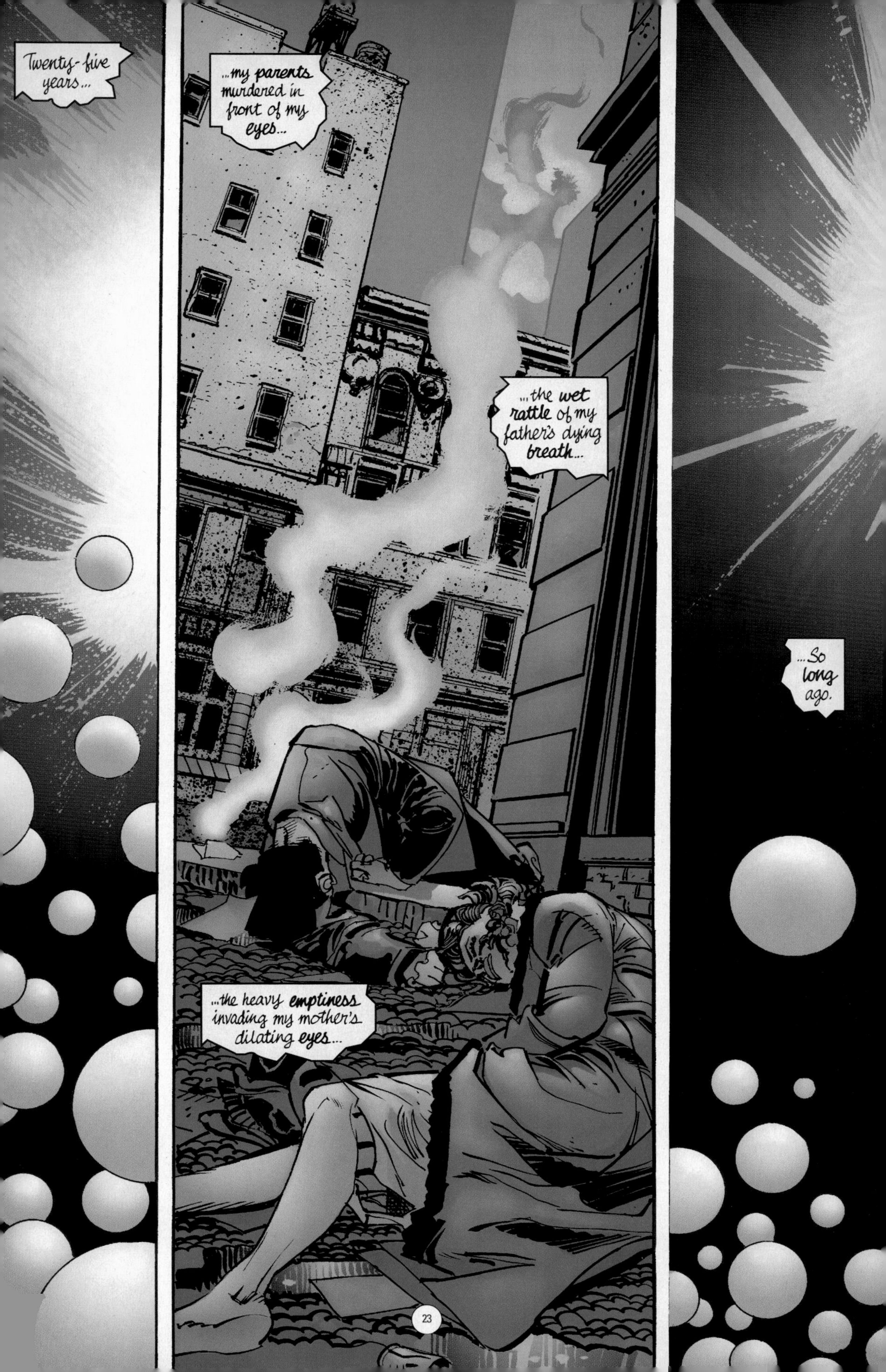
Twenty-five years...
...my parents murdered in front of my eyes...
...the wet rattle of my father's dying breath...
...the heavy emptiness invading my mother's dilating eyes...
...So long ago.

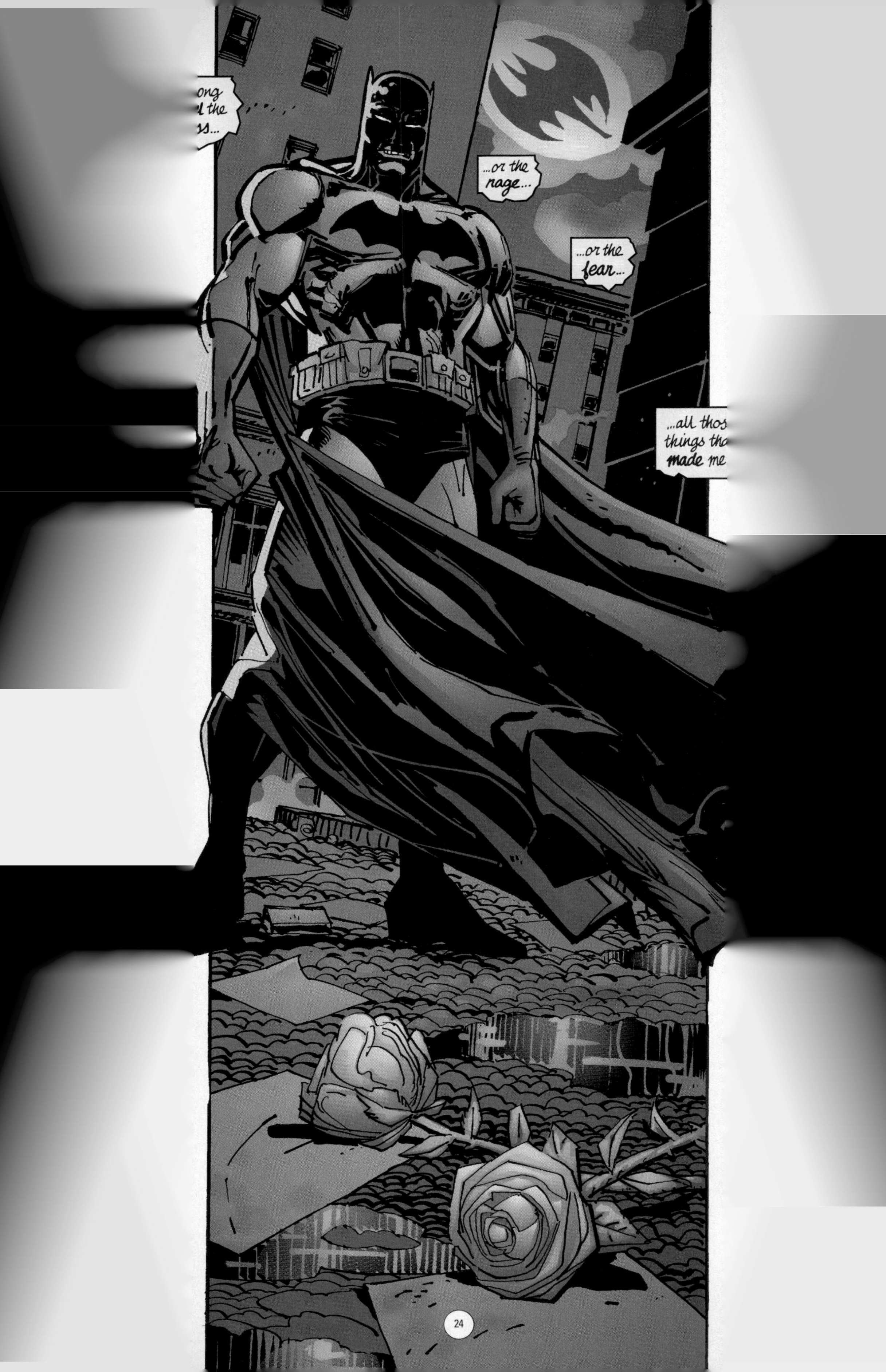
...or the rage...
...or the fear...
...all thos
things tha
made me

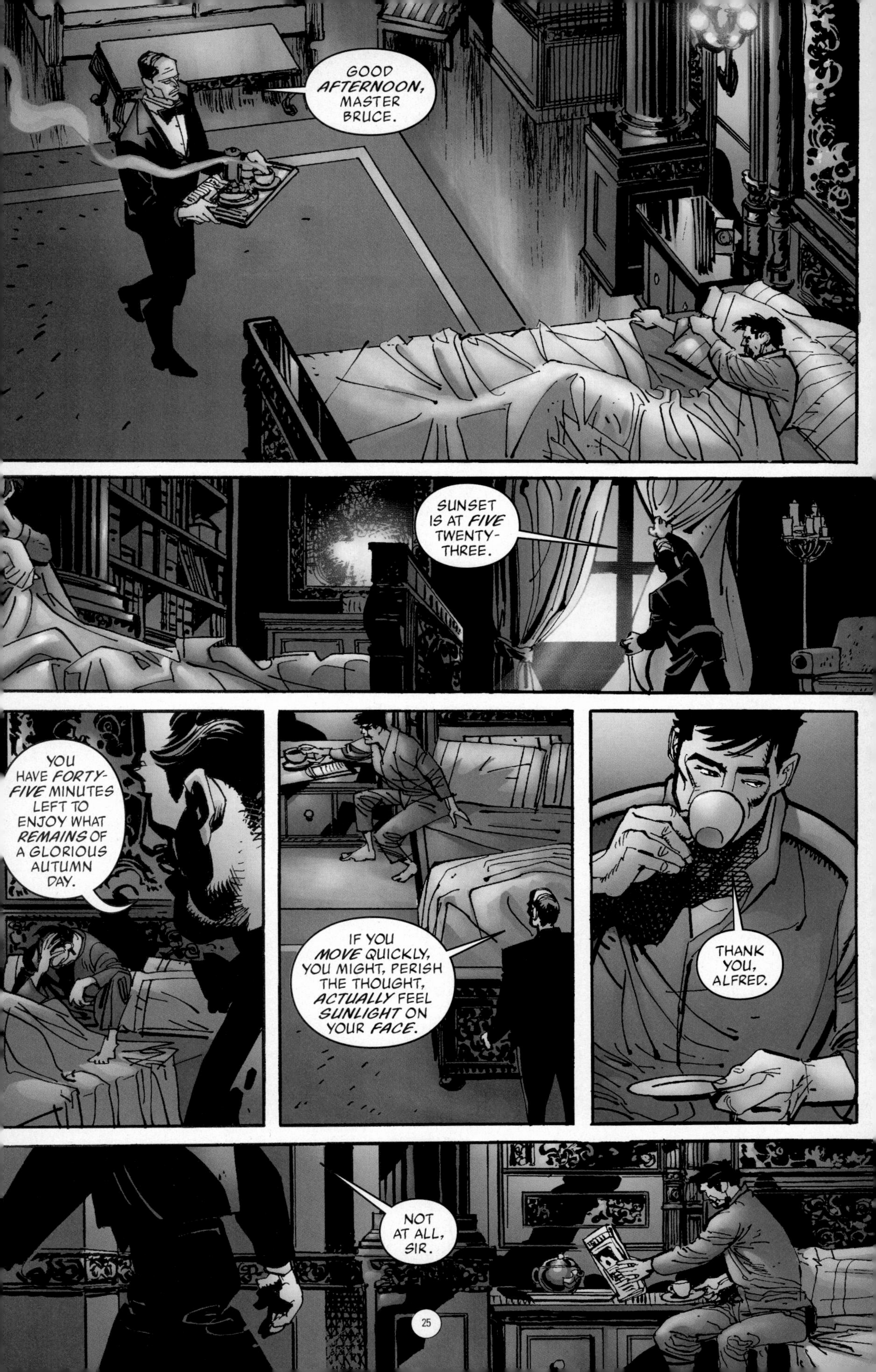
GOOD AFTERNOON, MASTER BRUCE.
SUNSET IS AT FIVE TWENTY-THREE.
YOU HAVE FORTY-FIVE MINUTES LEFT TO ENJOY WHAT REMAINS OF A GLORIOUS AUTUMN DAY.
IF YOU MOVE QUICKLY, YOU MIGHT, PERISH THE THOUGHT, ACTUALLY FEEL SUNLIGHT ON YOUR FACE.
THANK YOU, ALFRED.
NOT AT ALL, SIR.

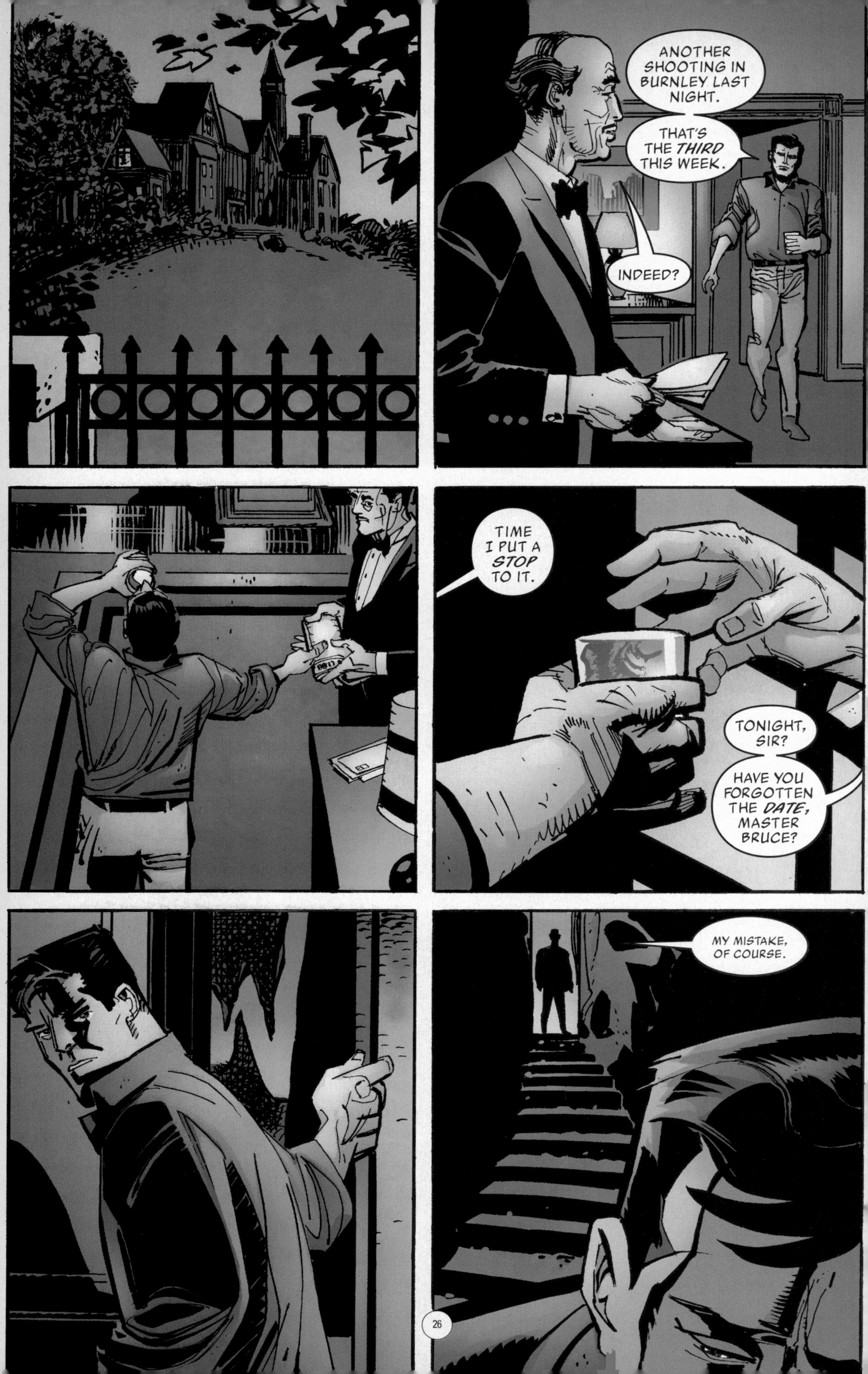
ANOTHER SHOOTING IN BURNLEY LAST NIGHT.
THAT'S THE *THIRD* THIS WEEK.
INDEED?
TIME I PUT A *STOP* TO IT.
TONIGHT, SIR?
HAVE YOU FORGOTTEN THE *DATE,* MASTER BRUCE?
MY MISTAKE, OF COURSE.

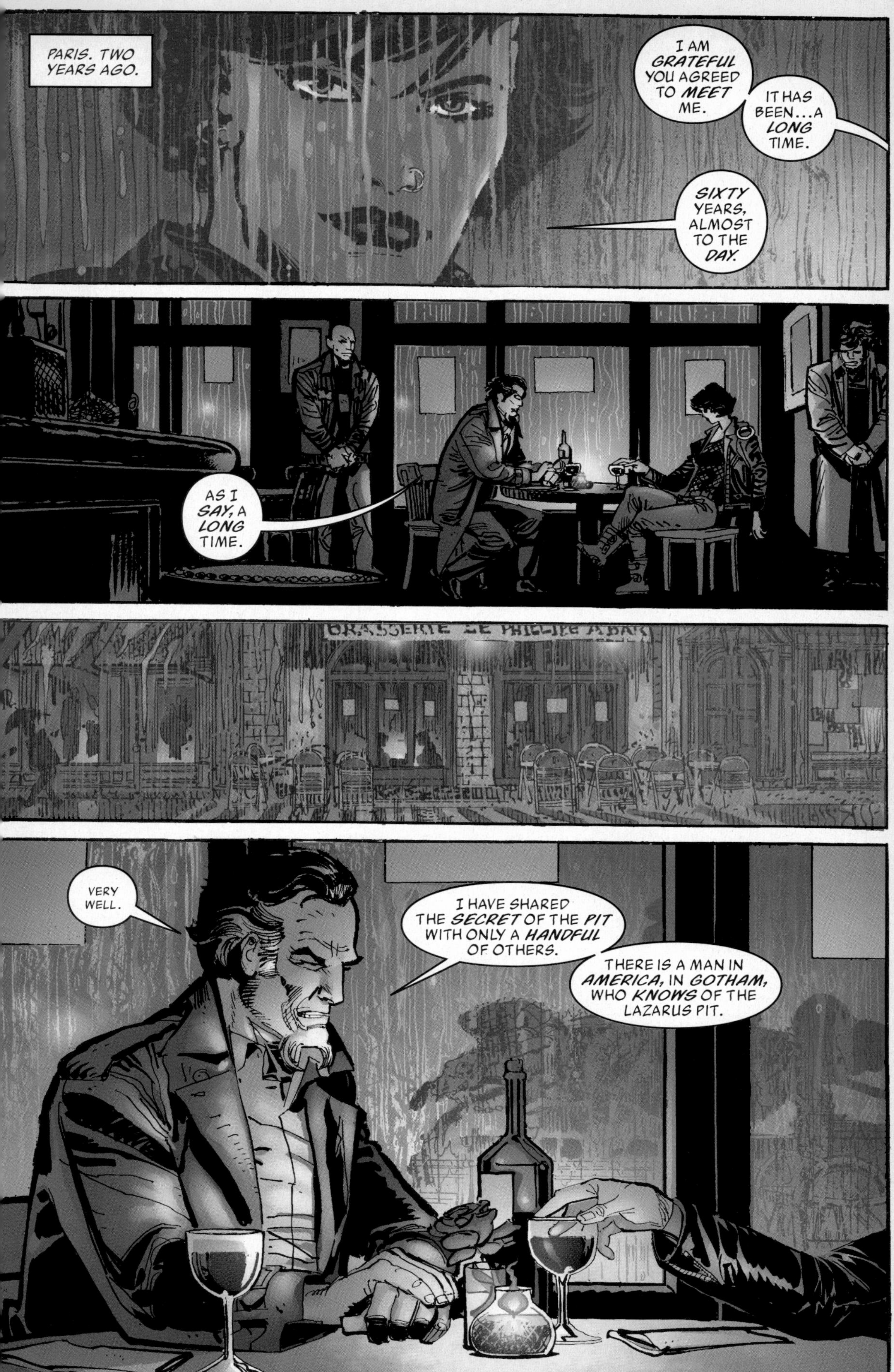
PARIS. TWO YEARS AGO.
I AM GRATEFUL YOU AGREED TO MEET ME.
IT HAS BEEN...A LONG TIME.
SIXTY YEARS, ALMOST TO THE DAY.
AS I SAY, A LONG TIME.
VERY WELL.
I HAVE SHARED THE SECRET OF THE PIT WITH ONLY A HANDFUL OF OTHERS.
THERE IS A MAN IN AMERICA, IN GOTHAM, WHO KNOWS OF THE LAZARUS PIT.

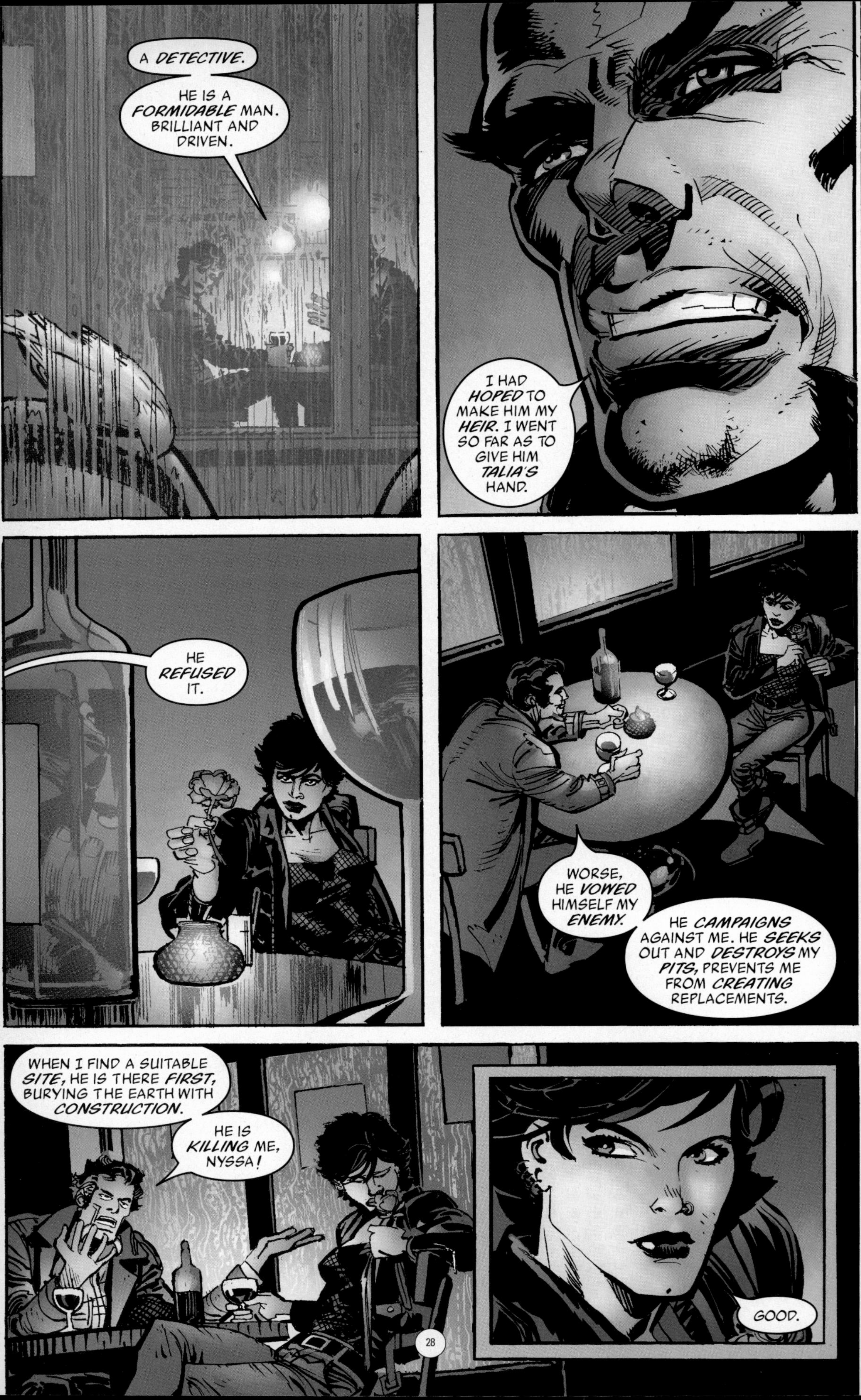
A DETECTIVE.
HE IS A FORMIDABLE MAN. BRILLIANT AND DRIVEN.
I HAD HOPED TO MAKE HIM MY HEIR. I WENT SO FAR AS TO GIVE HIM TALIA'S HAND.
HE REFUSED IT.
WORSE, HE VOWED HIMSELF MY ENEMY.
HE CAMPAIGNS AGAINST ME. HE SEEKS OUT AND DESTROYS MY PITS, PREVENTS ME FROM CREATING REPLACEMENTS.
WHEN I FIND A SUITABLE SITE, HE IS THERE FIRST, BURYING THE EARTH WITH CONSTRUCTION.
HE IS KILLING ME, NYSSA!
GOOD.

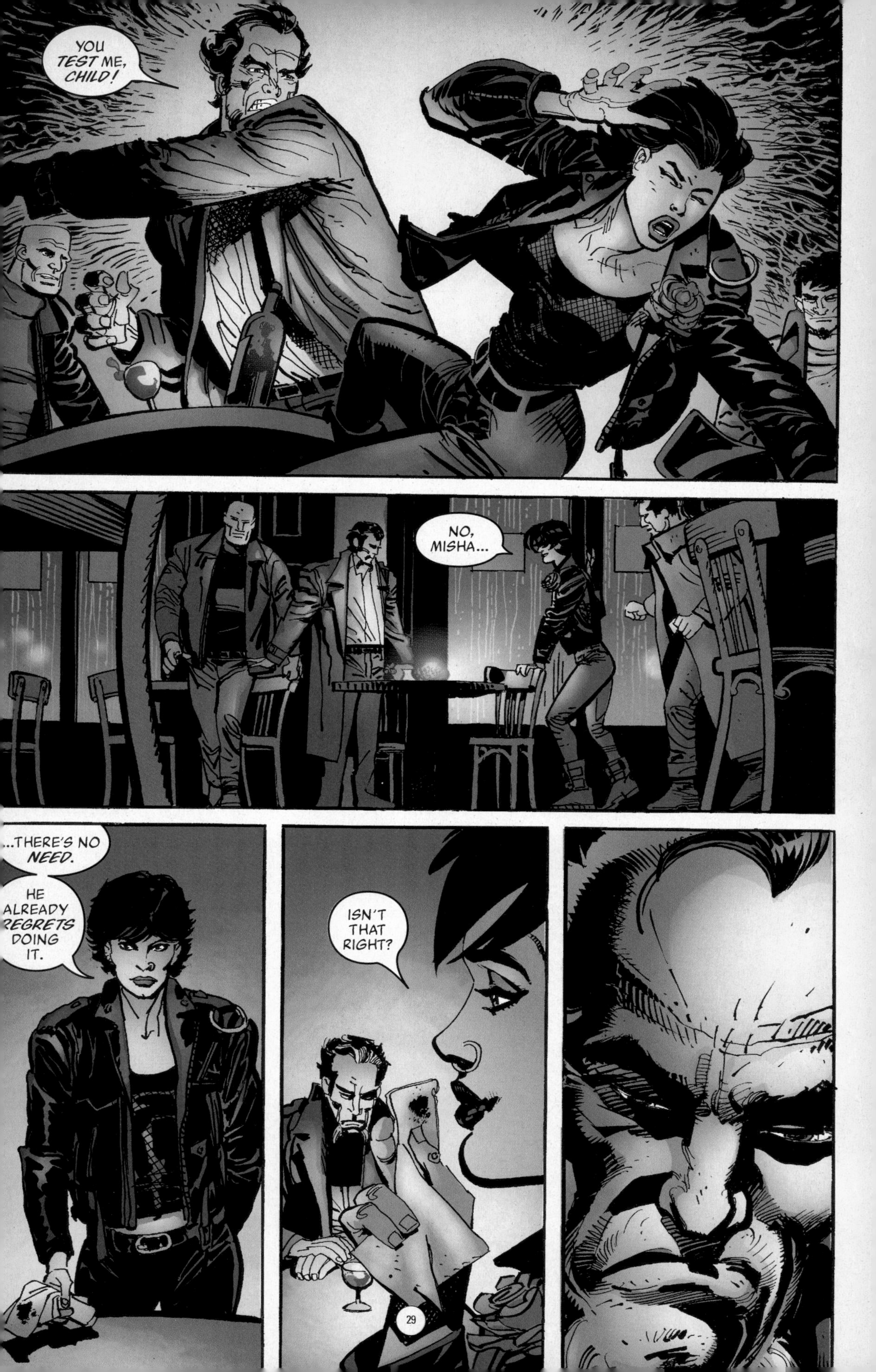

YOU TEST ME, CHILD!
NO, MISHA...
...THERE'S NO NEED.
HE ALREADY REGRETS DOING IT.
ISN'T THAT RIGHT?

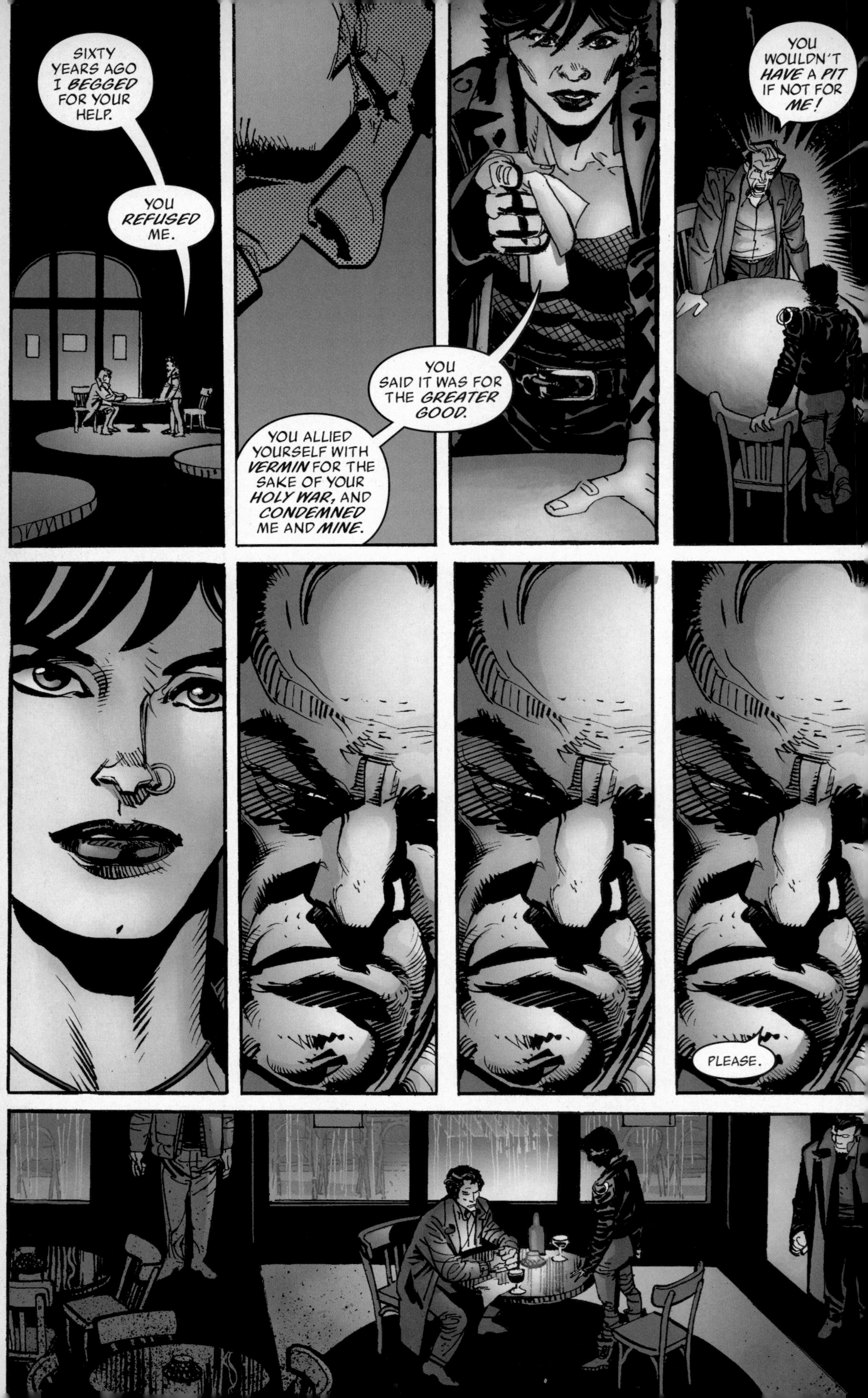

SIXTY YEARS AGO I *BEGGED* FOR YOUR HELP.
YOU *REFUSED* ME.
YOU SAID IT WAS FOR THE *GREATER GOOD*.
YOU ALLIED YOURSELF WITH *VERMIN* FOR THE SAKE OF YOUR *HOLY WAR*, AND *CONDEMNED* ME AND *MINE*.
YOU WOULDN'T *HAVE* A *PIT* IF NOT FOR *ME!*
PLEASE.

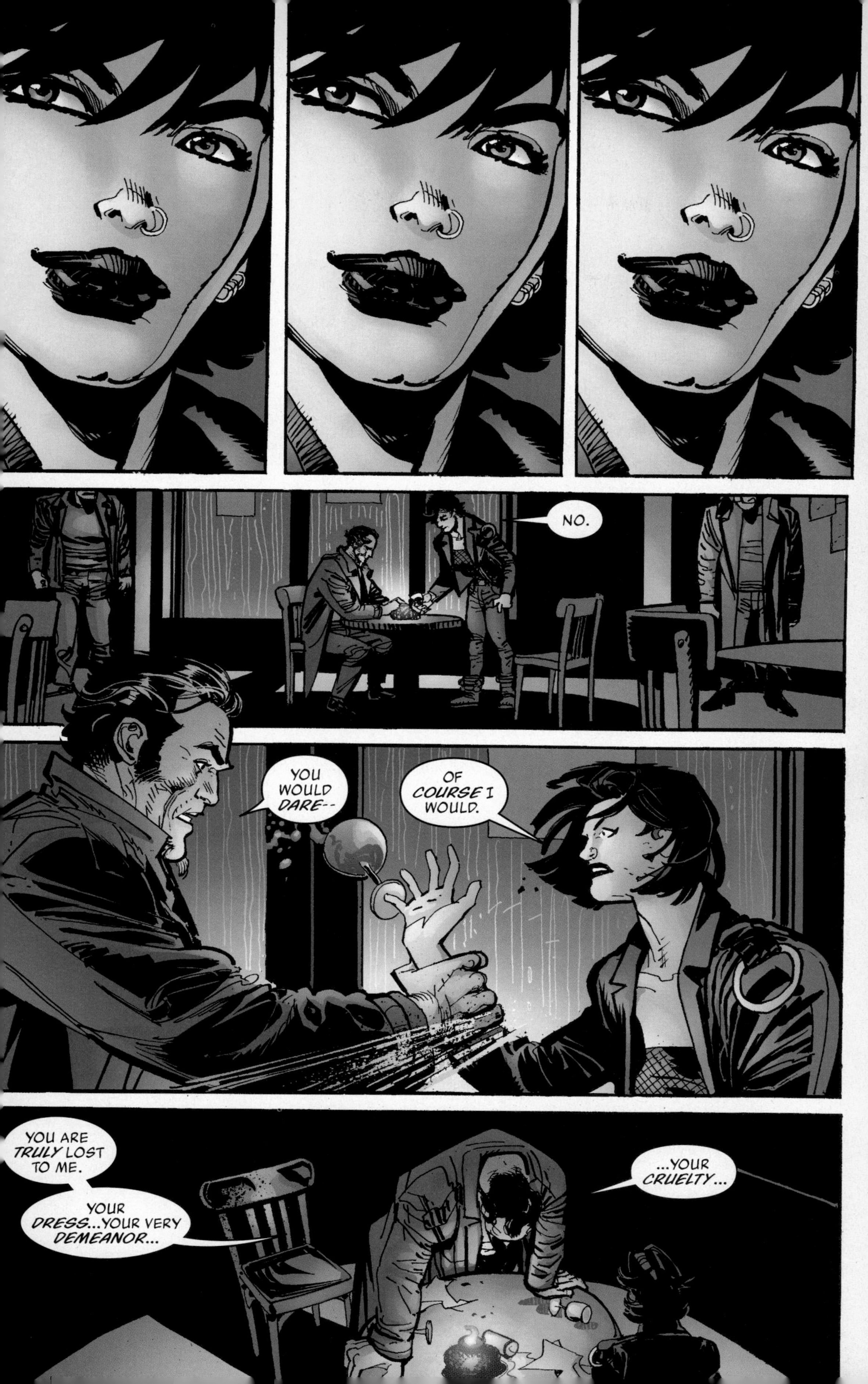
NO.
YOU WOULD DARE--
OF COURSE I WOULD.
YOU ARE TRULY LOST TO ME.
YOUR DRESS...YOUR VERY DEMEANOR...
...YOUR CRUELTY...

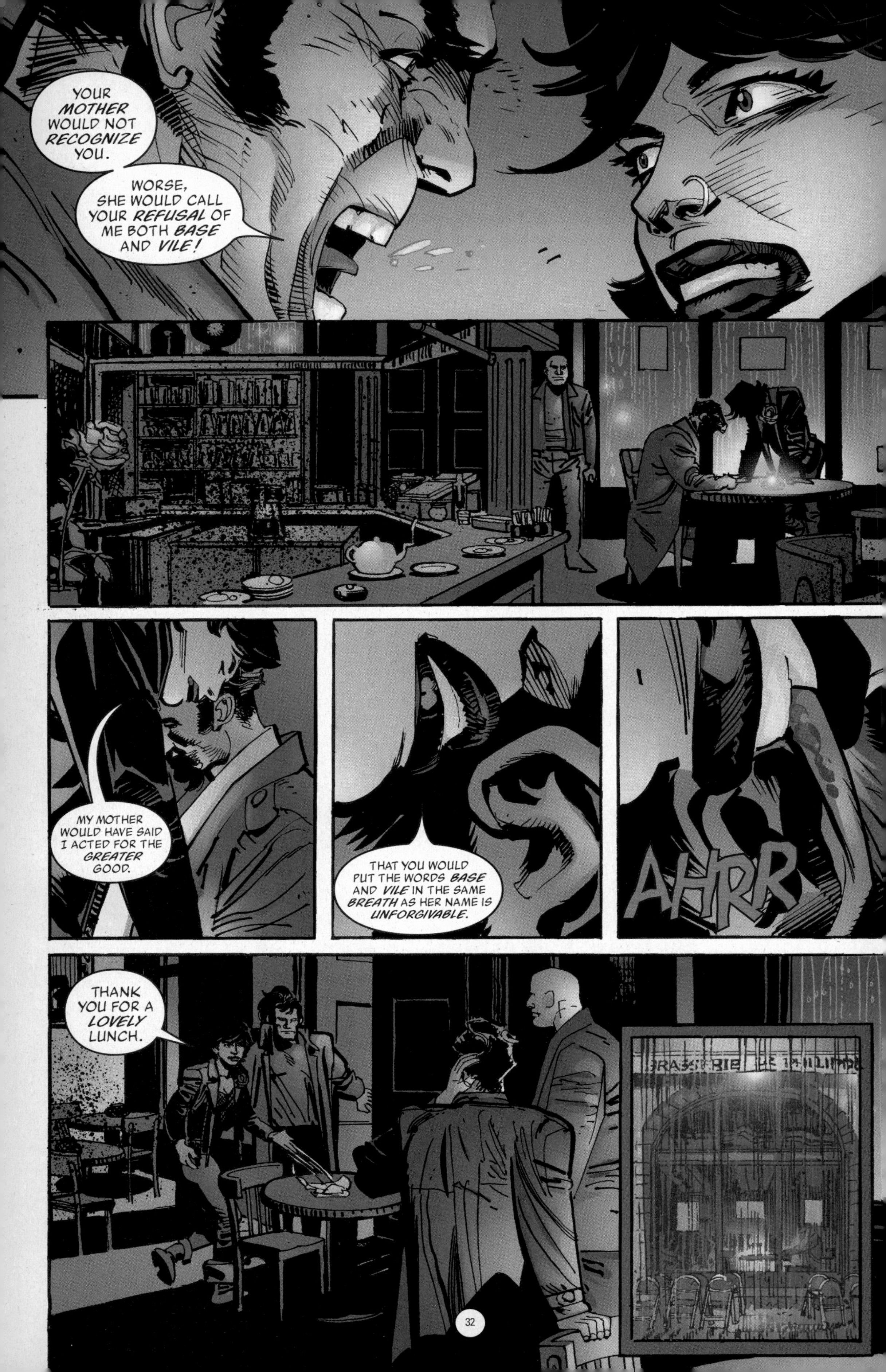

YOUR *MOTHER* WOULD NOT *RECOGNIZE* YOU.
WORSE, SHE WOULD CALL YOUR *REFUSAL* OF ME BOTH *BASE* AND *VILE*!
MY MOTHER WOULD HAVE SAID I ACTED FOR THE *GREATER* GOOD.
THAT YOU WOULD PUT THE WORDS *BASE* AND *VILE* IN THE SAME *BREATH* AS HER NAME IS *UNFORGIVABLE*.
AHRR
THANK YOU FOR A *LOVELY* LUNCH.

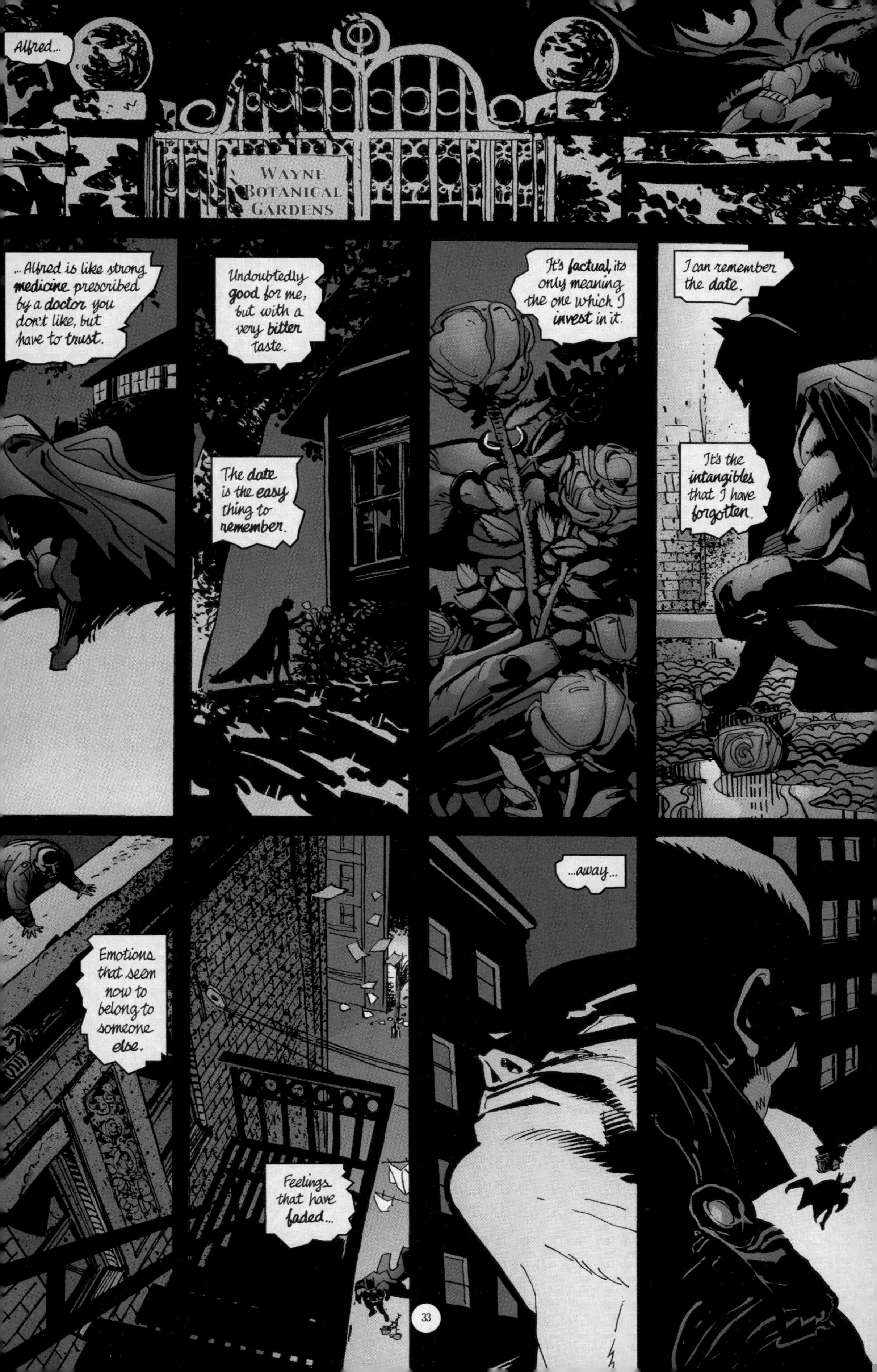
Alfred...
WAYNE BOTANICAL GARDENS
...Alfred is like strong medicine prescribed by a doctor you don't like, but have to trust.
Undoubtedly good for me, but with a very bitter taste.
The date is the easy thing to remember.
It's factual, its only meaning the one which I invest in it.
I can remember the date.
It's the intangibles that I have forgotten.
Emotions that seem now to belong to someone else.
Feelings that have faded...
...away...

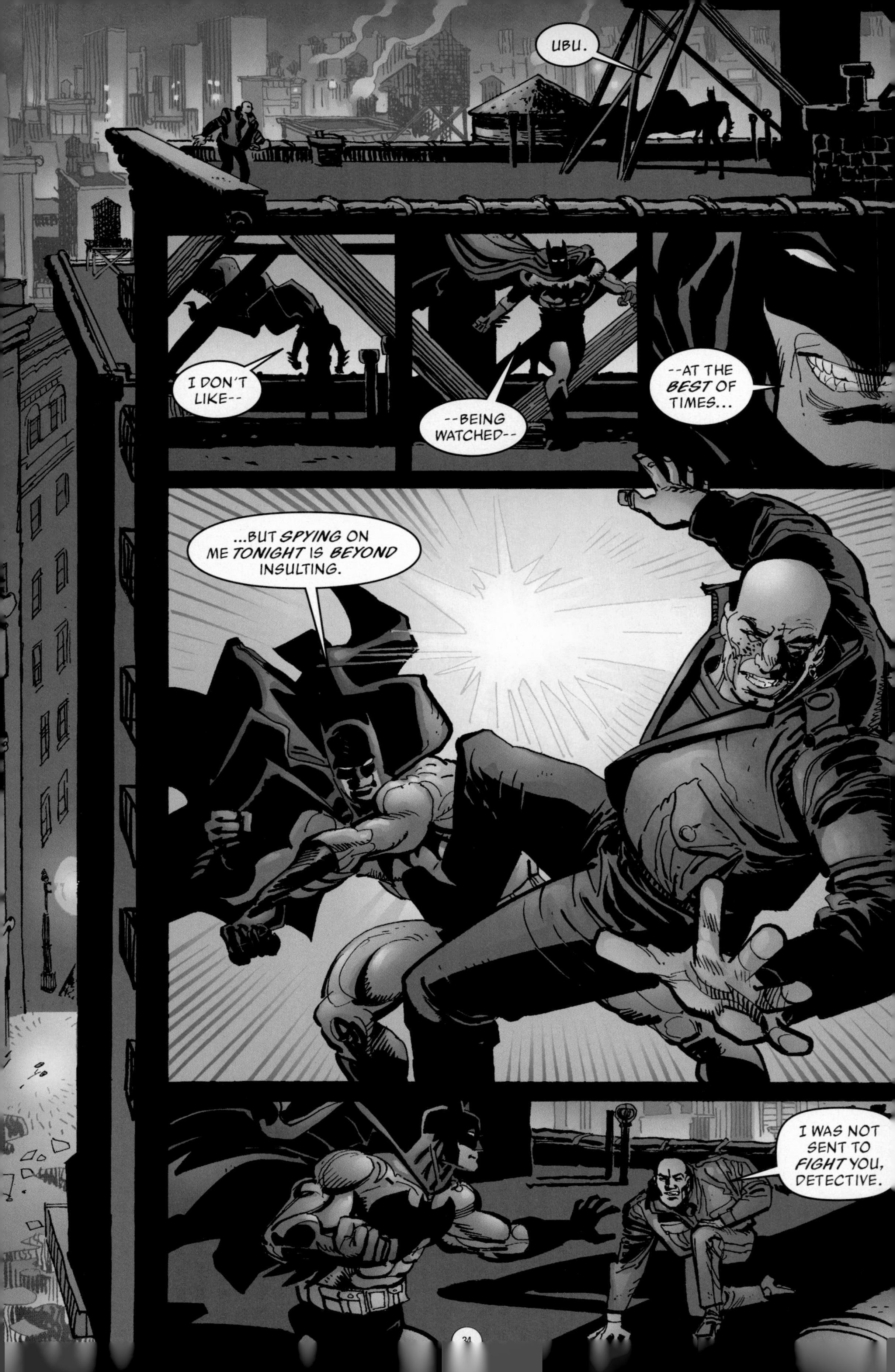
UBU.
I DON'T LIKE--
--BEING WATCHED--
--AT THE BEST OF TIMES...
...BUT SPYING ON ME TONIGHT IS BEYOND INSULTING.
I WAS NOT SENT TO FIGHT YOU, DETECTIVE.

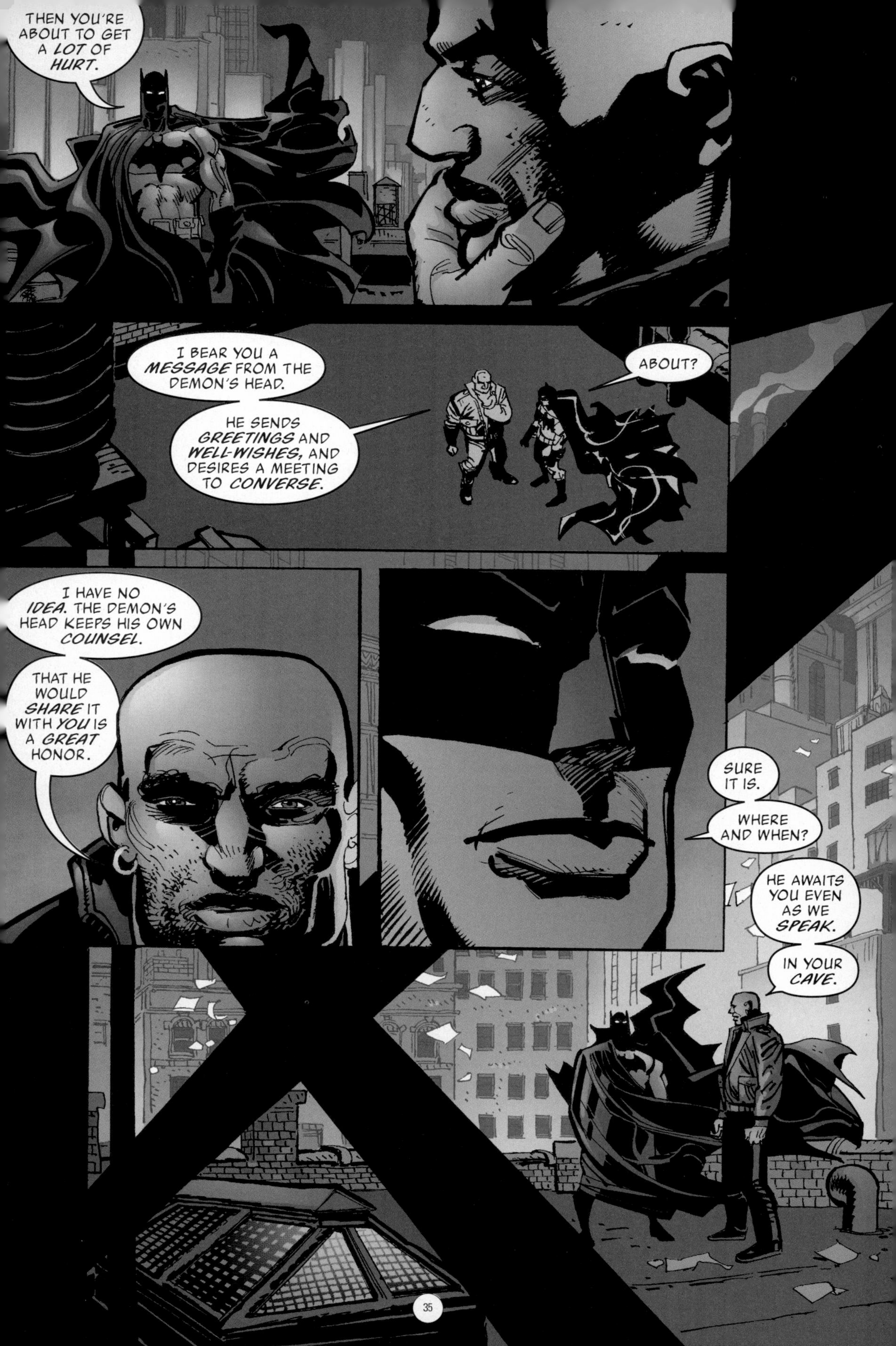

THEN YOU'RE ABOUT TO GET A *LOT* OF *HURT*.
I BEAR YOU A *MESSAGE* FROM THE DEMON'S HEAD.
HE SENDS *GREETINGS* AND *WELL-WISHES,* AND DESIRES A MEETING TO *CONVERSE*.
ABOUT?
I HAVE NO *IDEA*. THE DEMON'S HEAD KEEPS HIS OWN *COUNSEL*.
THAT HE WOULD *SHARE* IT WITH *YOU* IS A *GREAT* HONOR.
SURE IT IS.
WHERE AND WHEN?
HE AWAITS YOU EVEN AS WE *SPEAK*.
IN YOUR *CAVE*.

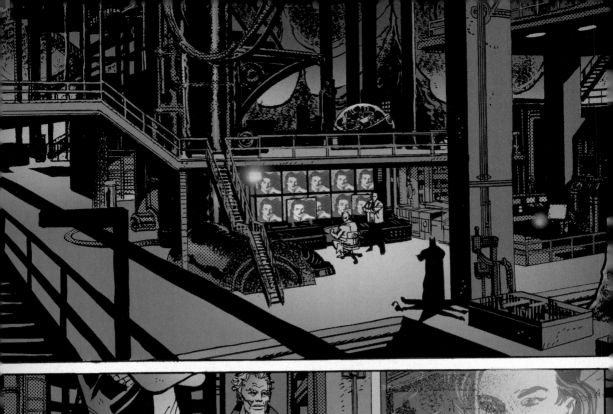

MY DAUGHTER *IS* BEAUTIFUL...

...I'M SURE YOU *AGREE,* DETECTIVE.

YOU SHOULD DO *SOMETHING* ABOUT YOUR ENCRYPTION.

AND MY *SECURITY.*

YES, THAT ALSO.

UBU, HELP ME *UP.*

THIS *MUST* BE A *SPECIAL* OCCASION.

I'VE *NEVER* KNOWN YOU TO TRAVEL WITH MORE THAN *ONE* UBU AT A *TIME*.

THEIR FAMILY HAS SERVED ME FOR *CENTURIES*.

THAT IS THEIR *PRIVILEGE*.

MY *CURRENT* HEALTH REQUIRES THE *ASSISTANCE* OF MORE THAN ONE AT A TIME, UNFORTUNATELY.

HOW MANY ARE THERE?

ONCE THE FAMILY *UBU* WAS *LEGION*, DETECTIVE.

NOW THEY ARE BUT A *HANDFUL*. THEY ARE *DYING*.

AS I AM *DYING*.

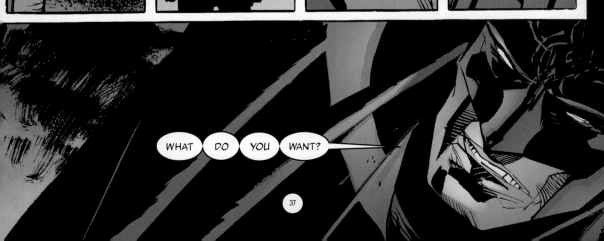

WHAT DO YOU WANT?

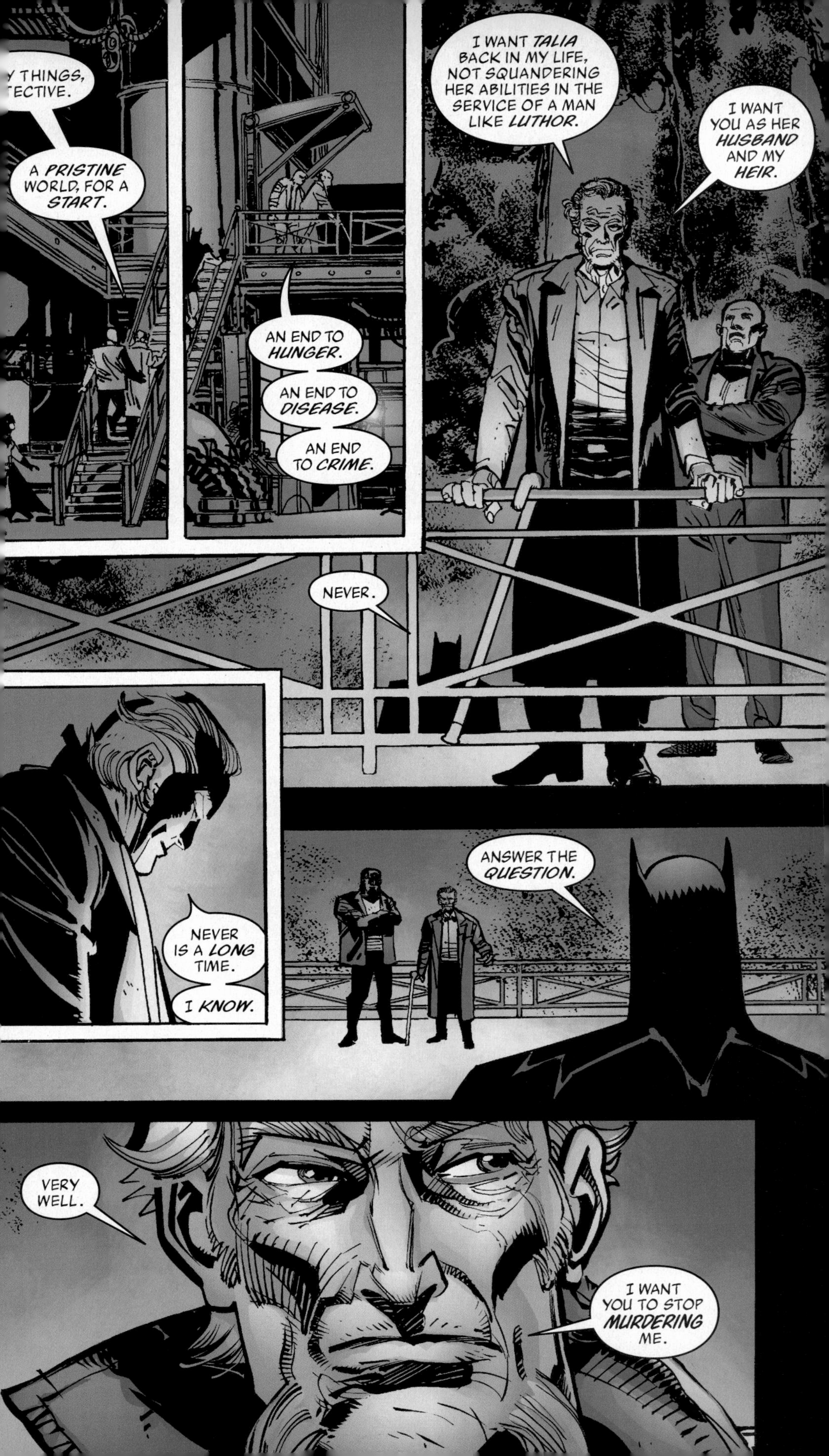
Y THINGS, TECTIVE.
A PRISTINE WORLD, FOR A START.
AN END TO HUNGER.
AN END TO DISEASE.
AN END TO CRIME.
I WANT TALIA BACK IN MY LIFE, NOT SQUANDERING HER ABILITIES IN THE SERVICE OF A MAN LIKE LUTHOR.
I WANT YOU AS HER HUSBAND AND MY HEIR.
NEVER.
NEVER IS A LONG TIME.
I KNOW.
ANSWER THE QUESTION.
VERY WELL.
I WANT YOU TO STOP MURDERING ME.

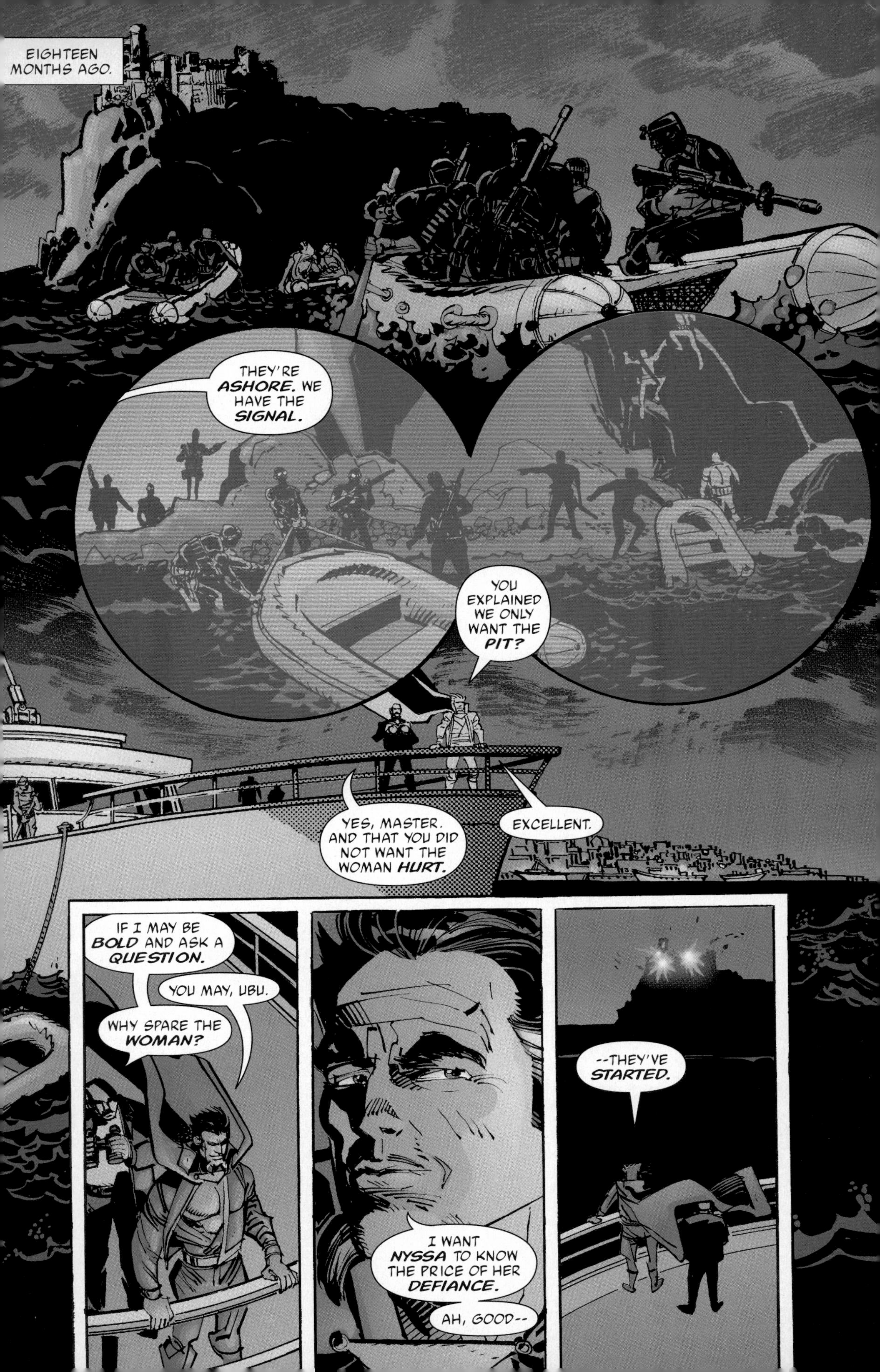

EIGHTEEN MONTHS AGO.
THEY'RE ASHORE. WE HAVE THE SIGNAL.
YOU EXPLAINED WE ONLY WANT THE PIT?
YES, MASTER. AND THAT YOU DID NOT WANT THE WOMAN HURT.
EXCELLENT.
IF I MAY BE BOLD AND ASK A QUESTION.
YOU MAY, UBU.
WHY SPARE THE WOMAN?
I WANT NYSSA TO KNOW THE PRICE OF HER DEFIANCE.
AH, GOOD--
--THEY'VE STARTED.

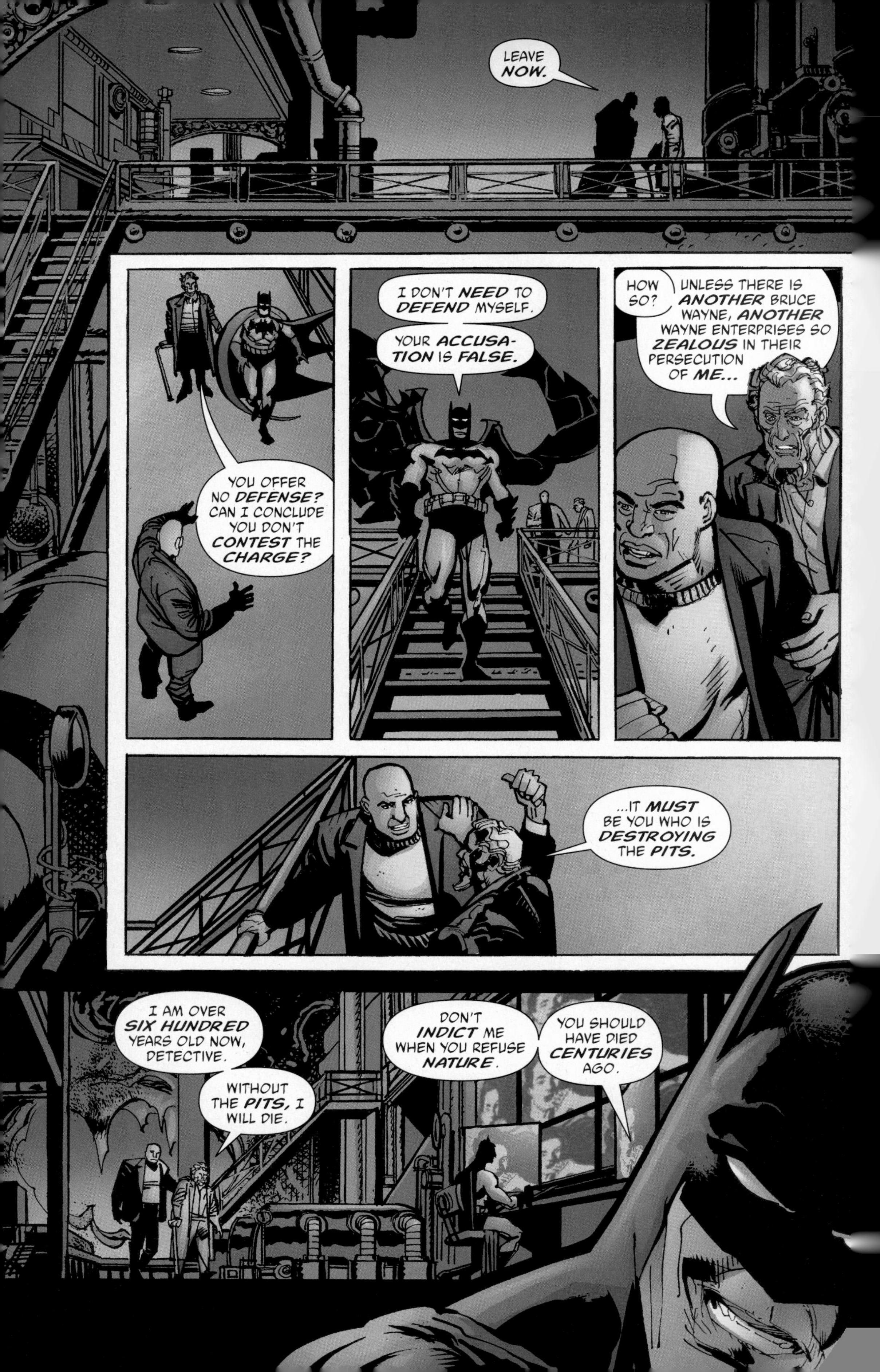
LEAVE NOW.
YOU OFFER NO DEFENSE? CAN I CONCLUDE YOU DON'T CONTEST THE CHARGE?
I DON'T NEED TO DEFEND MYSELF.
YOUR ACCUSATION IS FALSE.
HOW SO?
UNLESS THERE IS ANOTHER BRUCE WAYNE, ANOTHER WAYNE ENTERPRISES SO ZEALOUS IN THEIR PERSECUTION OF ME...
...IT MUST BE YOU WHO IS DESTROYING THE PITS.
I AM OVER SIX HUNDRED YEARS OLD NOW, DETECTIVE.
WITHOUT THE PITS, I WILL DIE.
DON'T INDICT ME WHEN YOU REFUSE NATURE.
YOU SHOULD HAVE DIED CENTURIES AGO.

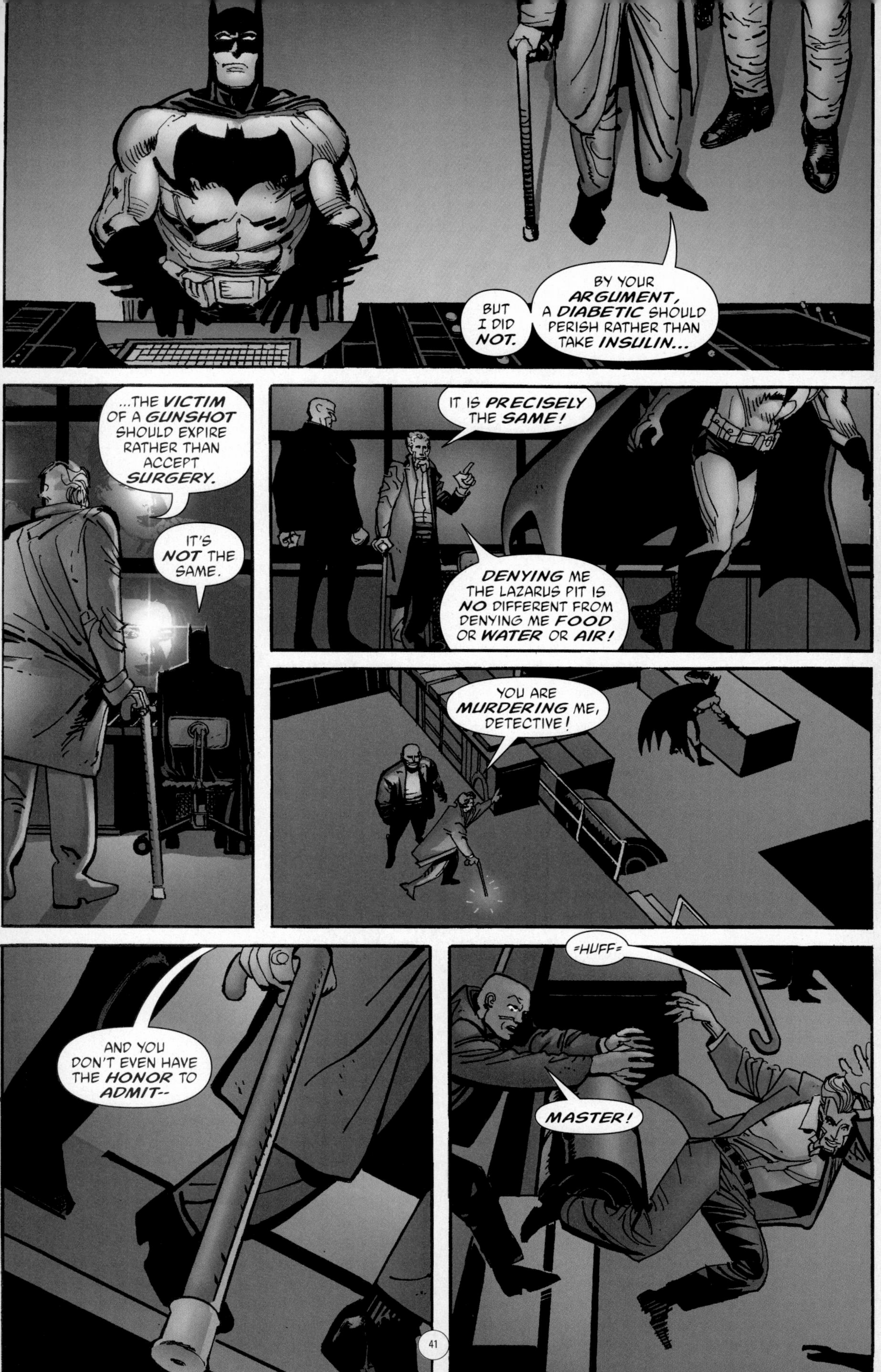
BY YOUR ARGUMENT, A DIABETIC SHOULD PERISH RATHER THAN TAKE INSULIN...
BUT I DID NOT.
...THE VICTIM OF A GUNSHOT SHOULD EXPIRE RATHER THAN ACCEPT SURGERY.
IT'S NOT THE SAME.
IT IS PRECISELY THE SAME!
DENYING ME THE LAZARUS PIT IS NO DIFFERENT FROM DENYING ME FOOD OR WATER OR AIR!
YOU ARE MURDERING ME, DETECTIVE!
AND YOU DON'T EVEN HAVE THE HONOR TO ADMIT--
=HUFF=
MASTER!

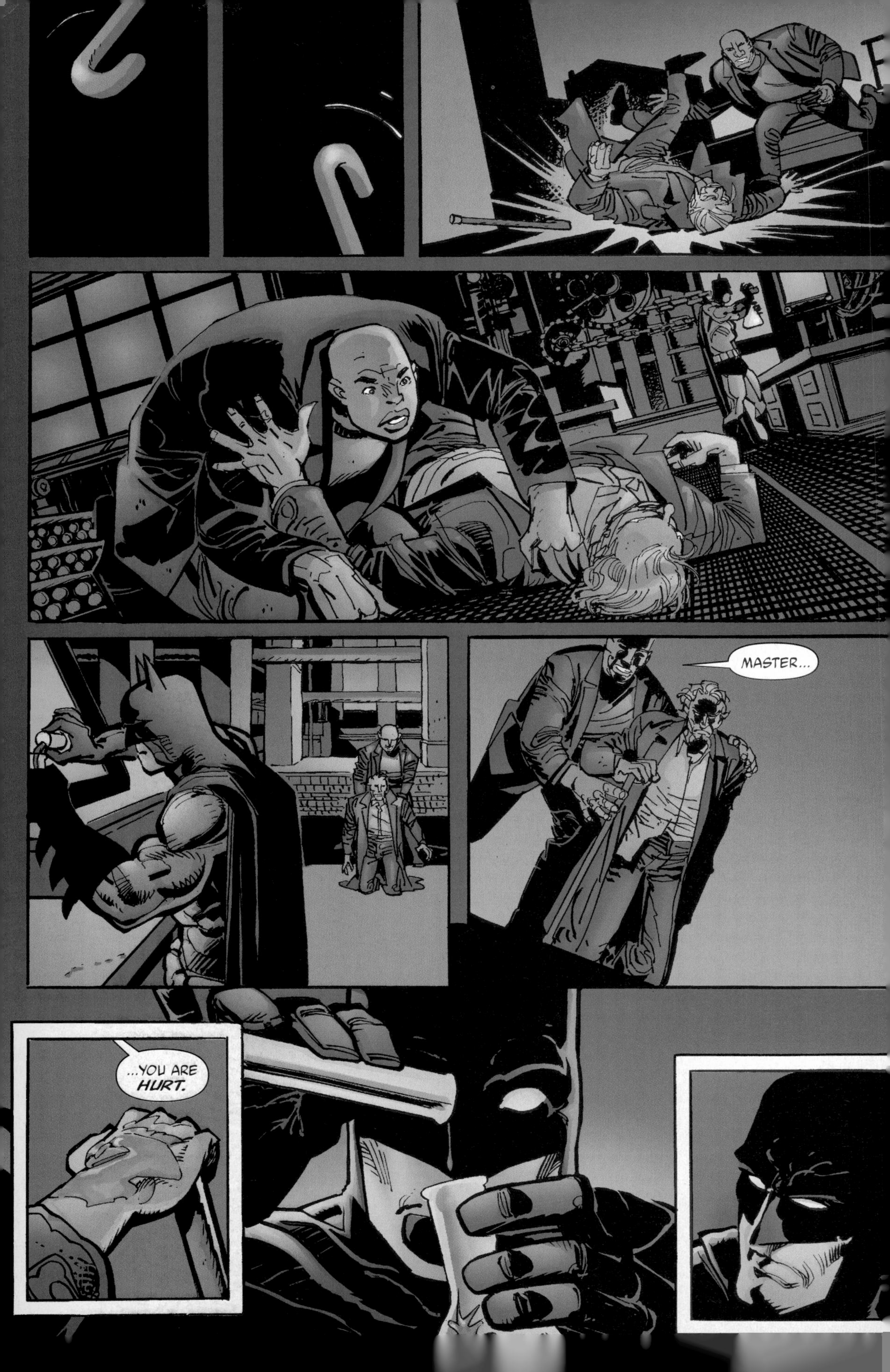
MASTER...
...YOU ARE **HURT.**

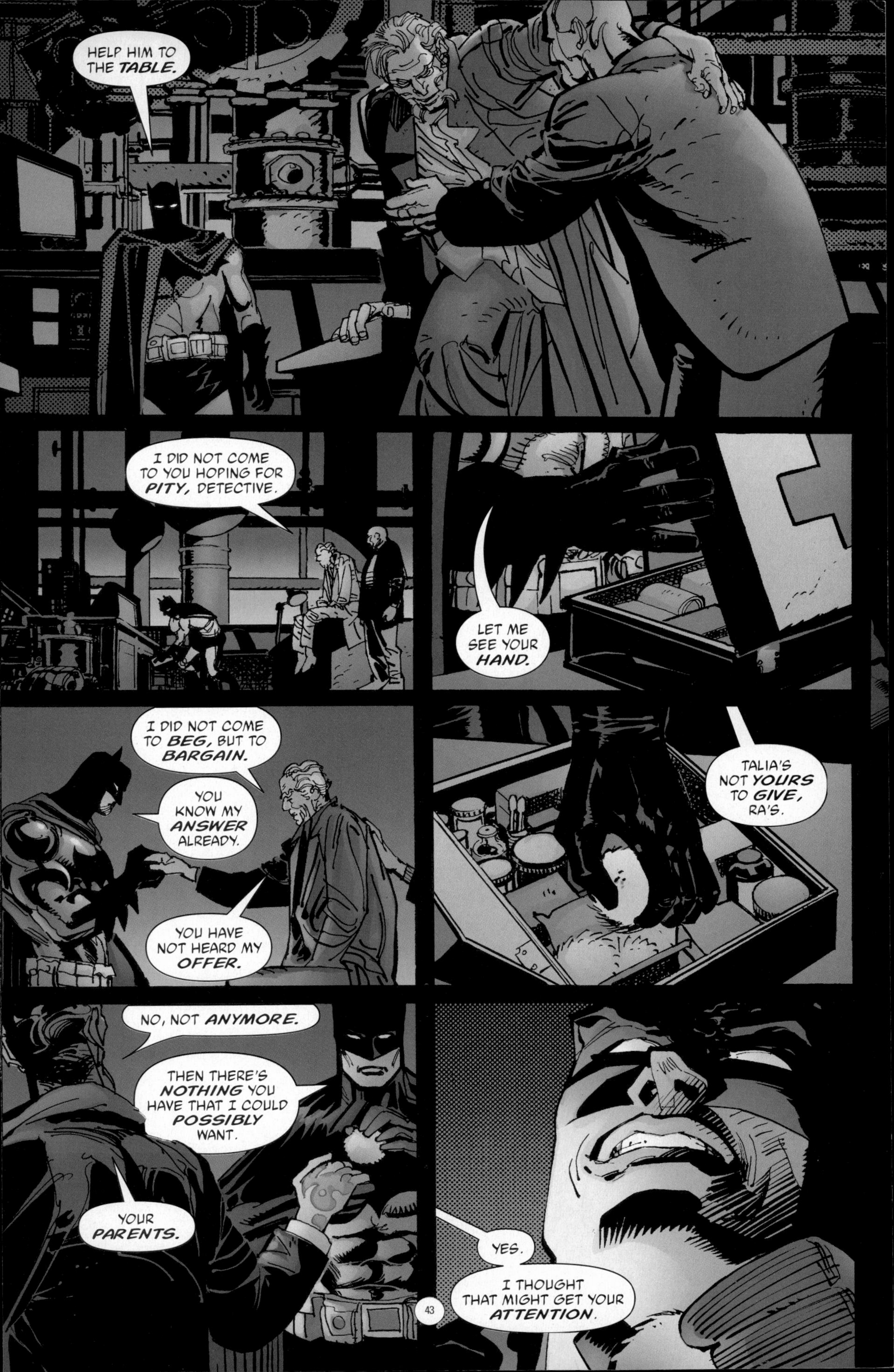
HELP HIM TO THE TABLE.
I DID NOT COME TO YOU HOPING FOR PITY, DETECTIVE.
LET ME SEE YOUR HAND.
I DID NOT COME TO BEG, BUT TO BARGAIN.
YOU KNOW MY ANSWER ALREADY.
YOU HAVE NOT HEARD MY OFFER.
TALIA'S NOT YOURS TO GIVE, RA'S.
NO, NOT ANYMORE.
THEN THERE'S NOTHING YOU HAVE THAT I COULD POSSIBLY WANT.
YOUR PARENTS.
YES.
I THOUGHT THAT MIGHT GET YOUR ATTENTION.

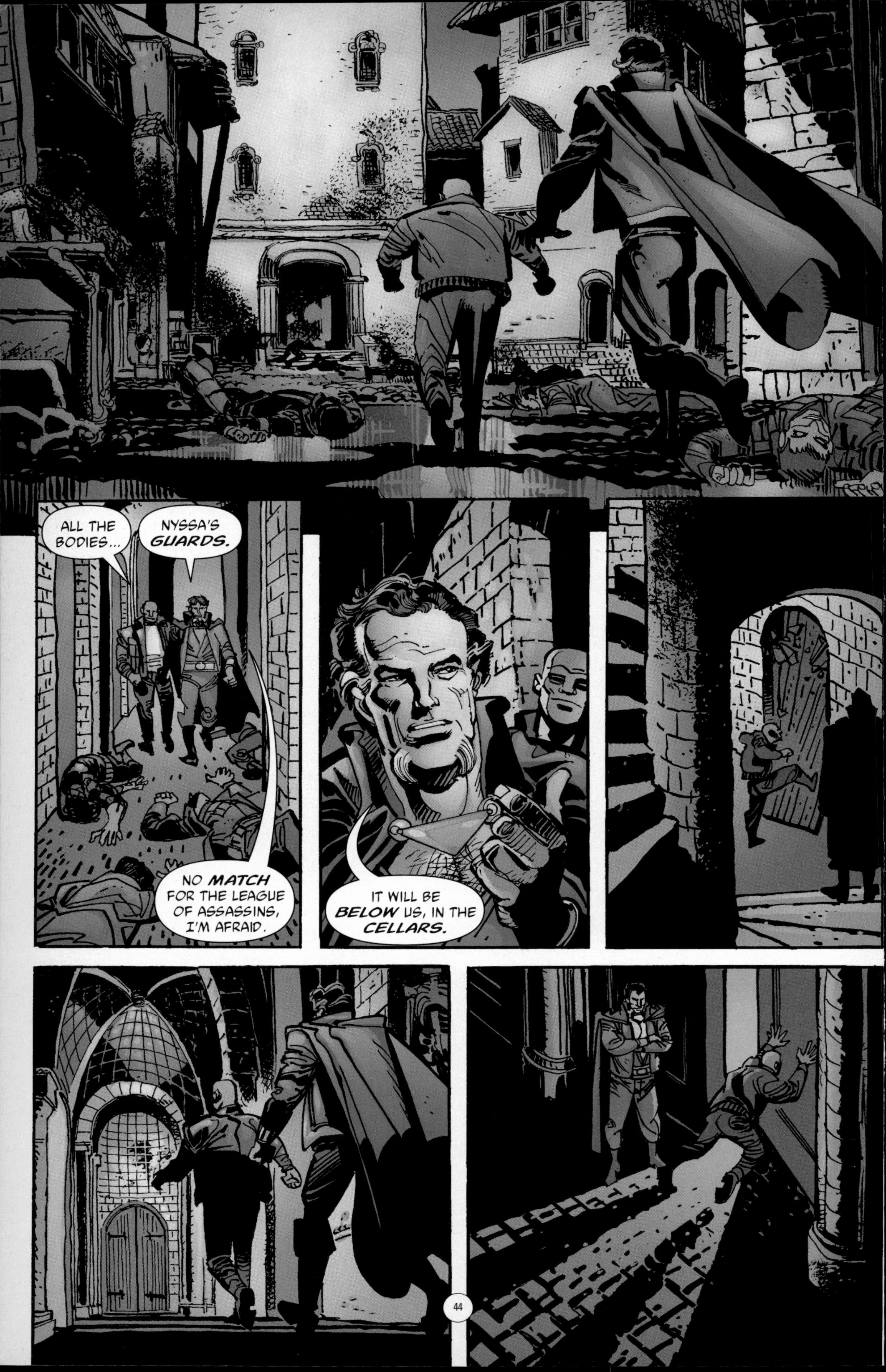
ALL THE BODIES...
NYSSA'S GUARDS.
NO MATCH FOR THE LEAGUE OF ASSASSINS, I'M AFRAID.
IT WILL BE BELOW US, IN THE CELLARS.

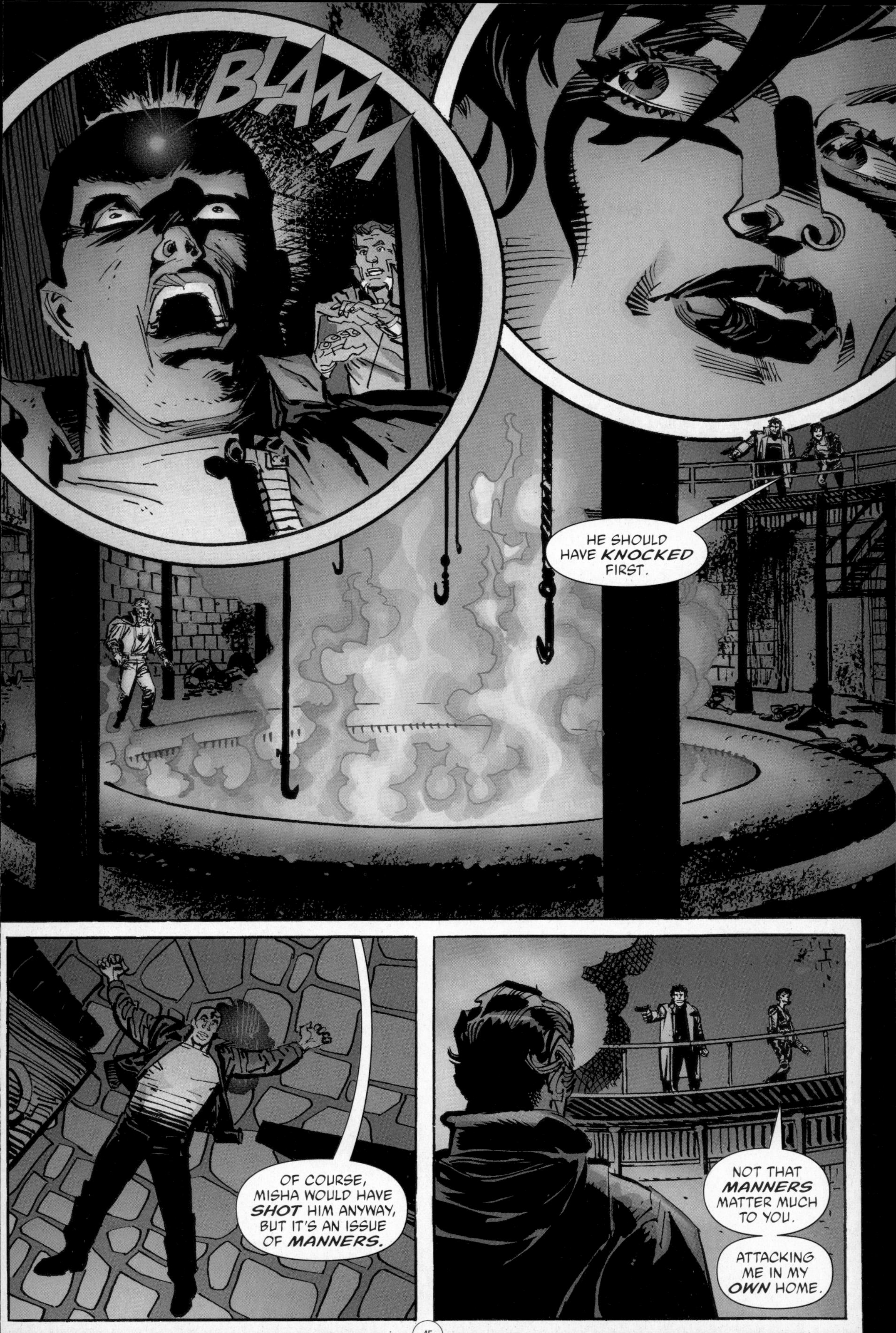
BLAMM
HE SHOULD HAVE KNOCKED FIRST.
OF COURSE, MISHA WOULD HAVE SHOT HIM ANYWAY, BUT IT'S AN ISSUE OF MANNERS.
NOT THAT MANNERS MATTER MUCH TO YOU.
ATTACKING ME IN MY OWN HOME.

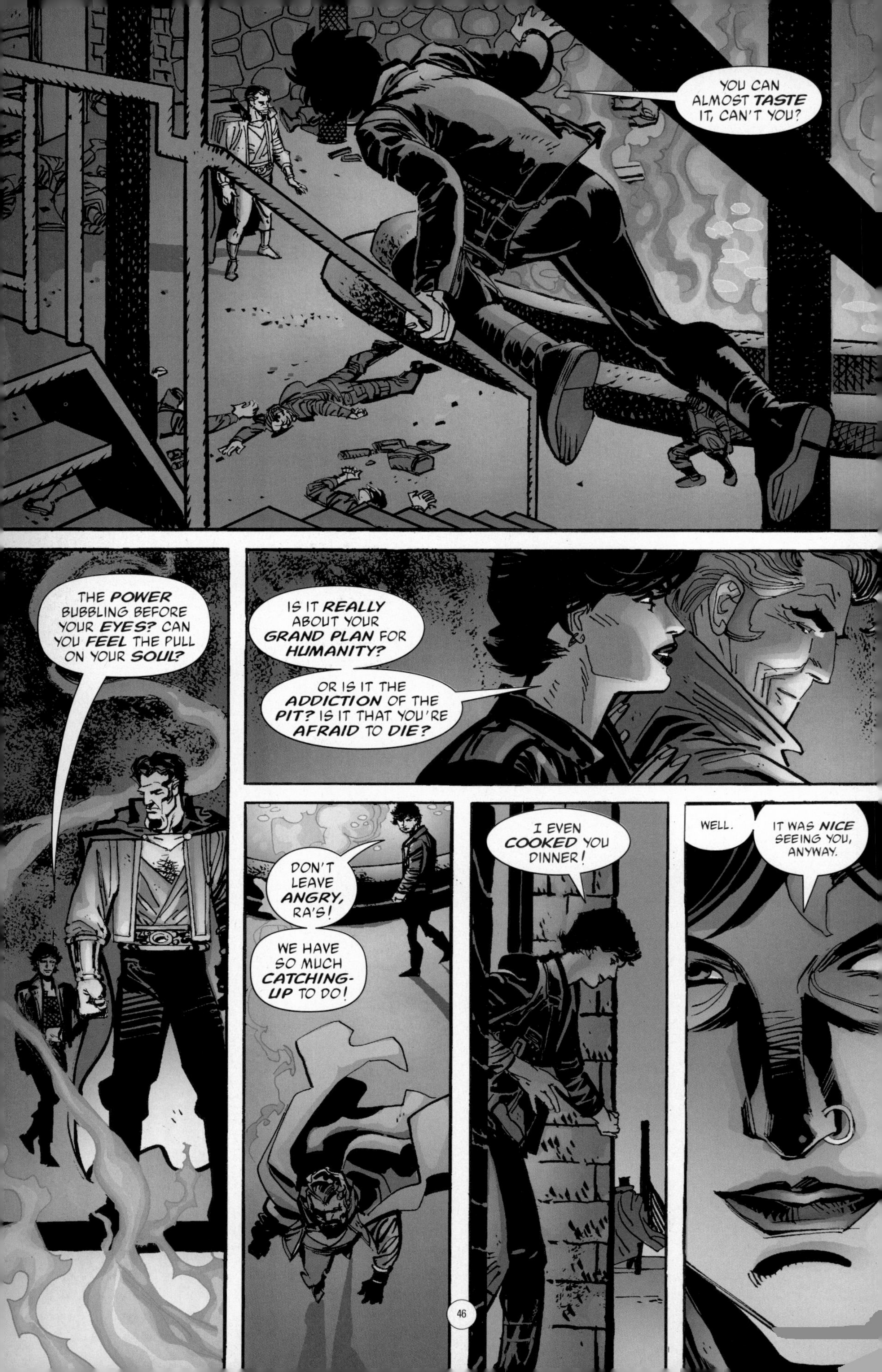

YOU CAN ALMOST TASTE IT, CAN'T YOU?
THE POWER BUBBLING BEFORE YOUR EYES? CAN YOU FEEL THE PULL ON YOUR SOUL?
IS IT REALLY ABOUT YOUR GRAND PLAN FOR HUMANITY?
OR IS IT THE ADDICTION OF THE PIT? IS IT THAT YOU'RE AFRAID TO DIE?
DON'T LEAVE ANGRY, RA'S!
WE HAVE SO MUCH CATCHING-UP TO DO!
I EVEN COOKED YOU DINNER!
WELL.
IT WAS NICE SEEING YOU, ANYWAY.

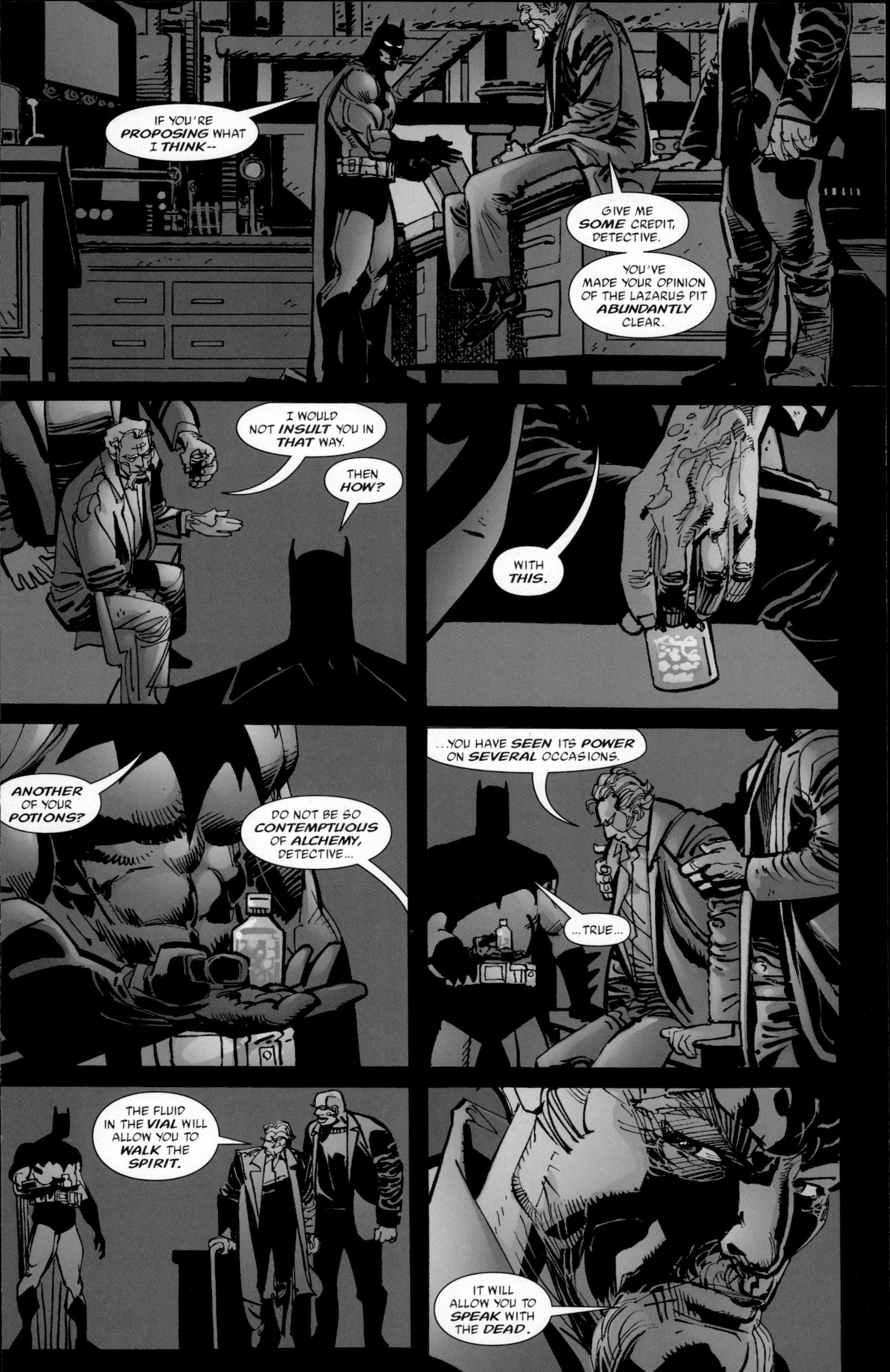
IF YOU'RE PROPOSING WHAT I THINK--
GIVE ME SOME CREDIT, DETECTIVE.
YOU'VE MADE YOUR OPINION OF THE LAZARUS PIT ABUNDANTLY CLEAR.
I WOULD NOT INSULT YOU IN THAT WAY.
THEN HOW?
WITH THIS.
ANOTHER OF YOUR POTIONS?
DO NOT BE SO CONTEMPTUOUS OF ALCHEMY, DETECTIVE...
...YOU HAVE SEEN ITS POWER ON SEVERAL OCCASIONS.
...TRUE...
THE FLUID IN THE VIAL WILL ALLOW YOU TO WALK THE SPIRIT.
IT WILL ALLOW YOU TO SPEAK WITH THE DEAD.

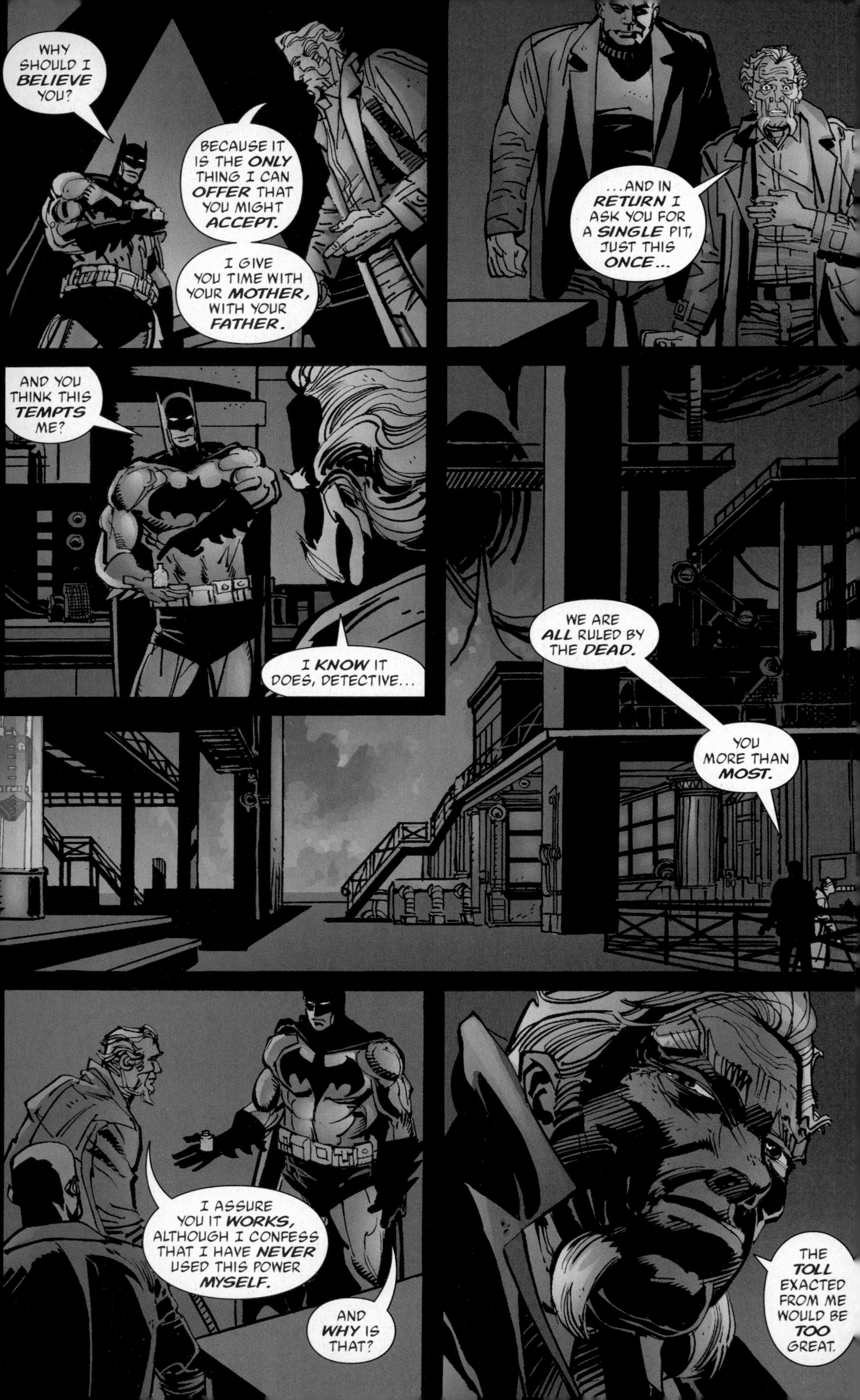
WHY SHOULD I BELIEVE YOU?
BECAUSE IT IS THE ONLY THING I CAN OFFER THAT YOU MIGHT ACCEPT.
I GIVE YOU TIME WITH YOUR MOTHER, WITH YOUR FATHER.
...AND IN RETURN I ASK YOU FOR A SINGLE PIT, JUST THIS ONCE...
AND YOU THINK THIS TEMPTS ME?
I KNOW IT DOES, DETECTIVE...
WE ARE ALL RULED BY THE DEAD.
YOU MORE THAN MOST.
I ASSURE YOU IT WORKS, ALTHOUGH I CONFESS THAT I HAVE NEVER USED THIS POWER MYSELF.
AND WHY IS THAT?
THE TOLL EXACTED FROM ME WOULD BE TOO GREAT.

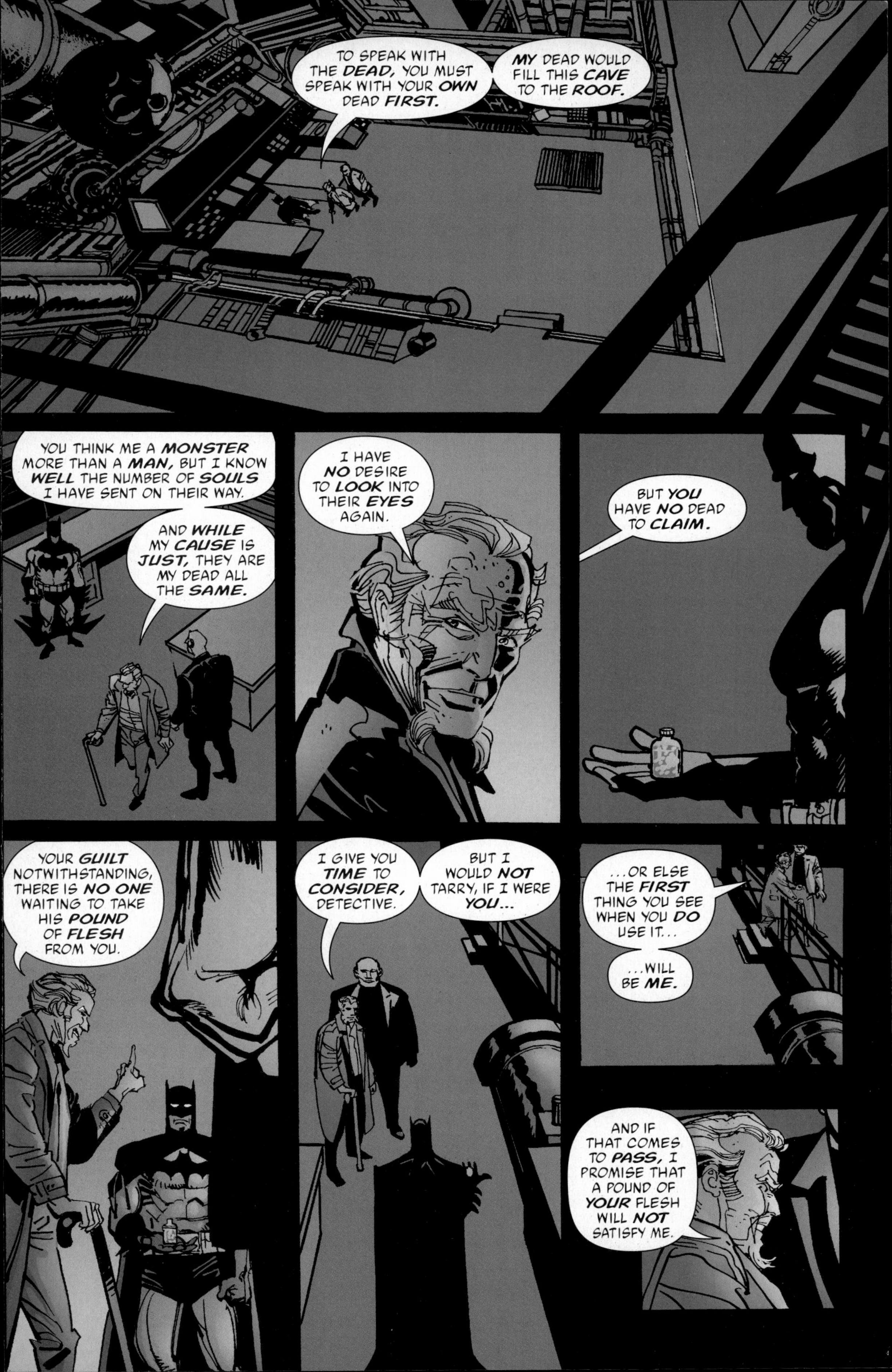

TO SPEAK WITH THE DEAD, YOU MUST SPEAK WITH YOUR OWN DEAD FIRST.
MY DEAD WOULD FILL THIS CAVE TO THE ROOF.
YOU THINK ME A MONSTER MORE THAN A MAN, BUT I KNOW WELL THE NUMBER OF SOULS I HAVE SENT ON THEIR WAY.
AND WHILE MY CAUSE IS JUST, THEY ARE MY DEAD ALL THE SAME.
I HAVE NO DESIRE TO LOOK INTO THEIR EYES AGAIN.
BUT YOU HAVE NO DEAD TO CLAIM.
YOUR GUILT NOTWITHSTANDING, THERE IS NO ONE WAITING TO TAKE HIS POUND OF FLESH FROM YOU.
I GIVE YOU TIME TO CONSIDER, DETECTIVE.
BUT I WOULD NOT TARRY, IF I WERE YOU...
...OR ELSE THE FIRST THING YOU SEE WHEN YOU DO USE IT...
...WILL BE ME.
AND IF THAT COMES TO PASS, I PROMISE THAT A POUND OF YOUR FLESH WILL NOT SATISFY ME.

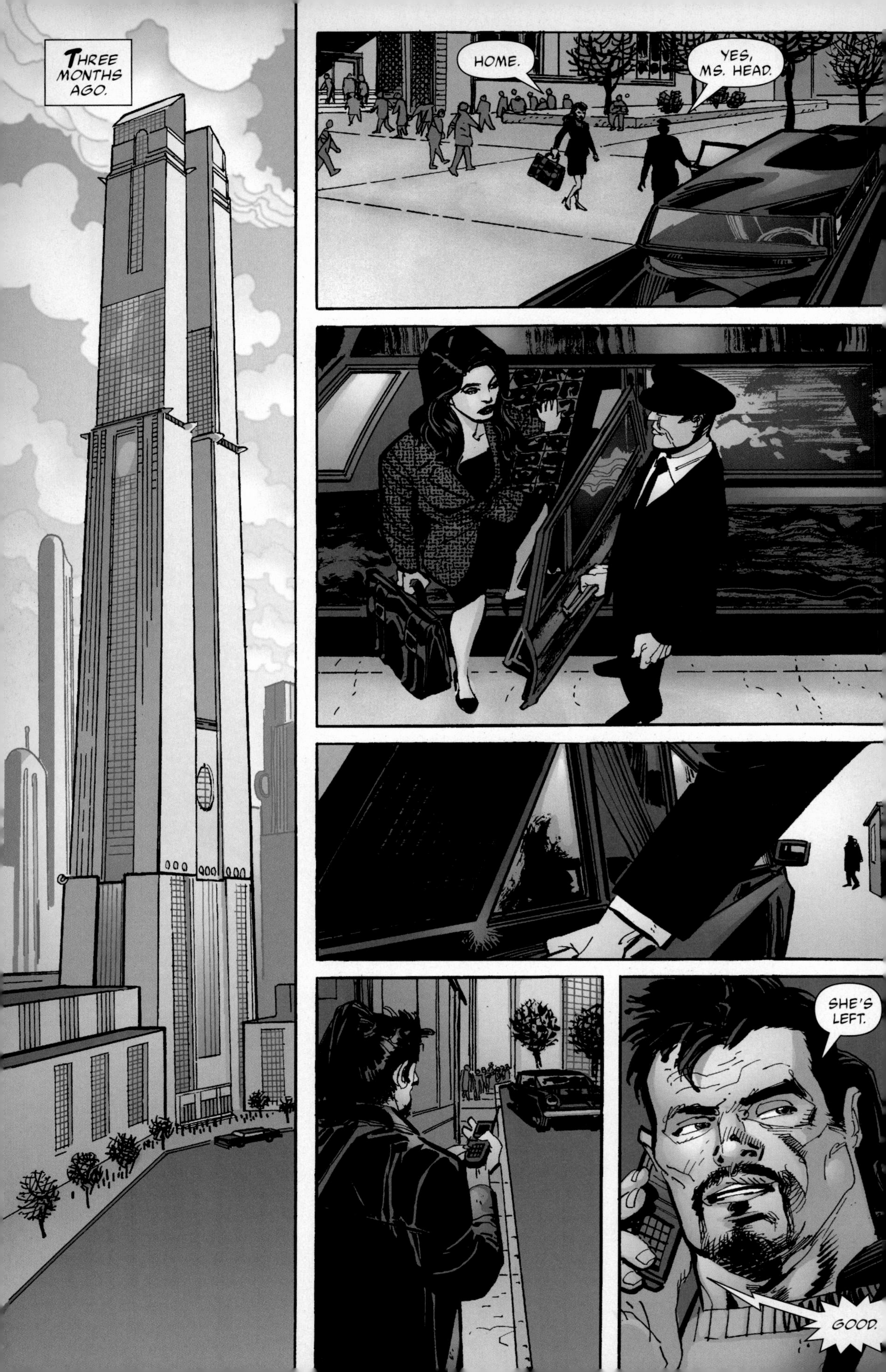
THREE MONTHS AGO.
HOME.
YES, MS. HEAD.
SHE'S LEFT.
GOOD.

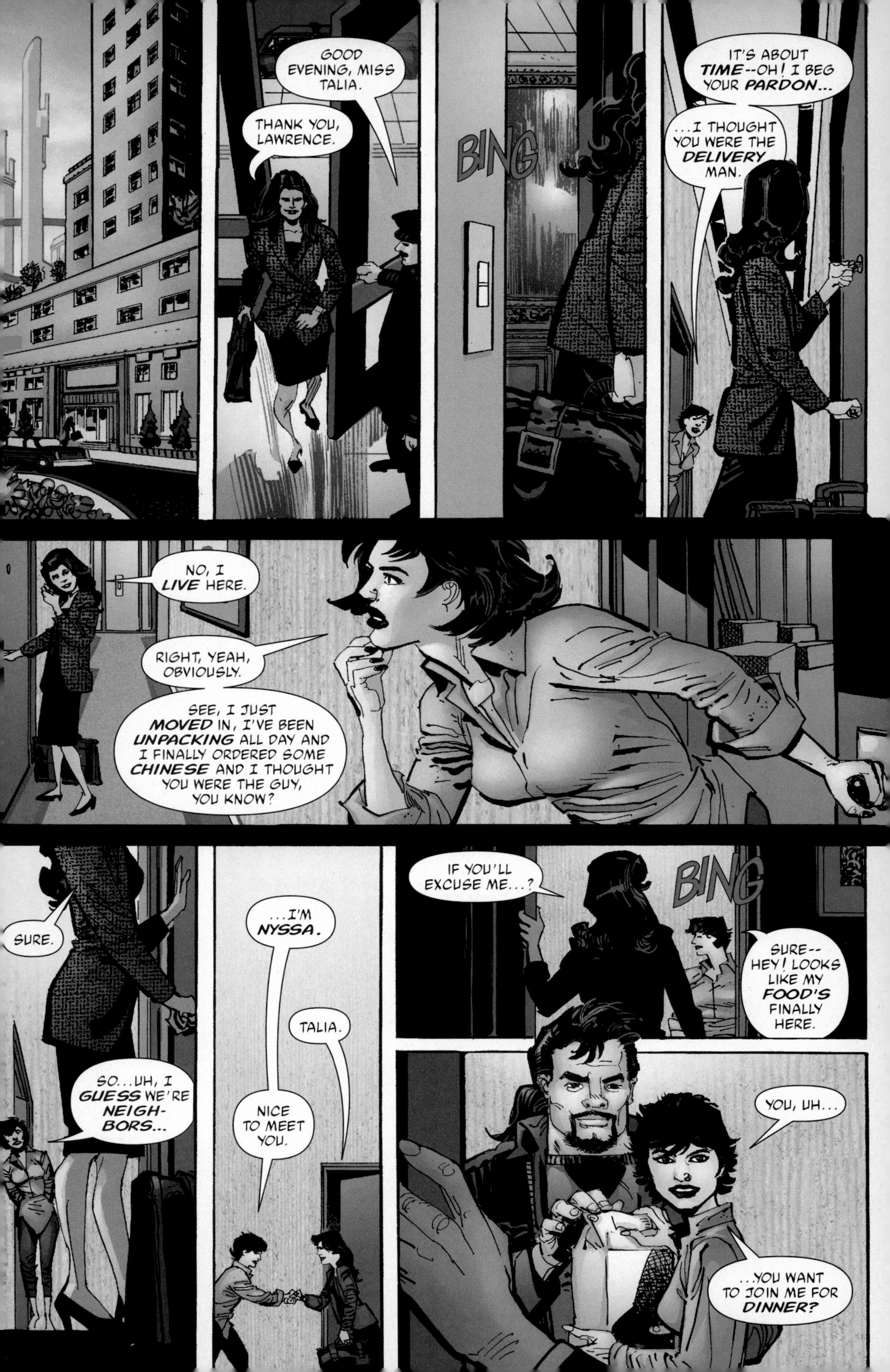

GOOD EVENING, MISS TALIA.
THANK YOU, LAWRENCE.
BING
IT'S ABOUT TIME--OH! I BEG YOUR PARDON...
...I THOUGHT YOU WERE THE DELIVERY MAN.
NO, I LIVE HERE.
RIGHT, YEAH, OBVIOUSLY.
SEE, I JUST MOVED IN, I'VE BEEN UNPACKING ALL DAY AND I FINALLY ORDERED SOME CHINESE AND I THOUGHT YOU WERE THE GUY, YOU KNOW?
SURE.
SO...UH, I GUESS WE'RE NEIGH-BORS...
...I'M NYSSA.
TALIA.
NICE TO MEET YOU.
IF YOU'LL EXCUSE ME...?
BING
SURE-- HEY! LOOKS LIKE MY FOOD'S FINALLY HERE.
YOU, UH...
...YOU WANT TO JOIN ME FOR DINNER?

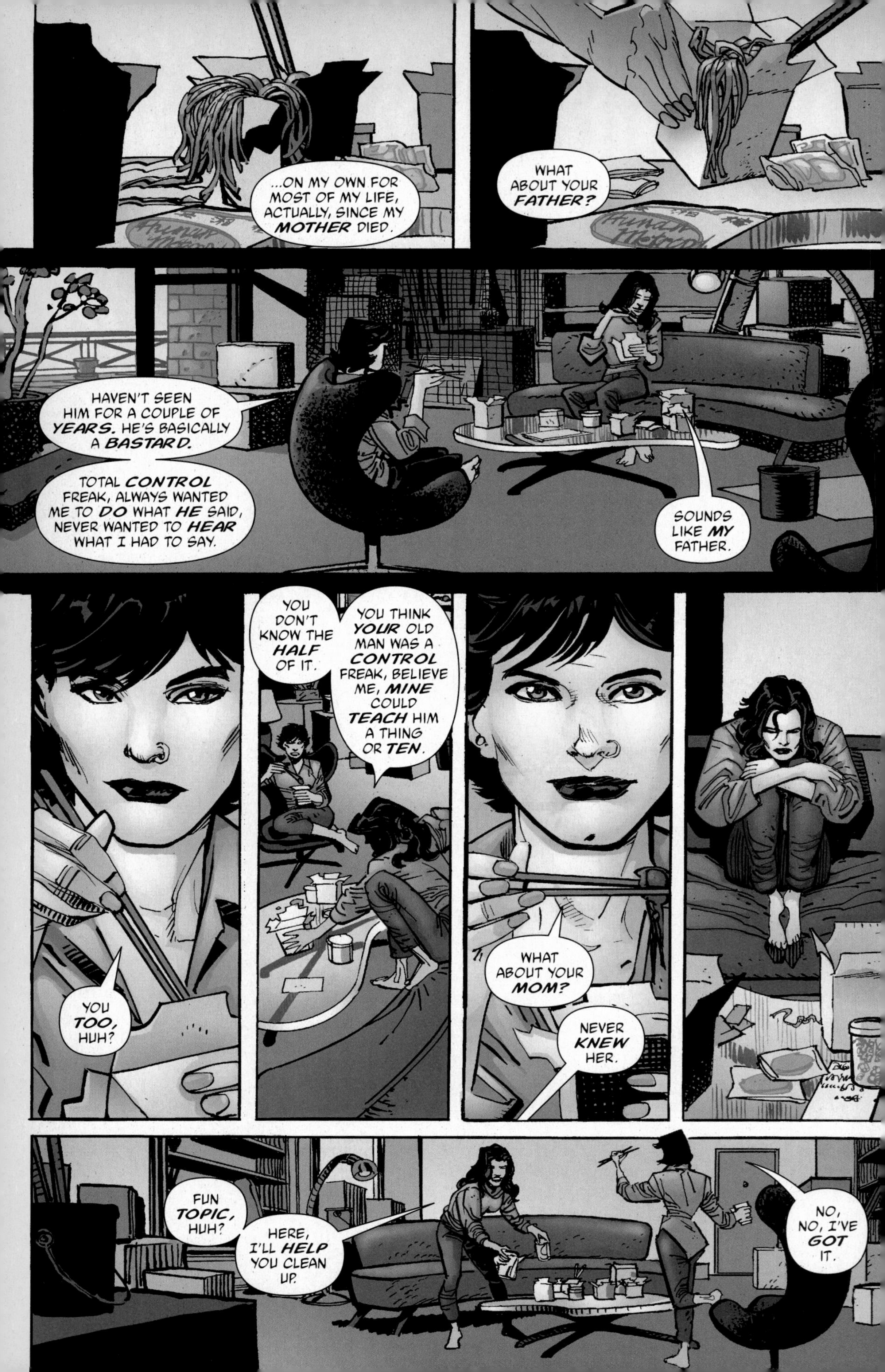

...ON MY OWN FOR MOST OF MY LIFE, ACTUALLY, SINCE MY MOTHER DIED.
WHAT ABOUT YOUR FATHER?
HAVEN'T SEEN HIM FOR A COUPLE OF YEARS. HE'S BASICALLY A BASTARD.
TOTAL CONTROL FREAK, ALWAYS WANTED ME TO DO WHAT HE SAID, NEVER WANTED TO HEAR WHAT I HAD TO SAY.
SOUNDS LIKE MY FATHER.
YOU TOO, HUH?
YOU DON'T KNOW THE HALF OF IT.
YOU THINK YOUR OLD MAN WAS A CONTROL FREAK, BELIEVE ME, MINE COULD TEACH HIM A THING OR TEN.
WHAT ABOUT YOUR MOM?
NEVER KNEW HER.
FUN TOPIC, HUH?
HERE, I'LL HELP YOU CLEAN UP.
NO, NO, I'VE GOT IT.

AFTER ALL, *I* INVITED *YOU.*

WHAT HAPPENED TO YOUR *ARM?*

WHAT DO YOU *MEAN?*

NOTHING, IT JUST LOOKS LIKE A *SCAR,* OR... NOTHING.

...I DIDN'T MEAN ANY *OFFENSE.*

NO. DON'T ...DON'T *WORRY.*

I JUST *FORGET* IT'S *THERE,* SOME- TIMES.

IT'S JUST... FROM A *LONG* TIME AGO.

THANKS FOR DINNER.

MAYBE WE CAN...DO IT AGAIN SOON?

I DON'T KNOW... I DON'T KNOW A LOT OF PEOPLE IN METROPOLIS...

I'D *LIKE* THAT.

HAVE A *GOOD NIGHT.*

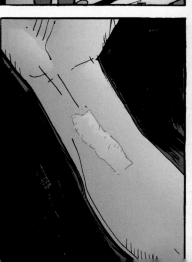

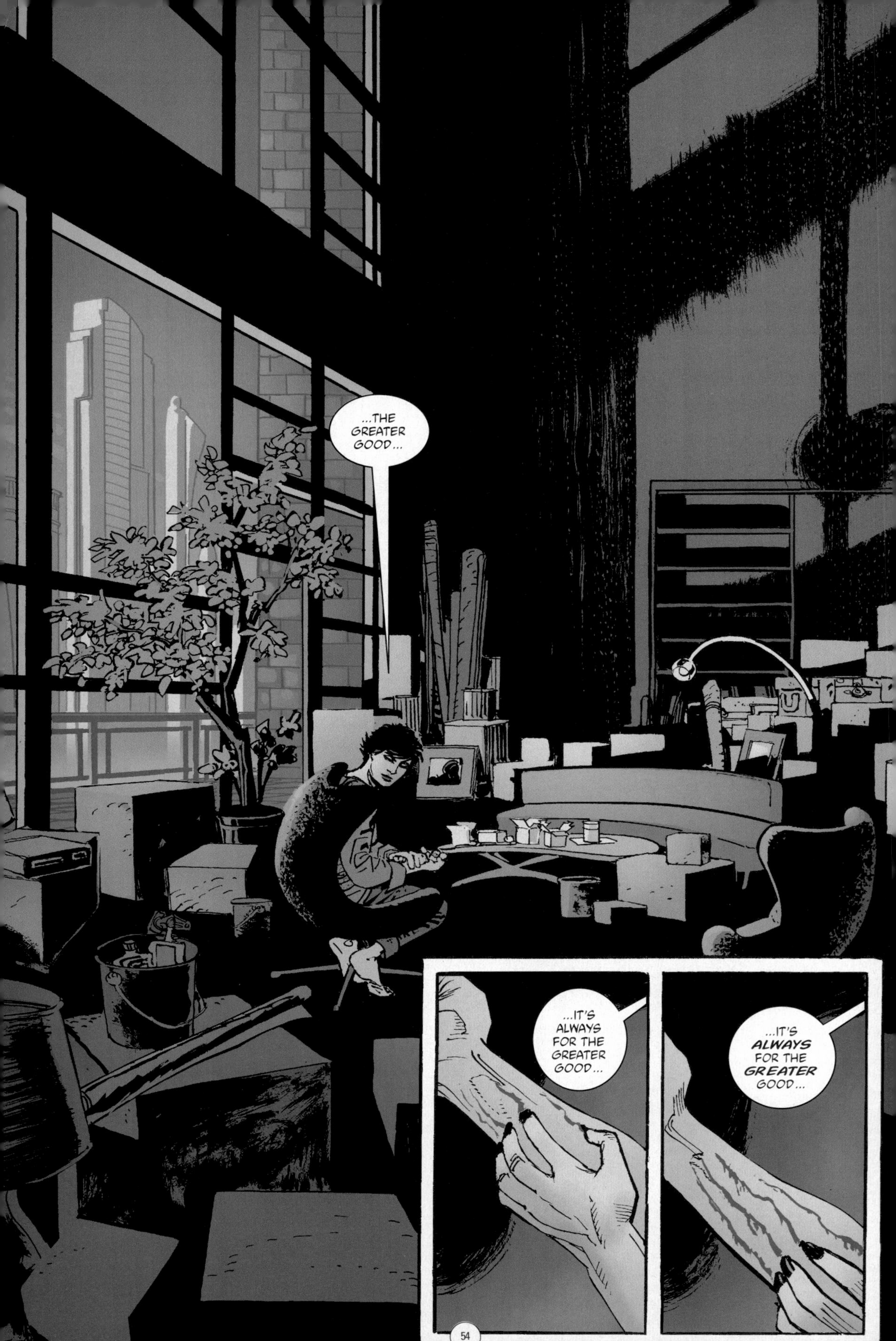
...THE GREATER GOOD...
...IT'S ALWAYS FOR THE GREATER GOOD...
...IT'S *ALWAYS* FOR THE *GREATER* GOOD...

In desperation, Ra's lies.

Offering the oldest promise ever to tempt man.

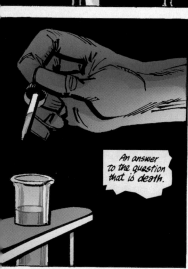

An answer to the question that is death.

Harry Houdini loved his mother so much that after her passing, he spent thousands trying to reach the other side.

...all for a chance to hear her voice once more.

In countless seances held by innumerable mediums...

...he found only promises made by frauds and swindlers...

...the tricks of men and women he termed villains of the highest order...

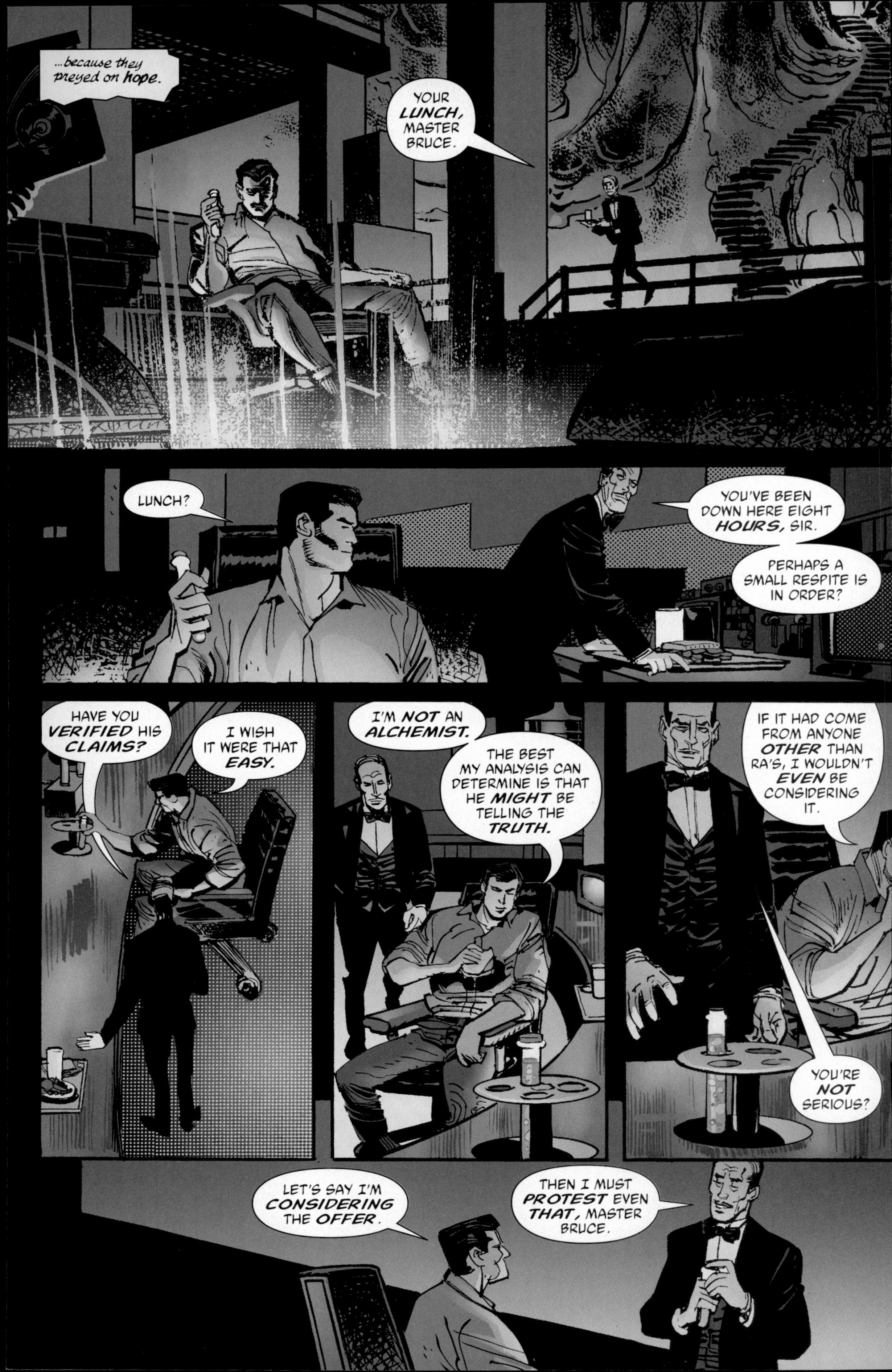
...because they preyed on hope.
YOUR LUNCH, MASTER BRUCE.
LUNCH?
YOU'VE BEEN DOWN HERE EIGHT HOURS, SIR.
PERHAPS A SMALL RESPITE IS IN ORDER?
HAVE YOU VERIFIED HIS CLAIMS?
I WISH IT WERE THAT EASY.
I'M NOT AN ALCHEMIST.
THE BEST MY ANALYSIS CAN DETERMINE IS THAT HE MIGHT BE TELLING THE TRUTH.
IF IT HAD COME FROM ANYONE OTHER THAN RA'S, I WOULDN'T EVEN BE CONSIDERING IT.
YOU'RE NOT SERIOUS?
LET'S SAY I'M CONSIDERING THE OFFER.
THEN I MUST PROTEST EVEN THAT, MASTER BRUCE.

ASIDE FROM THE *LEGION* OF ETHICAL AND MORAL QUESTIONS THAT ANY ATTEMPT TO SPEAK WITH THE *SPIRIT* BEGS...

...NEED I REMIND YOU THAT RA'S AL GHUL IS NOT SIMPLY *YOUR* ENEMY, BUT AN *ENEMY* OF ALL *HUMANITY*?

YOU *CANNOT* TRUST HIM.

IN THIS, PERHAPS I CAN. I HAVE SOMETHING HE DESPERATELY *WANTS*.

THAT YOU WOULD EVEN *CONSIDER* HIS OFFER IS *UNLIKE* YOU, AND FORCES ME TO CONCLUDE THAT THERE ARE *OTHER* FACTORS INVOLVED HERE OF WHICH I REMAIN *IGNORANT*.

THE *DEAD* HAVE *EARNED* THEIR *REST*, BRUCE...

...IT IS *NOT* YOUR PLACE TO *DISTURB* THEM.

DA DEET

IT APPEARS THERE IS *SOME-ONE* AT THE *DOOR*.

YOU GO UP, I'LL BE RIGHT THERE.

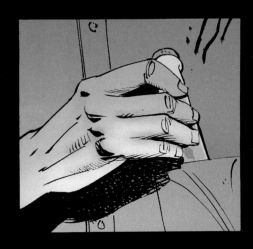

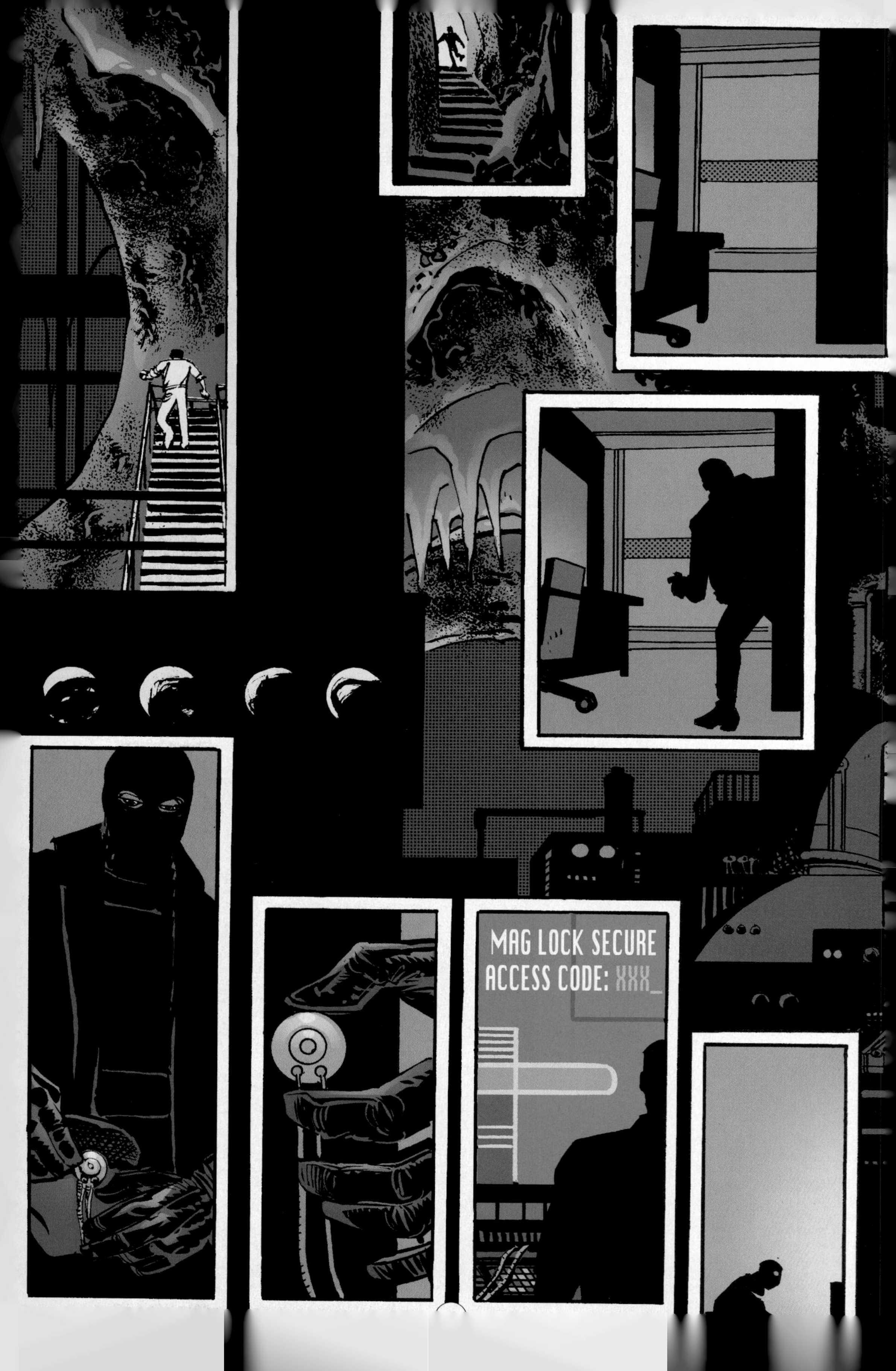
MAG LOCK SECURE
ACCESS CODE: XXX_

MAG LOCK SECURE
ACCESS CODE: XXXXXX
DENIED
COUNTERMEASURES
BEGIN IN: 5

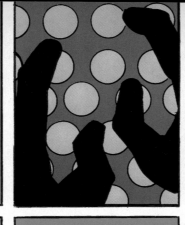

MAG LOCK SECURE
ACCESS CODE: XXX_
DENIED
COUNTERMEASURES
BEGIN IN: 3

:02

MAG LOCK SECURE
ACCESS CODE: XXXXXX_
CODE ACCEPTED
COUNTERMEASURES
RESET

SHHK

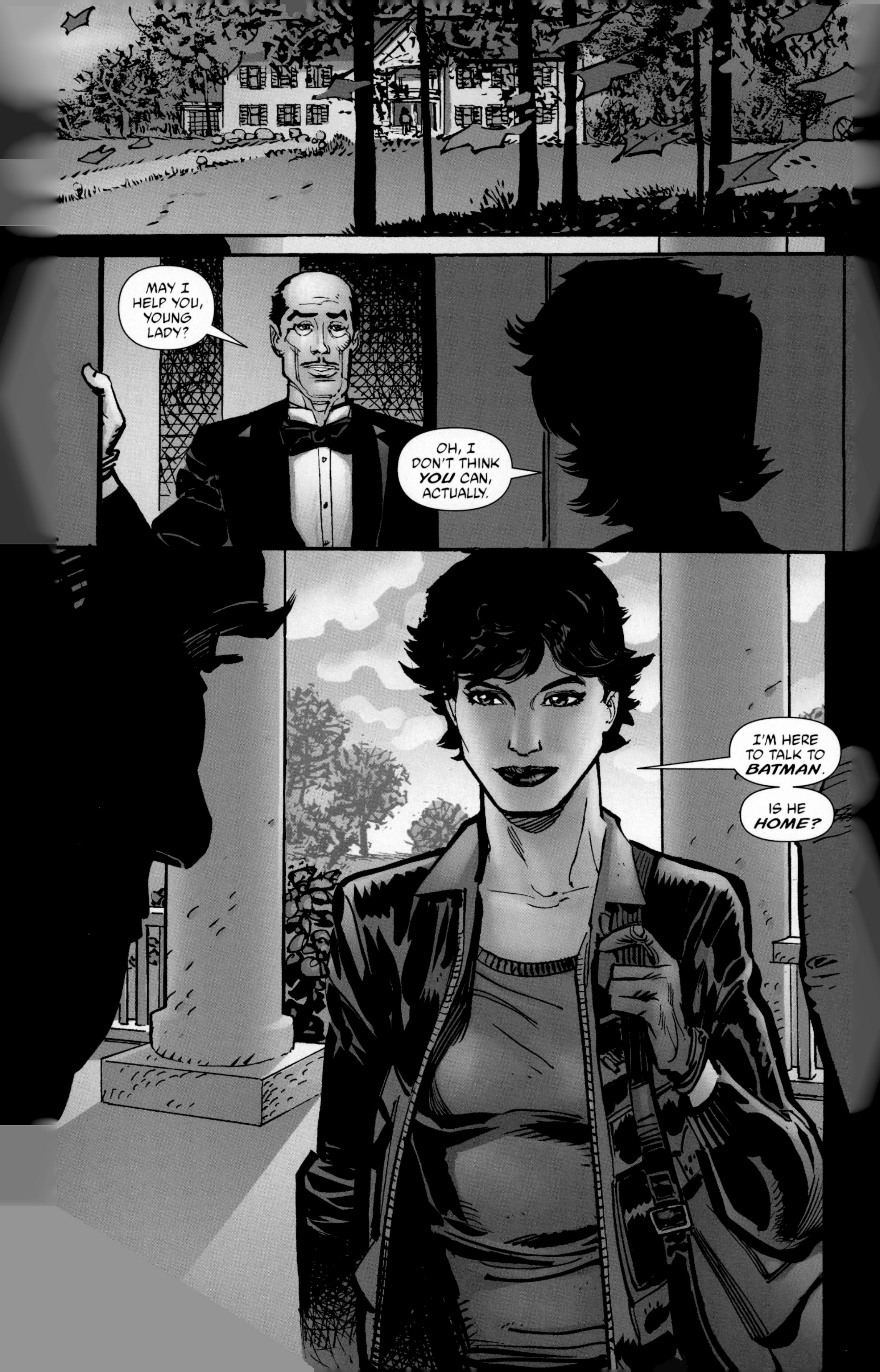
MAY I HELP YOU, YOUNG LADY?
OH, I DON'T THINK YOU CAN, ACTUALLY.
I'M HERE TO TALK TO BATMAN.
IS HE HOME?

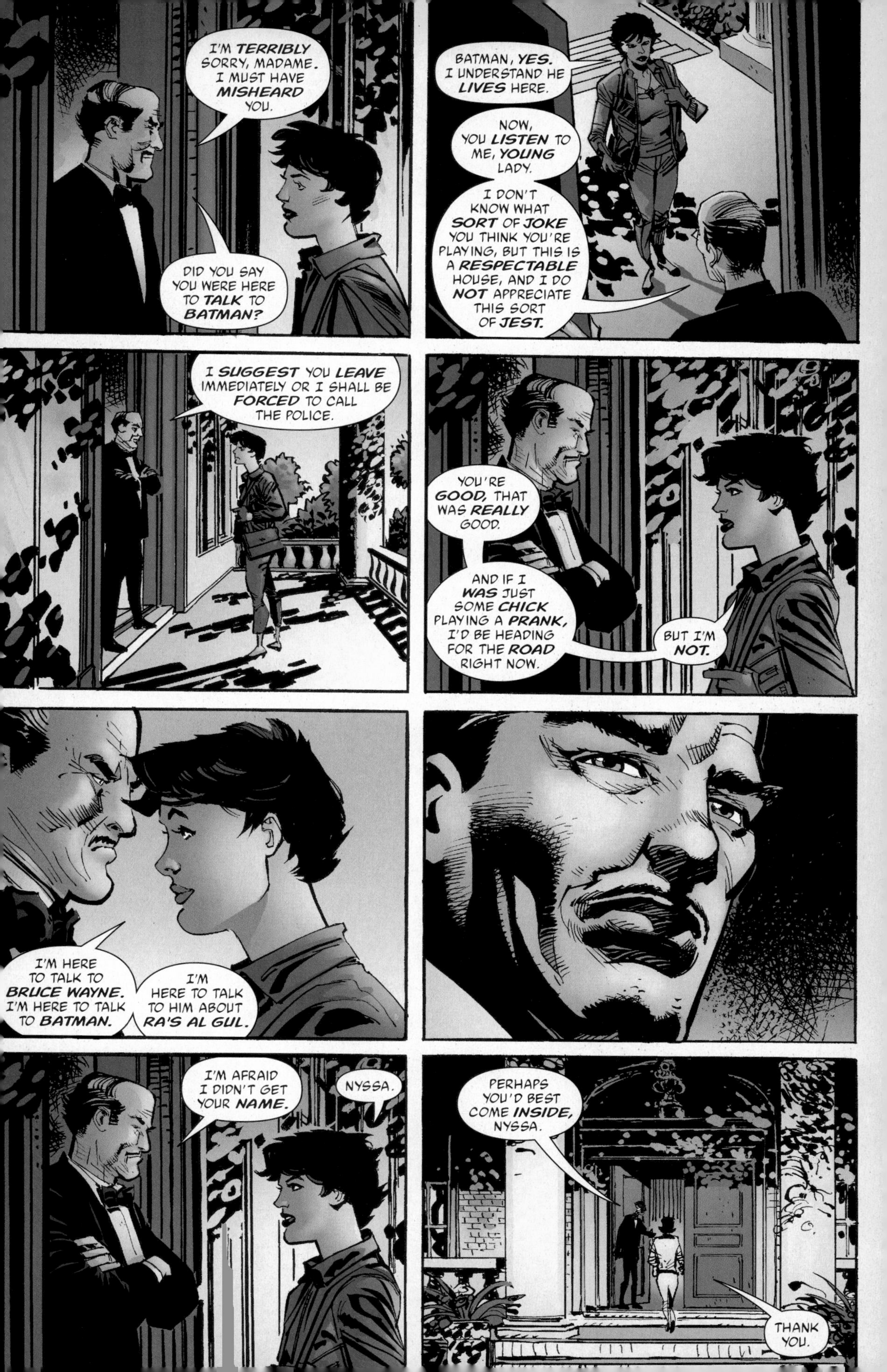
I'M TERRIBLY SORRY, MADAME. I MUST HAVE MISHEARD YOU.
DID YOU SAY YOU WERE HERE TO TALK TO BATMAN?
BATMAN, YES. I UNDERSTAND HE LIVES HERE.
NOW, YOU LISTEN TO ME, YOUNG LADY.
I DON'T KNOW WHAT SORT OF JOKE YOU THINK YOU'RE PLAYING, BUT THIS IS A RESPECTABLE HOUSE, AND I DO NOT APPRECIATE THIS SORT OF JEST.
I SUGGEST YOU LEAVE IMMEDIATELY OR I SHALL BE FORCED TO CALL THE POLICE.
YOU'RE GOOD, THAT WAS REALLY GOOD.
AND IF I WAS JUST SOME CHICK PLAYING A PRANK, I'D BE HEADING FOR THE ROAD RIGHT NOW.
BUT I'M NOT.
I'M HERE TO TALK TO BRUCE WAYNE. I'M HERE TO TALK TO BATMAN.
I'M HERE TO TALK TO HIM ABOUT RA'S AL GUL.
I'M AFRAID I DIDN'T GET YOUR NAME.
NYSSA.
PERHAPS YOU'D BEST COME INSIDE, NYSSA.
THANK YOU.

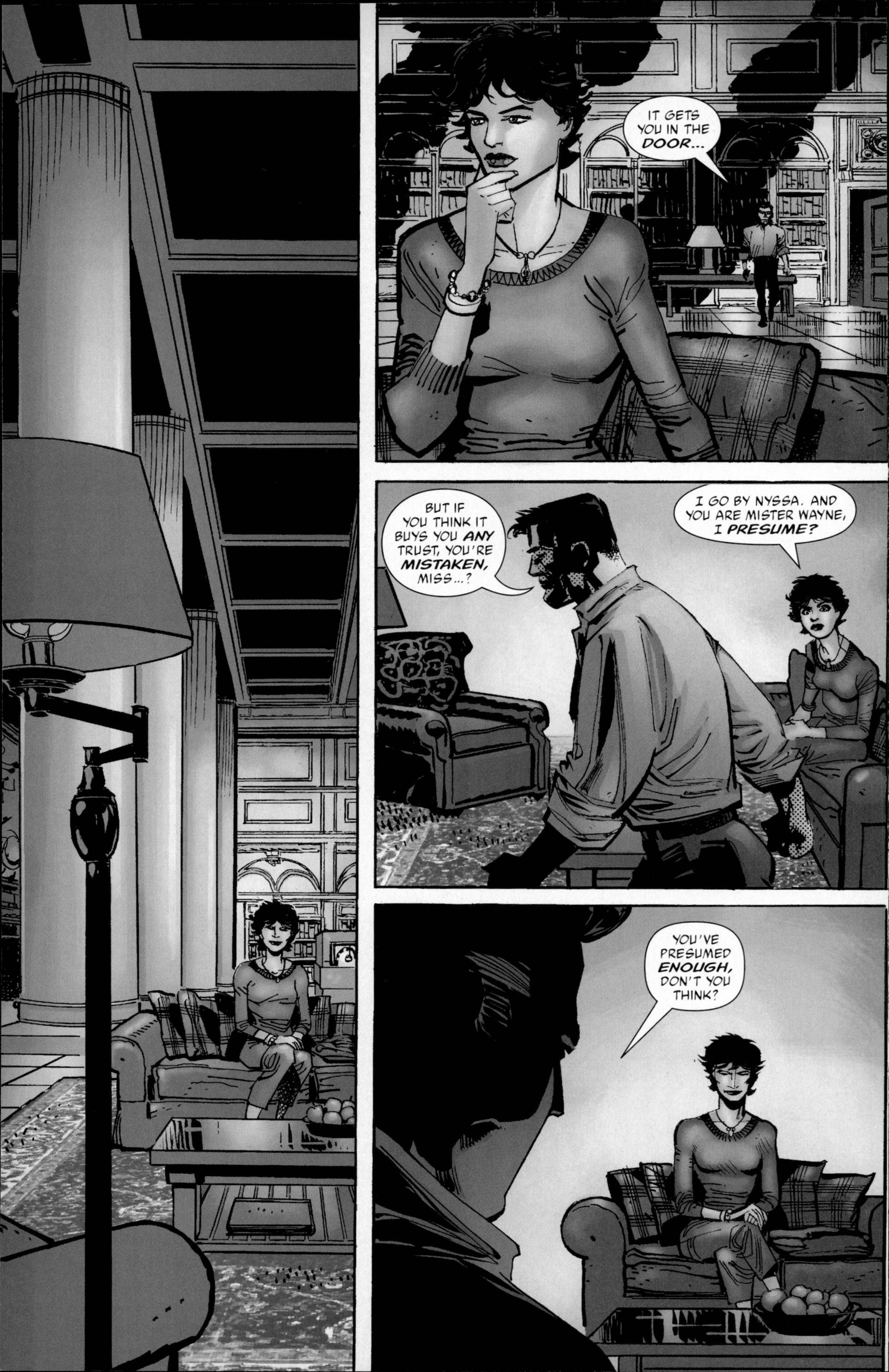
IT GETS YOU IN THE DOOR...
BUT IF YOU THINK IT BUYS YOU ANY TRUST, YOU'RE MISTAKEN, MISS...?
I GO BY NYSSA. AND YOU ARE MISTER WAYNE, I PRESUME?
YOU'VE PRESUMED ENOUGH, DON'T YOU THINK?

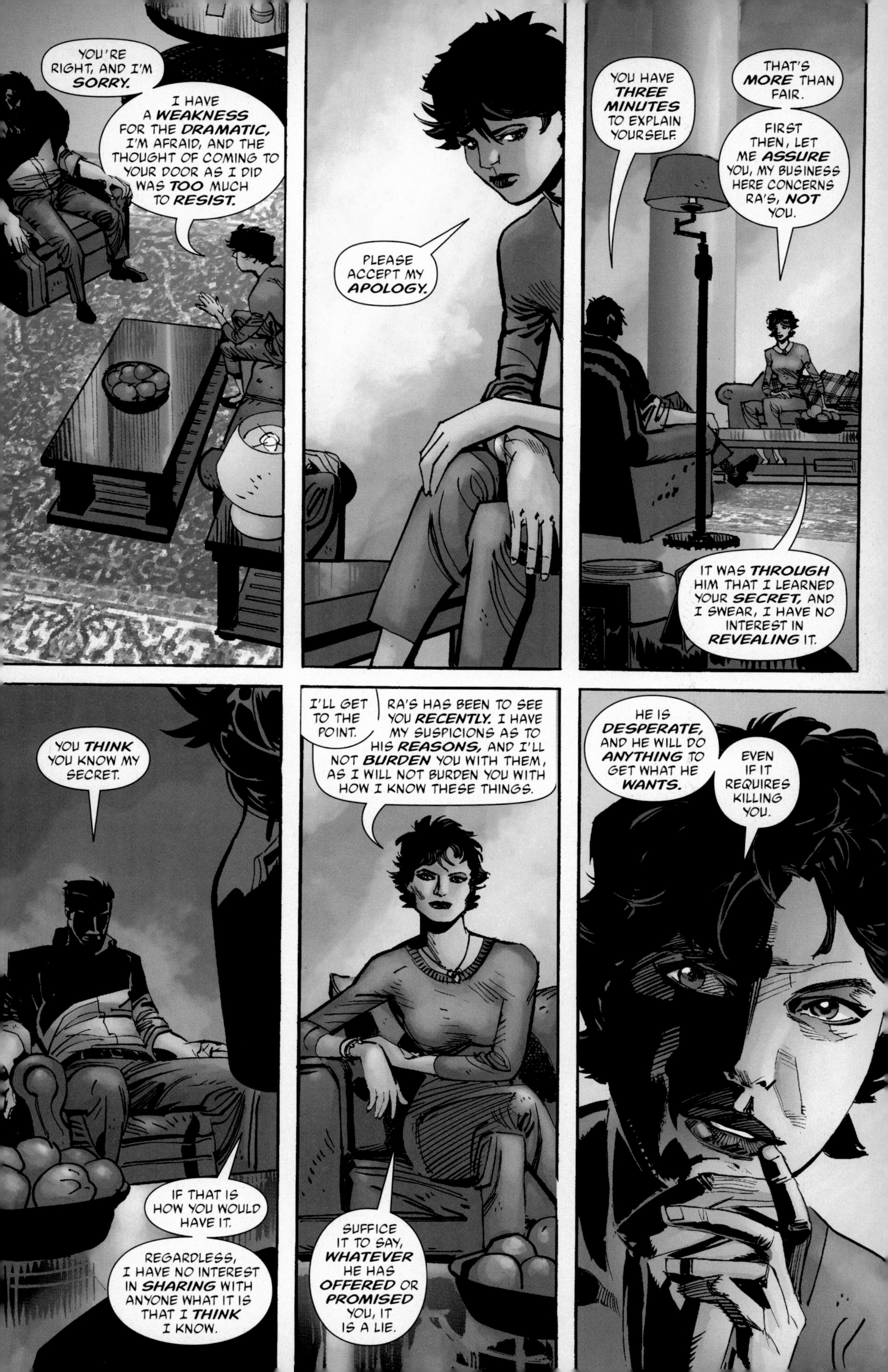
YOU'RE RIGHT, AND I'M SORRY.
I HAVE A WEAKNESS FOR THE DRAMATIC, I'M AFRAID, AND THE THOUGHT OF COMING TO YOUR DOOR AS I DID WAS TOO MUCH TO RESIST.
PLEASE ACCEPT MY APOLOGY.
YOU HAVE THREE MINUTES TO EXPLAIN YOURSELF.
THAT'S MORE THAN FAIR.
FIRST THEN, LET ME ASSURE YOU, MY BUSINESS HERE CONCERNS RA'S, NOT YOU.
IT WAS THROUGH HIM THAT I LEARNED YOUR SECRET, AND I SWEAR, I HAVE NO INTEREST IN REVEALING IT.
YOU THINK YOU KNOW MY SECRET.
IF THAT IS HOW YOU WOULD HAVE IT.
REGARDLESS, I HAVE NO INTEREST IN SHARING WITH ANYONE WHAT IT IS THAT I THINK I KNOW.
I'LL GET TO THE POINT.
RA'S HAS BEEN TO SEE YOU RECENTLY. I HAVE MY SUSPICIONS AS TO HIS REASONS, AND I'LL NOT BURDEN YOU WITH THEM, AS I WILL NOT BURDEN YOU WITH HOW I KNOW THESE THINGS.
SUFFICE IT TO SAY, WHATEVER HE HAS OFFERED OR PROMISED YOU, IT IS A LIE.
HE IS DESPERATE, AND HE WILL DO ANYTHING TO GET WHAT HE WANTS.
EVEN IF IT REQUIRES KILLING YOU.

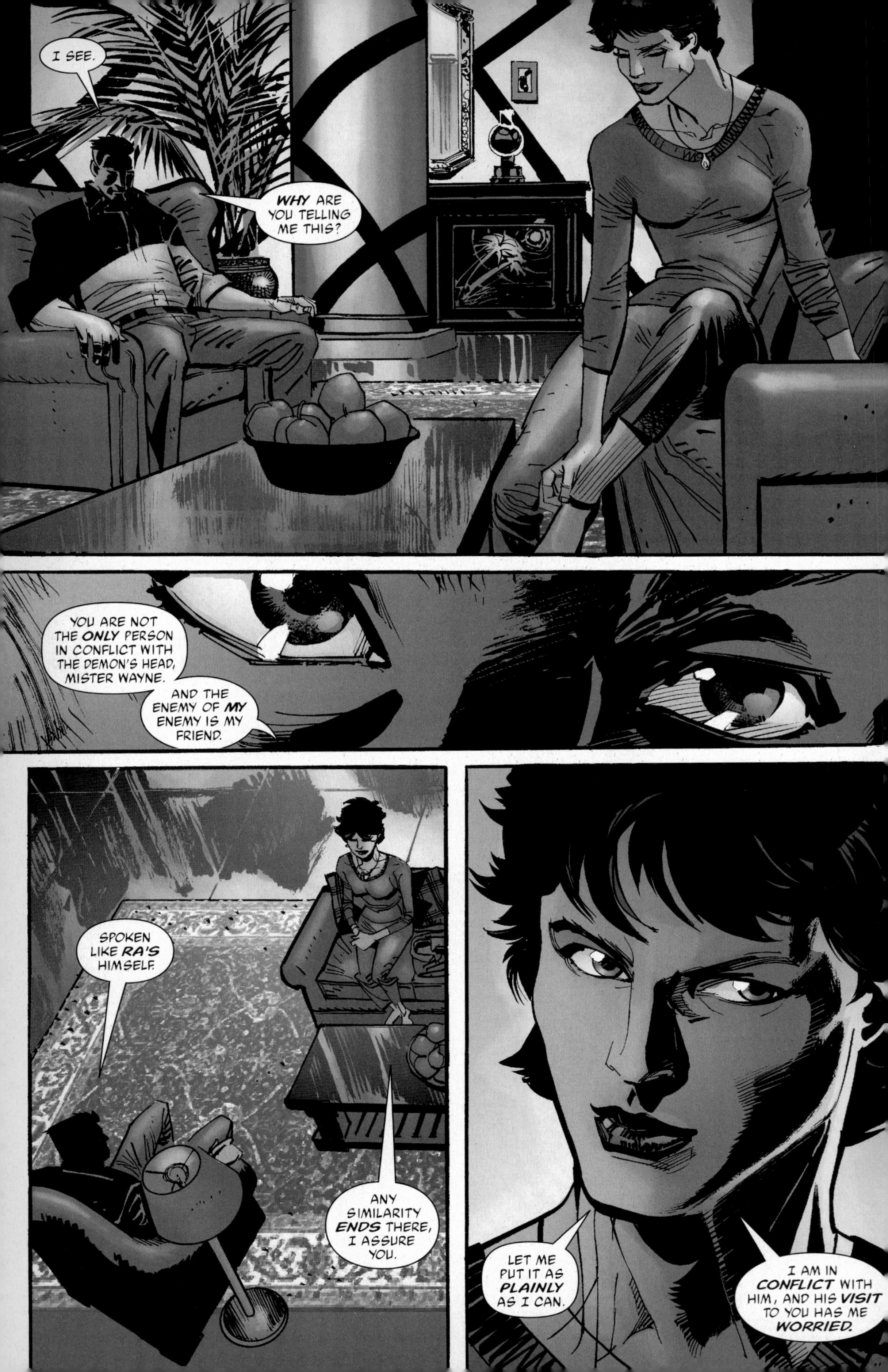

I SEE.
WHY ARE YOU TELLING ME THIS?
YOU ARE NOT THE ONLY PERSON IN CONFLICT WITH THE DEMON'S HEAD, MISTER WAYNE.
AND THE ENEMY OF MY ENEMY IS MY FRIEND.
SPOKEN LIKE RA'S HIMSELF.
ANY SIMILARITY ENDS THERE, I ASSURE YOU.
LET ME PUT IT AS PLAINLY AS I CAN.
I AM IN CONFLICT WITH HIM, AND HIS VISIT TO YOU HAS ME WORRIED.

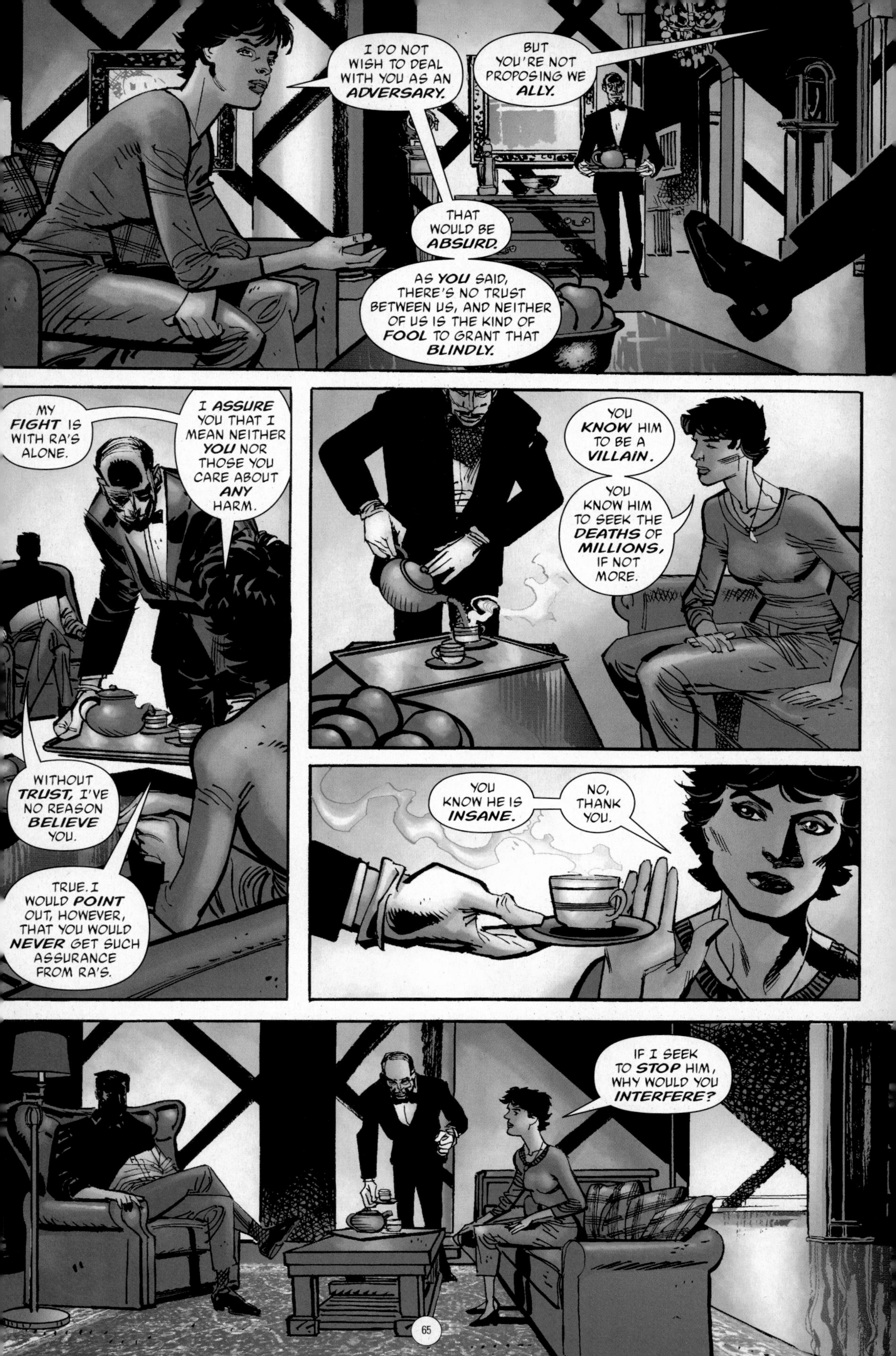
I DO NOT WISH TO DEAL WITH YOU AS AN ADVERSARY.
BUT YOU'RE NOT PROPOSING WE ALLY.
THAT WOULD BE ABSURD.
AS YOU SAID, THERE'S NO TRUST BETWEEN US, AND NEITHER OF US IS THE KIND OF FOOL TO GRANT THAT BLINDLY.
MY FIGHT IS WITH RA'S ALONE.
I ASSURE YOU THAT I MEAN NEITHER YOU NOR THOSE YOU CARE ABOUT ANY HARM.
WITHOUT TRUST, I'VE NO REASON BELIEVE YOU.
TRUE. I WOULD POINT OUT, HOWEVER, THAT YOU WOULD NEVER GET SUCH ASSURANCE FROM RA'S.
YOU KNOW HIM TO BE A VILLAIN.
YOU KNOW HIM TO SEEK THE DEATHS OF MILLIONS, IF NOT MORE.
YOU KNOW HE IS INSANE.
NO, THANK YOU.
IF I SEEK TO STOP HIM, WHY WOULD YOU INTERFERE?

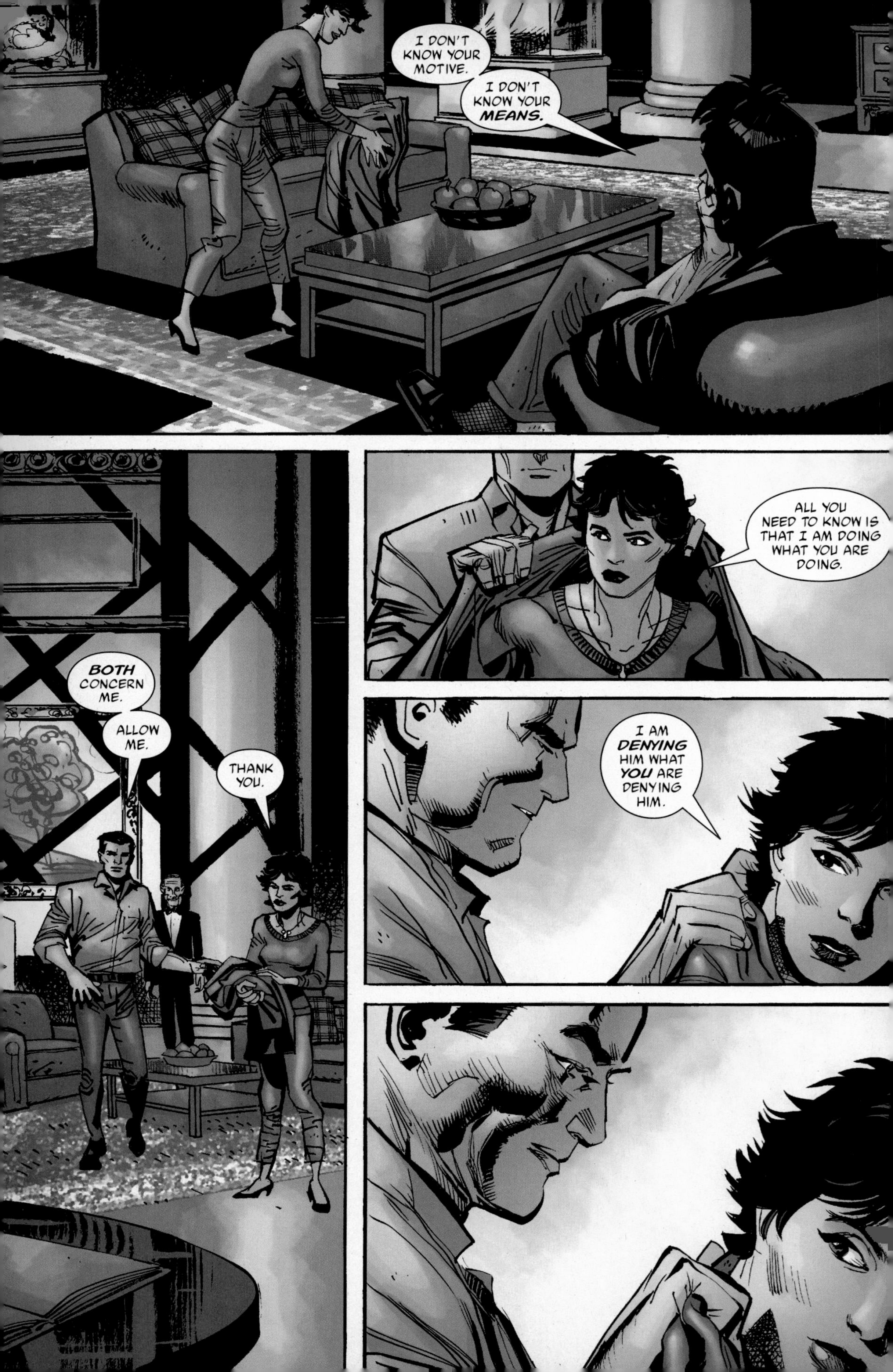
I DON'T KNOW YOUR MOTIVE.
I DON'T KNOW YOUR MEANS.
BOTH CONCERN ME.
ALLOW ME.
THANK YOU.
ALL YOU NEED TO KNOW IS THAT I AM DOING WHAT YOU ARE DOING.
I AM DENYING HIM WHAT YOU ARE DENYING HIM.

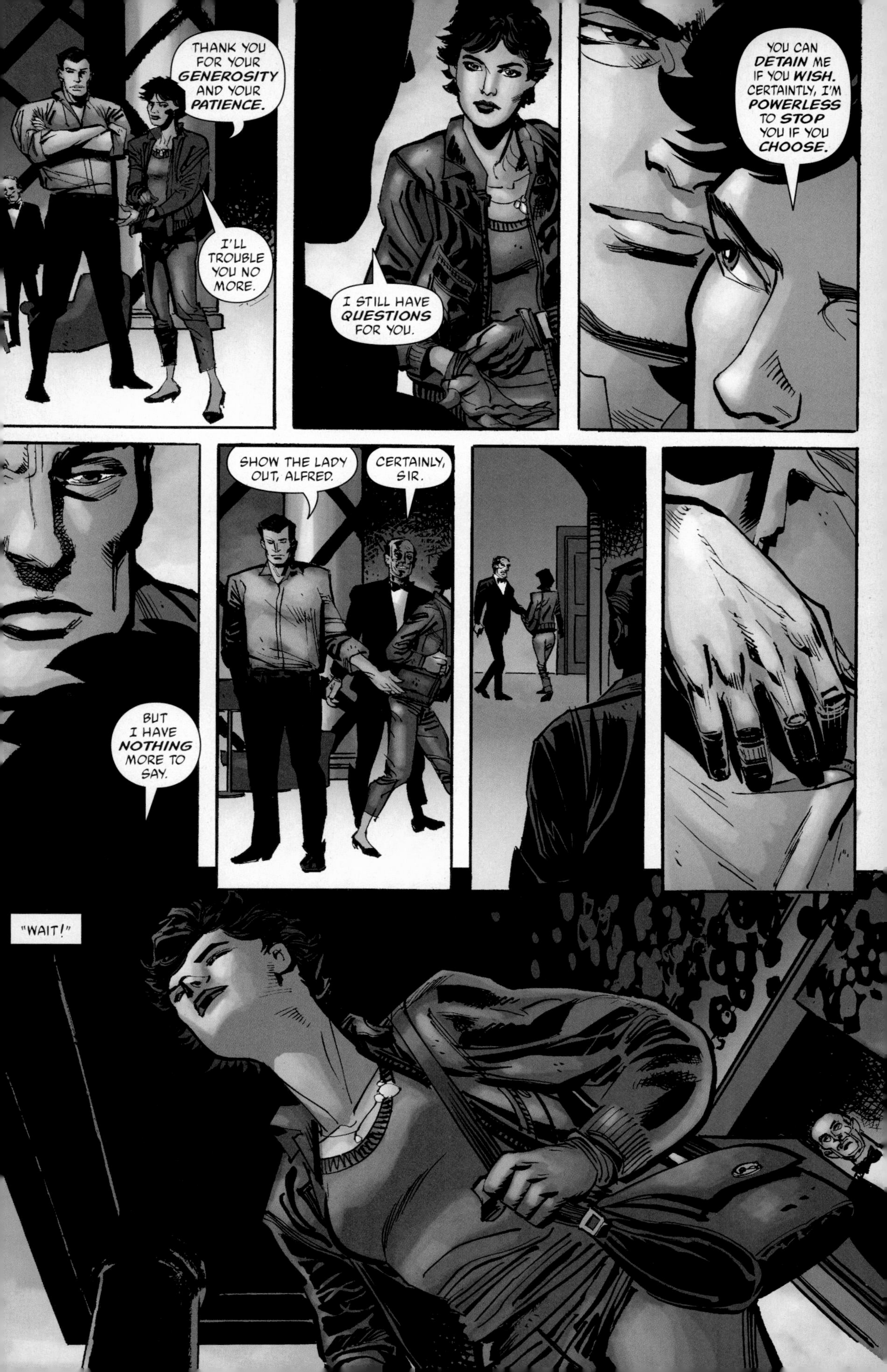

THANK YOU FOR YOUR GENEROSITY AND YOUR PATIENCE.
I'LL TROUBLE YOU NO MORE.
I STILL HAVE QUESTIONS FOR YOU.
YOU CAN DETAIN ME IF YOU WISH. CERTAINTLY, I'M POWERLESS TO STOP YOU IF YOU CHOOSE.
BUT I HAVE NOTHING MORE TO SAY.
SHOW THE LADY OUT, ALFRED.
CERTAINLY, SIR.
"WAIT!"

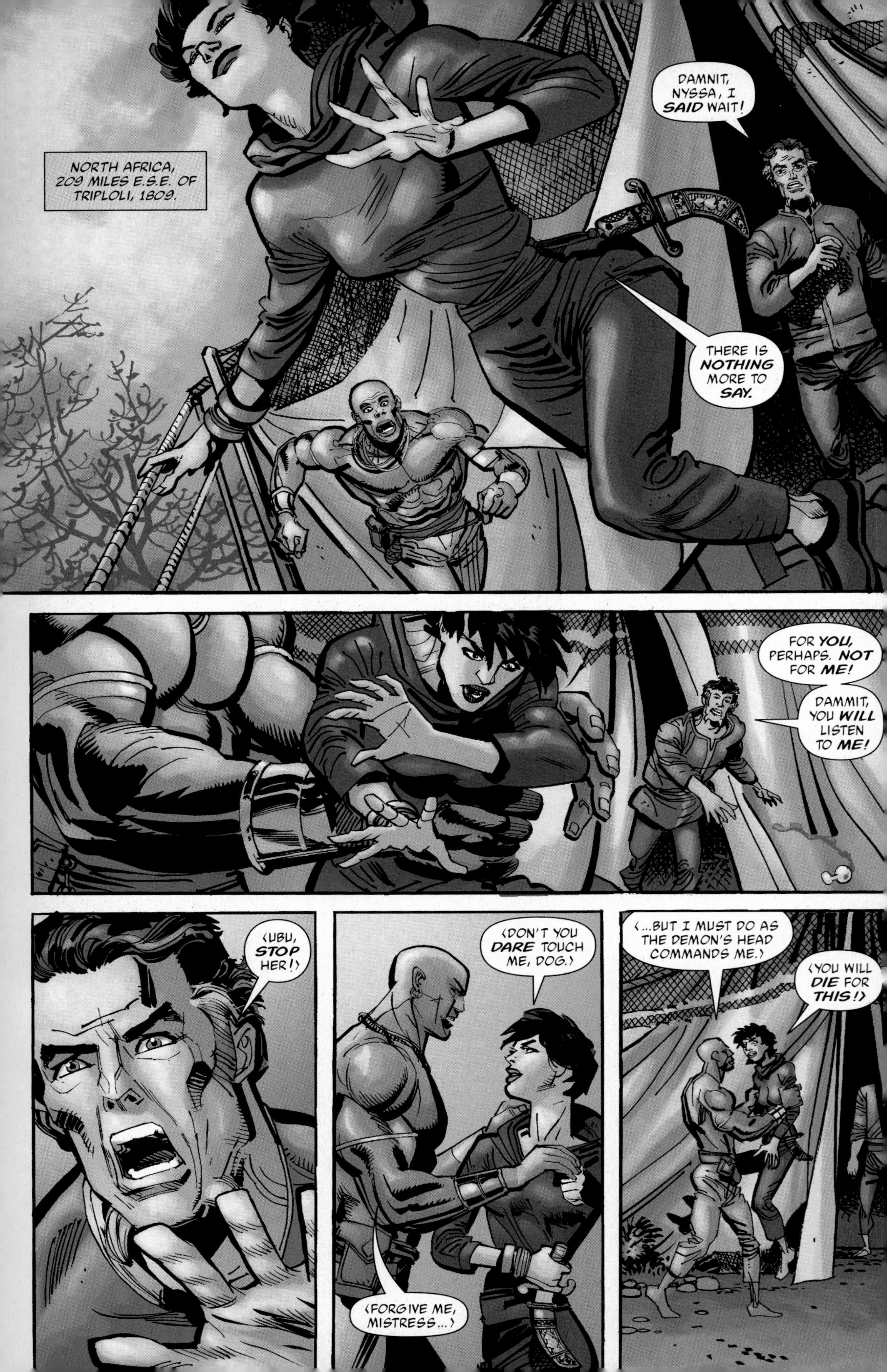
NORTH AFRICA, 209 MILES E.S.E. OF TRIPLOLI, 1809.
DAMNIT, NYSSA, I SAID WAIT!
THERE IS NOTHING MORE TO SAY.
FOR YOU, PERHAPS. NOT FOR ME!
DAMMIT, YOU WILL LISTEN TO ME!
‹UBU, STOP HER!›
‹DON'T YOU DARE TOUCH ME, DOG.›
‹FORGIVE ME, MISTRESS...›
‹...BUT I MUST DO AS THE DEMON'S HEAD COMMANDS ME.›
‹YOU WILL DIE FOR THIS!›

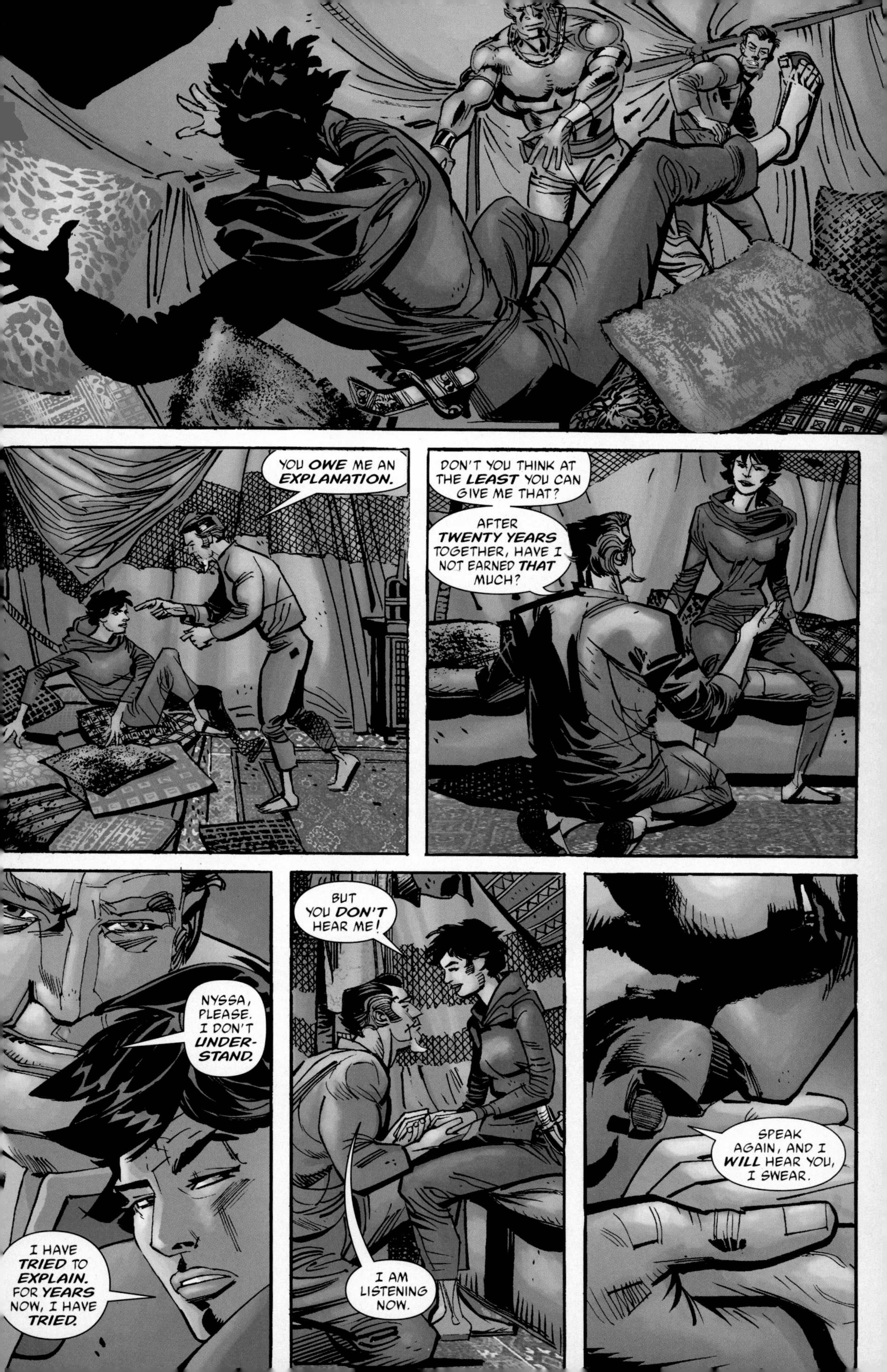
YOU OWE ME AN EXPLANATION.
DON'T YOU THINK AT THE LEAST YOU CAN GIVE ME THAT?
AFTER TWENTY YEARS TOGETHER, HAVE I NOT EARNED THAT MUCH?
NYSSA, PLEASE. I DON'T UNDER-STAND.
I HAVE TRIED TO EXPLAIN. FOR YEARS NOW, I HAVE TRIED.
BUT YOU DON'T HEAR ME!
I AM LISTENING NOW.
SPEAK AGAIN, AND I WILL HEAR YOU, I SWEAR.

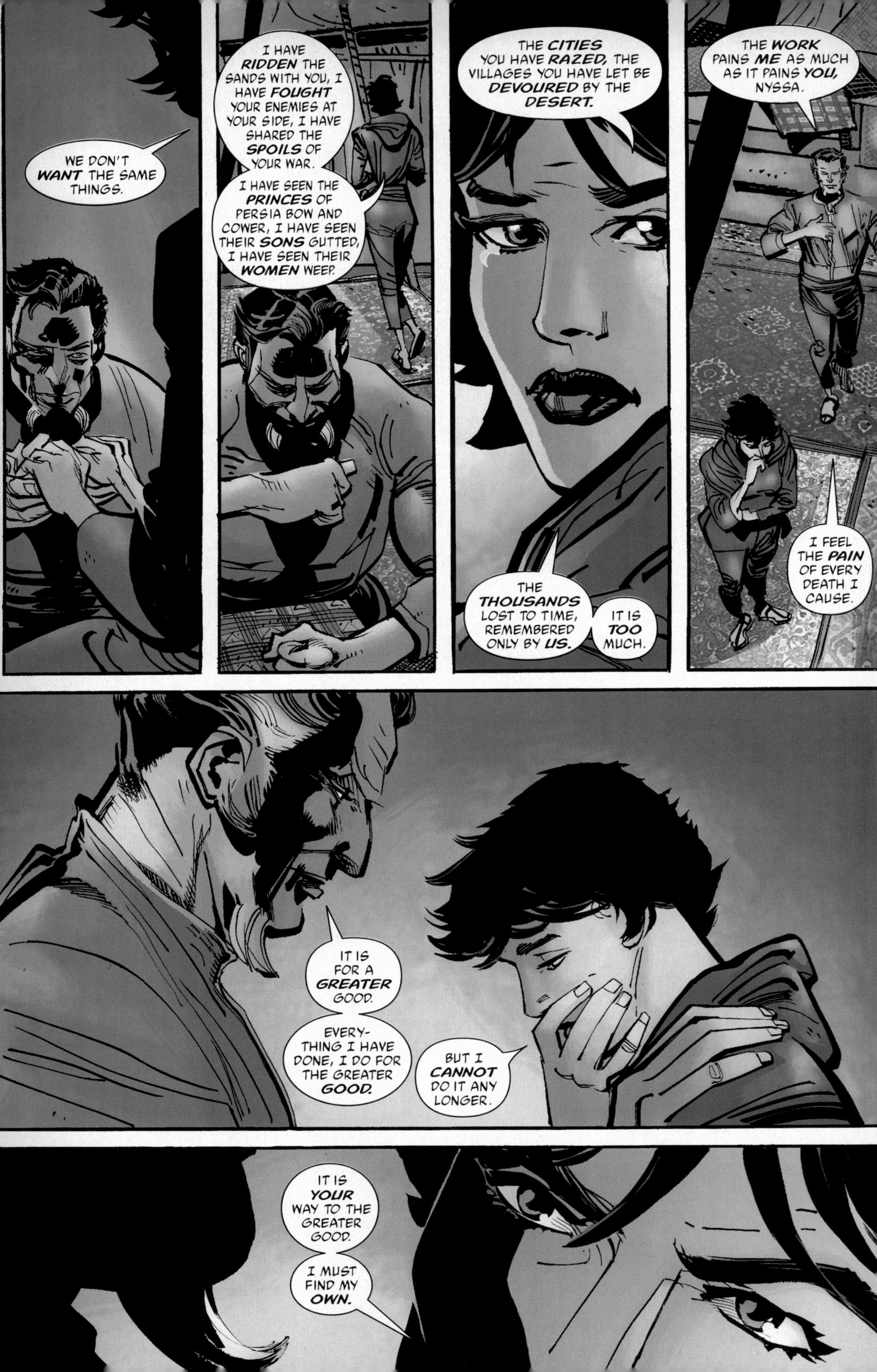

WE DON'T WANT THE SAME THINGS.
I HAVE RIDDEN THE SANDS WITH YOU, I HAVE FOUGHT YOUR ENEMIES AT YOUR SIDE, I HAVE SHARED THE SPOILS OF YOUR WAR.
I HAVE SEEN THE PRINCES OF PERSIA BOW AND COWER, I HAVE SEEN THEIR SONS GUTTED, I HAVE SEEN THEIR WOMEN WEEP.
THE CITIES YOU HAVE RAZED, THE VILLAGES YOU HAVE LET BE DEVOURED BY THE DESERT.
THE THOUSANDS LOST TO TIME, REMEMBERED ONLY BY US.
IT IS TOO MUCH.
THE WORK PAINS ME AS MUCH AS IT PAINS YOU, NYSSA.
I FEEL THE PAIN OF EVERY DEATH I CAUSE.
IT IS FOR A GREATER GOOD.
EVERY-THING I HAVE DONE, I DO FOR THE GREATER GOOD.
BUT I CANNOT DO IT ANY LONGER.
IT IS YOUR WAY TO THE GREATER GOOD.
I MUST FIND MY OWN.

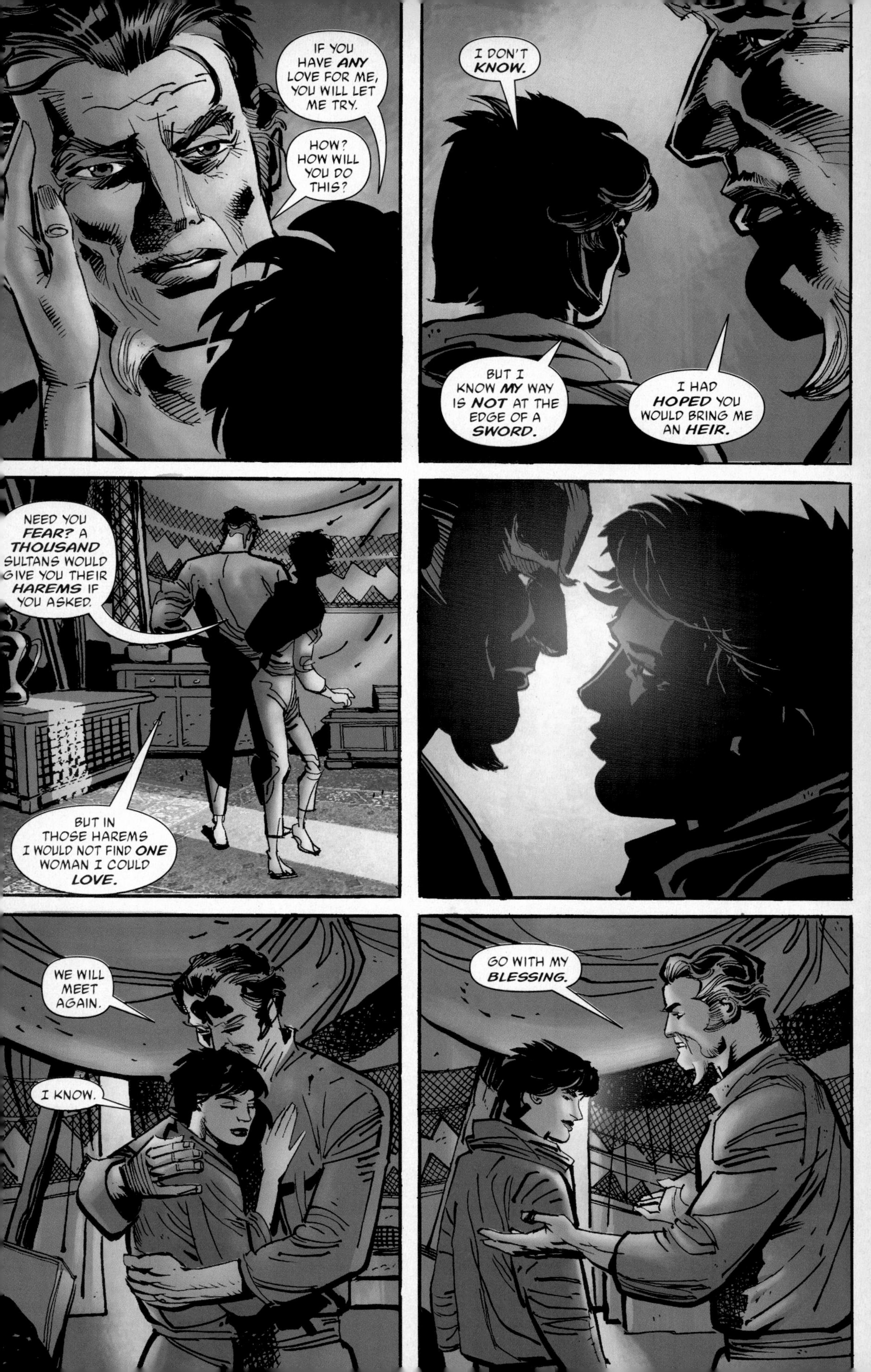
IF YOU HAVE ANY LOVE FOR ME, YOU WILL LET ME TRY.
HOW? HOW WILL YOU DO THIS?
I DON'T KNOW.
BUT I KNOW MY WAY IS NOT AT THE EDGE OF A SWORD.
I HAD HOPED YOU WOULD BRING ME AN HEIR.
NEED YOU FEAR? A THOUSAND SULTANS WOULD GIVE YOU THEIR HAREMS IF YOU ASKED.
BUT IN THOSE HAREMS I WOULD NOT FIND ONE WOMAN I COULD LOVE.
WE WILL MEET AGAIN.
I KNOW.
GO WITH MY BLESSING.

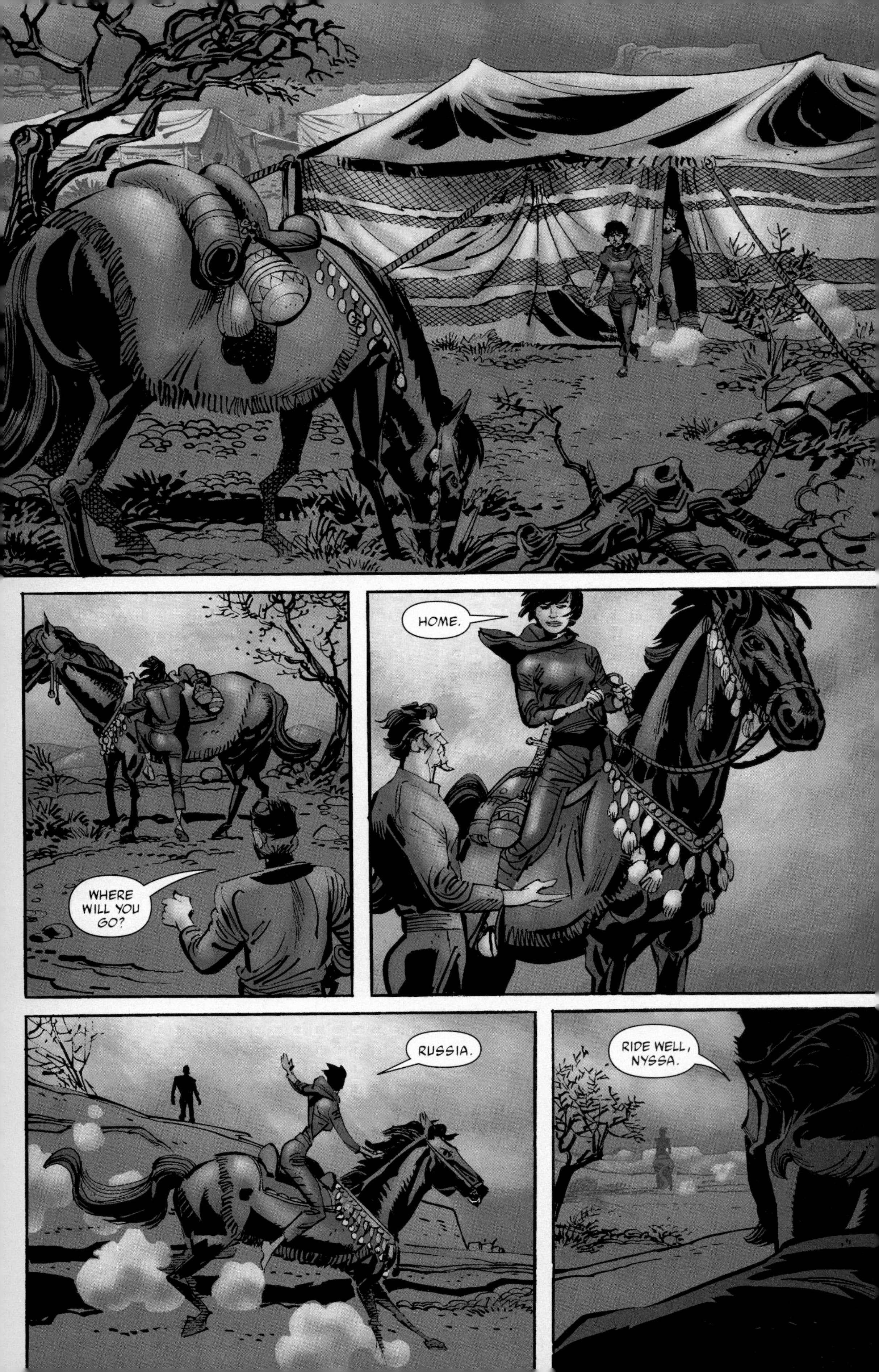
WHERE WILL YOU GO?
HOME.
RUSSIA.
RIDE WELL, NYSSA.

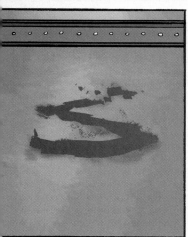

MAG LOCK SECURE
QUERY ACCESS_
CODE ••••••••

MAG LOCK SECURE
ACCESS LOG_
NO ACTIVITY

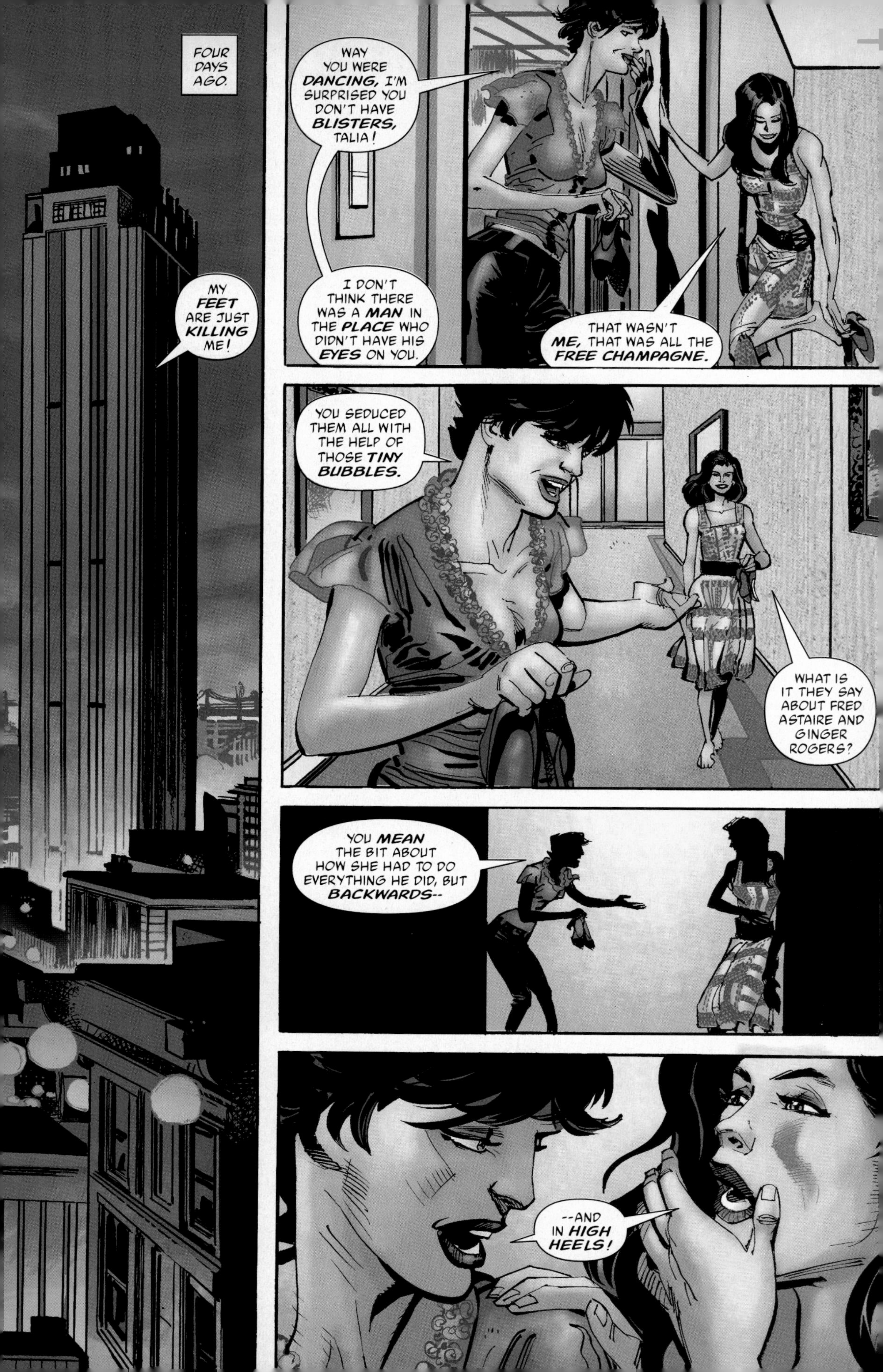
FOUR DAYS AGO.
MY FEET ARE JUST KILLING ME!
WAY YOU WERE DANCING, I'M SURPRISED YOU DON'T HAVE BLISTERS, TALIA!
I DON'T THINK THERE WAS A MAN IN THE PLACE WHO DIDN'T HAVE HIS EYES ON YOU.
THAT WASN'T ME, THAT WAS ALL THE FREE CHAMPAGNE.
YOU SEDUCED THEM ALL WITH THE HELP OF THOSE TINY BUBBLES.
WHAT IS IT THEY SAY ABOUT FRED ASTAIRE AND GINGER ROGERS?
YOU MEAN THE BIT ABOUT HOW SHE HAD TO DO EVERYTHING HE DID, BUT BACKWARDS--
--AND IN HIGH HEELS!

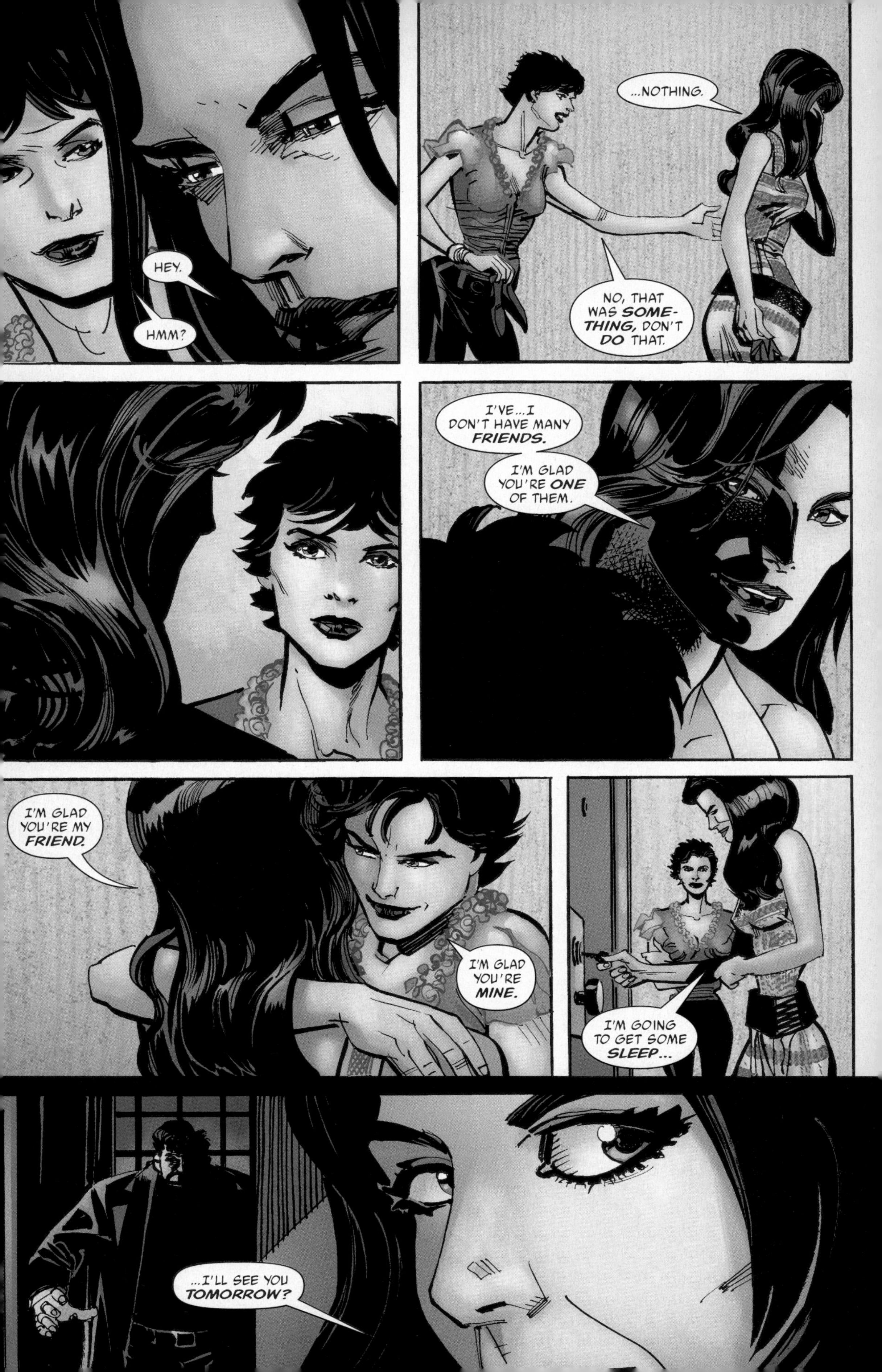
HEY.
HMM?
...NOTHING.
NO, THAT WAS SOME-THING, DON'T DO THAT.
I'VE...I DON'T HAVE MANY FRIENDS.
I'M GLAD YOU'RE ONE OF THEM.
I'M GLAD YOU'RE MY FRIEND.
I'M GLAD YOU'RE MINE.
I'M GOING TO GET SOME SLEEP...
...I'LL SEE YOU TOMORROW?

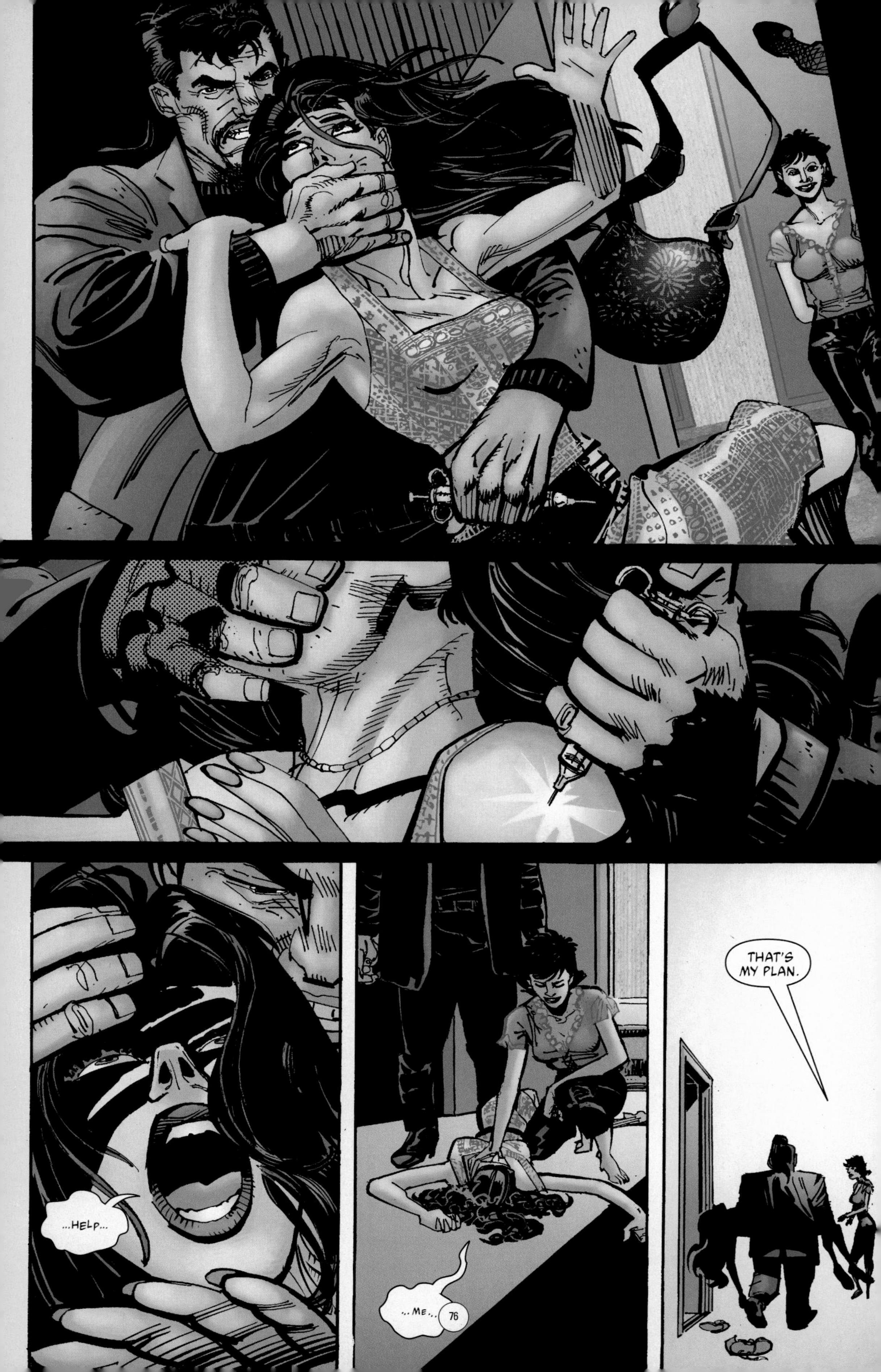
...HELP...
...ME...
THAT'S MY PLAN.

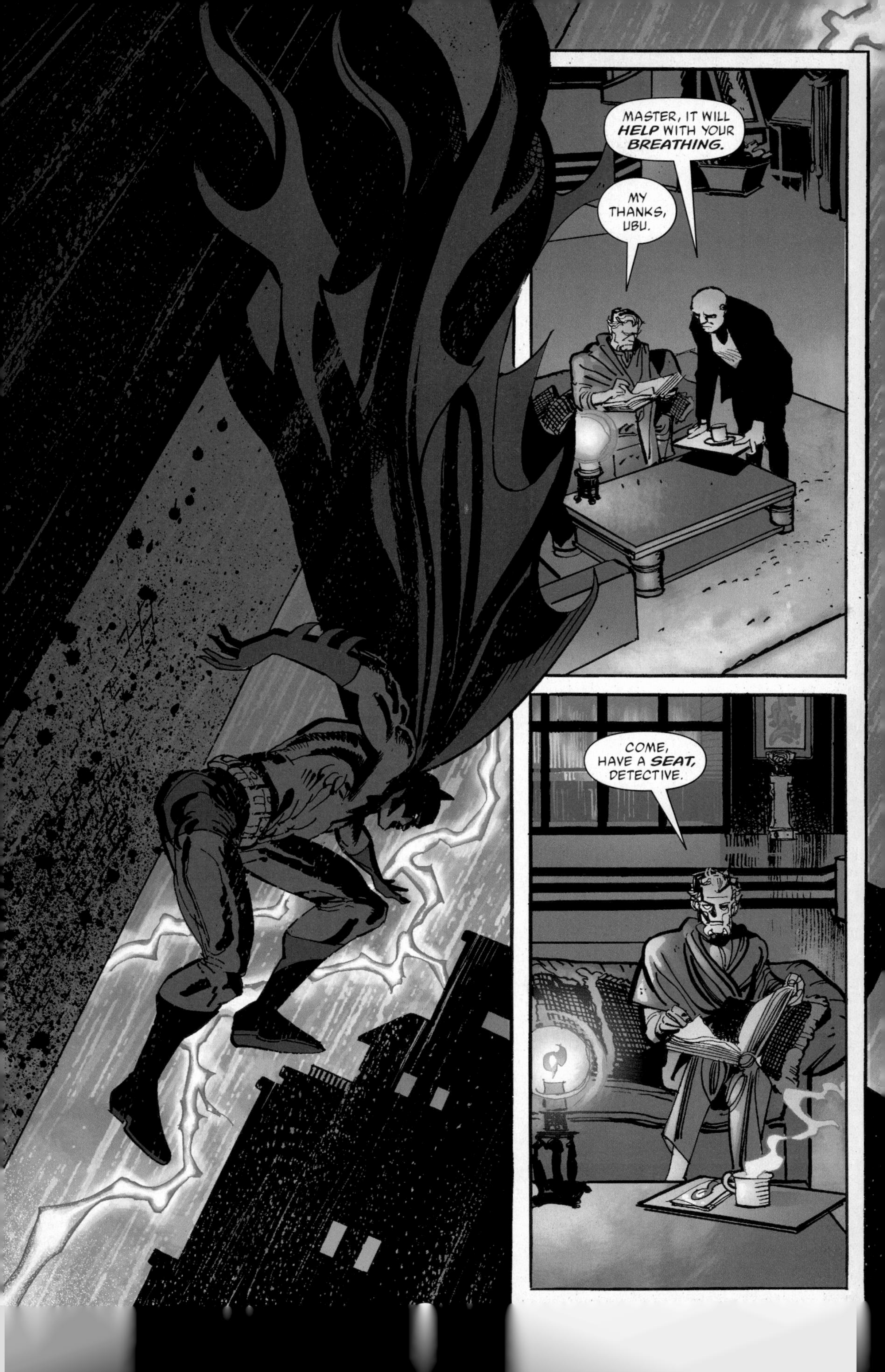
MASTER, IT WILL HELP WITH YOUR BREATHING.
MY THANKS, UBU.
COME, HAVE A SEAT, DETECTIVE.

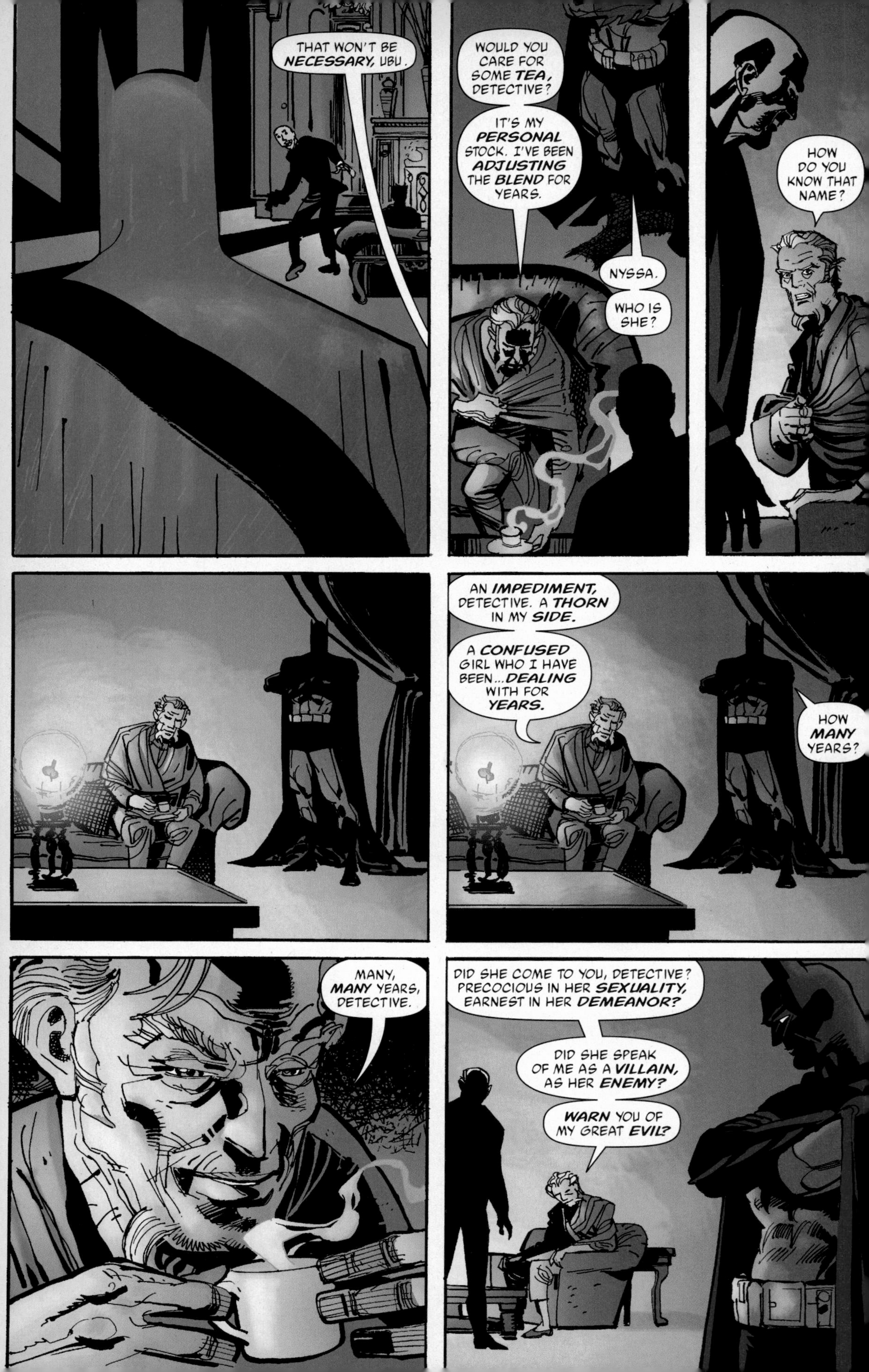
THAT WON'T BE NECESSARY, UBU.
WOULD YOU CARE FOR SOME TEA, DETECTIVE?
IT'S MY PERSONAL STOCK. I'VE BEEN ADJUSTING THE BLEND FOR YEARS.
NYSSA.
WHO IS SHE?
HOW DO YOU KNOW THAT NAME?
AN IMPEDIMENT, DETECTIVE. A THORN IN MY SIDE.
A CONFUSED GIRL WHO I HAVE BEEN...DEALING WITH FOR YEARS.
HOW MANY YEARS?
MANY, MANY YEARS, DETECTIVE.
DID SHE COME TO YOU, DETECTIVE? PRECOCIOUS IN HER SEXUALITY, EARNEST IN HER DEMEANOR?
DID SHE SPEAK OF ME AS A VILLAIN, AS HER ENEMY?
WARN YOU OF MY GREAT EVIL?

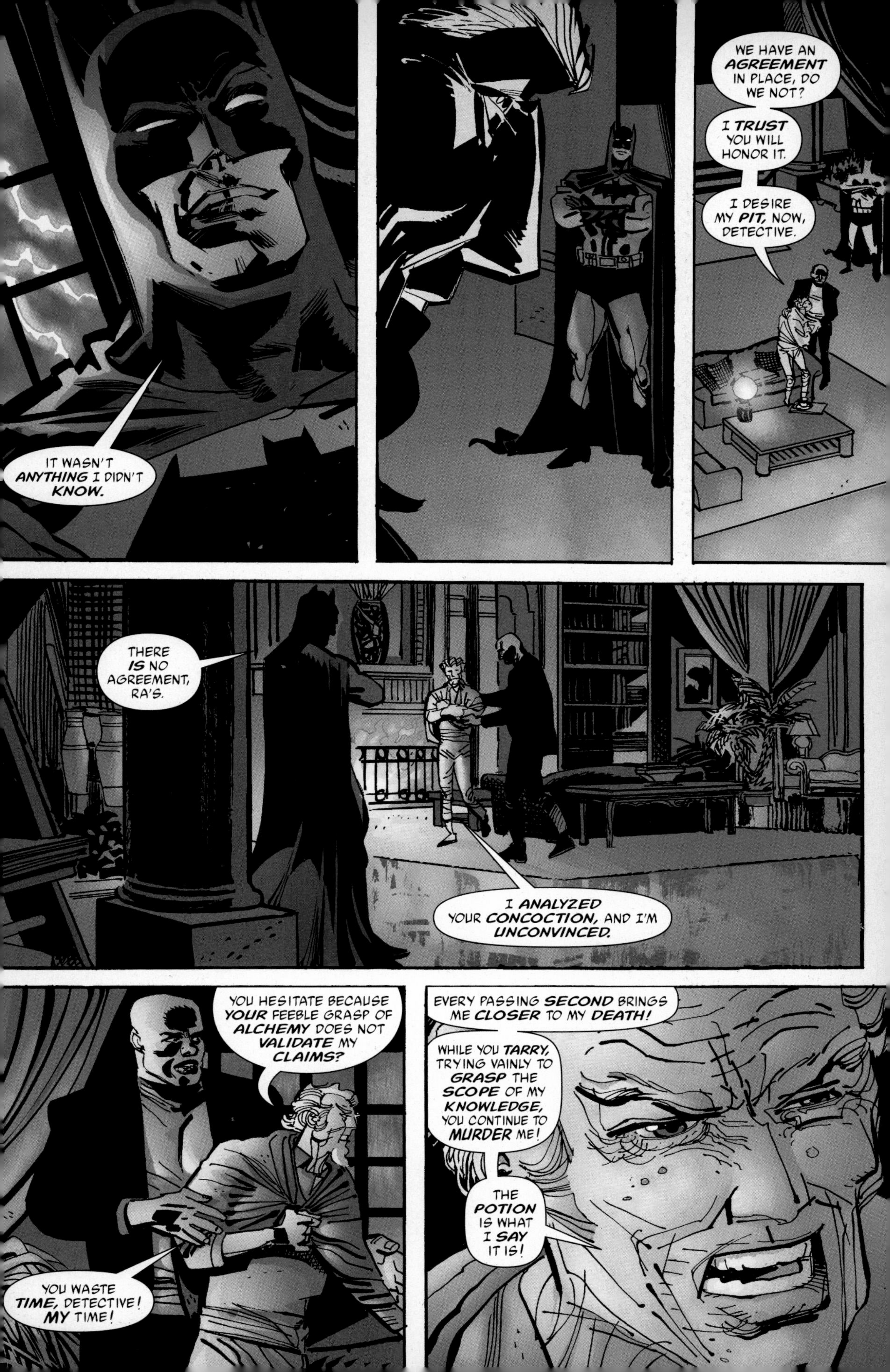
IT WASN'T ANYTHING I DIDN'T KNOW.
WE HAVE AN AGREEMENT IN PLACE, DO WE NOT?
I TRUST YOU WILL HONOR IT.
I DESIRE MY PIT, NOW, DETECTIVE.
THERE IS NO AGREEMENT, RA'S.
I ANALYZED YOUR CONCOCTION, AND I'M UNCONVINCED.
YOU HESITATE BECAUSE YOUR FEEBLE GRASP OF ALCHEMY DOES NOT VALIDATE MY CLAIMS?
YOU WASTE TIME, DETECTIVE! MY TIME!
EVERY PASSING SECOND BRINGS ME CLOSER TO MY DEATH!
WHILE YOU TARRY, TRYING VAINLY TO GRASP THE SCOPE OF MY KNOWLEDGE, YOU CONTINUE TO MURDER ME!
THE POTION IS WHAT I SAY IT IS!

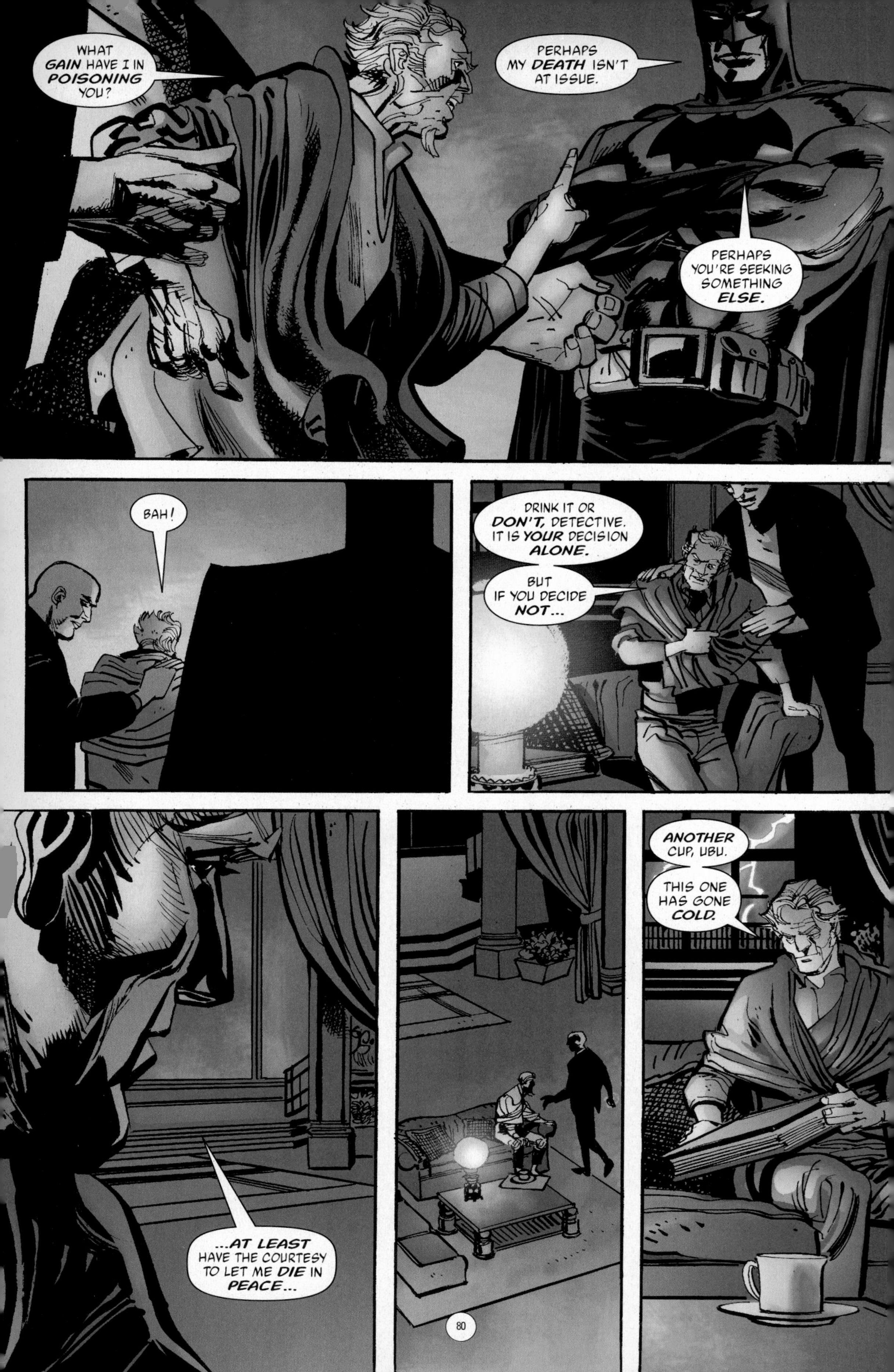
WHAT GAIN HAVE I IN POISONING YOU?
PERHAPS MY DEATH ISN'T AT ISSUE.
PERHAPS YOU'RE SEEKING SOMETHING ELSE.
BAH!
DRINK IT OR DON'T, DETECTIVE. IT IS YOUR DECISION ALONE.
BUT IF YOU DECIDE NOT...
...AT LEAST HAVE THE COURTESY TO LET ME DIE IN PEACE...
ANOTHER CUP, UBU.
THIS ONE HAS GONE COLD.

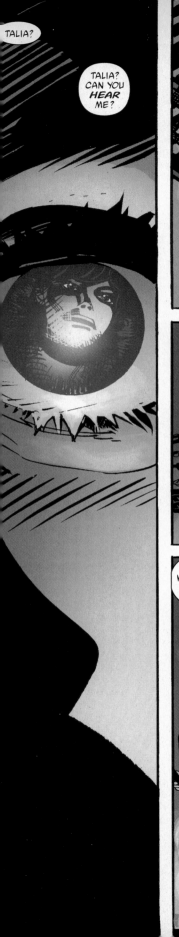

TALIA?

TALIA? CAN YOU **HEAR** ME?

NYSSA...

...WH...WHAT **HAPPENED?**

IT'S ALL RIGHT, NOW. YOU'RE **ALL** RIGHT.

WHERE... WHERE **AM** I? WHAT HAPPENED TO MY **CLOTHES?**

I TOOK THEM.

THEY WOULDN'T HAVE **SURVIVED** THE **PROCESS** ANYWAY.

PROCESS? WHAT ARE YOU **TALKING** ABOUT?

YOU'RE **SCARING** ME, NYSSA!

I KNOW.

I'M **SORRY...**

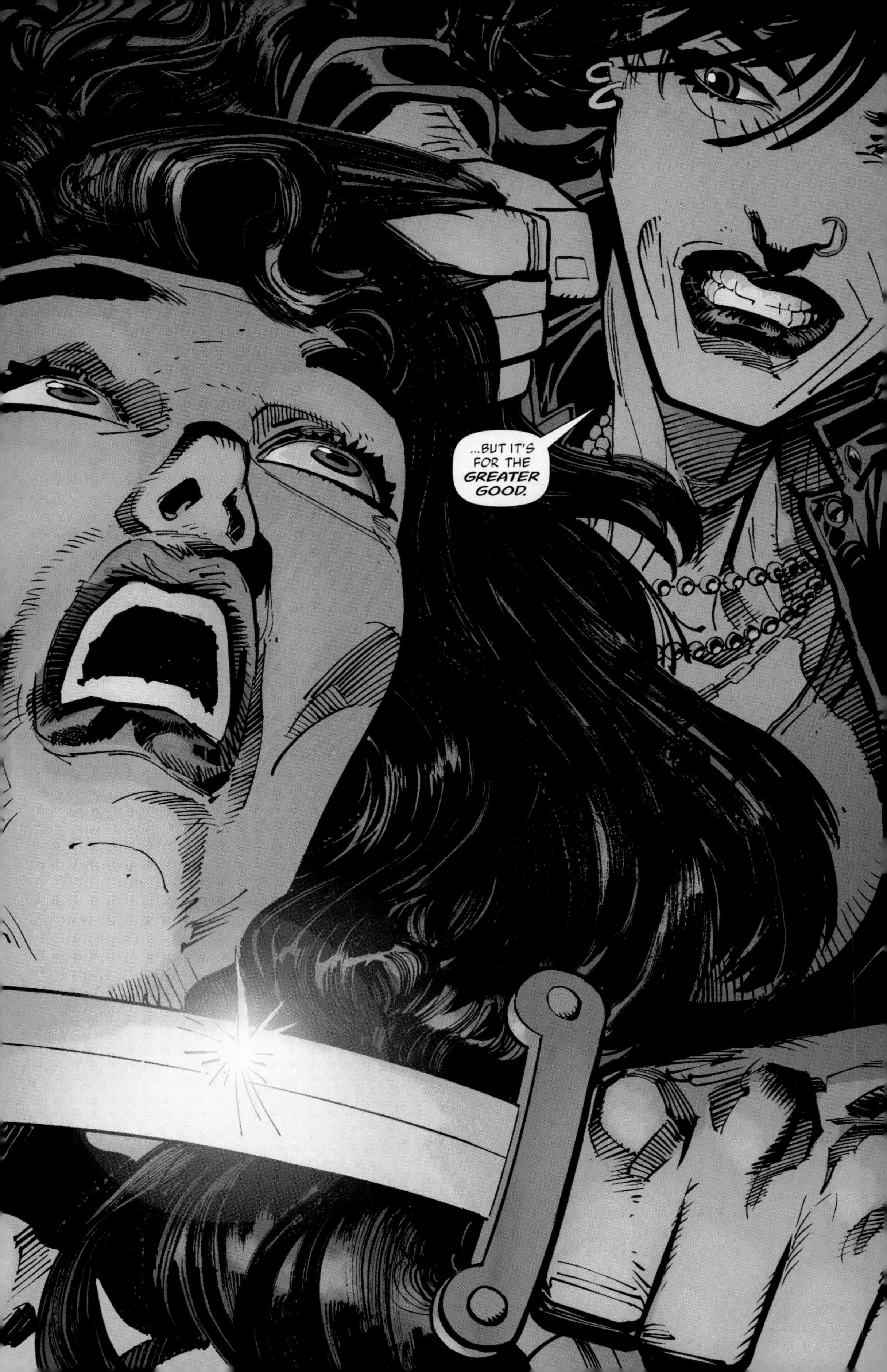
...BUT IT'S FOR THE GREATER GOOD.

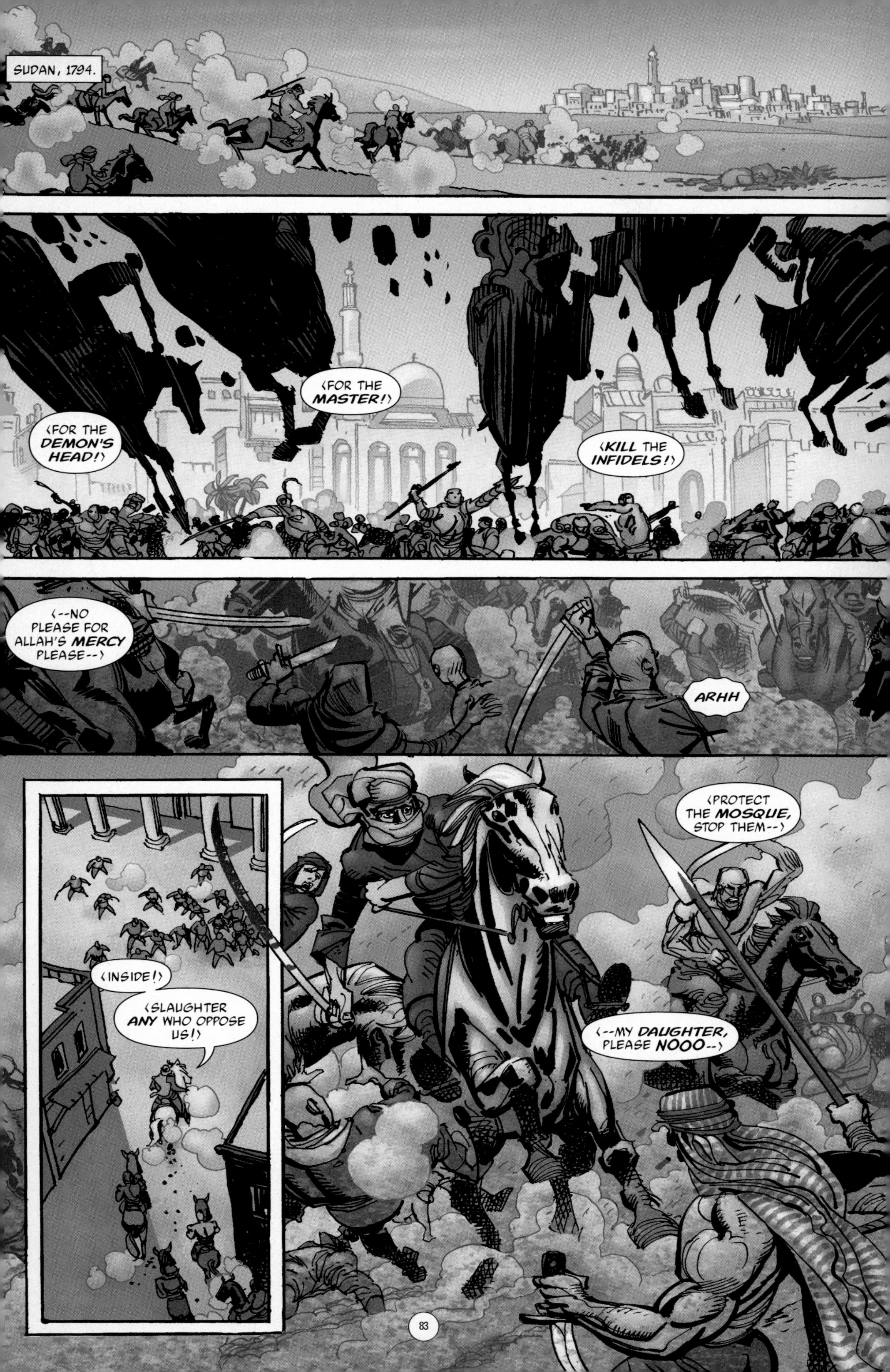
SUDAN, 1794.
‹FOR THE DEMON'S HEAD!›
‹FOR THE MASTER!›
‹KILL THE INFIDELS!›
‹--NO PLEASE FOR ALLAH'S MERCY PLEASE--›
ARHH
‹INSIDE!›
‹SLAUGHTER ANY WHO OPPOSE US!›
‹PROTECT THE MOSQUE, STOP THEM--›
‹--MY DAUGHTER, PLEASE NOOO--›

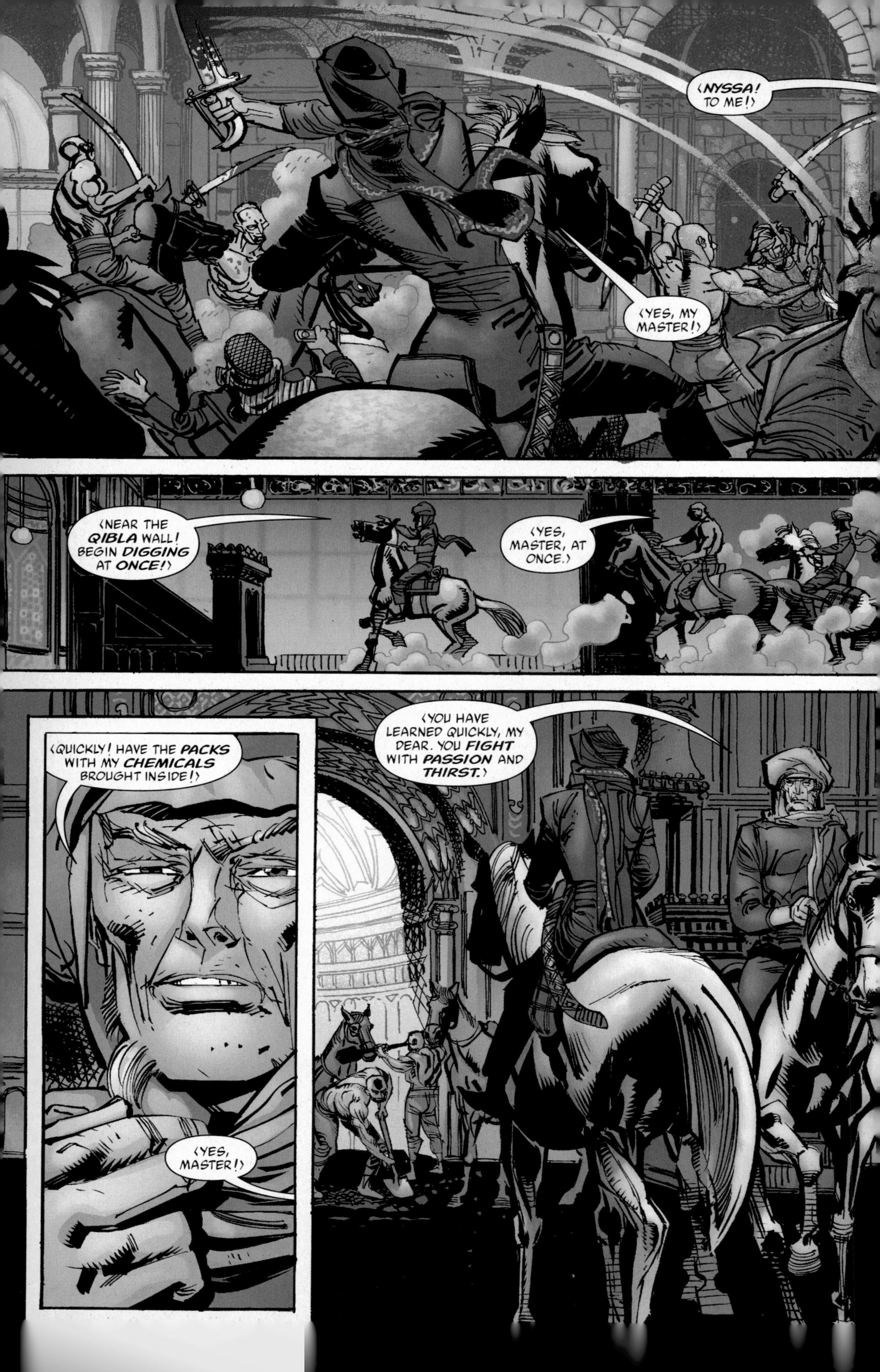
‹NYSSA! TO ME!›
‹YES, MY MASTER!›
‹NEAR THE QIBLA WALL! BEGIN DIGGING AT ONCE!›
‹YES, MASTER, AT ONCE.›
‹YOU HAVE LEARNED QUICKLY, MY DEAR. YOU FIGHT WITH PASSION AND THIRST.›
‹QUICKLY! HAVE THE PACKS WITH MY CHEMICALS BROUGHT INSIDE!›
‹YES, MASTER!›

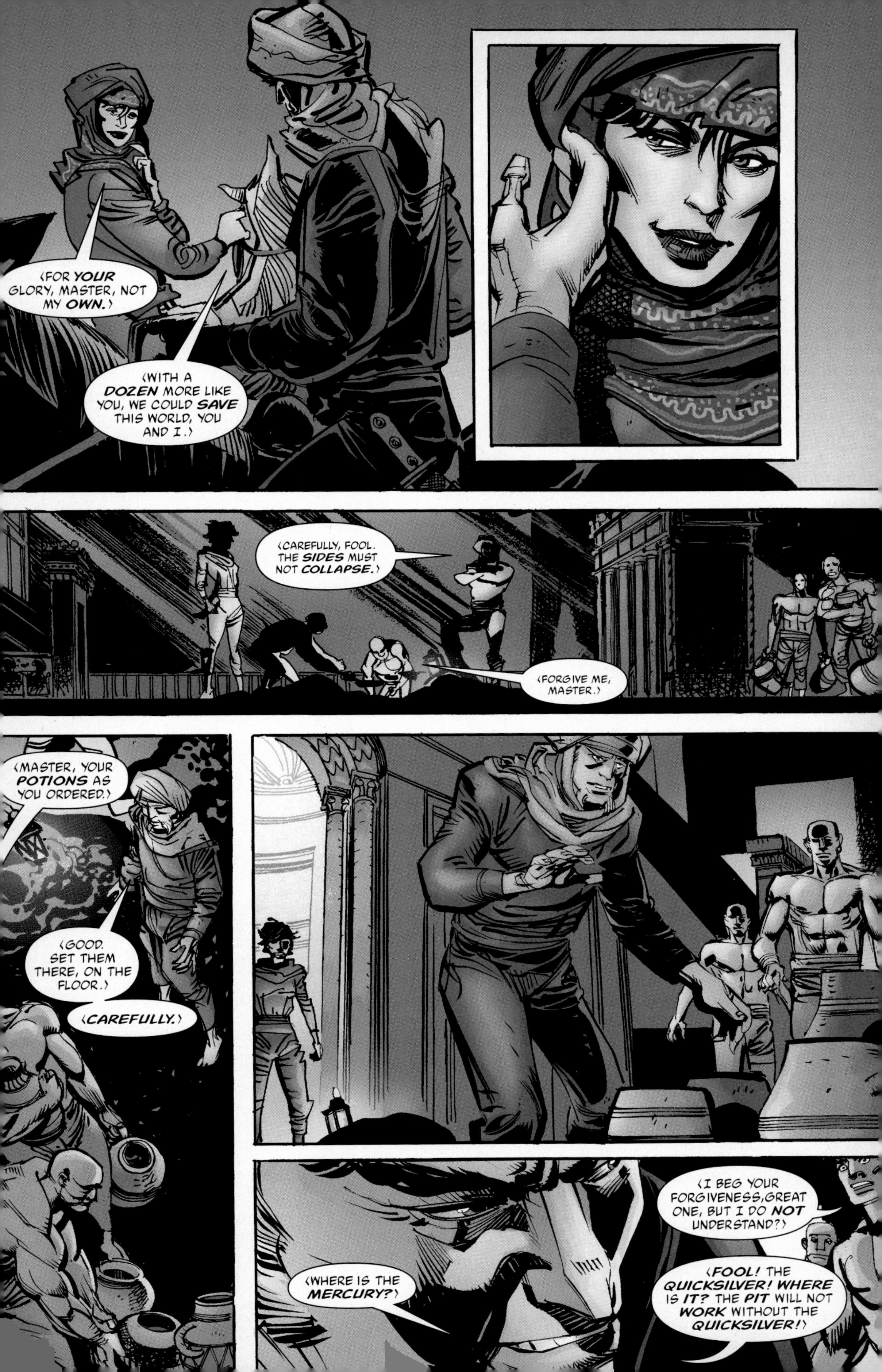
‹FOR YOUR GLORY, MASTER, NOT MY OWN.›
‹WITH A DOZEN MORE LIKE YOU, WE COULD SAVE THIS WORLD, YOU AND I.›
‹CAREFULLY, FOOL. THE SIDES MUST NOT COLLAPSE.›
‹FORGIVE ME, MASTER.›
‹MASTER, YOUR POTIONS AS YOU ORDERED.›
‹GOOD. SET THEM THERE, ON THE FLOOR.›
‹CAREFULLY.›
‹WHERE IS THE MERCURY?›
‹I BEG YOUR FORGIVENESS, GREAT ONE, BUT I DO NOT UNDERSTAND?›
‹FOOL! THE QUICKSILVER! WHERE IS IT? THE PIT WILL NOT WORK WITHOUT THE QUICKSILVER!›

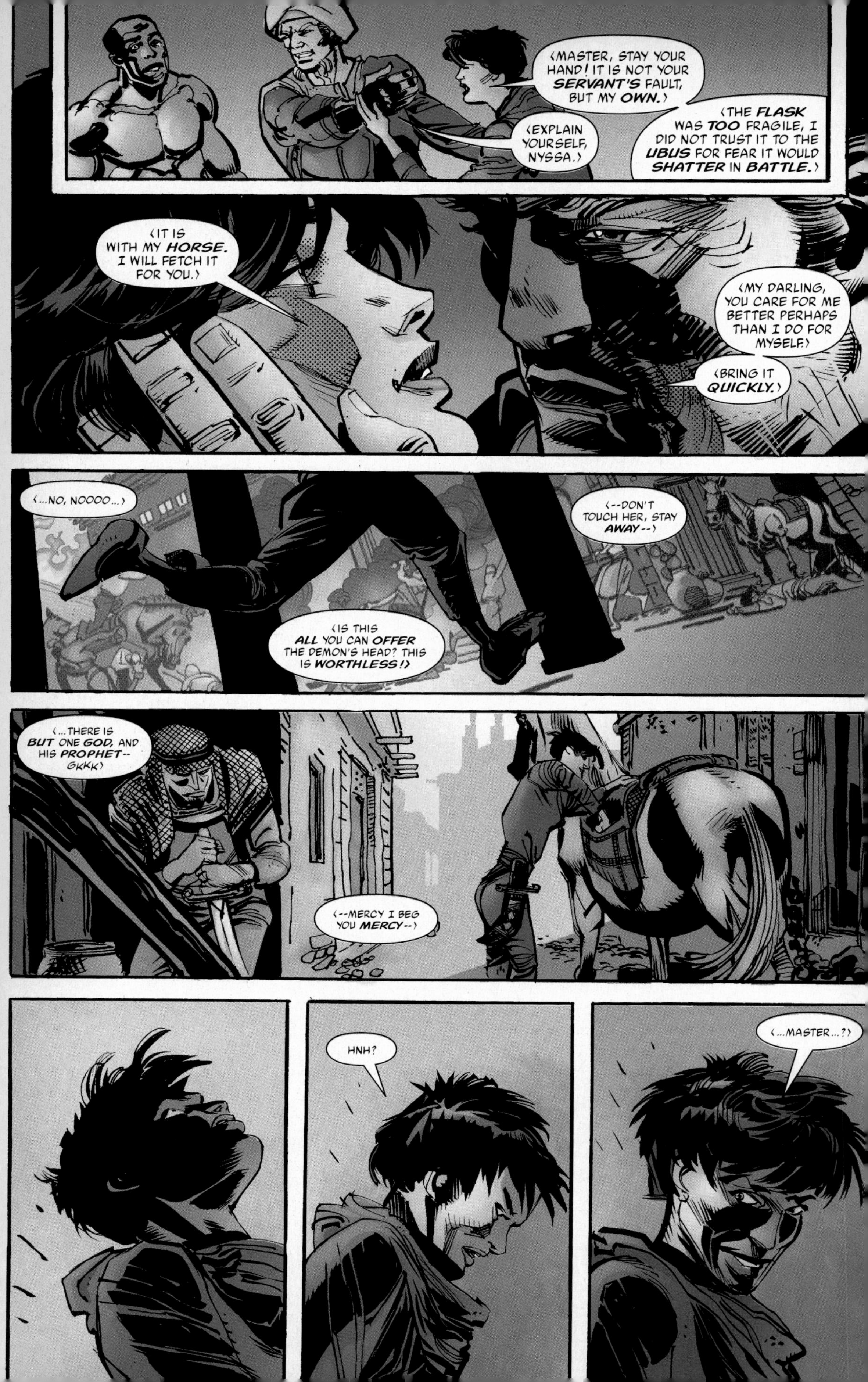
‹MASTER, STAY YOUR HAND! IT IS NOT YOUR SERVANT'S FAULT, BUT MY OWN.›
‹EXPLAIN YOURSELF, NYSSA.›
‹THE FLASK WAS TOO FRAGILE, I DID NOT TRUST IT TO THE UBUS FOR FEAR IT WOULD SHATTER IN BATTLE.›
‹IT IS WITH MY HORSE. I WILL FETCH IT FOR YOU.›
‹MY DARLING, YOU CARE FOR ME BETTER PERHAPS THAN I DO FOR MYSELF.›
‹BRING IT QUICKLY.›
‹...NO, NOOOO...›
‹--DON'T TOUCH HER, STAY AWAY--›
‹IS THIS ALL YOU CAN OFFER THE DEMON'S HEAD? THIS IS WORTHLESS!›
‹...THERE IS BUT ONE GOD, AND HIS PROPHET-- GKKK›
‹--MERCY I BEG YOU MERCY--›
HNH?
‹...MASTER...?›

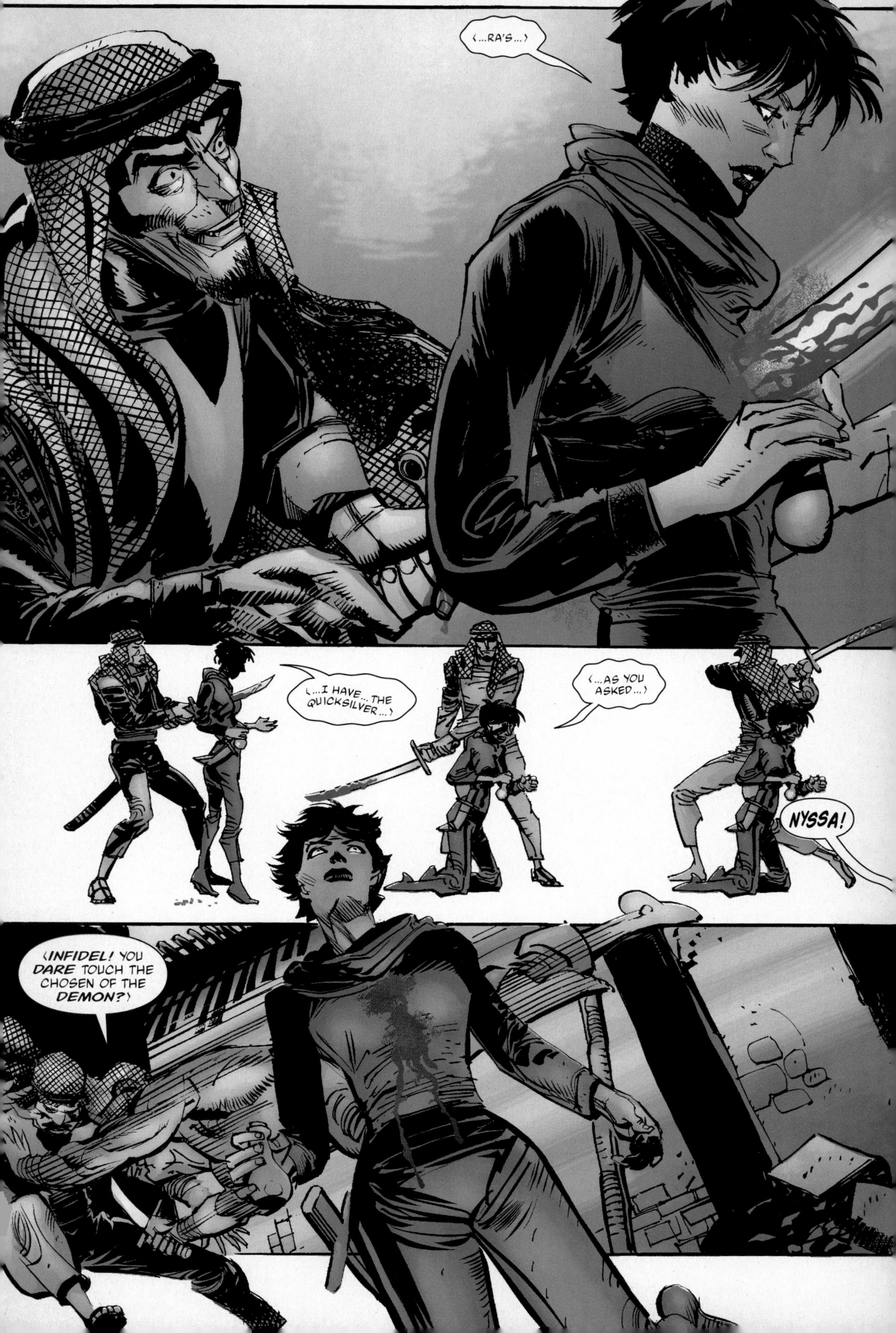
‹...RA'S...›
‹...I HAVE... THE QUICKSILVER...›
‹...AS YOU ASKED...›
NYSSA!
‹INFIDEL! YOU DARE TOUCH THE CHOSEN OF THE DEMON?›

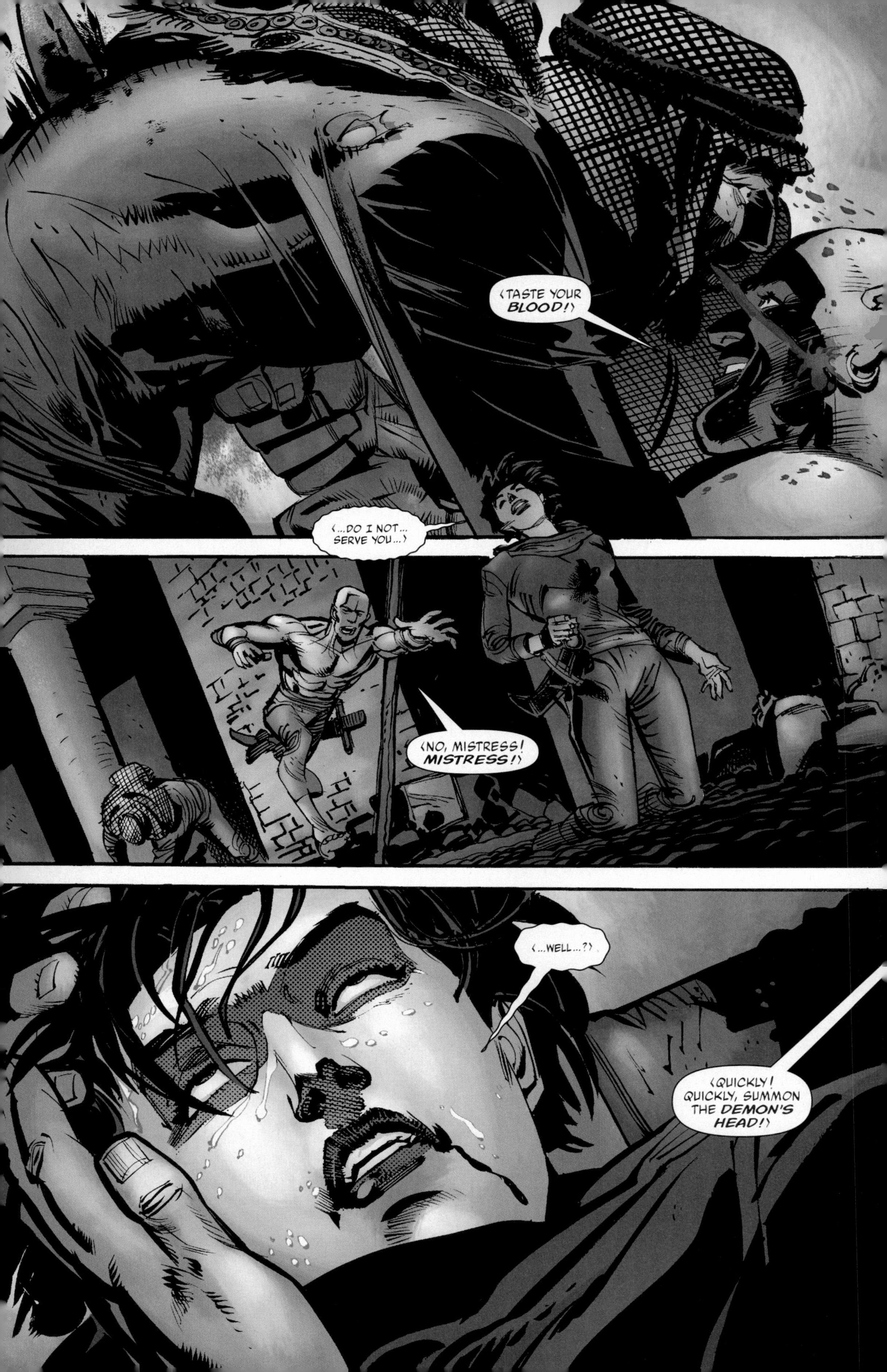
‹TASTE YOUR BLOOD!›
‹...DO I NOT... SERVE YOU...›
‹NO, MISTRESS! MISTRESS!›
‹...WELL...?›
‹QUICKLY! QUICKLY, SUMMON THE DEMON'S HEAD!›

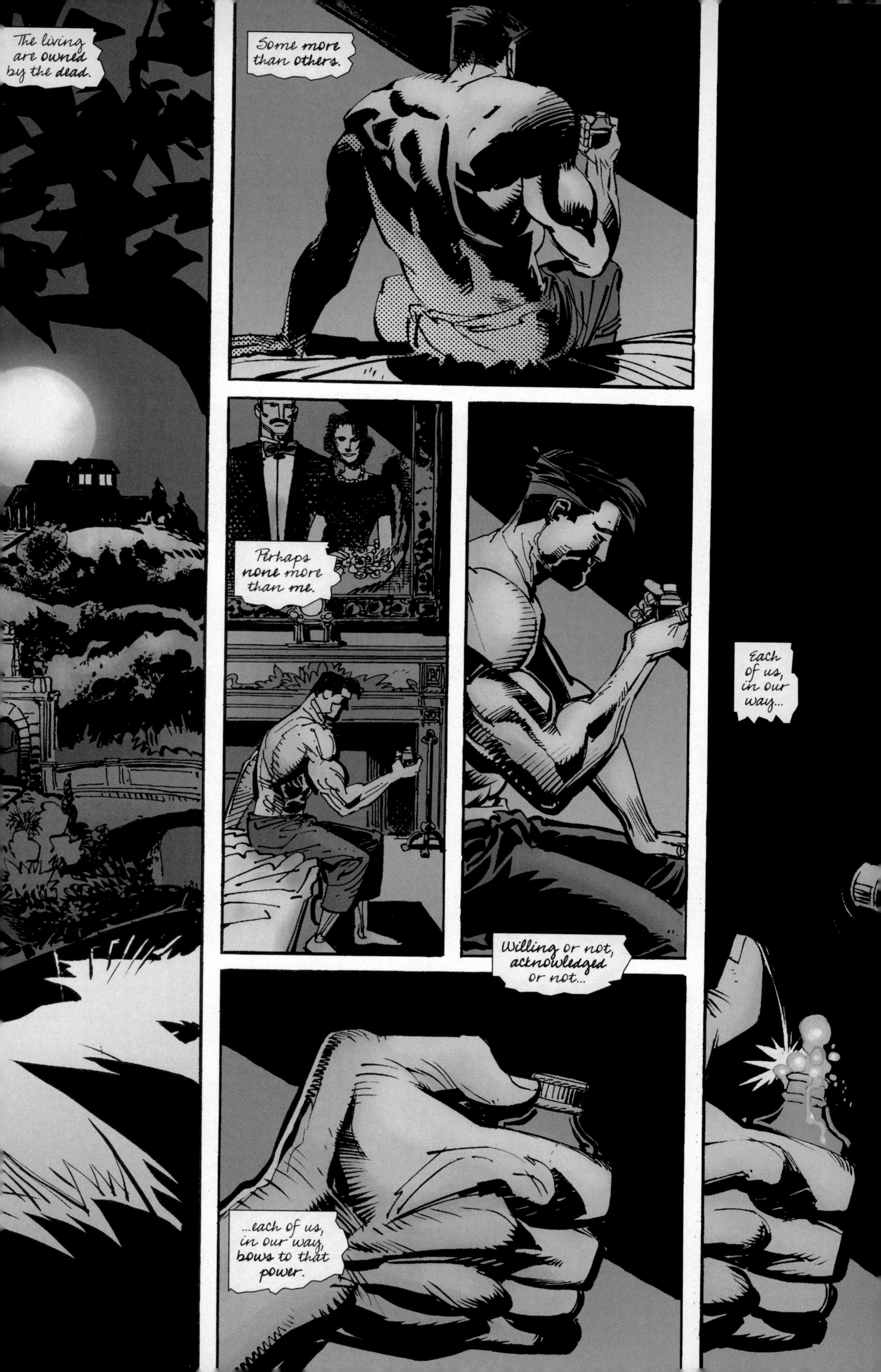

The living are owned by the dead.
Some more than others.
Perhaps none more than me.
Each of us, in our way...
Willing or not, acknowledged or not...
...each of us, in our way, bows to that power.

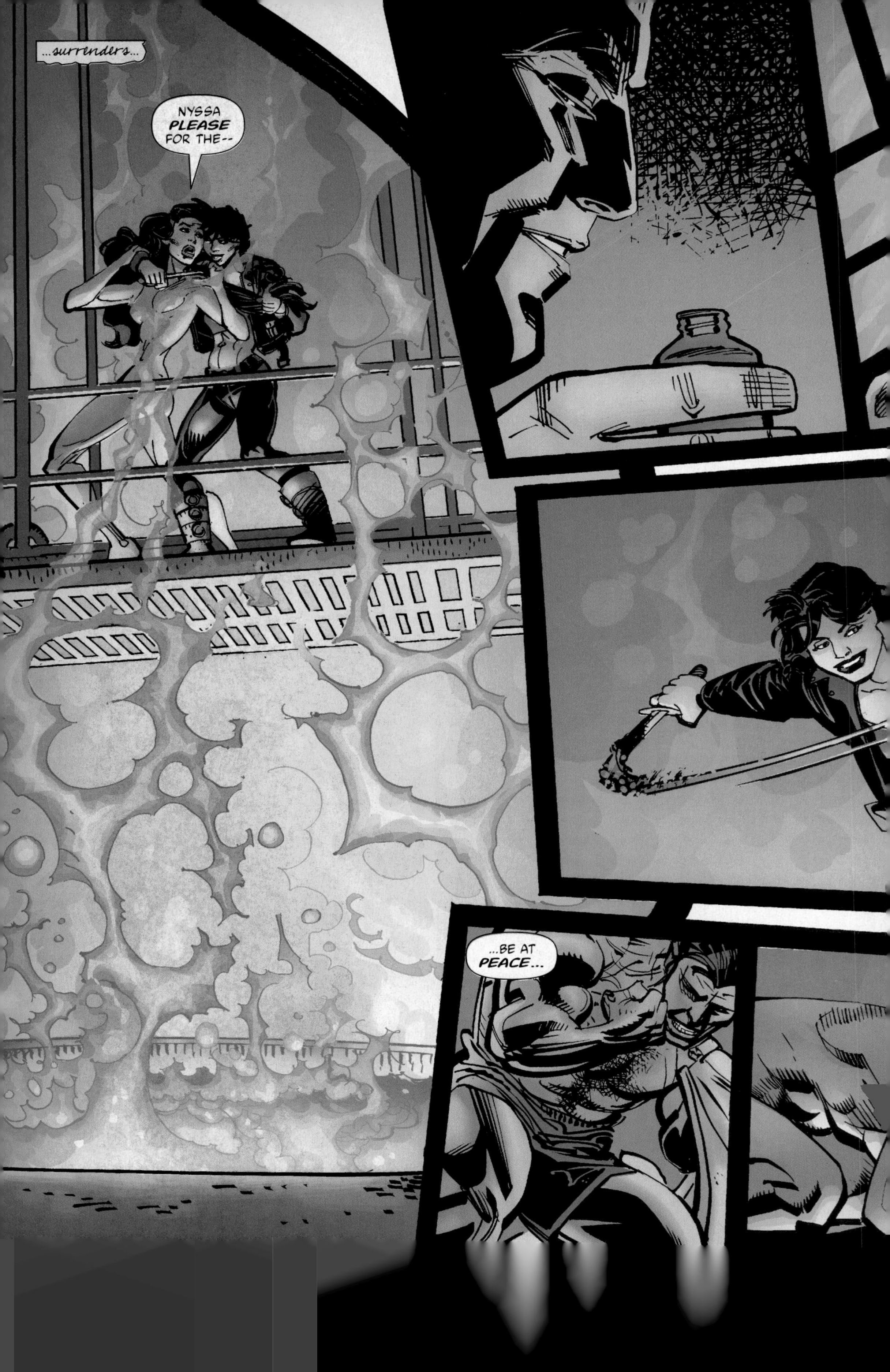
...surrenders...
NYSSA PLEASE FOR THE--
...BE AT PEACE...

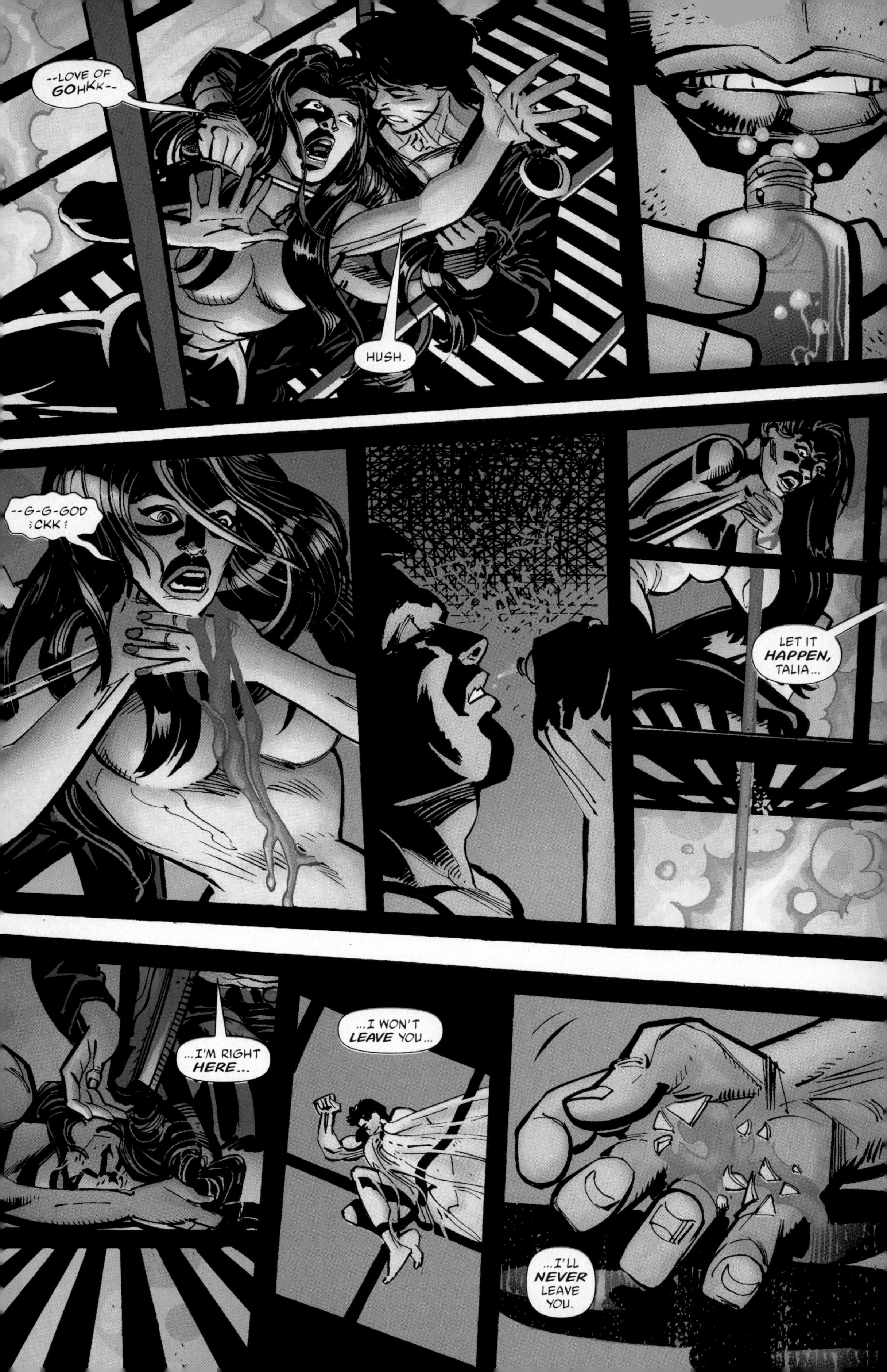
--LOVE OF GOHKK--
HUSH.
--G-G-GOD CKK
LET IT HAPPEN, TALIA...
...I'M RIGHT HERE...
...I WON'T LEAVE YOU...
...I'LL NEVER LEAVE YOU.

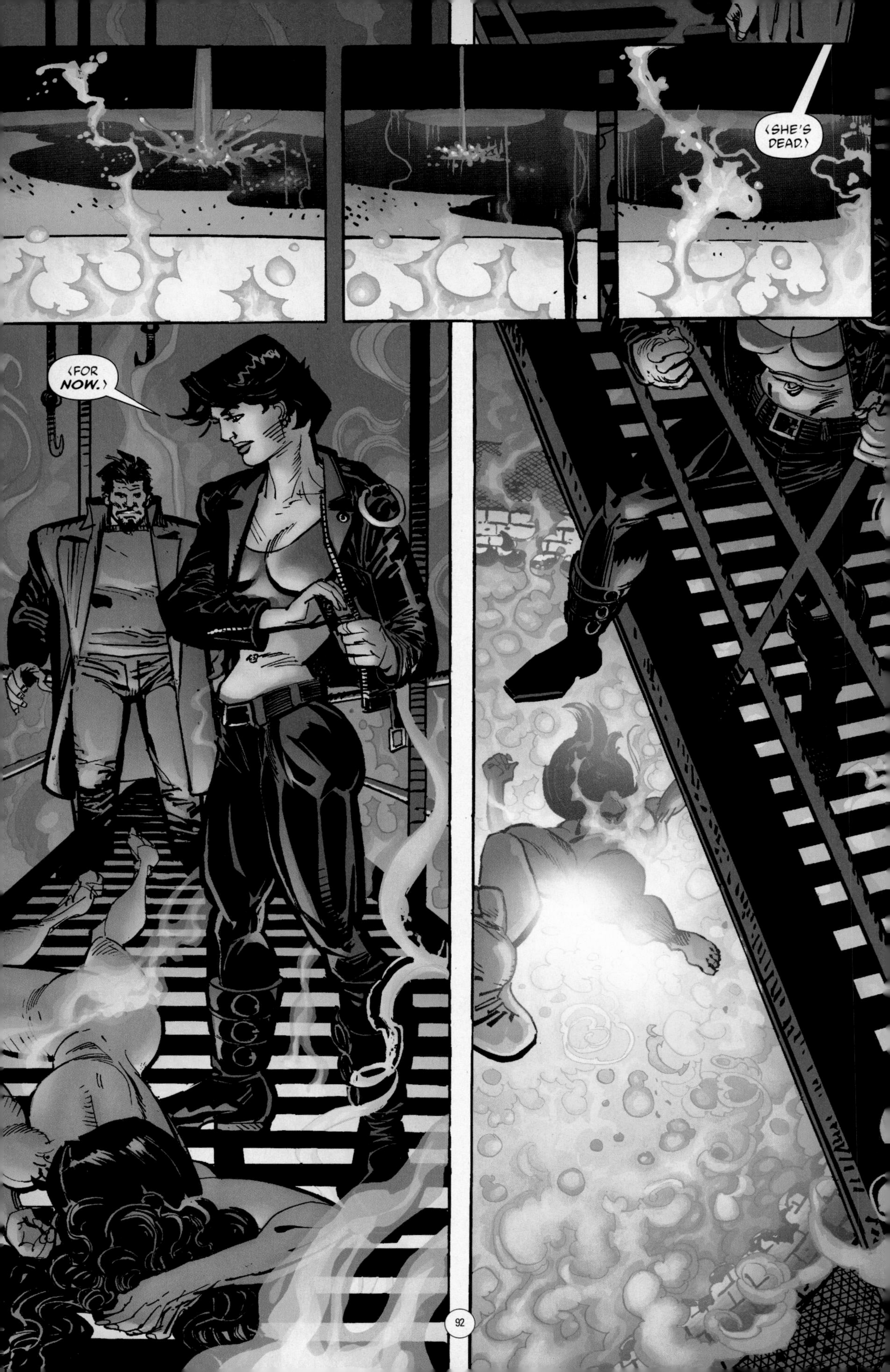
‹SHE'S DEAD.›
‹FOR NOW.›

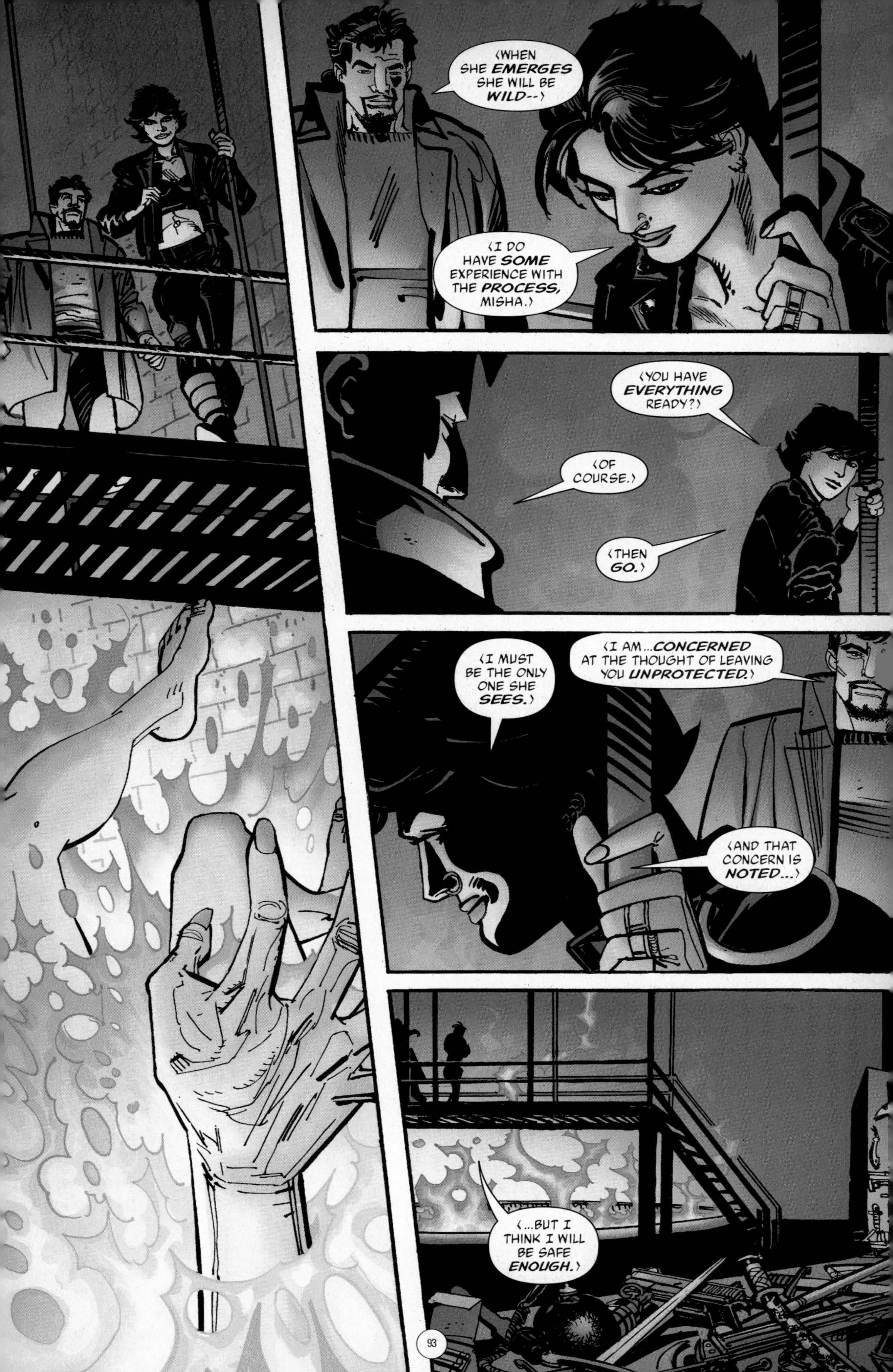
‹WHEN SHE EMERGES SHE WILL BE WILD--›
‹I DO HAVE SOME EXPERIENCE WITH THE PROCESS, MISHA.›
‹YOU HAVE EVERYTHING READY?›
‹OF COURSE.›
‹THEN GO.›
‹I AM...CONCERNED AT THE THOUGHT OF LEAVING YOU UNPROTECTED.›
‹I MUST BE THE ONLY ONE SHE SEES.›
‹AND THAT CONCERN IS NOTED...›
‹...BUT I THINK I WILL BE SAFE ENOUGH.›

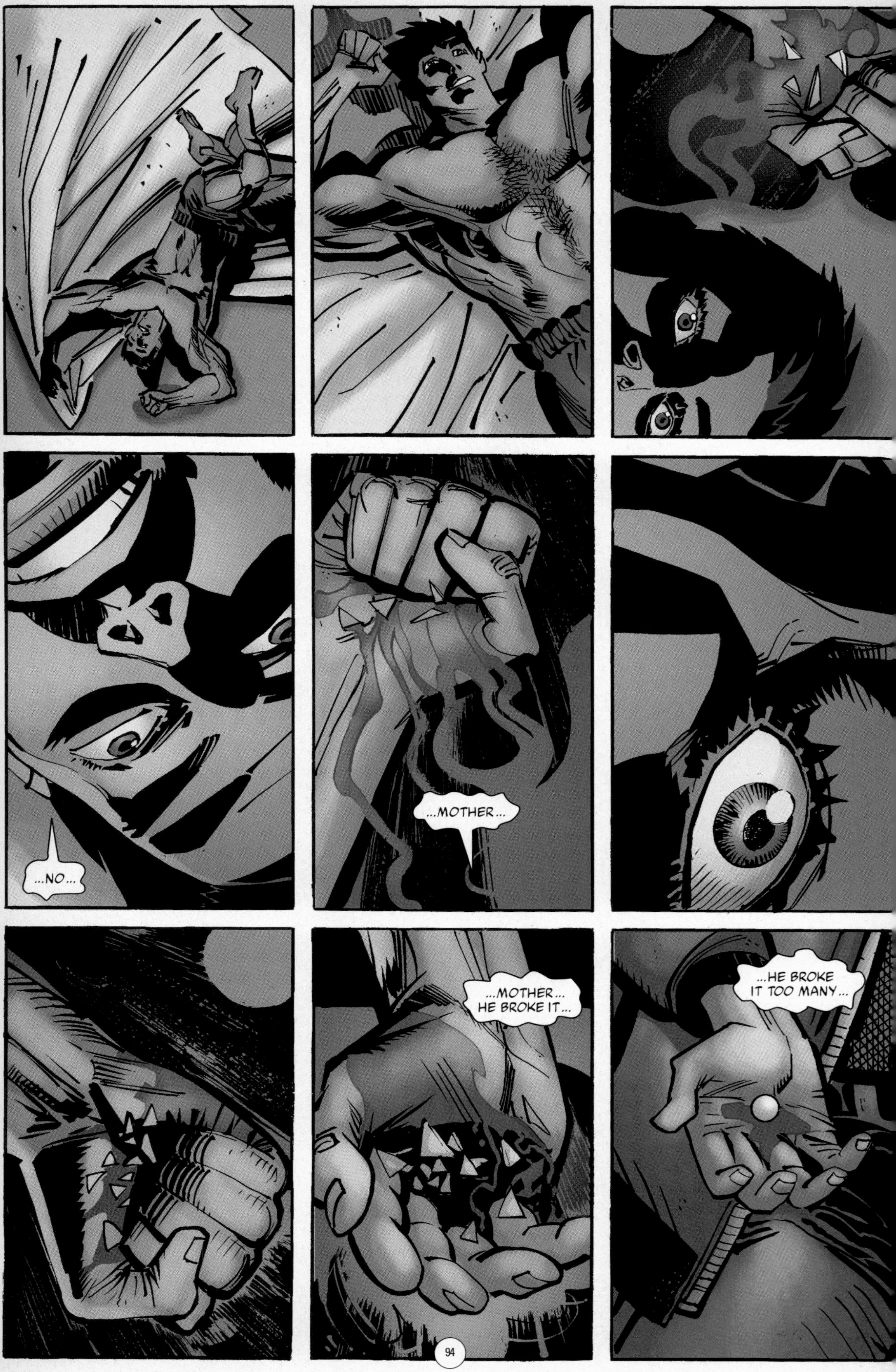
...NO...
...MOTHER...
...MOTHER... HE BROKE IT...
...HE BROKE IT TOO MANY...

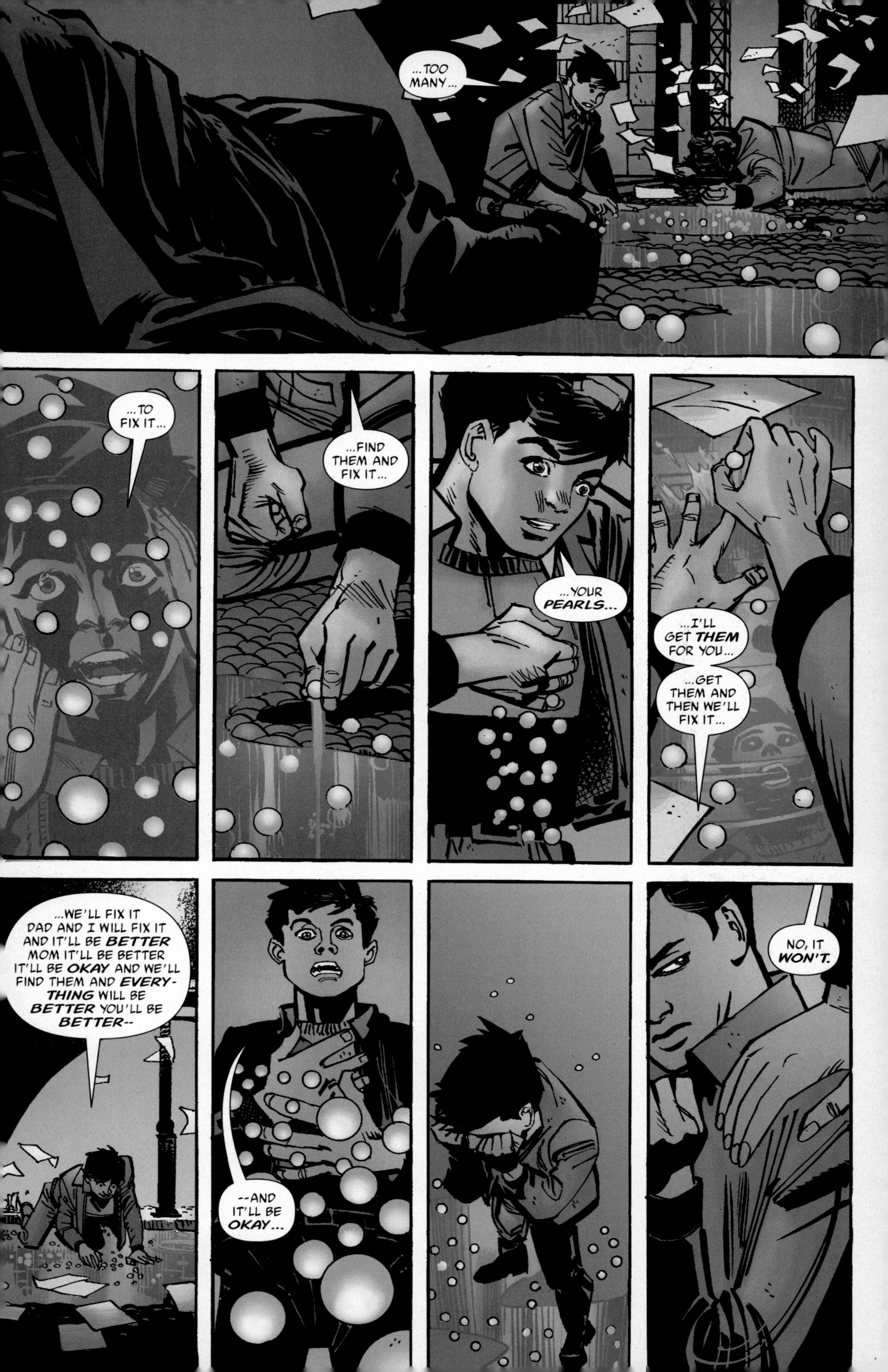
...TOO MANY...
...TO FIX IT...
...FIND THEM AND FIX IT...
...YOUR PEARLS...
...I'LL GET THEM FOR YOU...
...GET THEM AND THEN WE'LL FIX IT...
...WE'LL FIX IT DAD AND I WILL FIX IT AND IT'LL BE BETTER MOM IT'LL BE BETTER IT'LL BE OKAY AND WE'LL FIND THEM AND EVERY-THING WILL BE BETTER YOU'LL BE BETTER--
--AND IT'LL BE OKAY...
NO, IT WON'T.

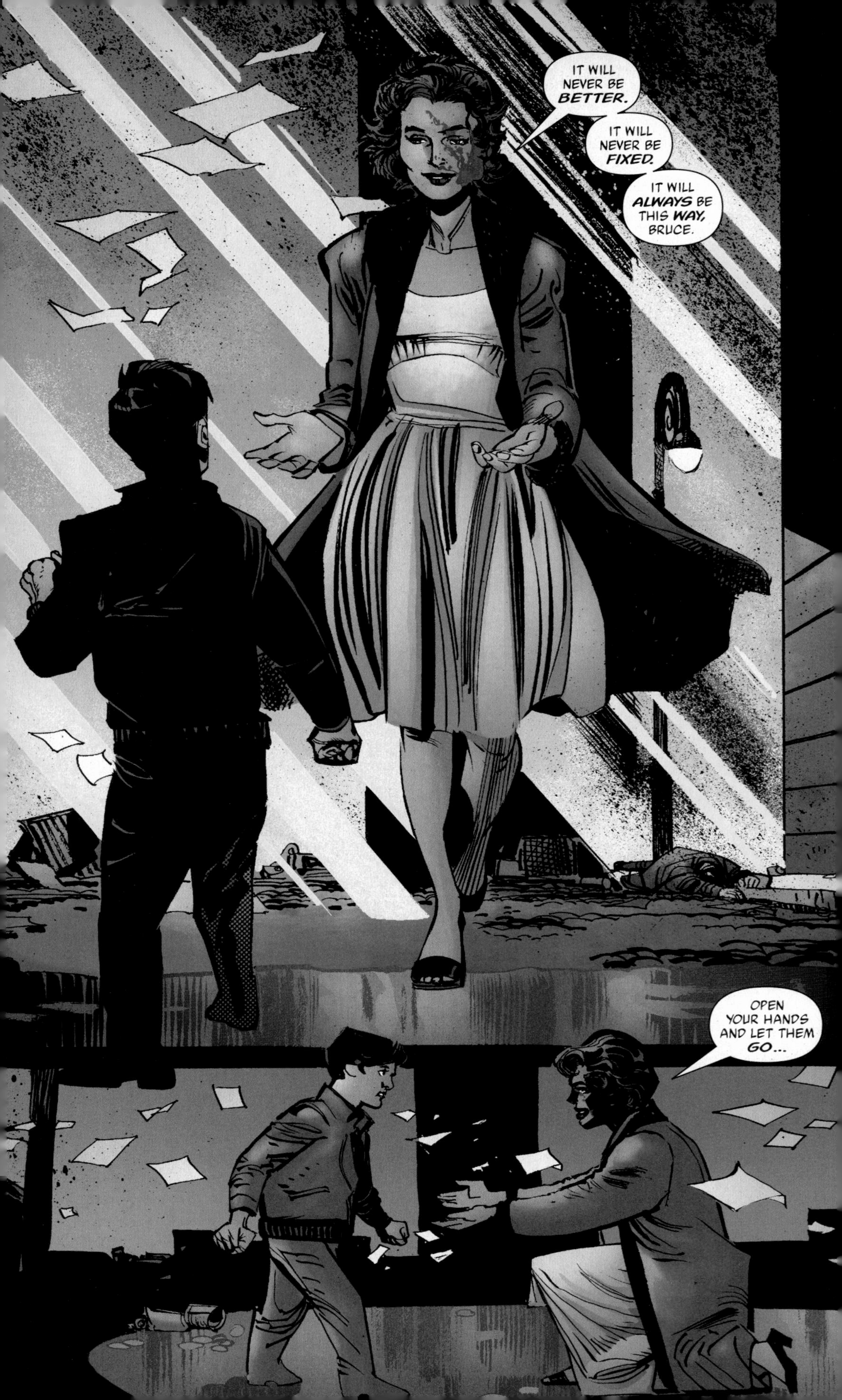
IT WILL NEVER BE BETTER.
IT WILL NEVER BE FIXED.
IT WILL ALWAYS BE THIS WAY, BRUCE.
OPEN YOUR HANDS AND LET THEM GO...

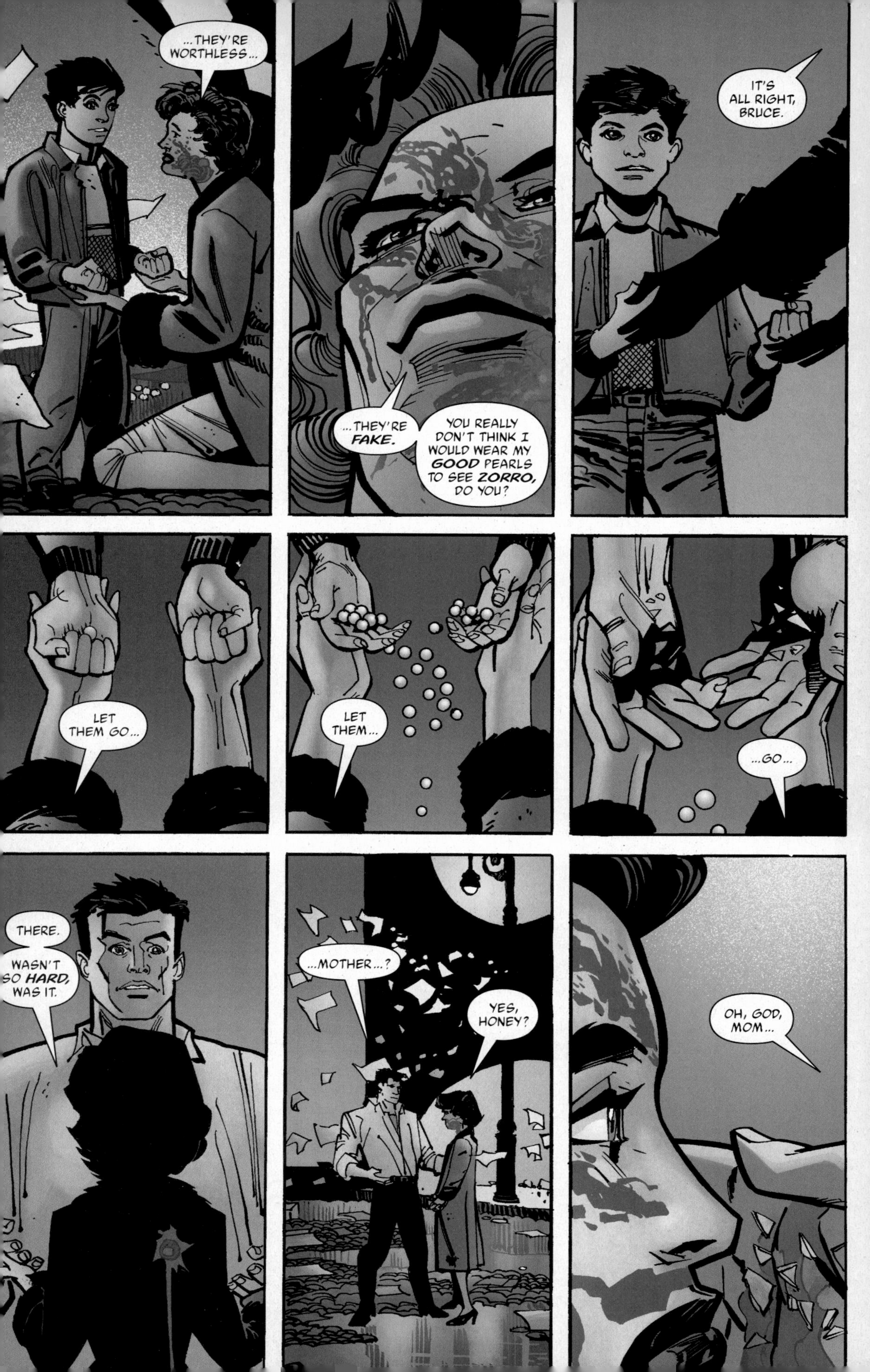

...THEY'RE WORTHLESS...
...THEY'RE FAKE.
YOU REALLY DON'T THINK I WOULD WEAR MY GOOD PEARLS TO SEE ZORRO, DO YOU?
IT'S ALL RIGHT, BRUCE.
LET THEM GO...
LET THEM...
...GO...
THERE.
WASN'T SO HARD, WAS IT.
...MOTHER...?
YES, HONEY?
OH, GOD, MOM...

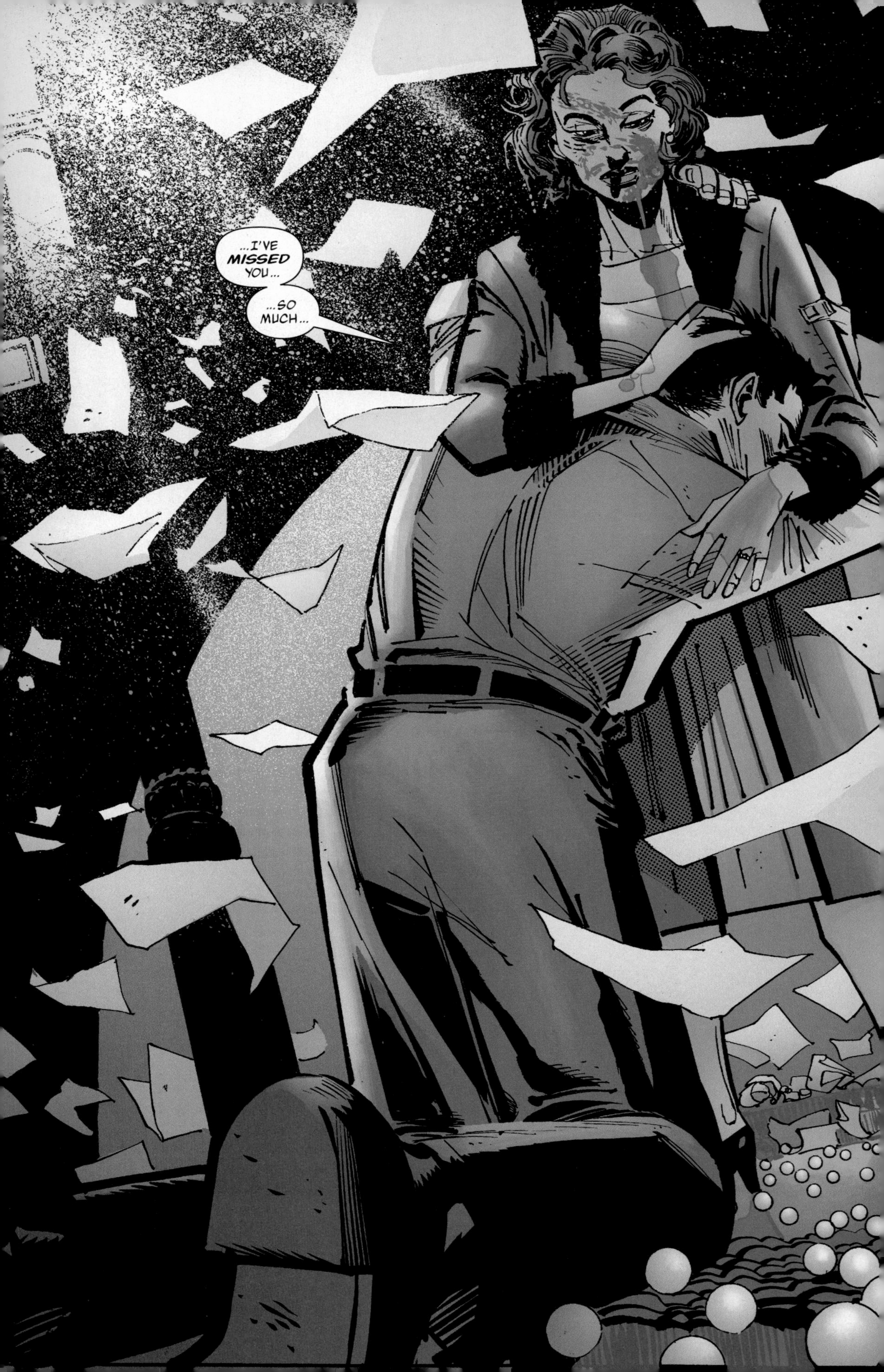
...I'VE MISSED YOU...
...SO MUCH...

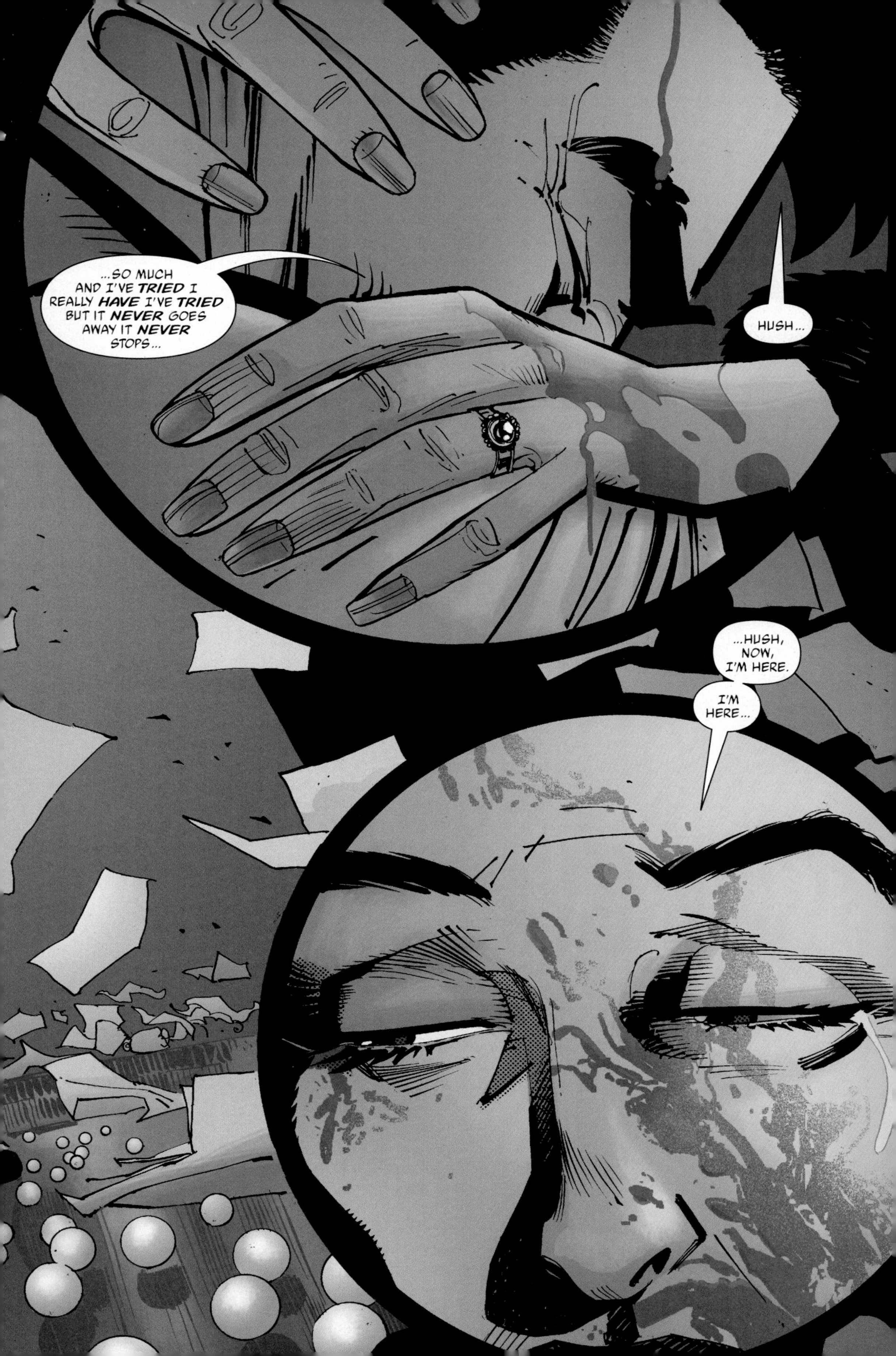
...SO MUCH AND I'VE TRIED I REALLY HAVE I'VE TRIED BUT IT NEVER GOES AWAY IT NEVER STOPS...
HUSH...
...HUSH, NOW, I'M HERE.
I'M HERE...

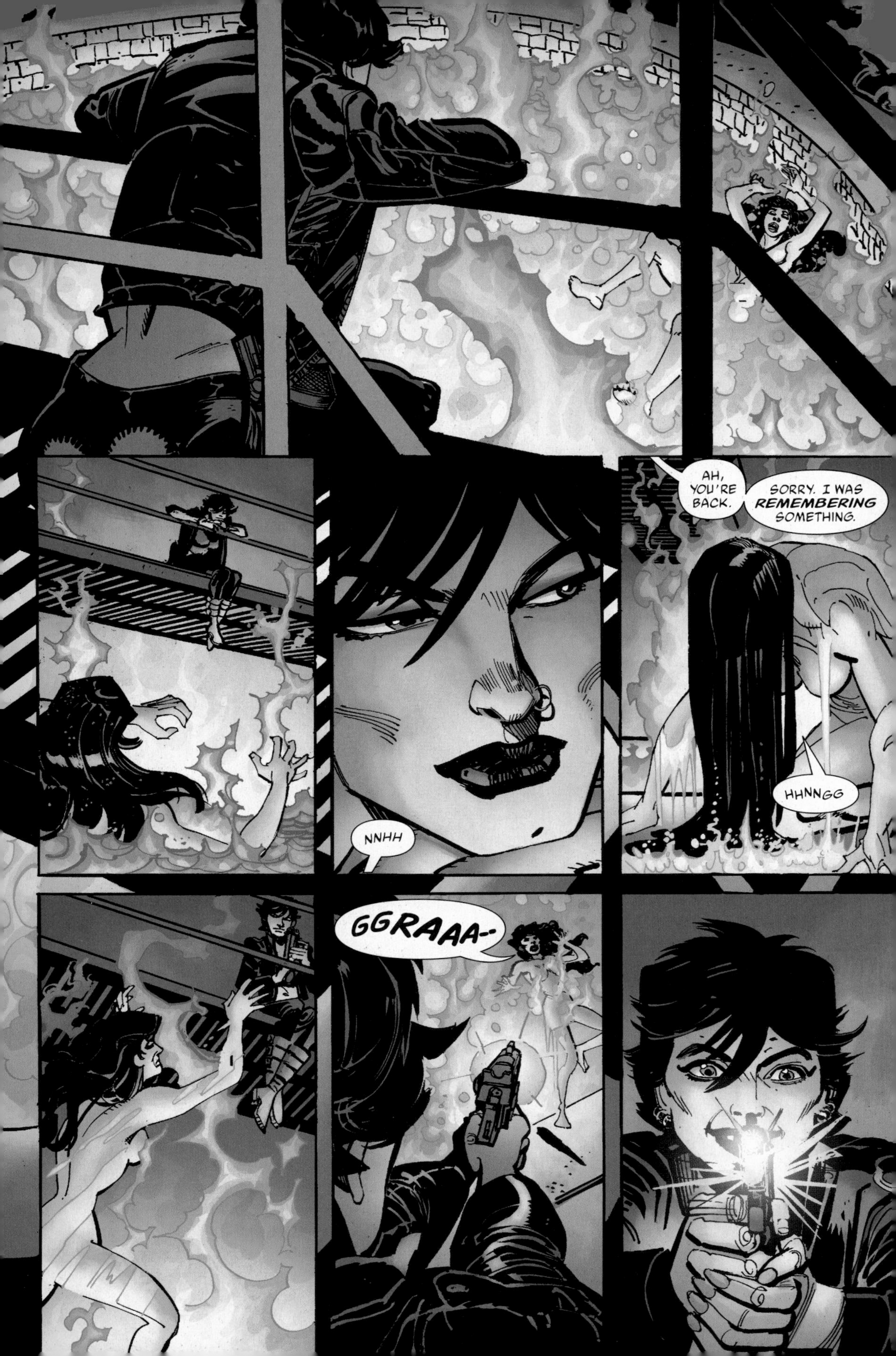

NNHH
AH, YOU'RE BACK.
SORRY. I WAS **REMEMBERING** SOMETHING.
HHNNGG
GGRAAA-

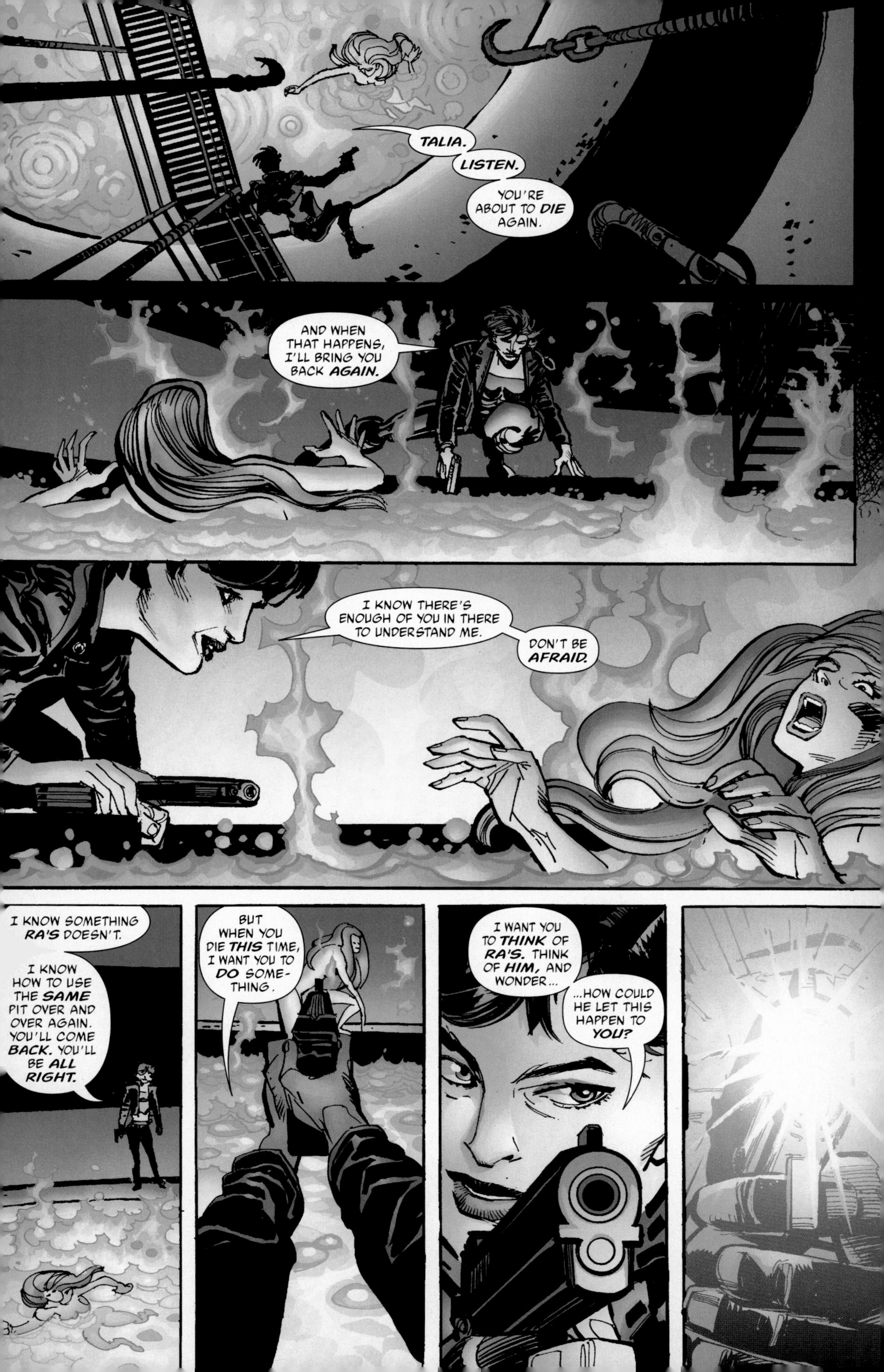
TALIA.
LISTEN.
YOU'RE ABOUT TO DIE AGAIN.
AND WHEN THAT HAPPENS, I'LL BRING YOU BACK AGAIN.
I KNOW THERE'S ENOUGH OF YOU IN THERE TO UNDERSTAND ME.
DON'T BE AFRAID.
I KNOW SOMETHING RA'S DOESN'T.
I KNOW HOW TO USE THE SAME PIT OVER AND OVER AGAIN. YOU'LL COME BACK. YOU'LL BE ALL RIGHT.
BUT WHEN YOU DIE THIS TIME, I WANT YOU TO DO SOME-THING.
I WANT YOU TO THINK OF RA'S. THINK OF HIM, AND WONDER...
...HOW COULD HE LET THIS HAPPEN TO YOU?

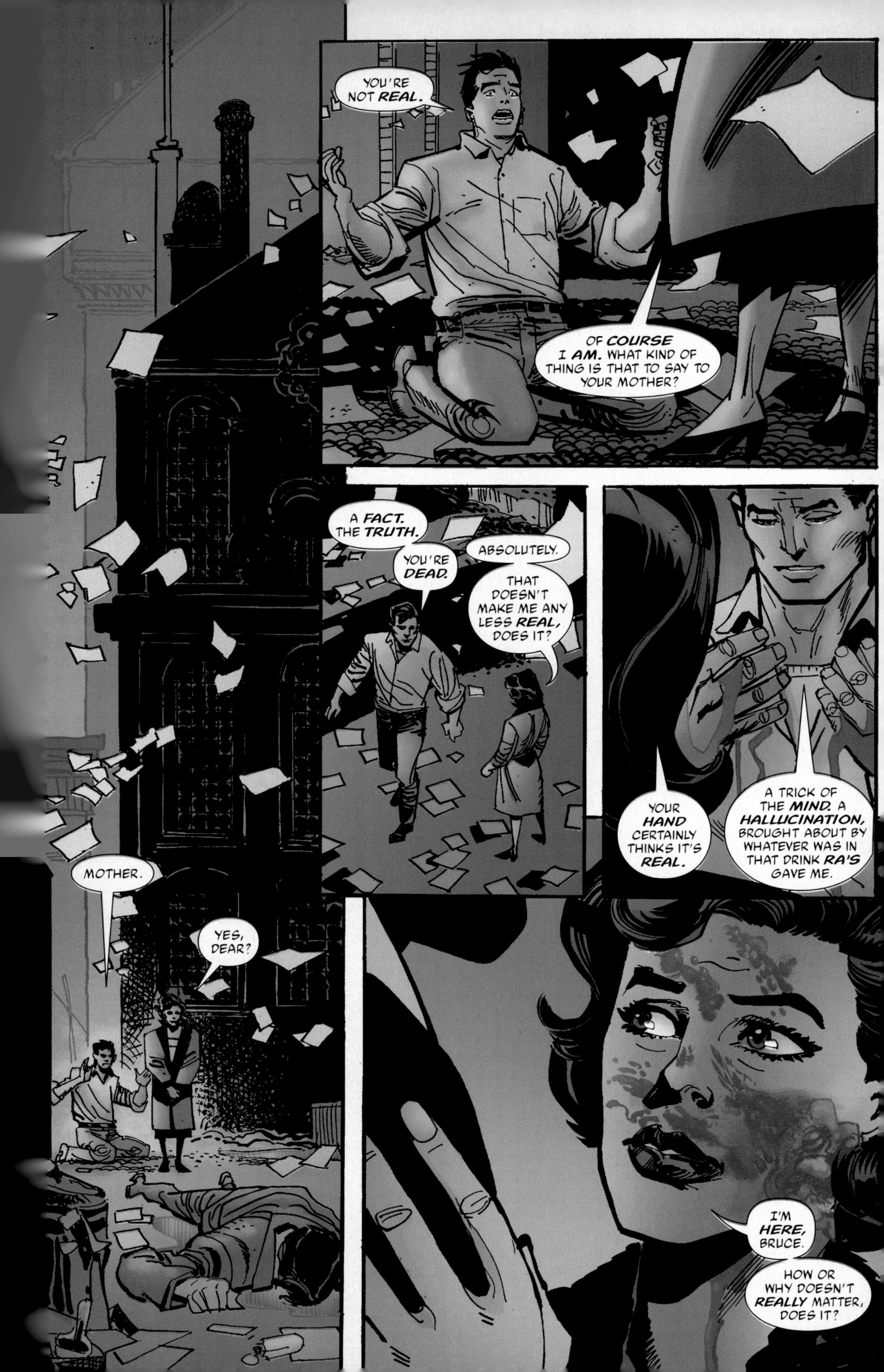
YOU'RE NOT REAL.
OF COURSE I AM. WHAT KIND OF THING IS THAT TO SAY TO YOUR MOTHER?
A FACT. THE TRUTH.
YOU'RE DEAD.
ABSOLUTELY.
THAT DOESN'T MAKE ME ANY LESS REAL, DOES IT?
A TRICK OF THE MIND. A HALLUCINATION, BROUGHT ABOUT BY WHATEVER WAS IN THAT DRINK RA'S GAVE ME.
YOUR HAND CERTAINLY THINKS IT'S REAL.
MOTHER.
YES, DEAR?
I'M HERE, BRUCE.
HOW OR WHY DOESN'T REALLY MATTER, DOES IT?

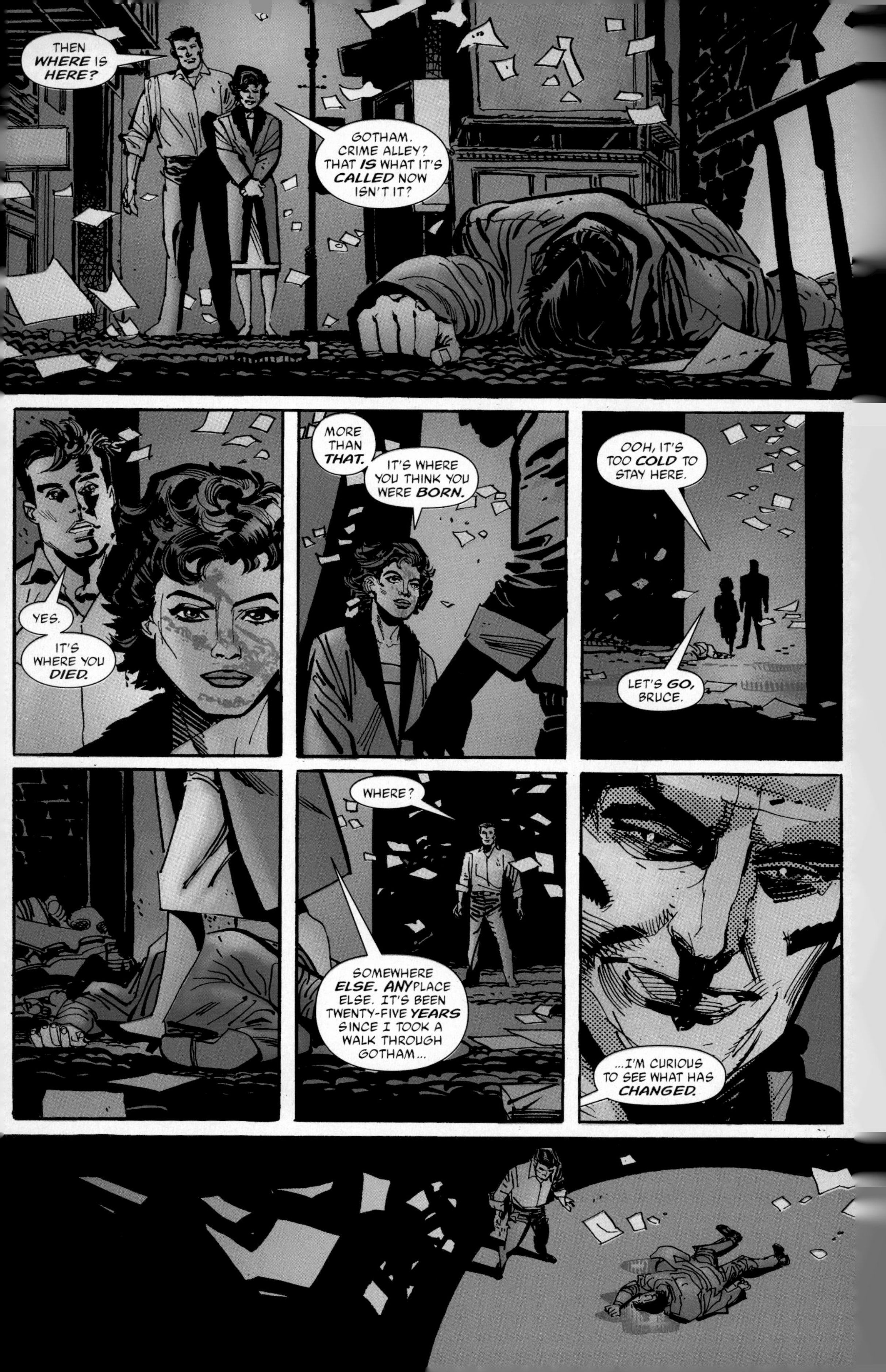
THEN WHERE IS HERE?
GOTHAM. CRIME ALLEY? THAT IS WHAT IT'S CALLED NOW ISN'T IT?
YES.
IT'S WHERE YOU DIED.
MORE THAN THAT.
IT'S WHERE YOU THINK YOU WERE BORN.
OOH, IT'S TOO COLD TO STAY HERE.
LET'S GO, BRUCE.
WHERE?
SOMEWHERE ELSE. ANYPLACE ELSE. IT'S BEEN TWENTY-FIVE YEARS SINCE I TOOK A WALK THROUGH GOTHAM...
...I'M CURIOUS TO SEE WHAT HAS CHANGED.

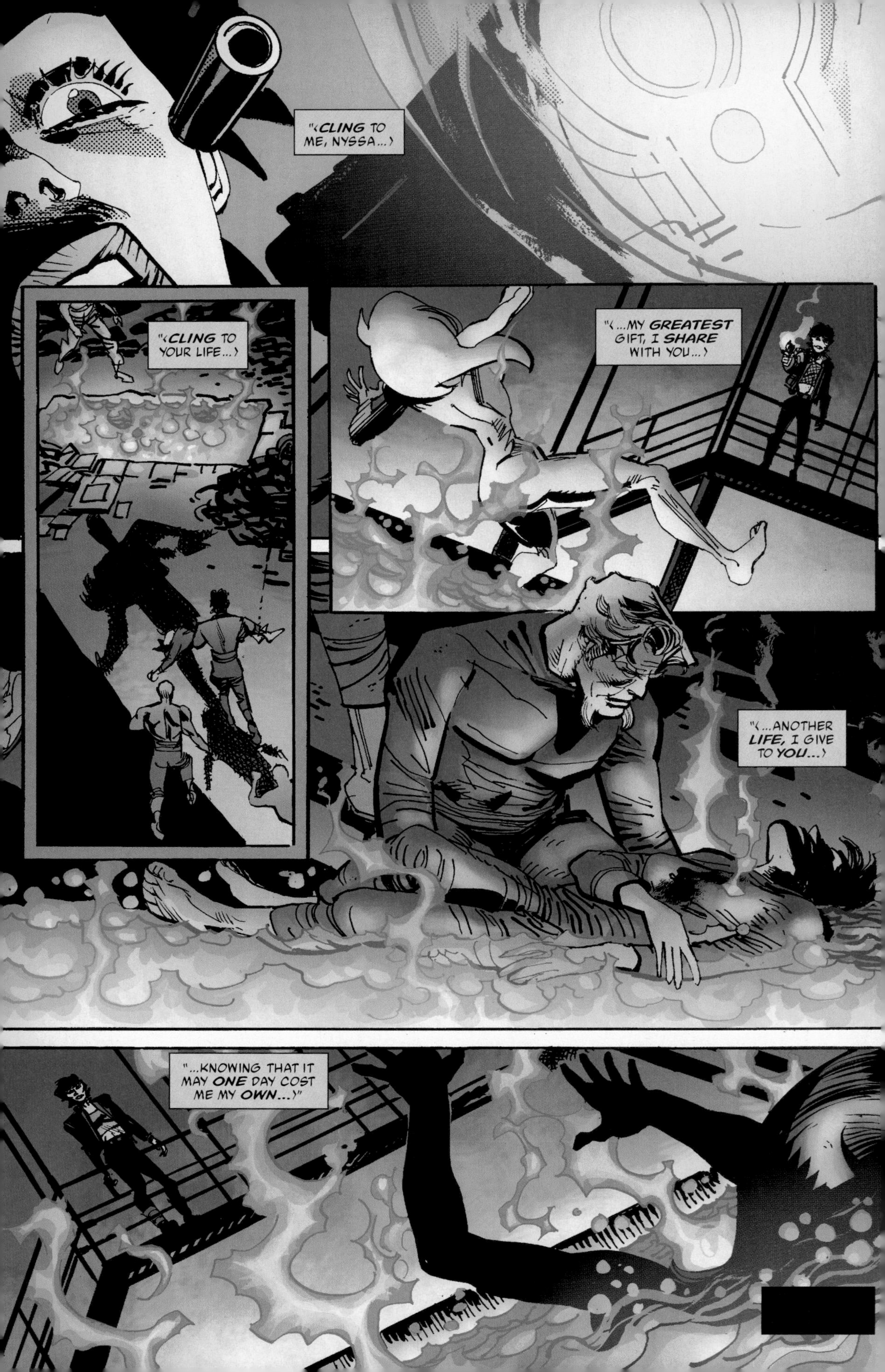
"‹CLING TO ME, NYSSA...›
"‹CLING TO YOUR LIFE...›
"‹...MY GREATEST GIFT, I SHARE WITH YOU...›
"‹...ANOTHER LIFE, I GIVE TO YOU...›
"...KNOWING THAT IT MAY ONE DAY COST ME MY OWN...›"

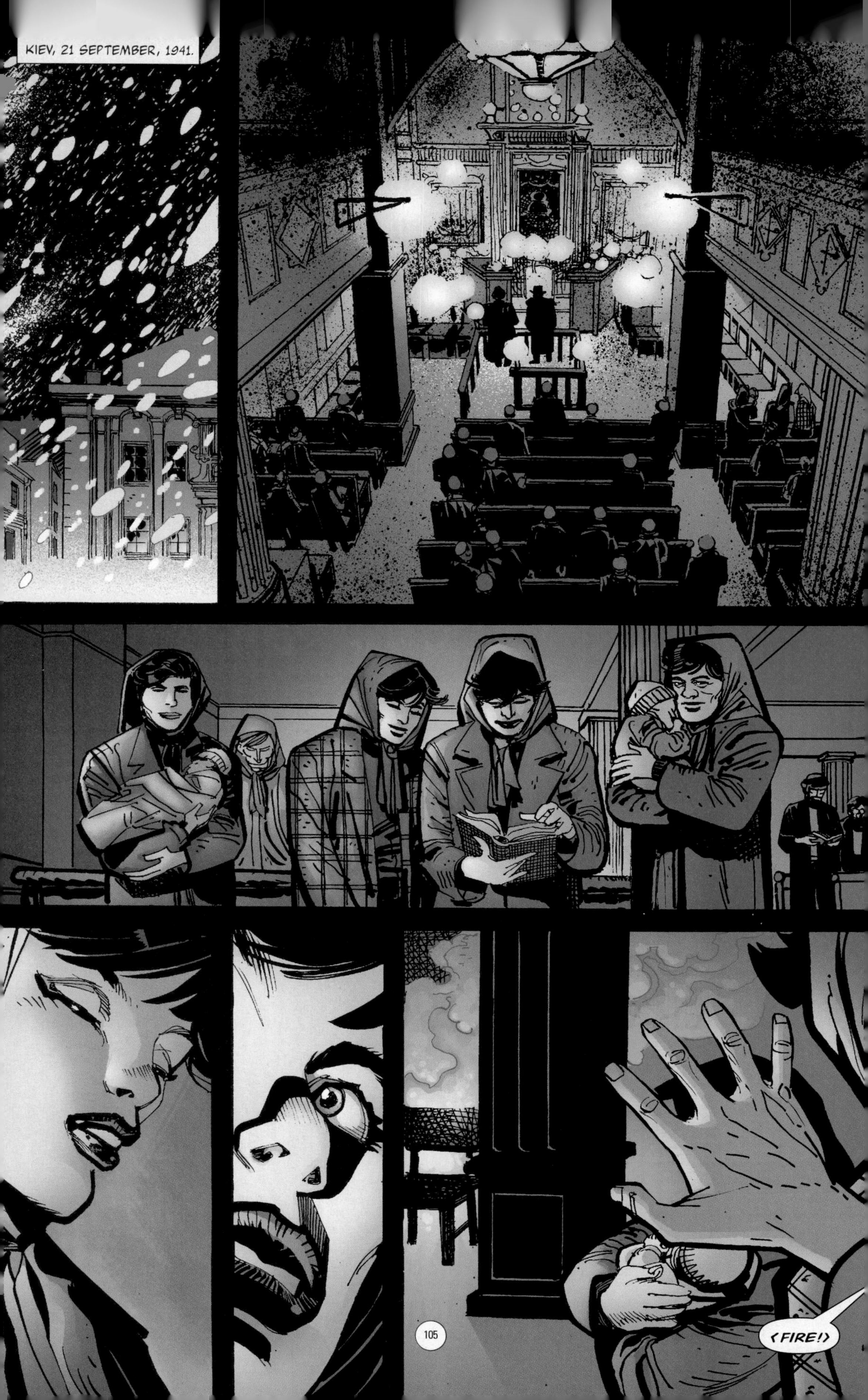
KIEV, 21 SEPTEMBER, 1941.
‹FIRE!›

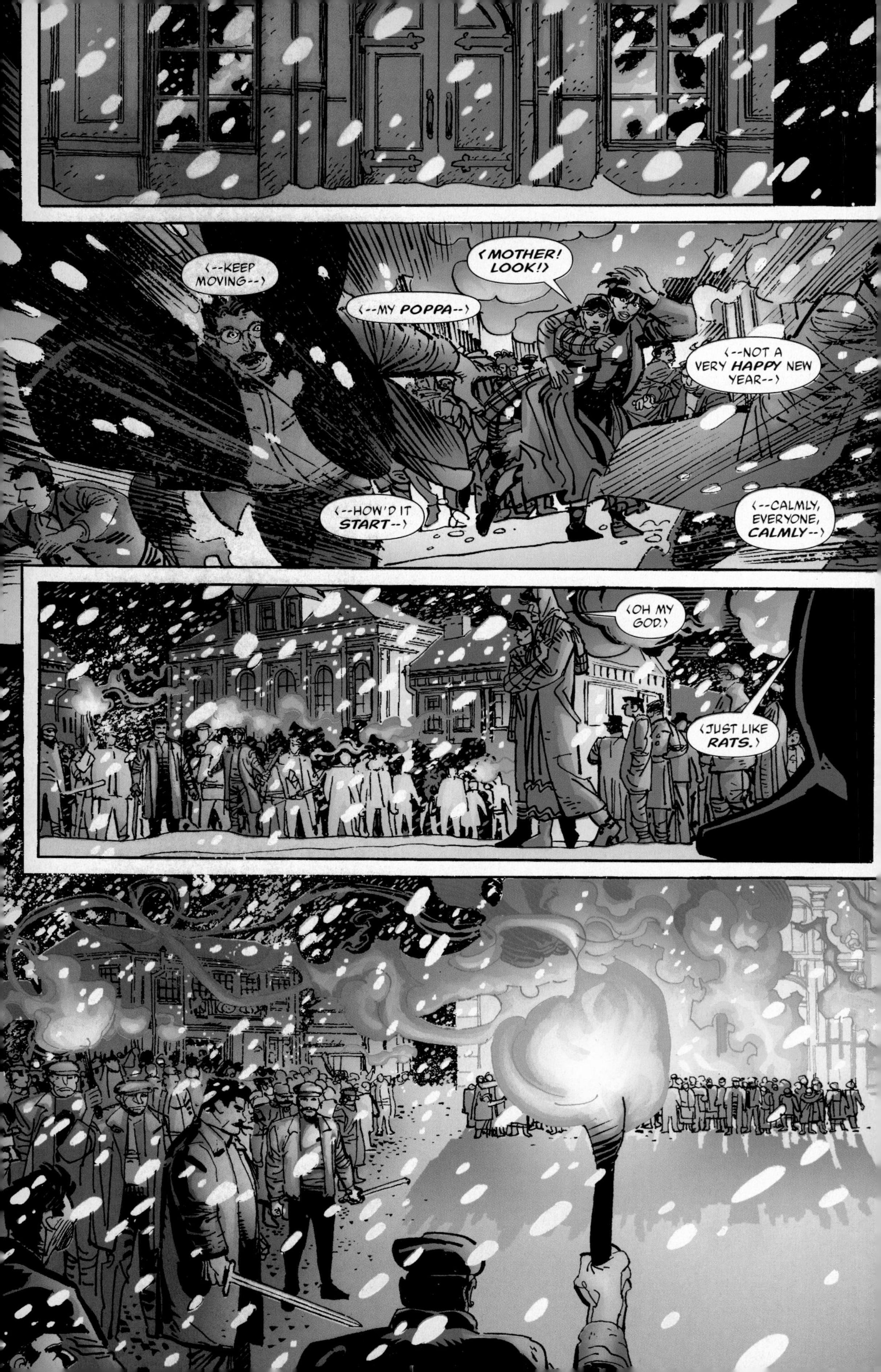

‹--KEEP MOVING--›
‹--MY POPPA--›
‹MOTHER! LOOK!›
‹--NOT A VERY HAPPY NEW YEAR--›
‹--HOW'D IT START--›
‹--CALMLY, EVERYONE, CALMLY--›
‹OH MY GOD.›
‹JUST LIKE RATS.›

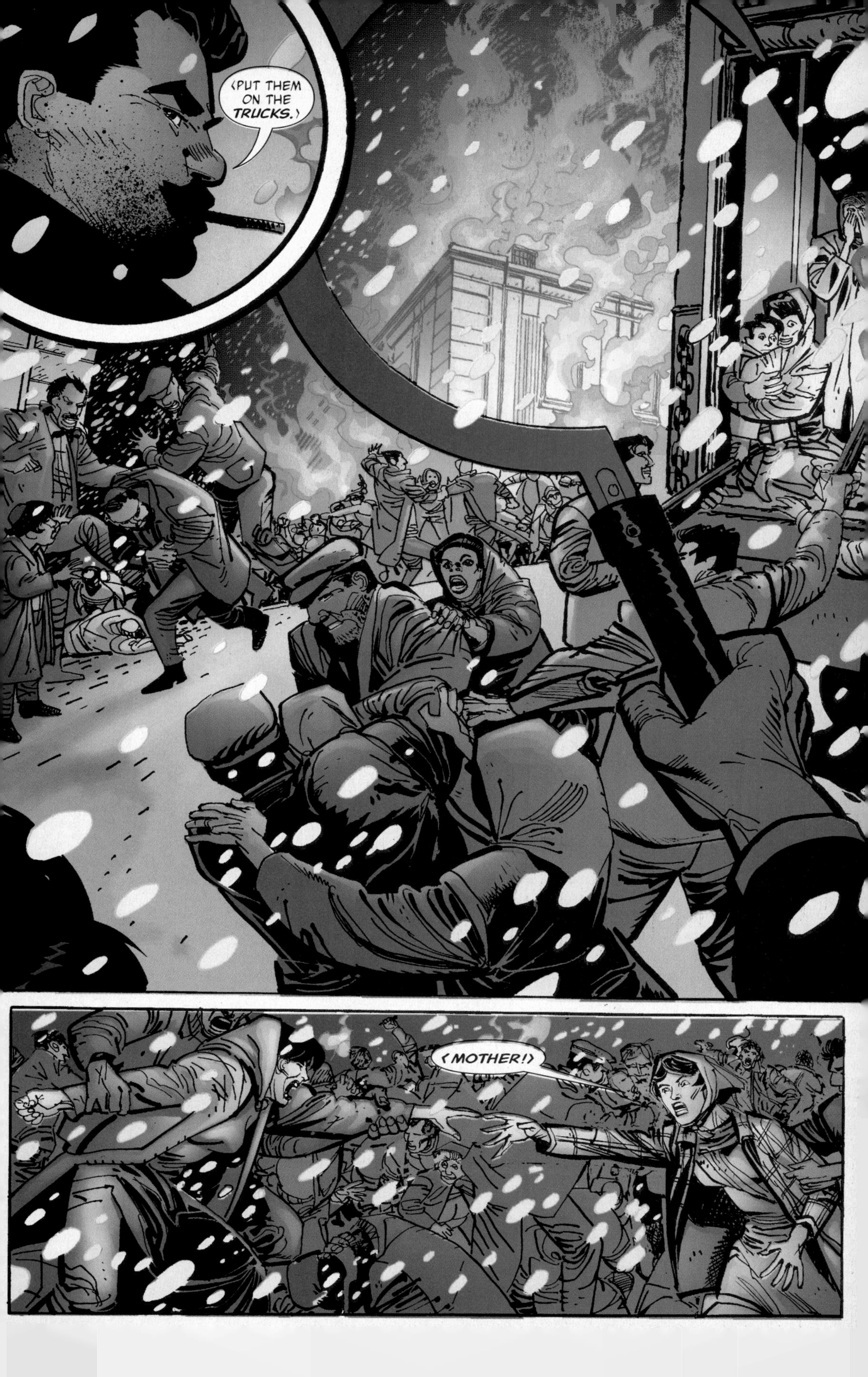
‹PUT THEM ON THE TRUCKS.›
‹MOTHER!›

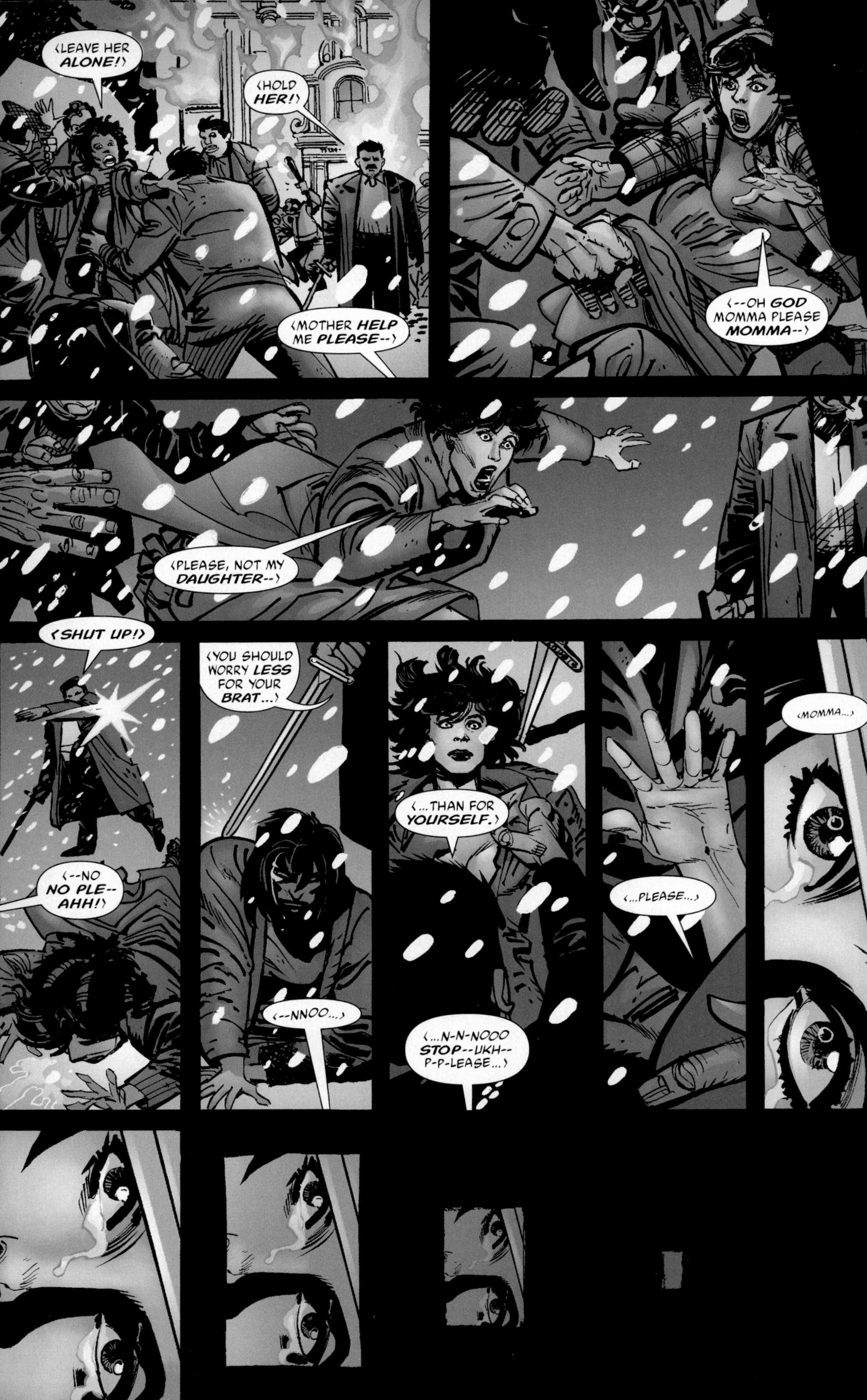
‹LEAVE HER ALONE!›
‹HOLD HER!›
‹MOTHER HELP ME PLEASE--›
‹--OH GOD MOMMA PLEASE MOMMA--›
‹PLEASE, NOT MY DAUGHTER--›
‹SHUT UP!›
‹--NO NO PLE-- AHH!›
‹YOU SHOULD WORRY LESS FOR YOUR BRAT...›
‹--NNOO...›
‹...THAN FOR YOURSELF.›
‹...N-N-NOOO STOP--UKH-- P-P-LEASE...›
‹...PLEASE...›
‹MOMMA...›

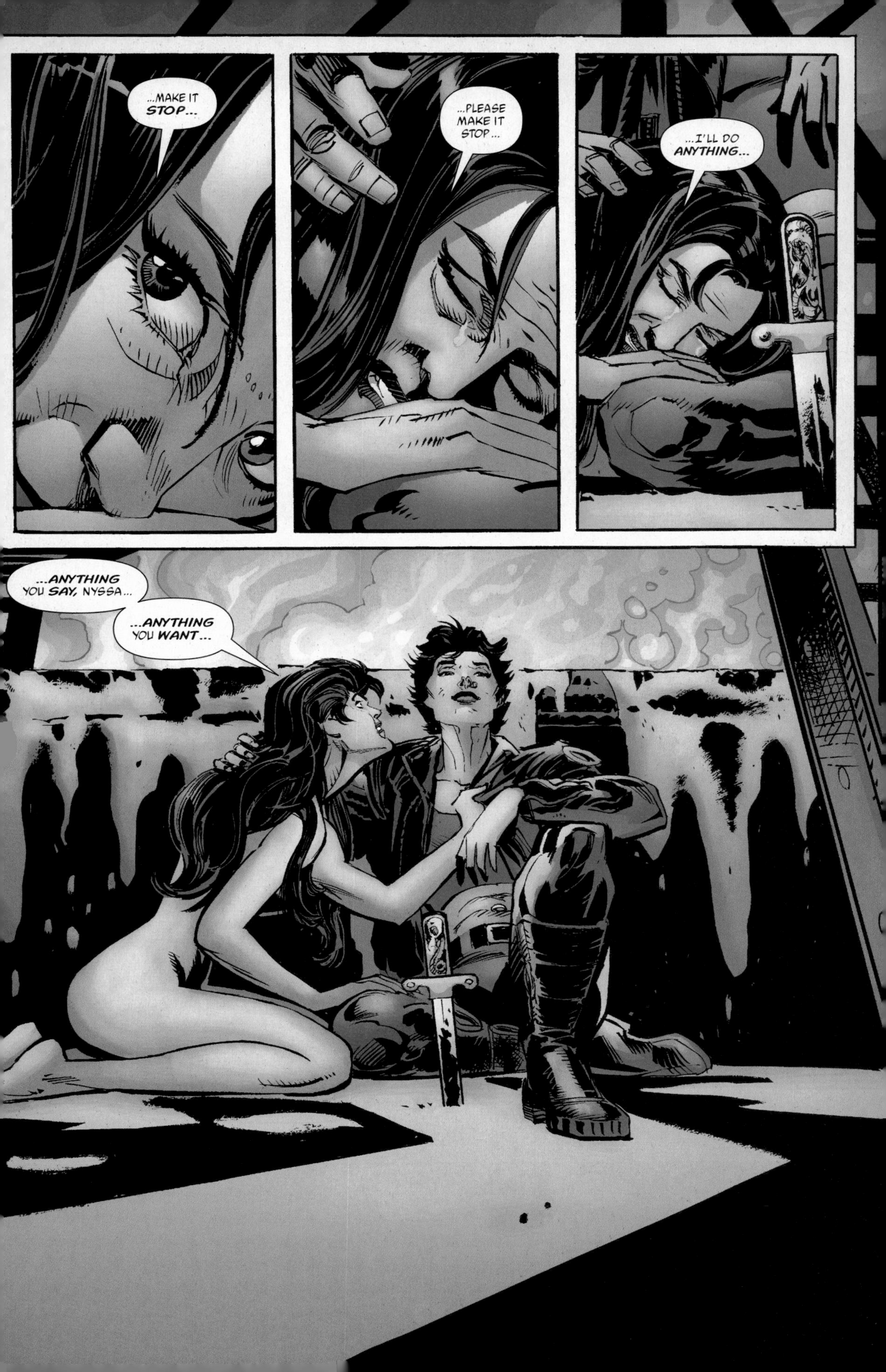
...MAKE IT STOP...
...PLEASE MAKE IT STOP...
...I'LL DO ANYTHING...
...ANYTHING YOU SAY, NYSSA...
...ANYTHING YOU WANT...

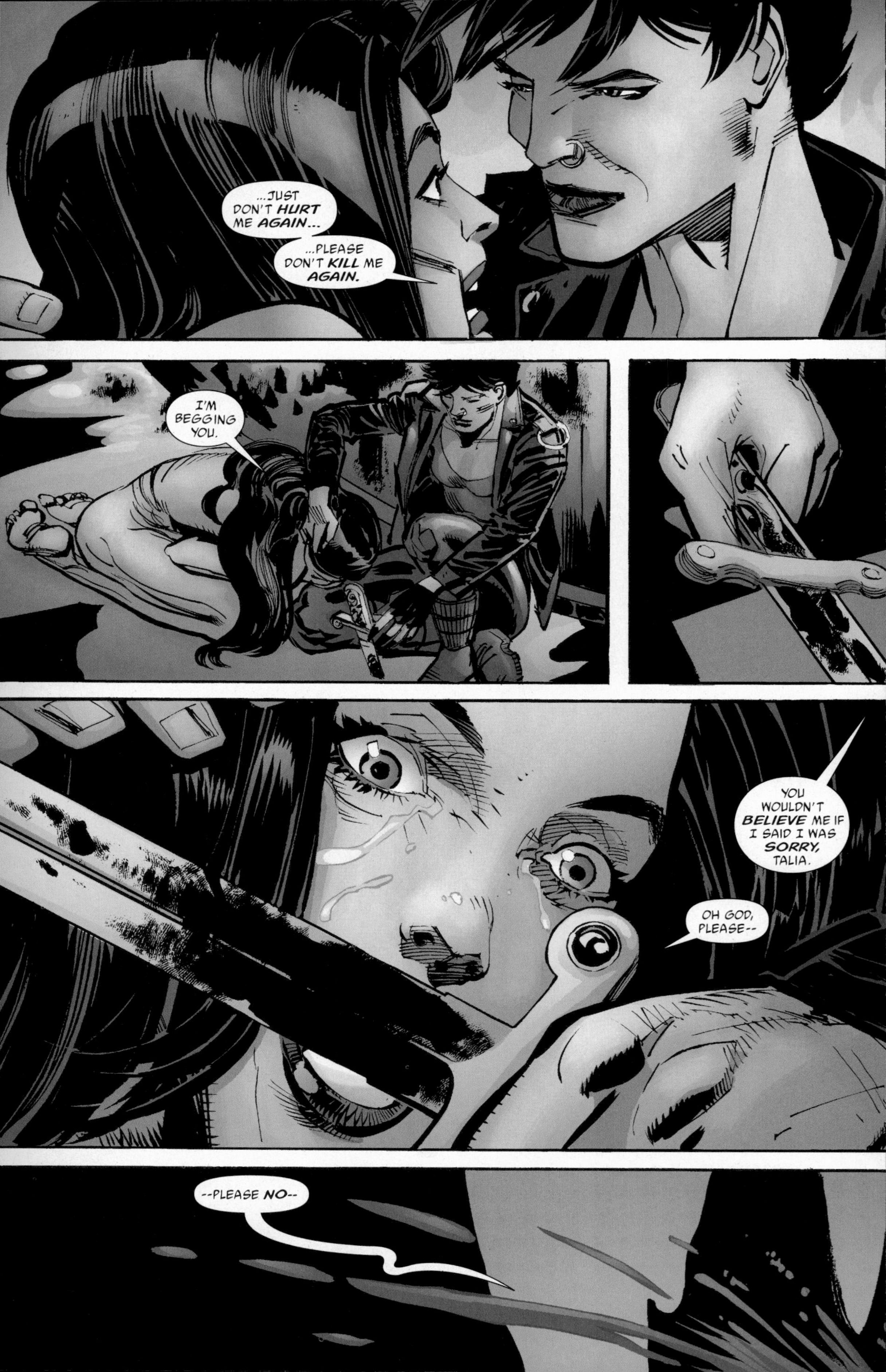
...JUST DON'T HURT ME AGAIN...
...PLEASE DON'T KILL ME AGAIN.
I'M BEGGING YOU.
YOU WOULDN'T BELIEVE ME IF I SAID I WAS SORRY, TALIA.
OH GOD, PLEASE--
--PLEASE NO--

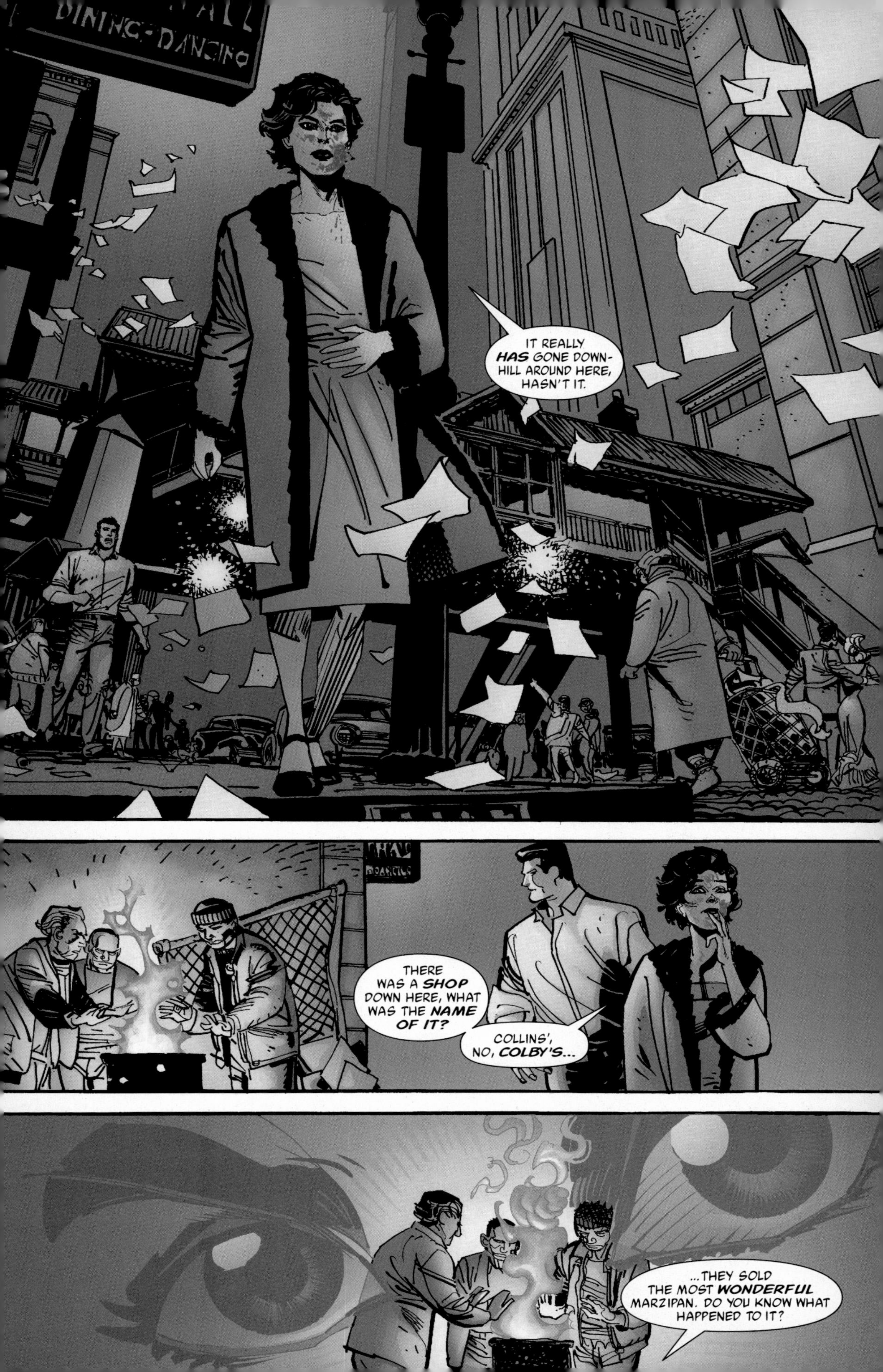

DINING-DANCING
IT REALLY HAS GONE DOWN-HILL AROUND HERE, HASN'T IT.
THERE WAS A SHOP DOWN HERE, WHAT WAS THE NAME OF IT?
COLLINS', NO, COLBY'S...
...THEY SOLD THE MOST WONDERFUL MARZIPAN. DO YOU KNOW WHAT HAPPENED TO IT?

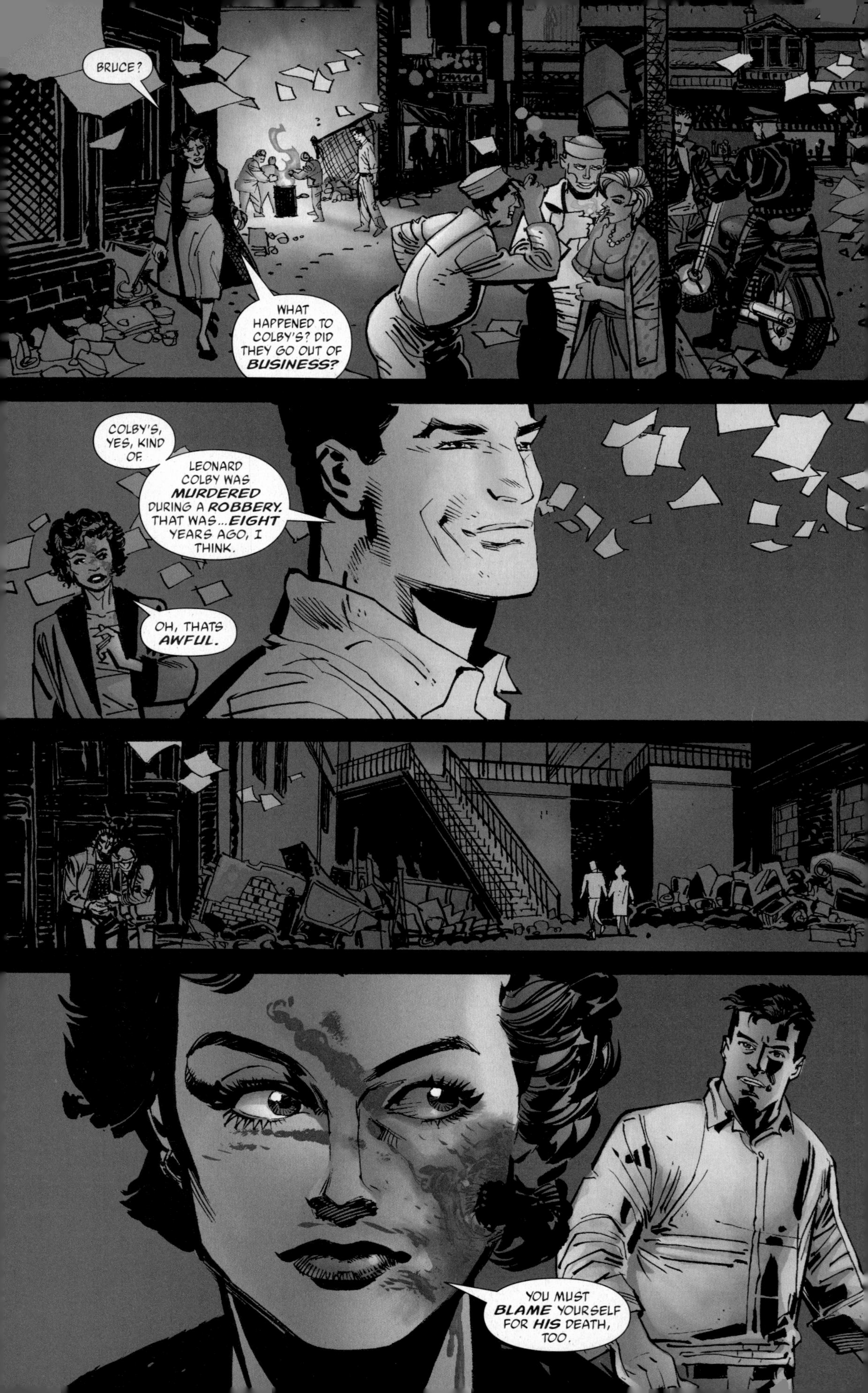
BRUCE?
WHAT HAPPENED TO COLBY'S? DID THEY GO OUT OF BUSINESS?
COLBY'S, YES, KIND OF.
LEONARD COLBY WAS MURDERED DURING A ROBBERY. THAT WAS... EIGHT YEARS AGO, I THINK.
OH, THATS AWFUL.
YOU MUST BLAME YOURSELF FOR HIS DEATH, TOO.

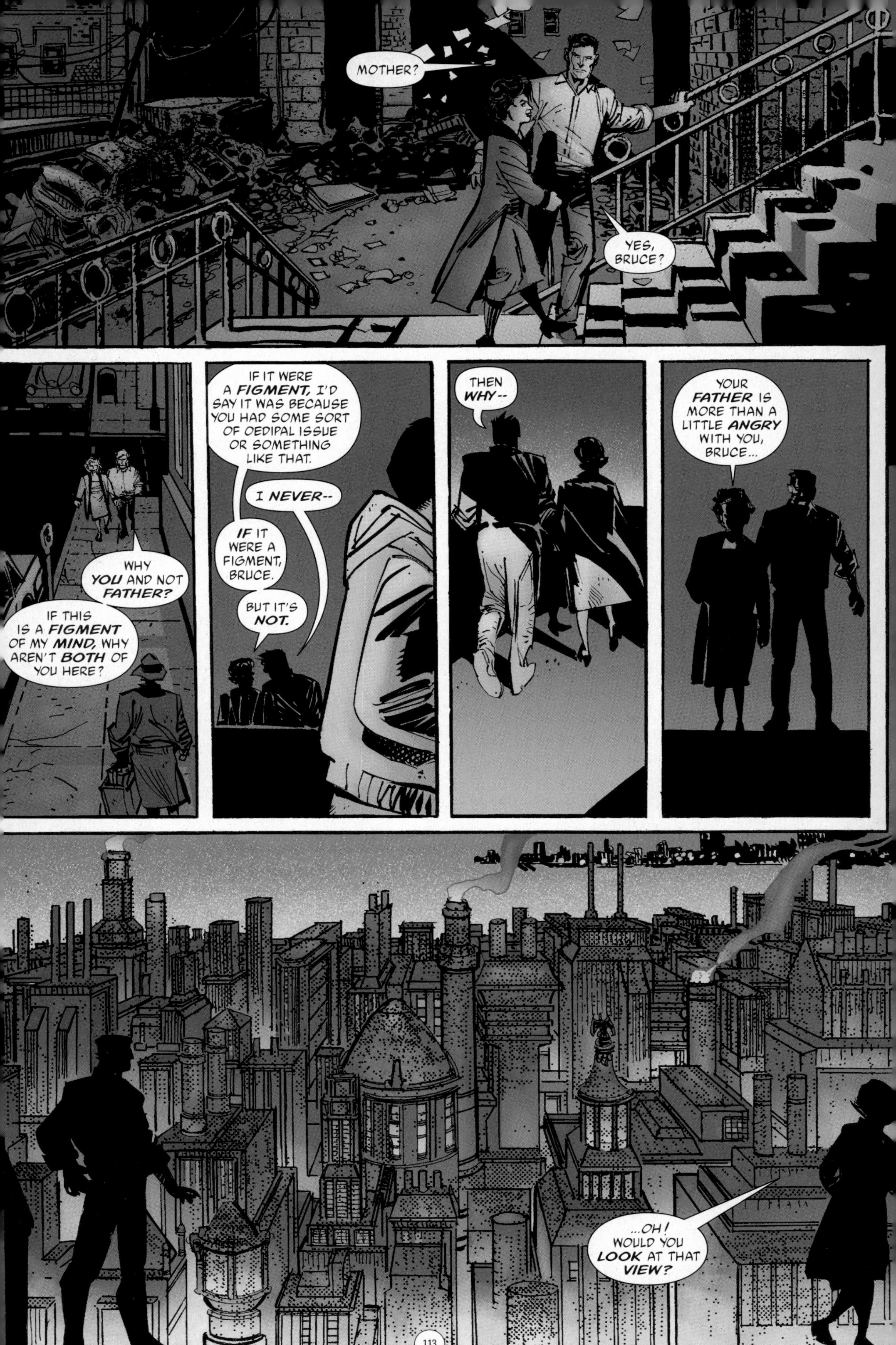
MOTHER?
YES, BRUCE?
IF THIS IS A FIGMENT OF MY MIND, WHY AREN'T BOTH OF YOU HERE?
WHY YOU AND NOT FATHER?
IF IT WERE A FIGMENT, I'D SAY IT WAS BECAUSE YOU HAD SOME SORT OF OEDIPAL ISSUE OR SOMETHING LIKE THAT.
I NEVER--
IF IT WERE A FIGMENT, BRUCE.
BUT IT'S NOT.
THEN WHY--
YOUR FATHER IS MORE THAN A LITTLE ANGRY WITH YOU, BRUCE...
...OH! WOULD YOU LOOK AT THAT VIEW?

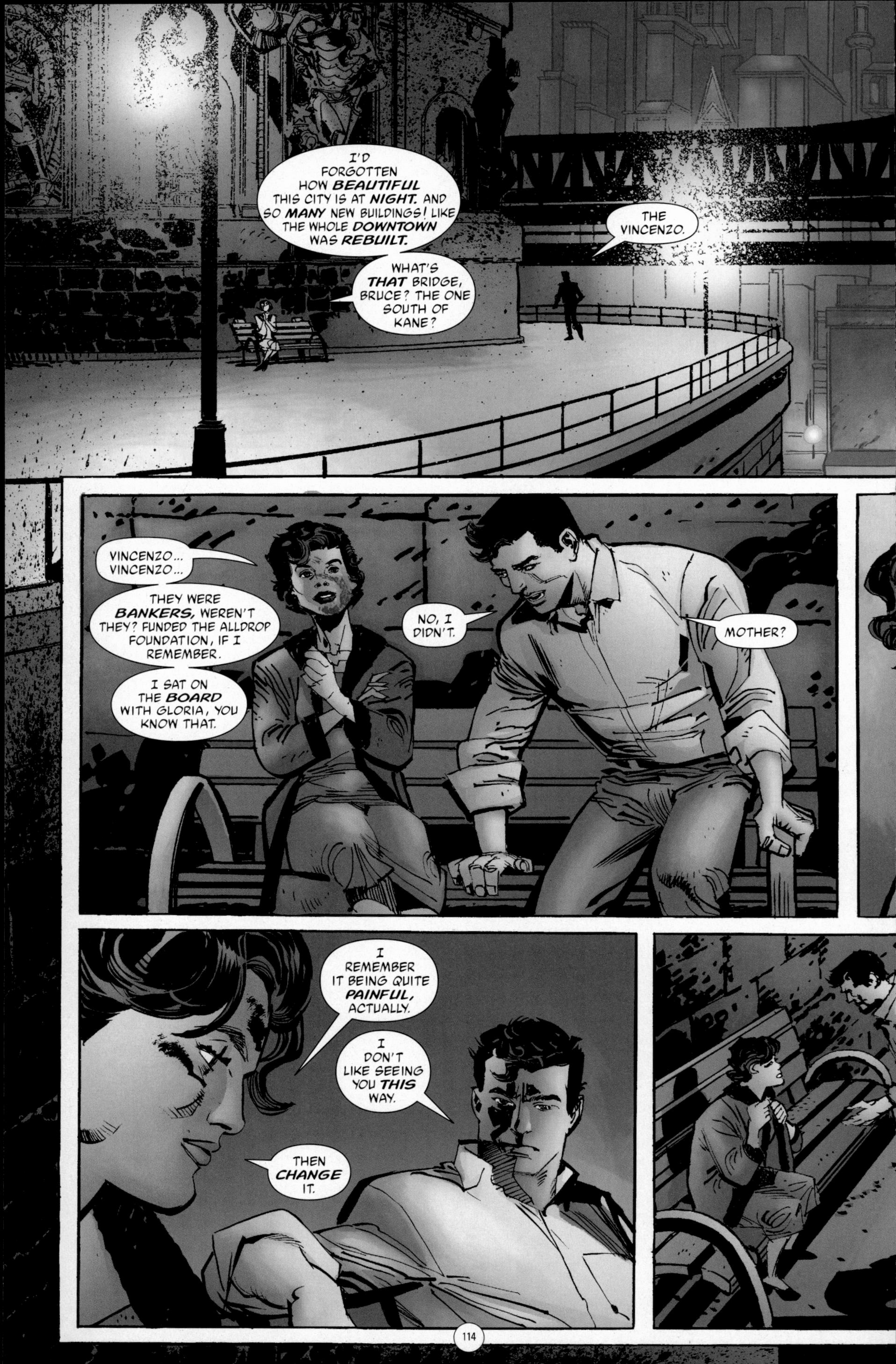

I'D FORGOTTEN HOW BEAUTIFUL THIS CITY IS AT NIGHT. AND SO MANY NEW BUILDINGS! LIKE THE WHOLE DOWNTOWN WAS REBUILT.
WHAT'S THAT BRIDGE, BRUCE? THE ONE SOUTH OF KANE?
THE VINCENZO.
VINCENZO... VINCENZO...
THEY WERE BANKERS, WEREN'T THEY? FUNDED THE ALLDROP FOUNDATION, IF I REMEMBER.
I SAT ON THE BOARD WITH GLORIA, YOU KNOW THAT.
NO, I DIDN'T.
MOTHER?
I REMEMBER IT BEING QUITE PAINFUL, ACTUALLY.
I DON'T LIKE SEEING YOU THIS WAY.
THEN CHANGE IT.

YES, BRUCE?

WHY DO YOU HAVE *THAT*... *WOUND?*

YOU *KNOW* WHY.

I WAS *SHOT.*

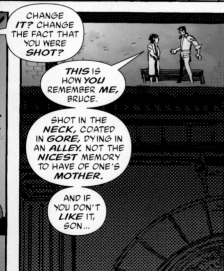

CHANGE *IT?* CHANGE THE FACT THAT YOU WERE *SHOT?*

THIS IS HOW *YOU* REMEMBER *ME,* BRUCE.

SHOT IN THE *NECK,* COATED IN *GORE,* DYING IN AN *ALLEY.* NOT THE *NICEST* MEMORY TO HAVE OF ONE'S *MOTHER.*

AND IF YOU DON'T *LIKE* IT, SON...

...MAYBE YOU SHOULD REMEMBER ME IN A *DIFFERENT* WAY.

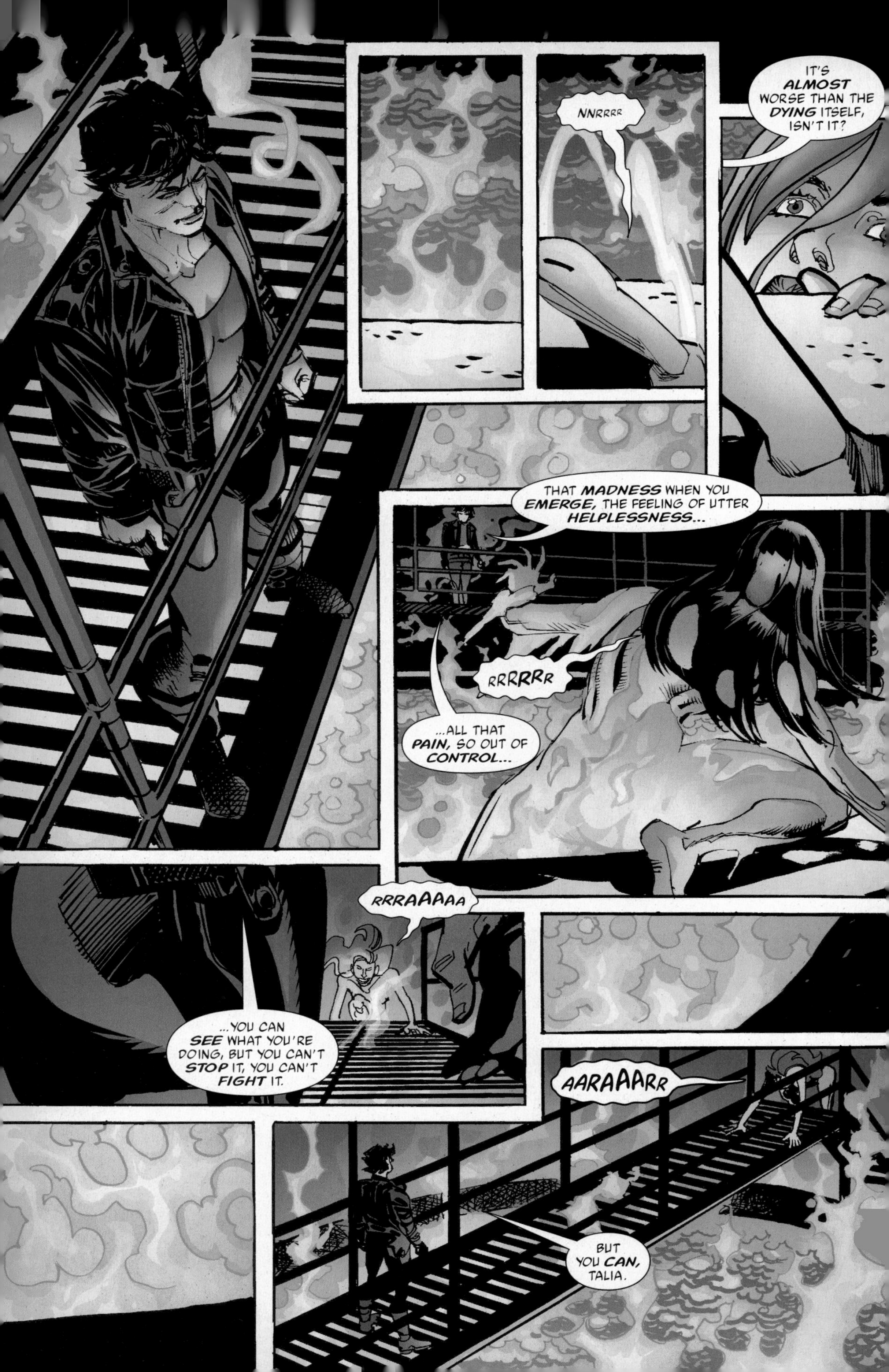

NNRRRR
IT'S ALMOST WORSE THAN THE DYING ITSELF, ISN'T IT?
THAT MADNESS WHEN YOU EMERGE, THE FEELING OF UTTER HELPLESSNESS...
RRRRRR
...ALL THAT PAIN, SO OUT OF CONTROL...
RRRAAAAA
...YOU CAN SEE WHAT YOU'RE DOING, BUT YOU CAN'T STOP IT, YOU CAN'T FIGHT IT.
AARAAARR
BUT YOU CAN, TALIA.

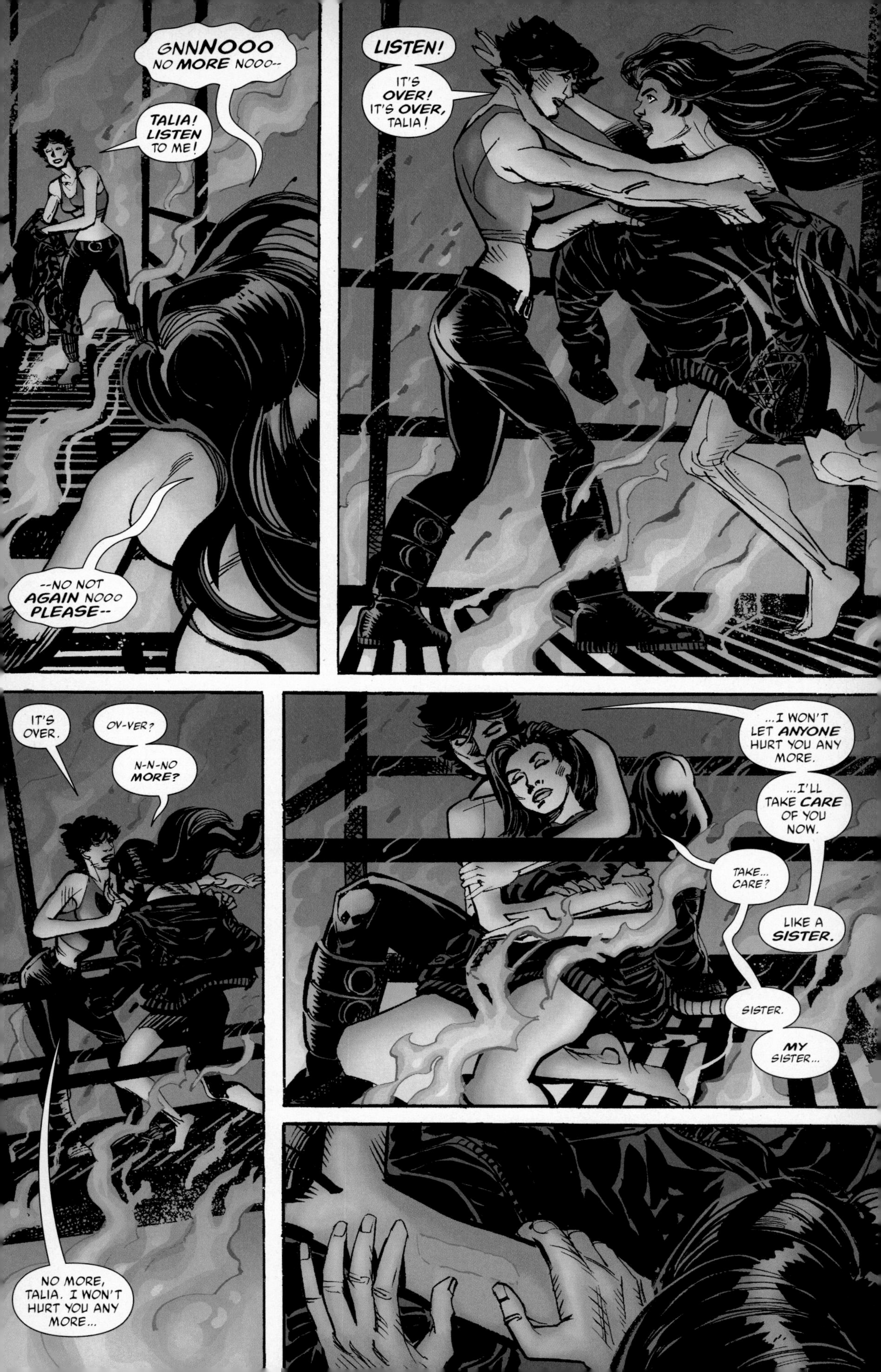
GNNNOOO NO MORE NOOO--
TALIA! LISTEN TO ME!
--NO NOT AGAIN NOOO PLEASE--
LISTEN!
IT'S OVER! IT'S OVER, TALIA!
IT'S OVER.
OV-VER?
N-N-NO MORE?
NO MORE, TALIA. I WON'T HURT YOU ANY MORE...
...I WON'T LET ANYONE HURT YOU ANY MORE.
...I'LL TAKE CARE OF YOU NOW.
TAKE... CARE?
LIKE A SISTER.
SISTER.
MY SISTER...

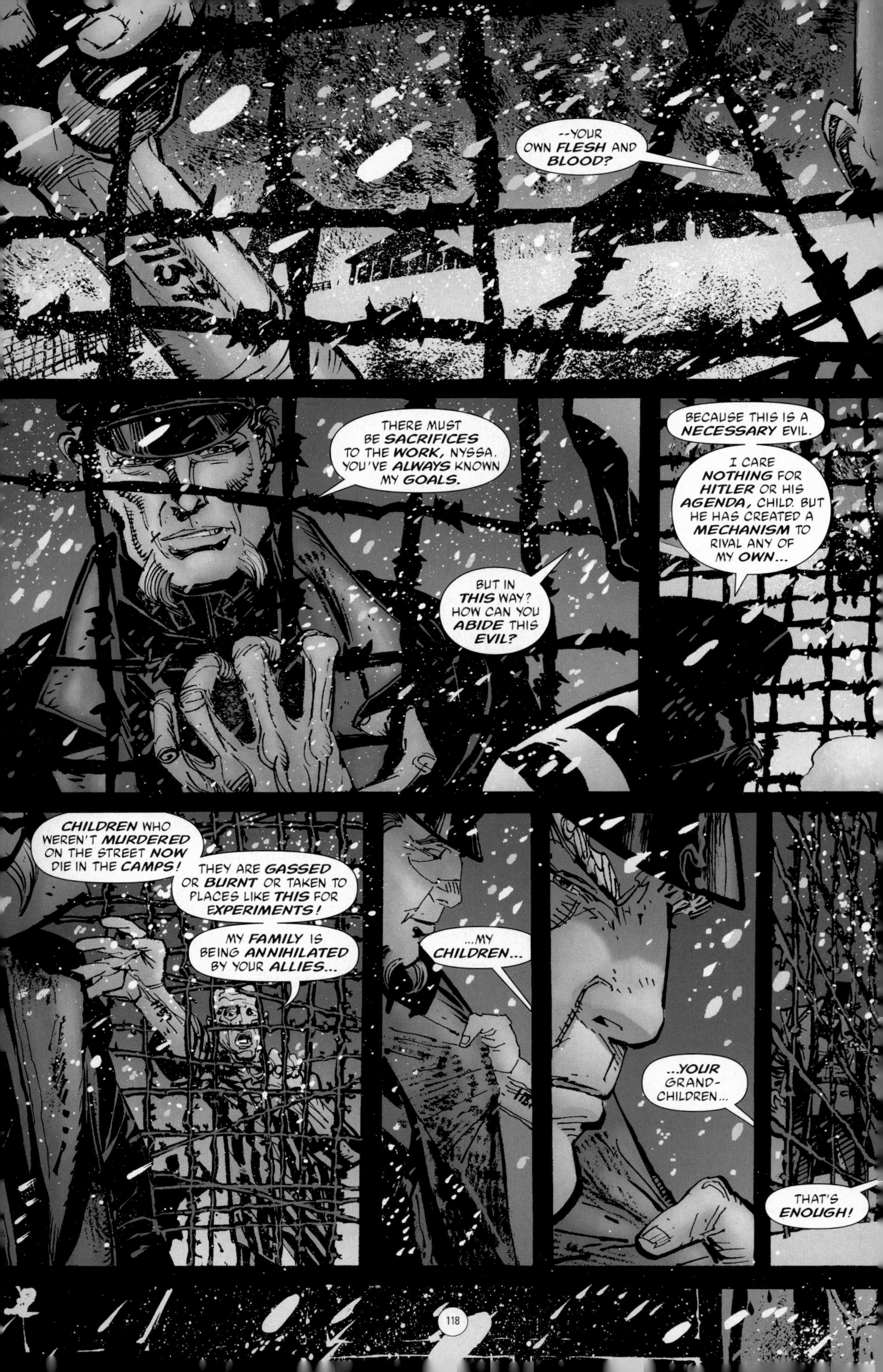
--YOUR OWN FLESH AND BLOOD?
THERE MUST BE SACRIFICES TO THE WORK, NYSSA. YOU'VE ALWAYS KNOWN MY GOALS.
BUT IN THIS WAY? HOW CAN YOU ABIDE THIS EVIL?
BECAUSE THIS IS A NECESSARY EVIL.
I CARE NOTHING FOR HITLER OR HIS AGENDA, CHILD. BUT HE HAS CREATED A MECHANISM TO RIVAL ANY OF MY OWN...
CHILDREN WHO WEREN'T MURDERED ON THE STREET NOW DIE IN THE CAMPS!
THEY ARE GASSED OR BURNT OR TAKEN TO PLACES LIKE THIS FOR EXPERIMENTS!
MY FAMILY IS BEING ANNIHILATED BY YOUR ALLIES...
...MY CHILDREN...
...YOUR GRAND-CHILDREN...
THAT'S ENOUGH!

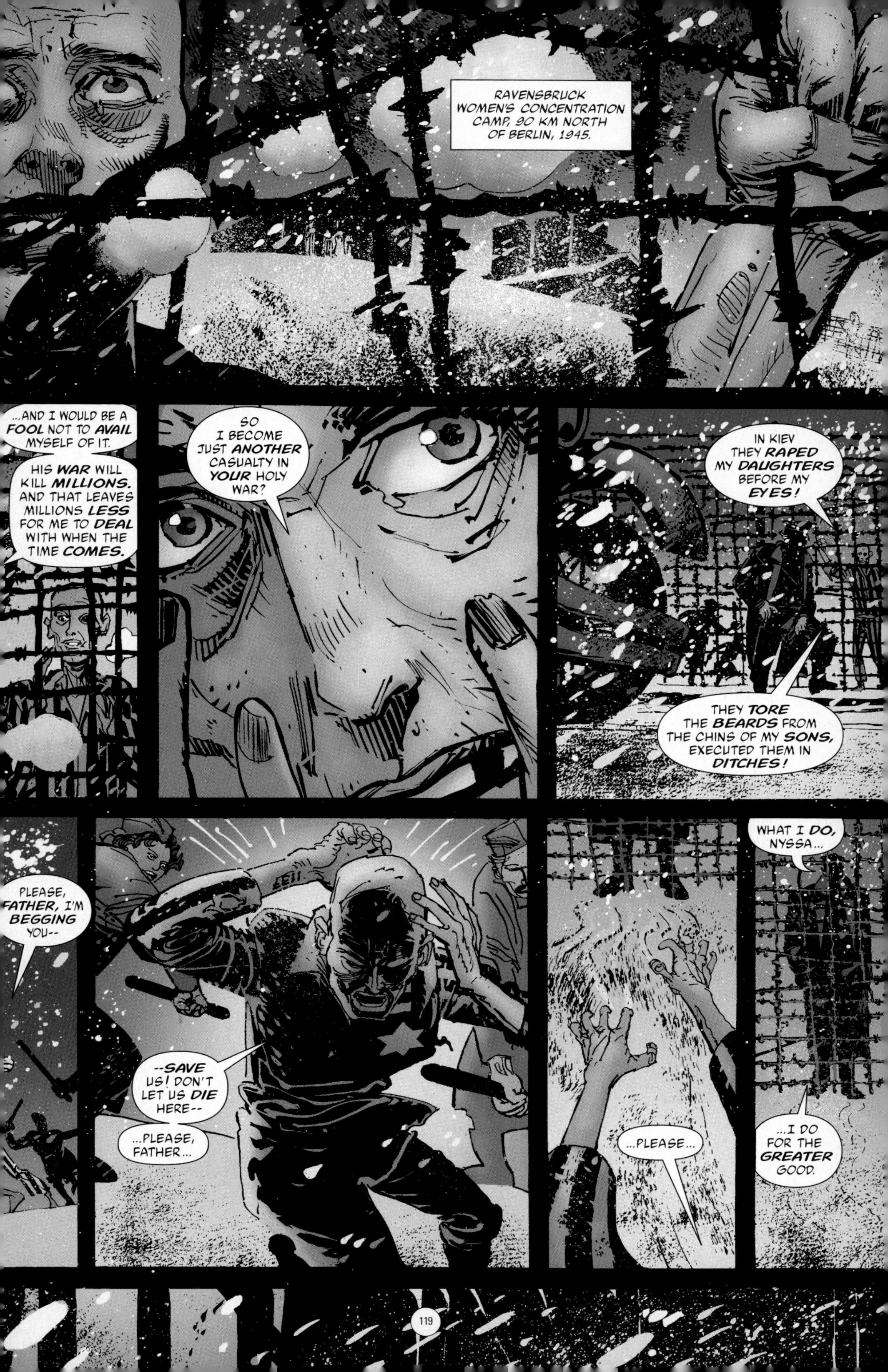
RAVENSBRUCK WOMEN'S CONCENTRATION CAMP, 90 KM NORTH OF BERLIN, 1945.
...AND I WOULD BE A FOOL NOT TO AVAIL MYSELF OF IT.
HIS WAR WILL KILL MILLIONS. AND THAT LEAVES MILLIONS LESS FOR ME TO DEAL WITH WHEN THE TIME COMES.
SO I BECOME JUST ANOTHER CASUALTY IN YOUR HOLY WAR?
IN KIEV THEY RAPED MY DAUGHTERS BEFORE MY EYES!
THEY TORE THE BEARDS FROM THE CHINS OF MY SONS, EXECUTED THEM IN DITCHES!
PLEASE, FATHER, I'M BEGGING YOU--
--SAVE US! DON'T LET US DIE HERE--
...PLEASE, FATHER...
...PLEASE...
WHAT I DO, NYSSA...
...I DO FOR THE GREATER GOOD.

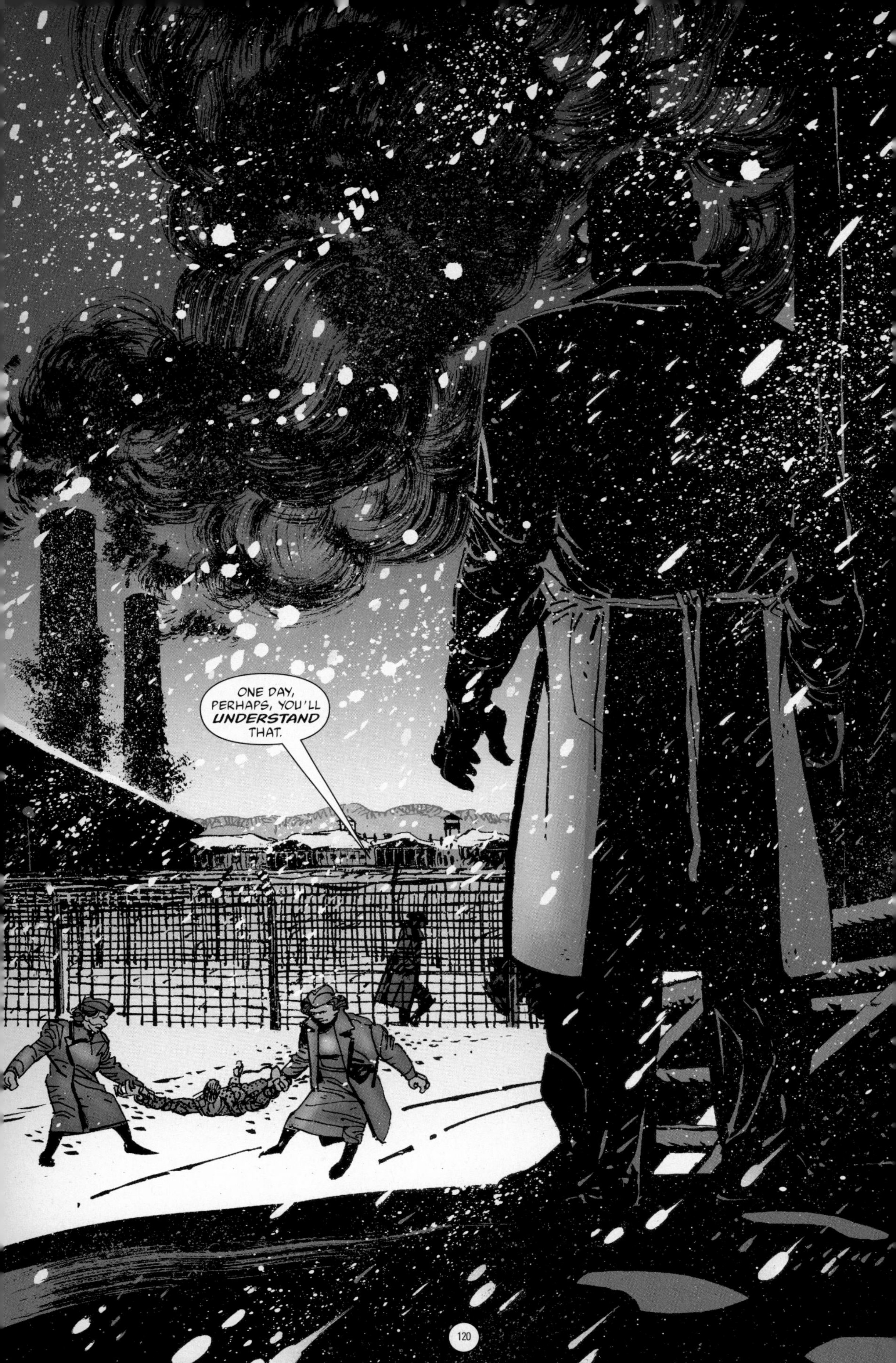
ONE DAY, PERHAPS, YOU'LL **UNDERSTAND** THAT.

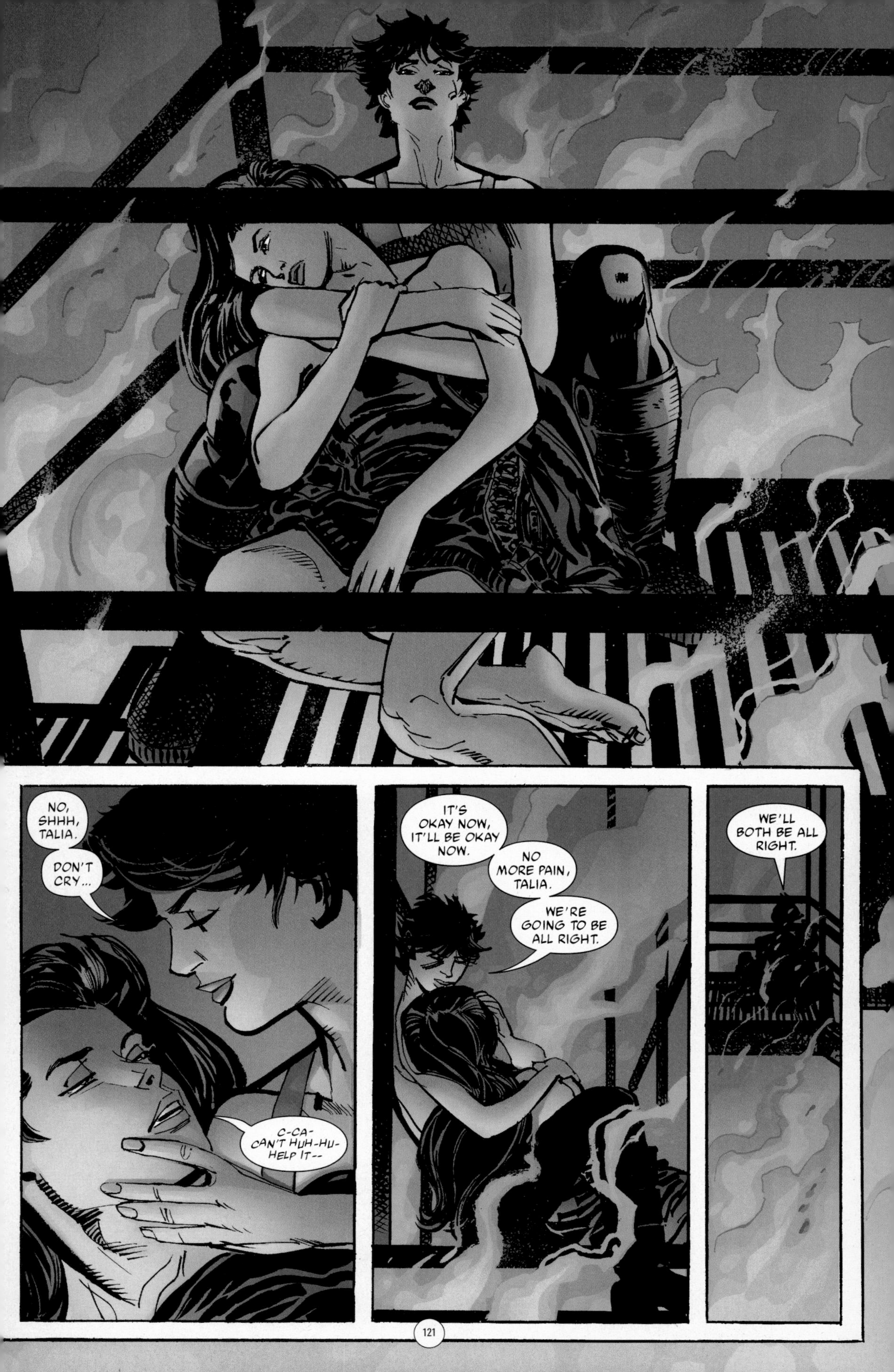
NO, SHHH, TALIA.
DON'T CRY...
C-CA-CAN'T HUH-HU-HELP IT--
IT'S OKAY NOW, IT'LL BE OKAY NOW.
NO MORE PAIN, TALIA.
WE'RE GOING TO BE ALL RIGHT.
WE'LL BOTH BE ALL RIGHT.

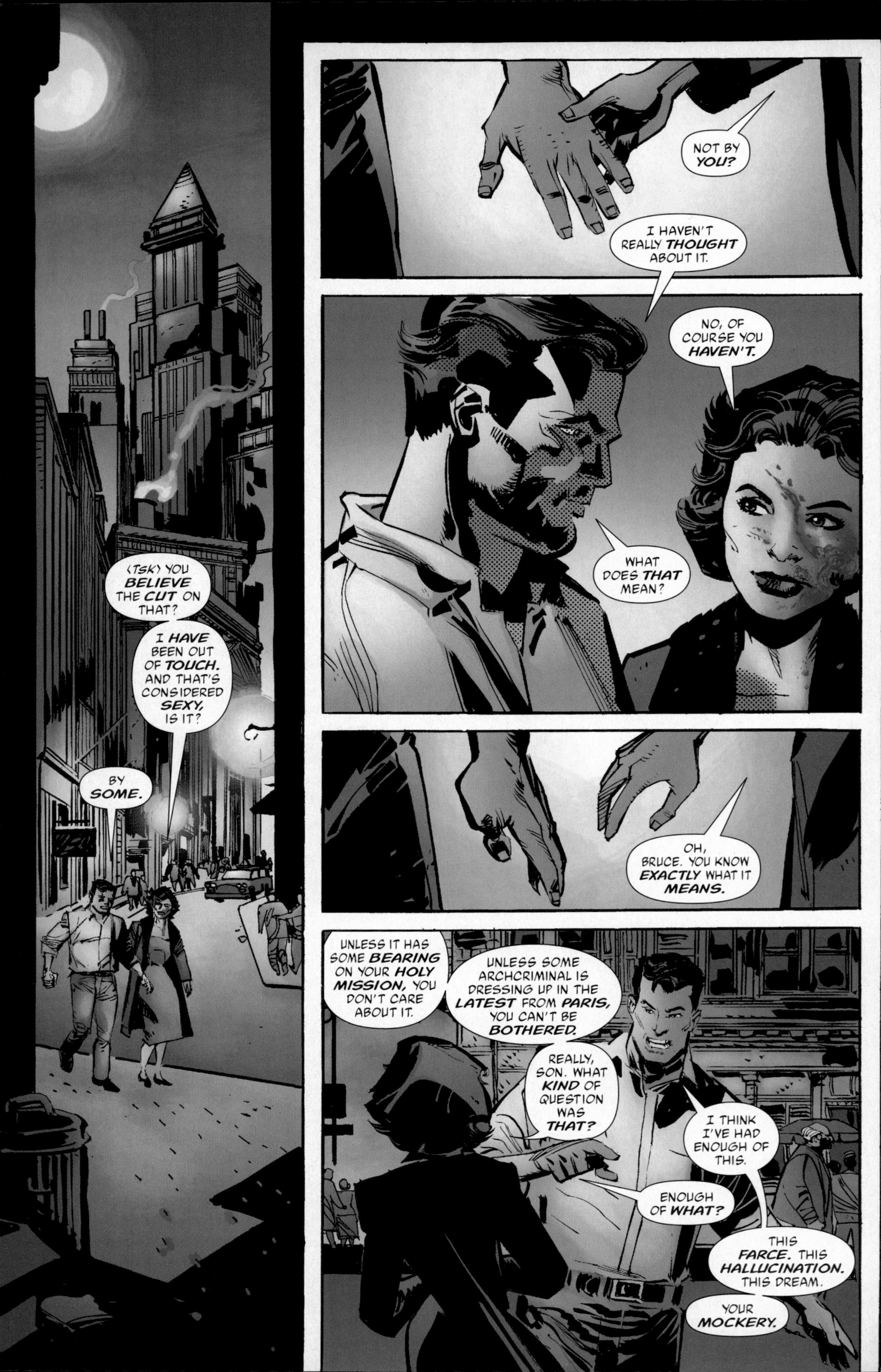

(TSK) YOU BELIEVE THE CUT ON THAT?
I HAVE BEEN OUT OF TOUCH. AND THAT'S CONSIDERED SEXY, IS IT?
BY SOME.
NOT BY YOU?
I HAVEN'T REALLY THOUGHT ABOUT IT.
NO, OF COURSE YOU HAVEN'T.
WHAT DOES THAT MEAN?
OH, BRUCE. YOU KNOW EXACTLY WHAT IT MEANS.
UNLESS IT HAS SOME BEARING ON YOUR HOLY MISSION, YOU DON'T CARE ABOUT IT.
UNLESS SOME ARCHCRIMINAL IS DRESSING UP IN THE LATEST FROM PARIS, YOU CAN'T BE BOTHERED.
REALLY, SON. WHAT KIND OF QUESTION WAS THAT?
I THINK I'VE HAD ENOUGH OF THIS.
ENOUGH OF WHAT?
THIS FARCE. THIS HALLUCINATION. THIS DREAM.
YOUR MOCKERY.

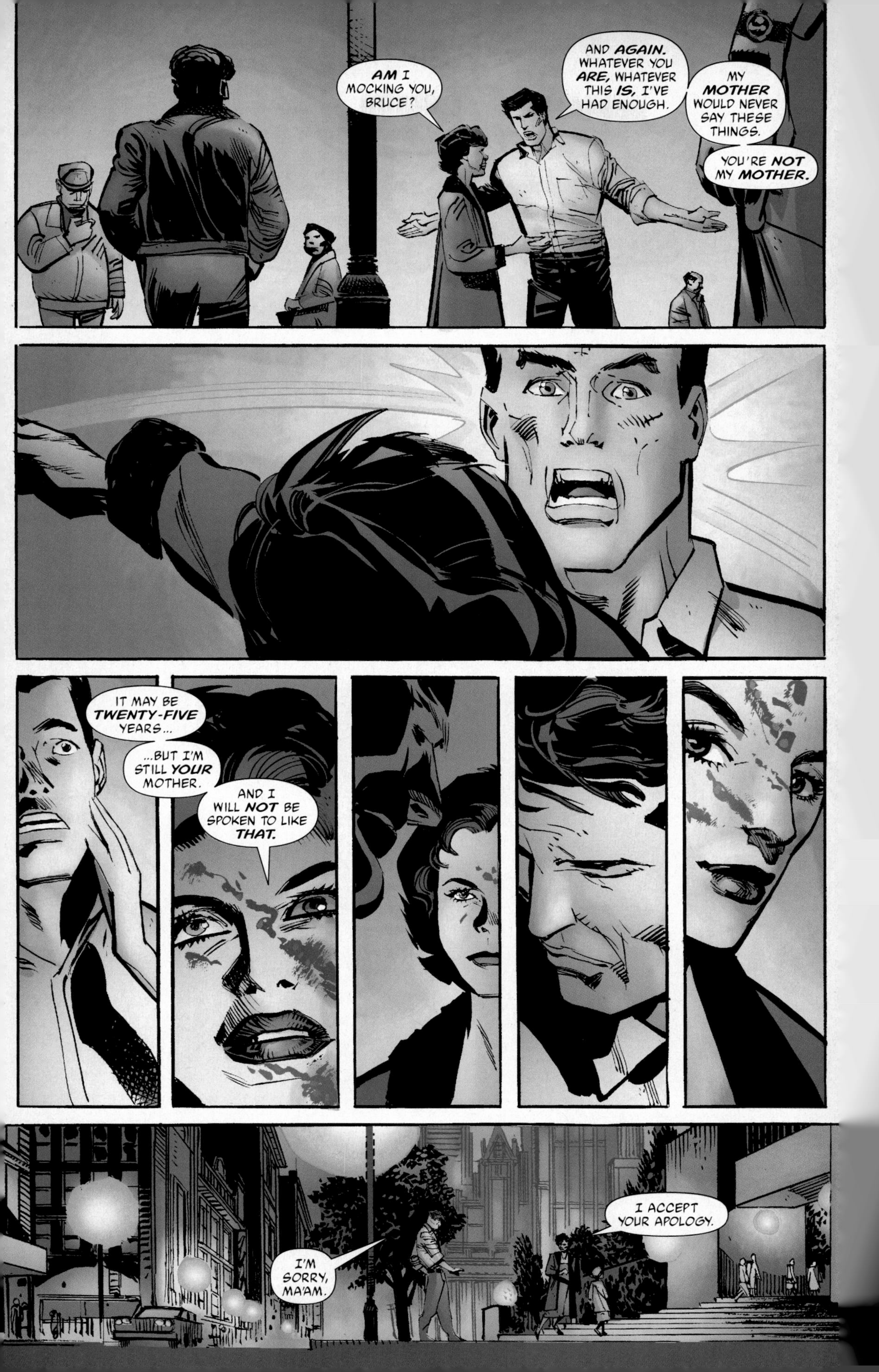
AM I MOCKING YOU, BRUCE?
AND AGAIN. WHATEVER YOU ARE, WHATEVER THIS IS, I'VE HAD ENOUGH.
MY MOTHER WOULD NEVER SAY THESE THINGS.
YOU'RE NOT MY MOTHER.
IT MAY BE TWENTY-FIVE YEARS...
...BUT I'M STILL YOUR MOTHER.
AND I WILL NOT BE SPOKEN TO LIKE THAT.
I'M SORRY, MA'AM.
I ACCEPT YOUR APOLOGY.

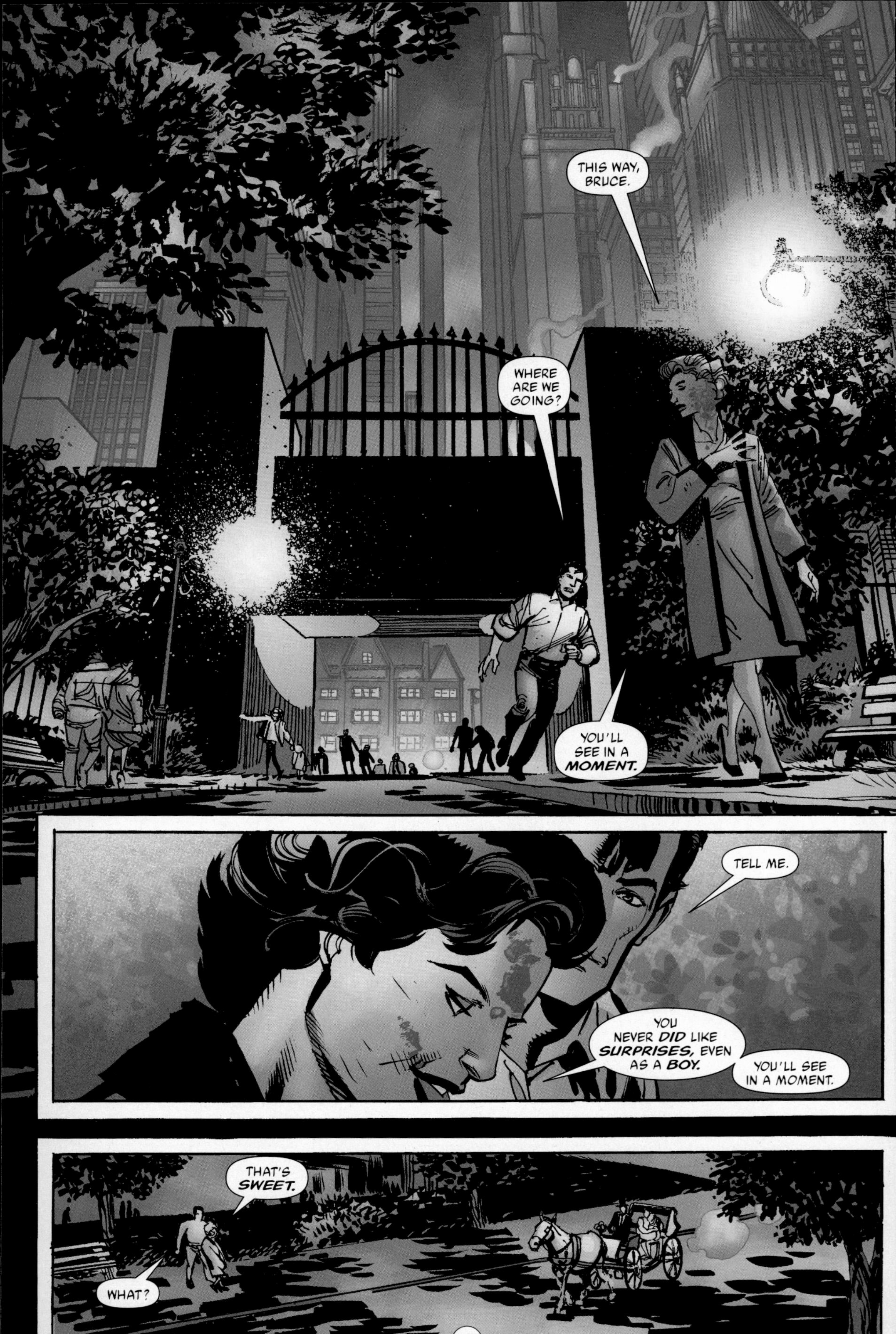
THIS WAY, BRUCE.
WHERE ARE WE GOING?
YOU'LL SEE IN A MOMENT.
TELL ME.
YOU NEVER DID LIKE SURPRISES, EVEN AS A BOY.
YOU'LL SEE IN A MOMENT.
THAT'S SWEET.
WHAT?

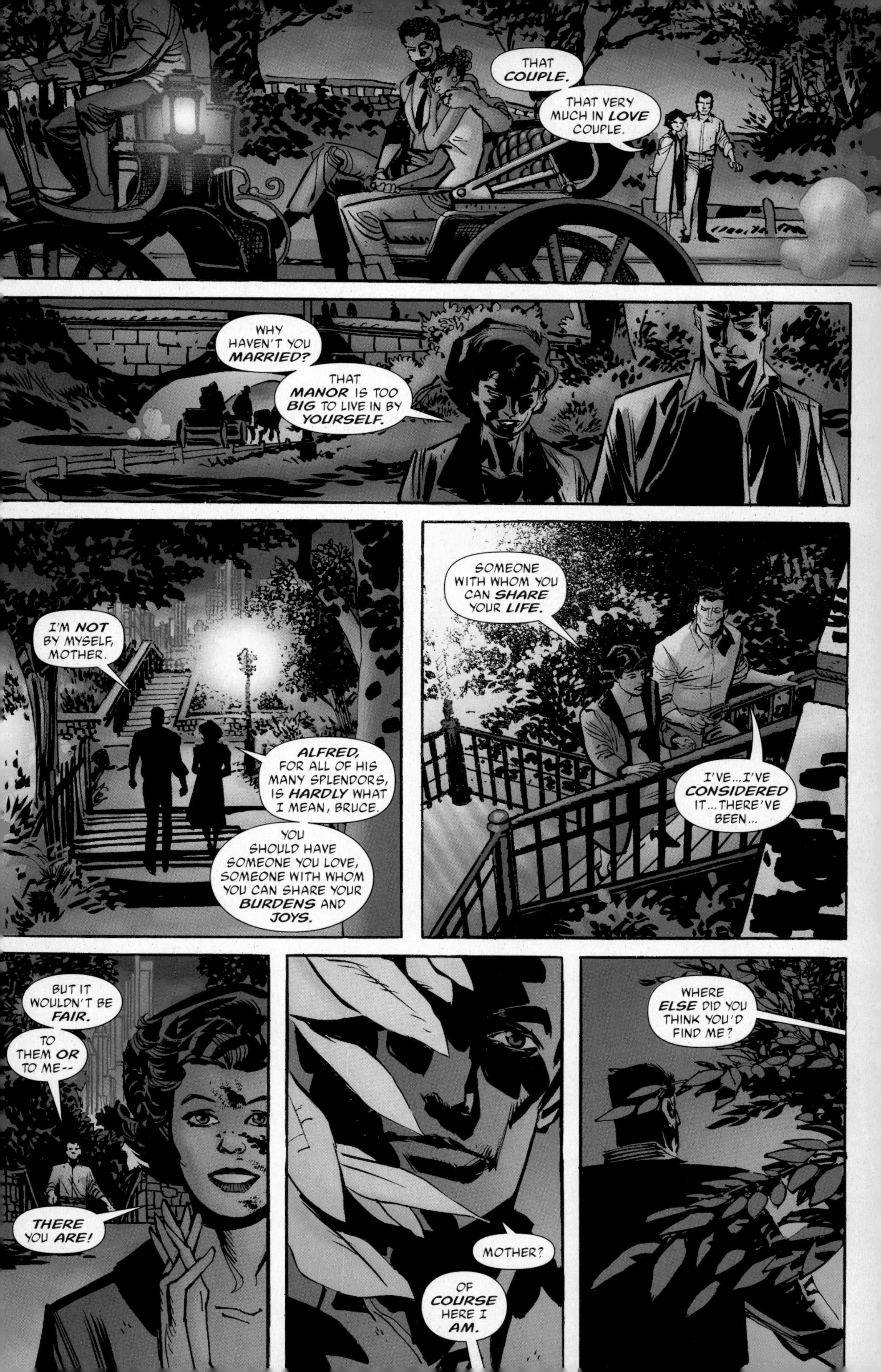

THAT COUPLE.
THAT VERY MUCH IN LOVE COUPLE.
WHY HAVEN'T YOU MARRIED?
THAT MANOR IS TOO BIG TO LIVE IN BY YOURSELF.
I'M NOT BY MYSELF, MOTHER.
ALFRED, FOR ALL OF HIS MANY SPLENDORS, IS HARDLY WHAT I MEAN, BRUCE.
YOU SHOULD HAVE SOMEONE YOU LOVE, SOMEONE WITH WHOM YOU CAN SHARE YOUR BURDENS AND JOYS.
SOMEONE WITH WHOM YOU CAN SHARE YOUR LIFE.
I'VE...I'VE CONSIDERED IT...THERE'VE BEEN...
BUT IT WOULDN'T BE FAIR.
TO THEM OR TO ME--
THERE YOU ARE!
MOTHER?
OF COURSE HERE I AM.
WHERE ELSE DID YOU THINK YOU'D FIND ME?

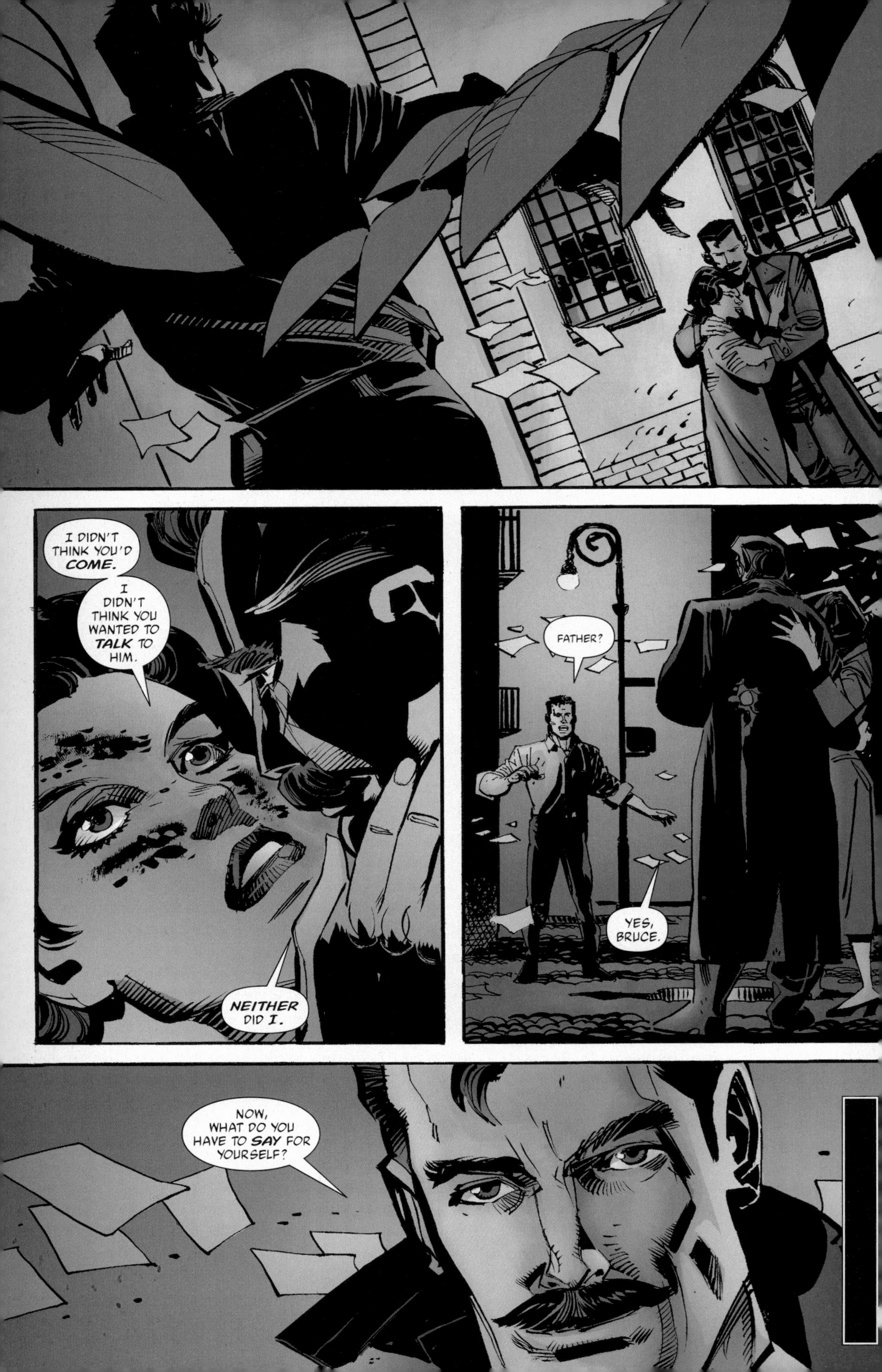

I DIDN'T THINK YOU'D COME.
I DIDN'T THINK YOU WANTED TO TALK TO HIM.
NEITHER DID I.
FATHER?
YES, BRUCE.
NOW, WHAT DO YOU HAVE TO SAY FOR YOURSELF?

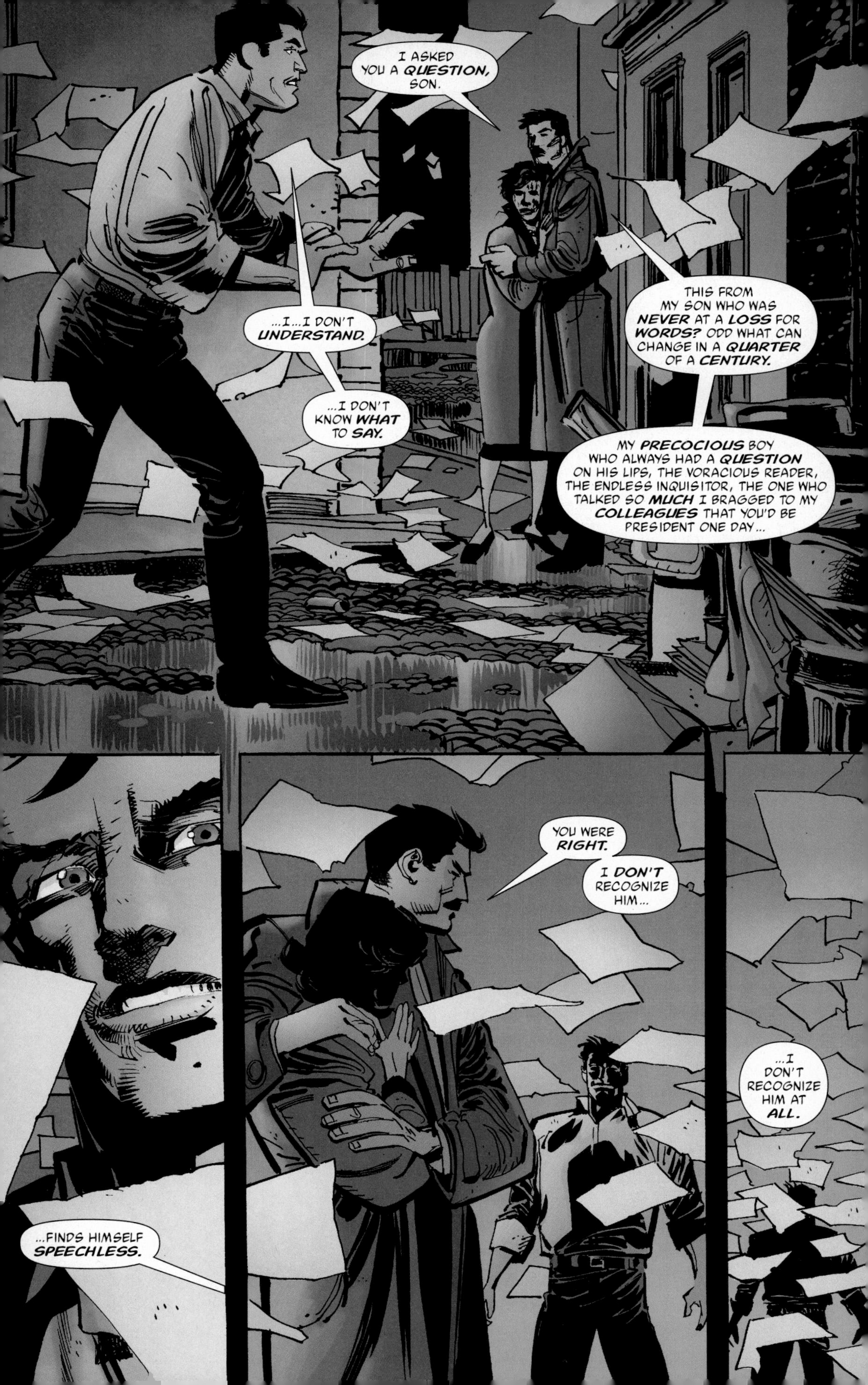
I ASKED YOU A QUESTION, SON.
...I...I DON'T UNDERSTAND.
...I DON'T KNOW WHAT TO SAY.
THIS FROM MY SON WHO WAS NEVER AT A LOSS FOR WORDS? ODD WHAT CAN CHANGE IN A QUARTER OF A CENTURY.
MY PRECOCIOUS BOY WHO ALWAYS HAD A QUESTION ON HIS LIPS, THE VORACIOUS READER, THE ENDLESS INQUISITOR, THE ONE WHO TALKED SO MUCH I BRAGGED TO MY COLLEAGUES THAT YOU'D BE PRESIDENT ONE DAY...
...FINDS HIMSELF SPEECHLESS.
YOU WERE RIGHT.
I DON'T RECOGNIZE HIM...
...I DON'T RECOGNIZE HIM AT ALL.

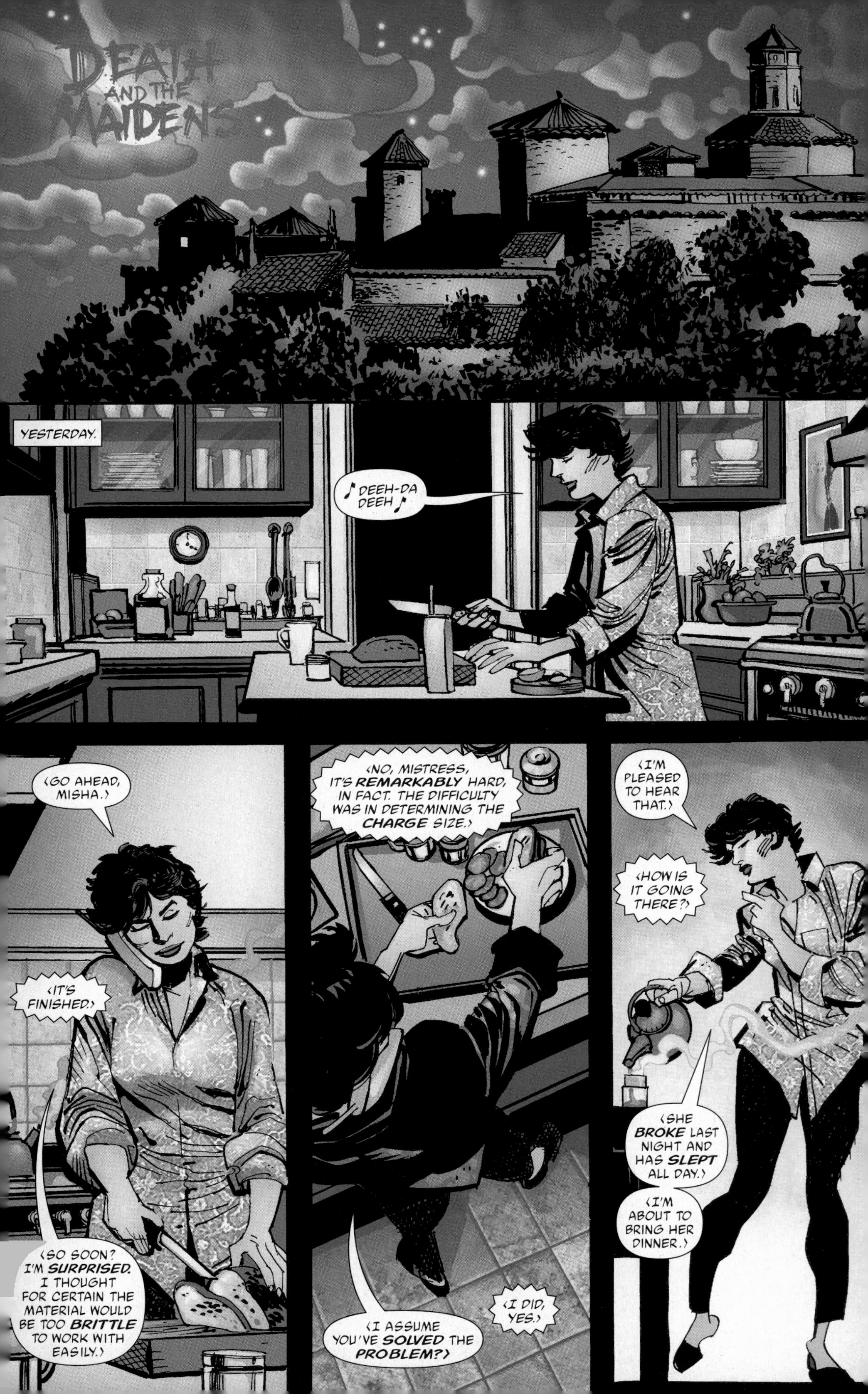
DEATH AND THE MAIDENS
YESTERDAY.
♪ DEEH-DA DEEH ♪
‹GO AHEAD, MISHA.›
‹IT'S FINISHED.›
‹SO SOON? I'M SURPRISED. I THOUGHT FOR CERTAIN THE MATERIAL WOULD BE TOO BRITTLE TO WORK WITH EASILY.›
‹NO, MISTRESS, IT'S REMARKABLY HARD, IN FACT. THE DIFFICULTY WAS IN DETERMINING THE CHARGE SIZE.›
‹I ASSUME YOU'VE SOLVED THE PROBLEM?›
‹I DID, YES.›
‹I'M PLEASED TO HEAR THAT.›
‹HOW IS IT GOING THERE?›
‹SHE BROKE LAST NIGHT AND HAS SLEPT ALL DAY.›
‹I'M ABOUT TO BRING HER DINNER.›

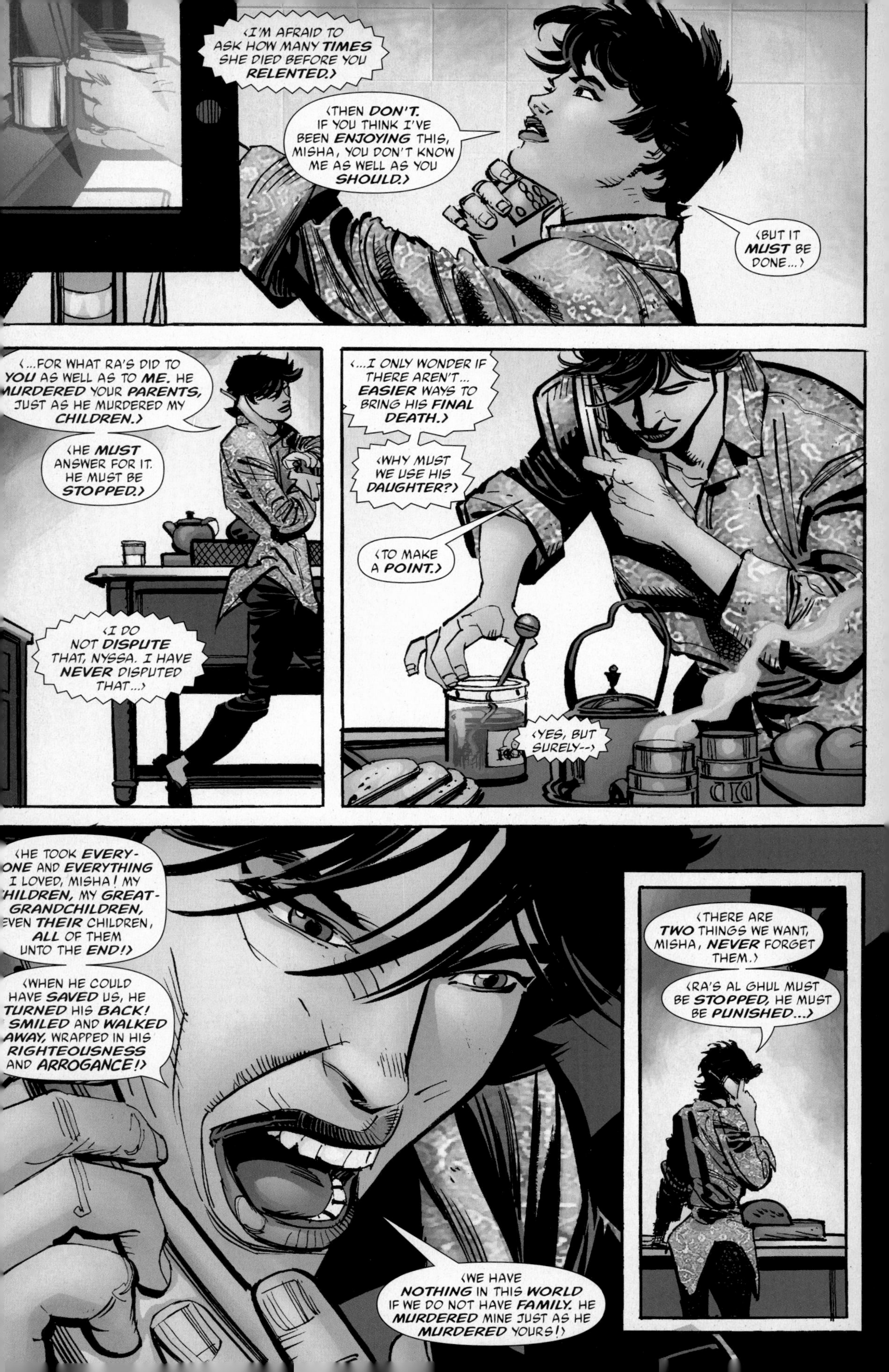
‹I'M AFRAID TO ASK HOW MANY TIMES SHE DIED BEFORE YOU RELENTED.›
‹THEN DON'T. IF YOU THINK I'VE BEEN ENJOYING THIS, MISHA, YOU DON'T KNOW ME AS WELL AS YOU SHOULD.›
‹BUT IT MUST BE DONE...›
‹...FOR WHAT RA'S DID TO YOU AS WELL AS TO ME. HE MURDERED YOUR PARENTS, JUST AS HE MURDERED MY CHILDREN.›
‹HE MUST ANSWER FOR IT. HE MUST BE STOPPED.›
‹I DO NOT DISPUTE THAT, NYSSA. I HAVE NEVER DISPUTED THAT...›
‹...I ONLY WONDER IF THERE AREN'T... EASIER WAYS TO BRING HIS FINAL DEATH.›
‹WHY MUST WE USE HIS DAUGHTER?›
‹TO MAKE A POINT.›
‹YES, BUT SURELY--›
‹HE TOOK EVERY-ONE AND EVERYTHING I LOVED, MISHA! MY CHILDREN, MY GREAT-GRANDCHILDREN, EVEN THEIR CHILDREN, ALL OF THEM UNTO THE END!›
‹WHEN HE COULD HAVE SAVED US, HE TURNED HIS BACK! SMILED AND WALKED AWAY, WRAPPED IN HIS RIGHTEOUSNESS AND ARROGANCE!›
‹WE HAVE NOTHING IN THIS WORLD IF WE DO NOT HAVE FAMILY. HE MURDERED MINE JUST AS HE MURDERED YOURS!›
‹THERE ARE TWO THINGS WE WANT, MISHA, NEVER FORGET THEM.›
‹RA'S AL GHUL MUST BE STOPPED, HE MUST BE PUNISHED...›

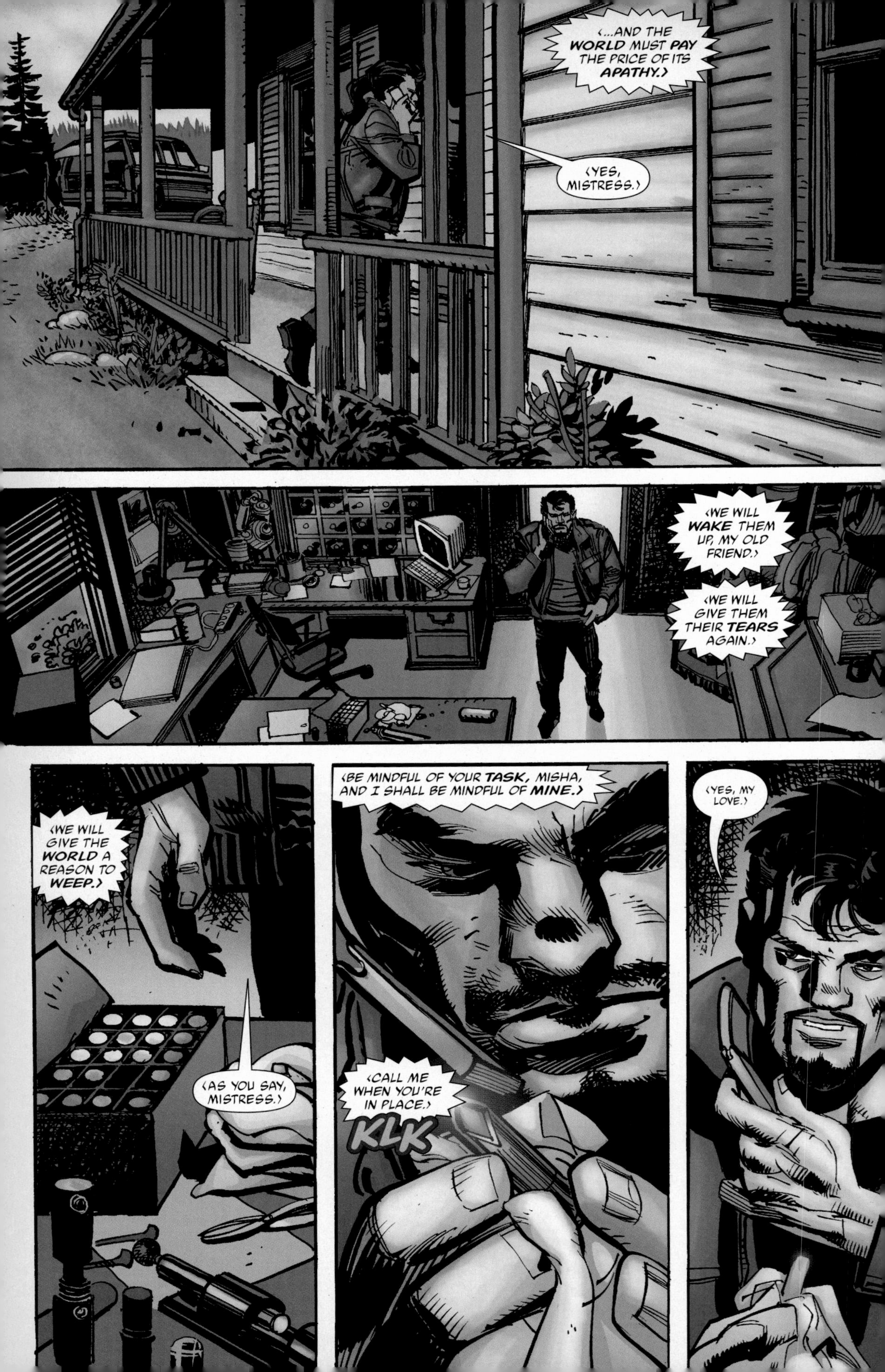
‹...AND THE WORLD MUST PAY THE PRICE OF ITS APATHY.›
‹YES, MISTRESS.›
‹WE WILL WAKE THEM UP, MY OLD FRIEND.›
‹WE WILL GIVE THEM THEIR TEARS AGAIN.›
‹WE WILL GIVE THE WORLD A REASON TO WEEP.›
‹AS YOU SAY, MISTRESS.›
‹BE MINDFUL OF YOUR TASK, MISHA, AND I SHALL BE MINDFUL OF MINE.›
‹CALL ME WHEN YOU'RE IN PLACE.›
KLK
‹YES, MY LOVE.›

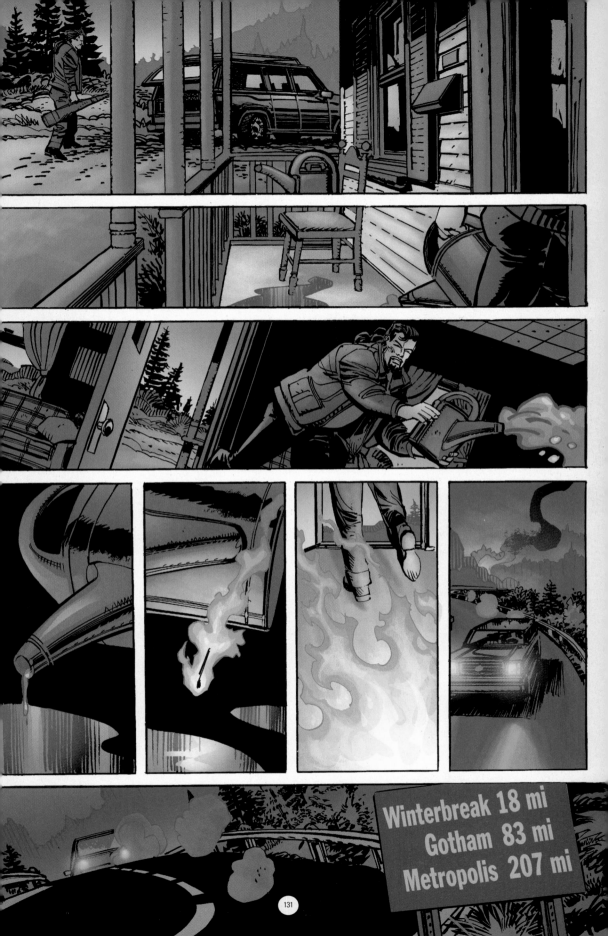

Winterbreak 18 mi
Gotham 83 mi
Metropolis 207 mi

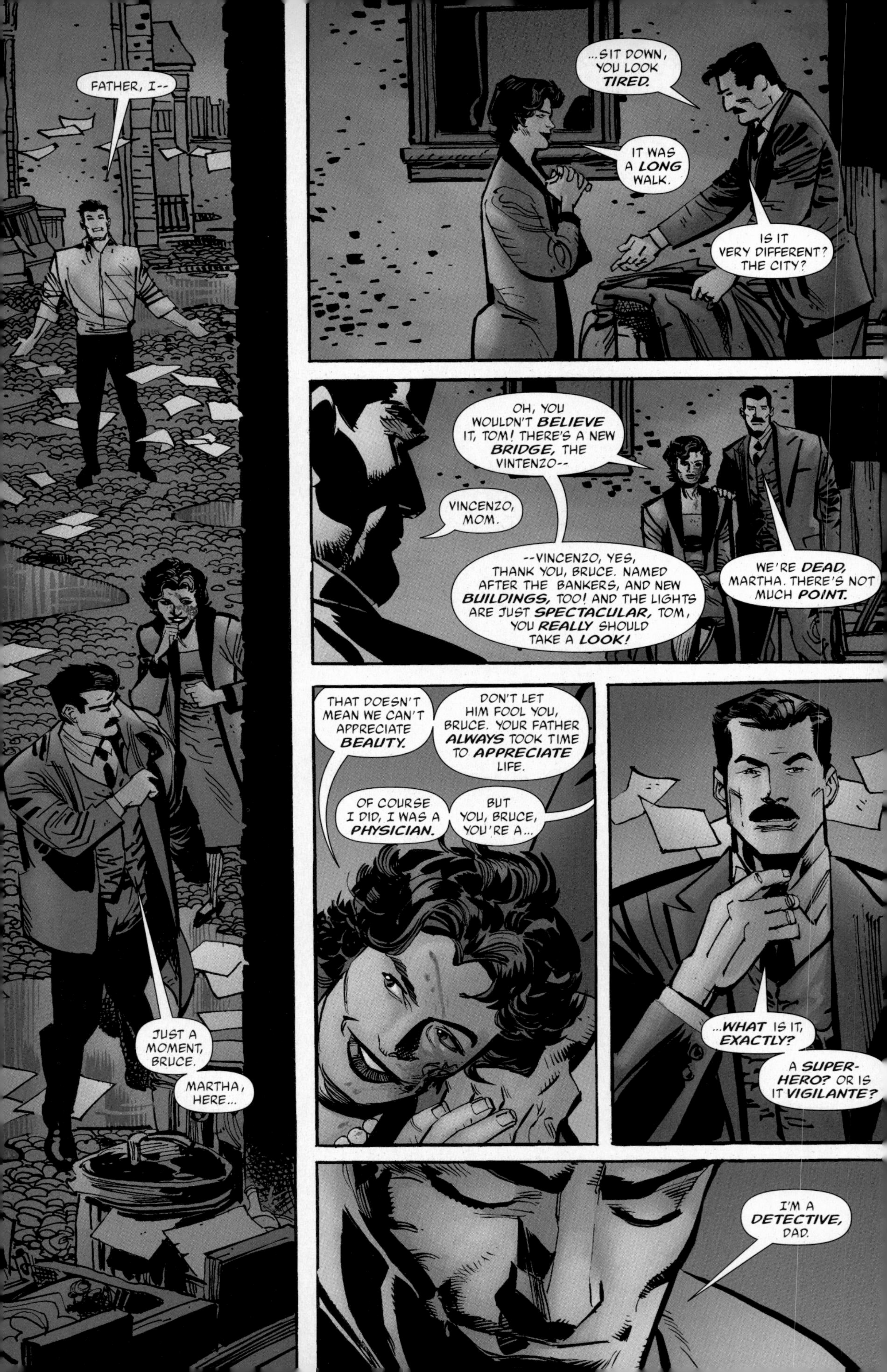

FATHER, I--
JUST A MOMENT, BRUCE.
MARTHA, HERE...
...SIT DOWN, YOU LOOK TIRED.
IT WAS A LONG WALK.
IS IT VERY DIFFERENT? THE CITY?
OH, YOU WOULDN'T BELIEVE IT, TOM! THERE'S A NEW BRIDGE, THE VINTENZO--
VINCENZO, MOM.
--VINCENZO, YES, THANK YOU, BRUCE. NAMED AFTER THE BANKERS, AND NEW BUILDINGS, TOO! AND THE LIGHTS ARE JUST SPECTACULAR, TOM, YOU REALLY SHOULD TAKE A LOOK!
WE'RE DEAD, MARTHA. THERE'S NOT MUCH POINT.
THAT DOESN'T MEAN WE CAN'T APPRECIATE BEAUTY.
DON'T LET HIM FOOL YOU, BRUCE. YOUR FATHER ALWAYS TOOK TIME TO APPRECIATE LIFE.
OF COURSE I DID, I WAS A PHYSICIAN.
BUT YOU, BRUCE, YOU'RE A...
...WHAT IS IT, EXACTLY?
A SUPER-HERO? OR IS IT VIGILANTE?
I'M A DETECTIVE, DAD.

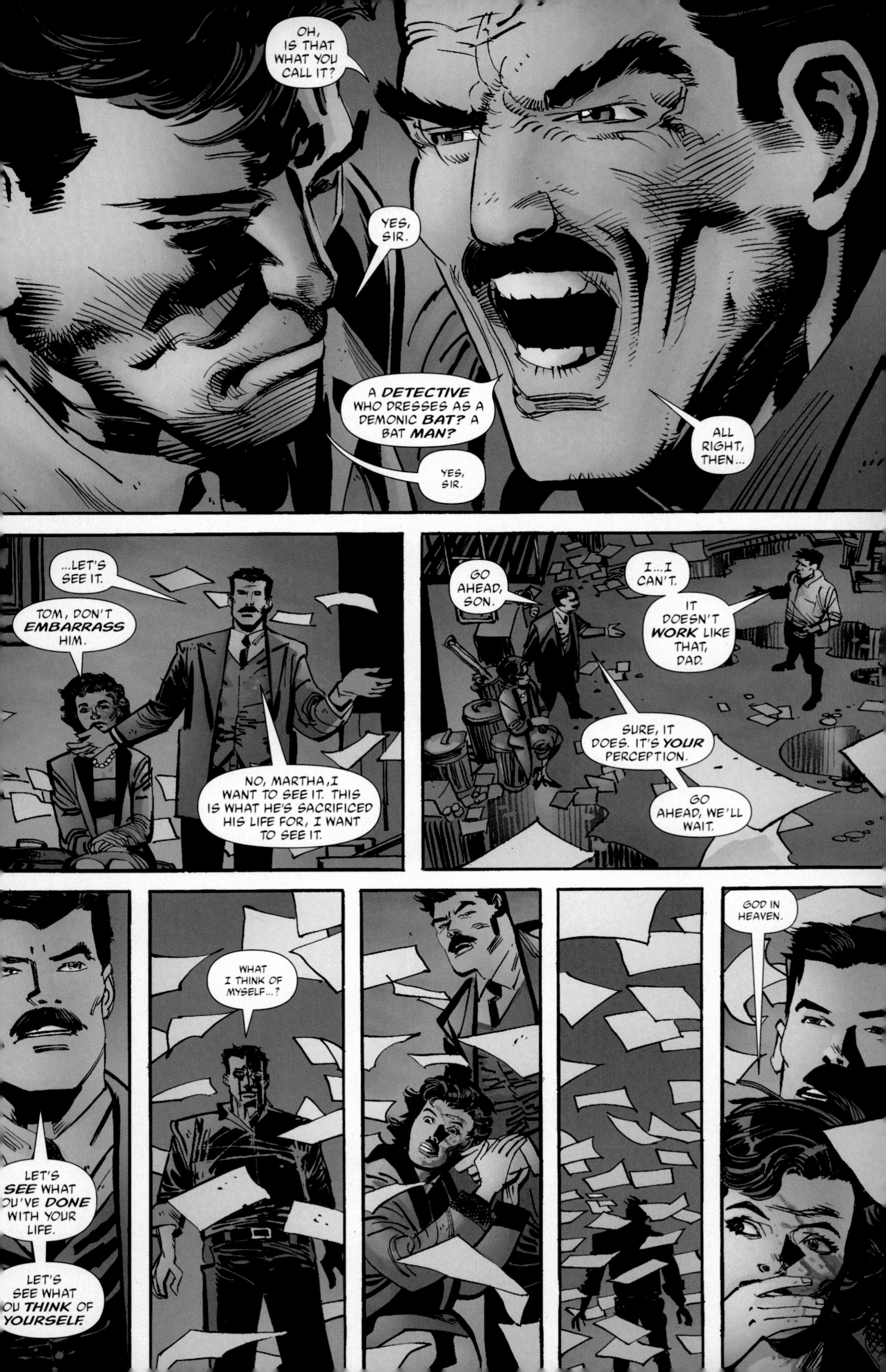
OH, IS THAT WHAT YOU CALL IT?
YES, SIR.
A DETECTIVE WHO DRESSES AS A DEMONIC BAT? A BAT MAN?
YES, SIR.
ALL RIGHT, THEN...
...LET'S SEE IT.
TOM, DON'T EMBARRASS HIM.
NO, MARTHA, I WANT TO SEE IT. THIS IS WHAT HE'S SACRIFICED HIS LIFE FOR, I WANT TO SEE IT.
GO AHEAD, SON.
I...I CAN'T.
IT DOESN'T WORK LIKE THAT, DAD.
SURE, IT DOES. IT'S YOUR PERCEPTION.
GO AHEAD, WE'LL WAIT.
LET'S SEE WHAT OU'VE DONE WITH YOUR LIFE.
LET'S SEE WHAT OU THINK OF YOURSELF.
WHAT I THINK OF MYSELF...?
GOD IN HEAVEN.

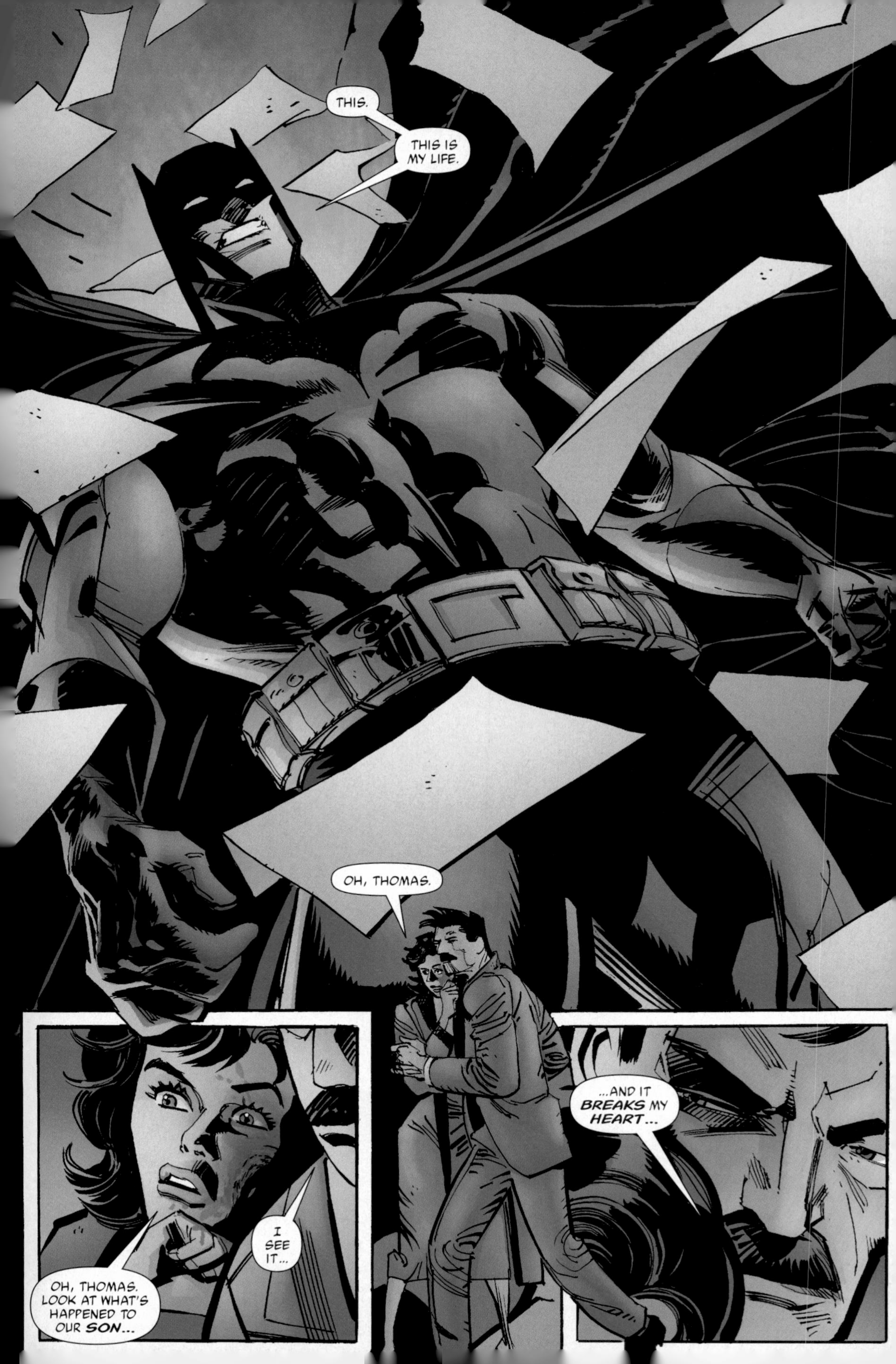

THIS.
THIS IS MY LIFE.
OH, THOMAS.
OH, THOMAS. LOOK AT WHAT'S HAPPENED TO OUR **SON**...
I SEE IT...
...AND IT **BREAKS** MY **HEART**...

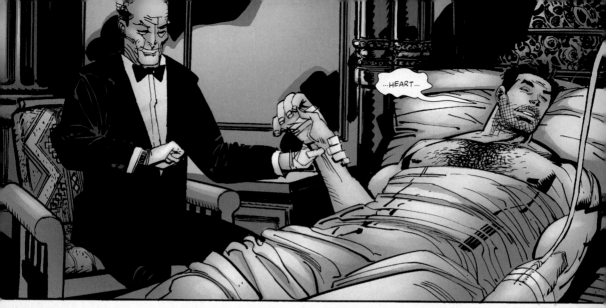

...HEART...

...NNH SWORE A VOW...

...NEVER AGAIN...

BEEP BEEP BEEP

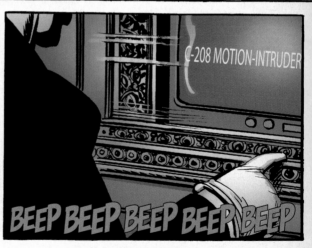

C-208 MOTION-INTRUDER

BEEP BEEP BEEP BEEP BEEP

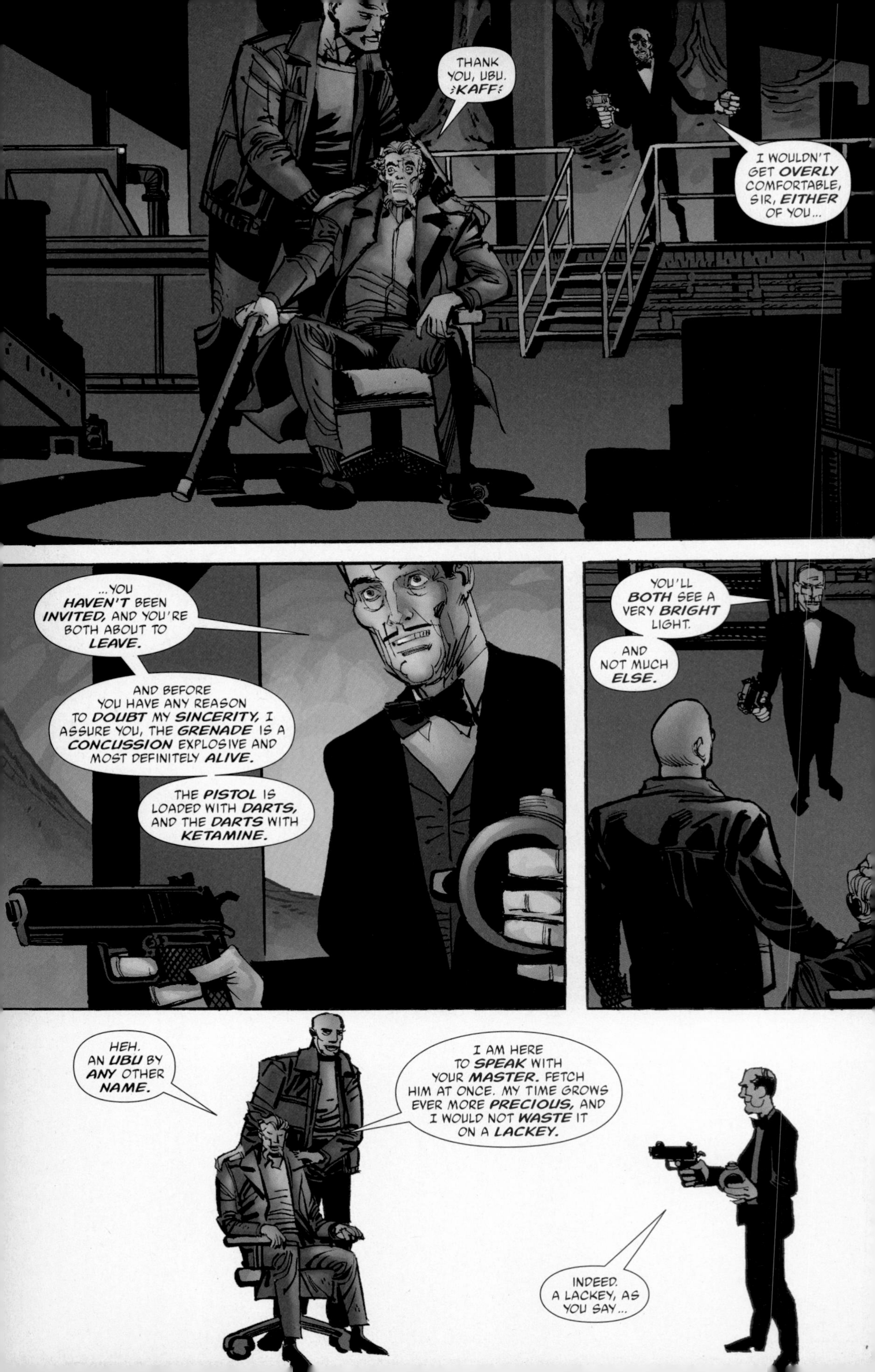
THANK YOU, UBU. ⋄KAFF⋄
I WOULDN'T GET OVERLY COMFORTABLE, SIR, EITHER OF YOU...
...YOU HAVEN'T BEEN INVITED, AND YOU'RE BOTH ABOUT TO LEAVE.
AND BEFORE YOU HAVE ANY REASON TO DOUBT MY SINCERITY, I ASSURE YOU, THE GRENADE IS A CONCUSSION EXPLOSIVE AND MOST DEFINITELY ALIVE.
THE PISTOL IS LOADED WITH DARTS, AND THE DARTS WITH KETAMINE.
YOU'LL BOTH SEE A VERY BRIGHT LIGHT.
AND NOT MUCH ELSE.
HEH. AN UBU BY ANY OTHER NAME.
I AM HERE TO SPEAK WITH YOUR MASTER. FETCH HIM AT ONCE. MY TIME GROWS EVER MORE PRECIOUS, AND I WOULD NOT WASTE IT ON A LACKEY.
INDEED. A LACKEY, AS YOU SAY...

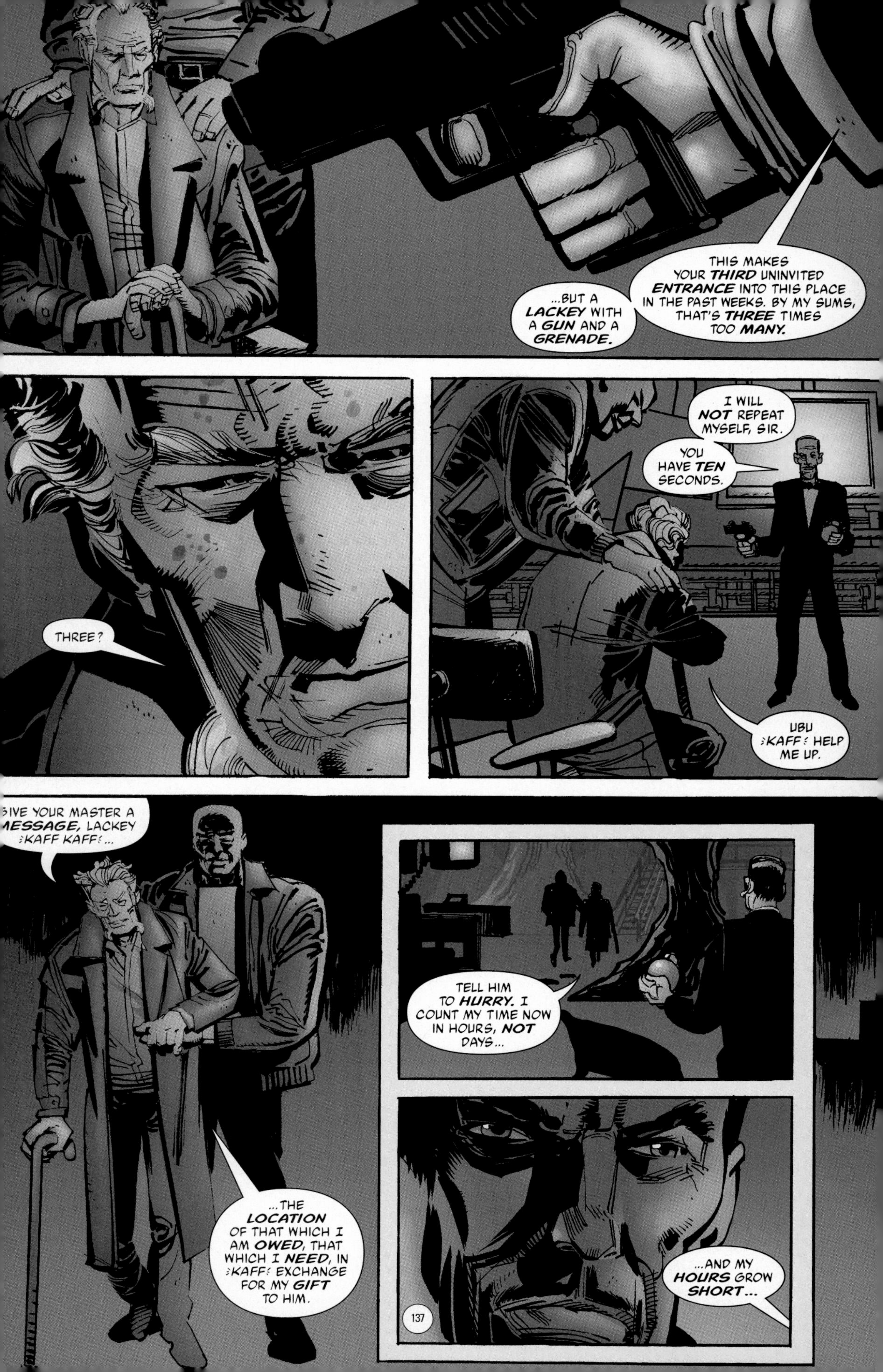

...BUT A LACKEY WITH A GUN AND A GRENADE.
THIS MAKES YOUR THIRD UNINVITED ENTRANCE INTO THIS PLACE IN THE PAST WEEKS. BY MY SUMS, THAT'S THREE TIMES TOO MANY.
THREE?
I WILL NOT REPEAT MYSELF, SIR.
YOU HAVE TEN SECONDS.
UBU ≷KAFF≷ HELP ME UP.
GIVE YOUR MASTER A MESSAGE, LACKEY ≷KAFF KAFF≷...
...THE LOCATION OF THAT WHICH I AM OWED, THAT WHICH I NEED, IN ≷KAFF≷ EXCHANGE FOR MY GIFT TO HIM.
TELL HIM TO HURRY. I COUNT MY TIME NOW IN HOURS, NOT DAYS...
...AND MY HOURS GROW SHORT...

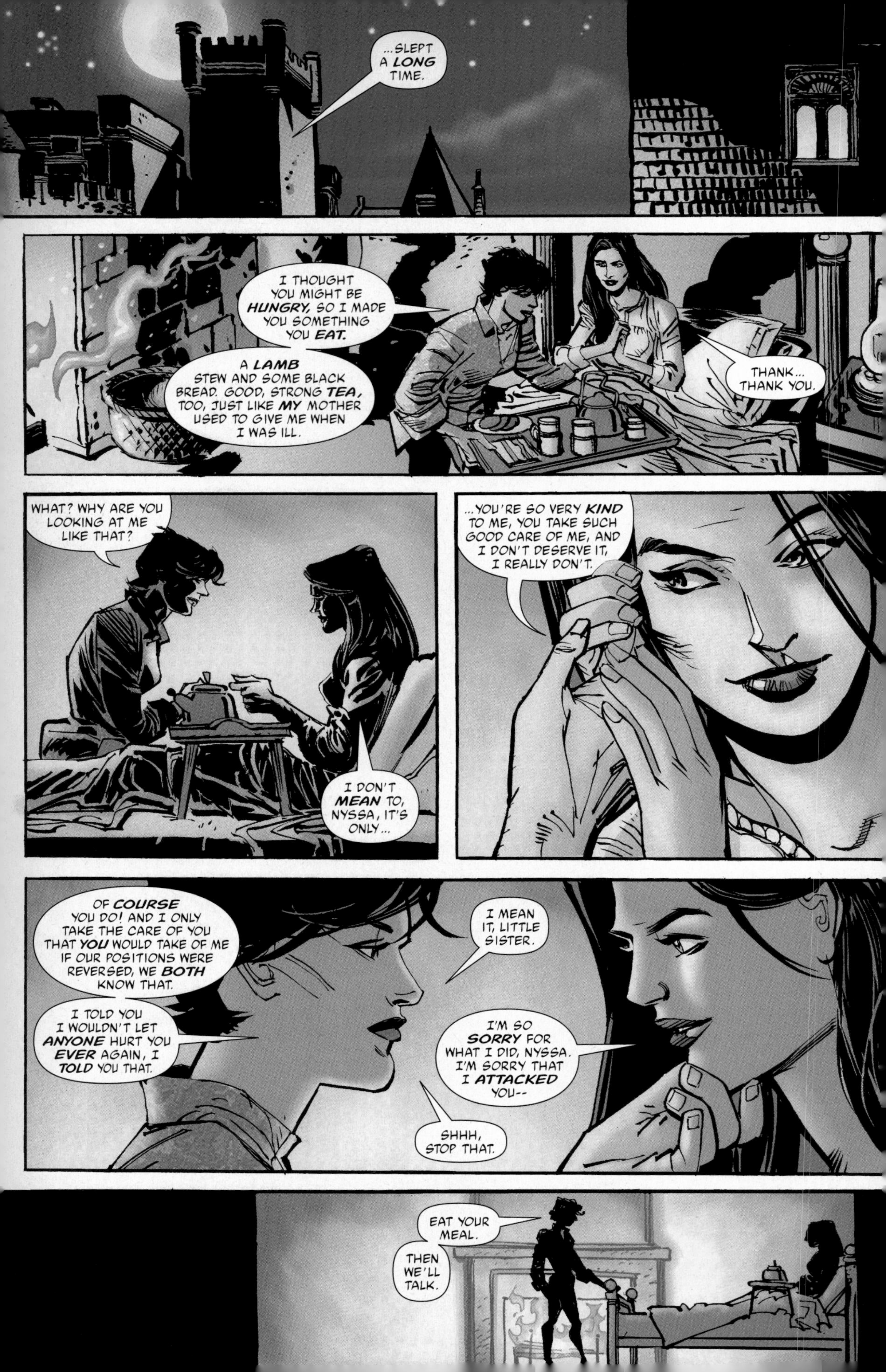
...SLEPT A LONG TIME.
I THOUGHT YOU MIGHT BE HUNGRY, SO I MADE YOU SOMETHING YOU EAT.
A LAMB STEW AND SOME BLACK BREAD. GOOD, STRONG TEA, TOO, JUST LIKE MY MOTHER USED TO GIVE ME WHEN I WAS ILL.
THANK... THANK YOU.
WHAT? WHY ARE YOU LOOKING AT ME LIKE THAT?
I DON'T MEAN TO, NYSSA, IT'S ONLY...
...YOU'RE SO VERY KIND TO ME, YOU TAKE SUCH GOOD CARE OF ME, AND I DON'T DESERVE IT, I REALLY DON'T.
OF COURSE YOU DO! AND I ONLY TAKE THE CARE OF YOU THAT YOU WOULD TAKE OF ME IF OUR POSITIONS WERE REVERSED, WE BOTH KNOW THAT.
I MEAN IT, LITTLE SISTER.
I TOLD YOU I WOULDN'T LET ANYONE HURT YOU EVER AGAIN, I TOLD YOU THAT.
I'M SO SORRY FOR WHAT I DID, NYSSA. I'M SORRY THAT I ATTACKED YOU--
SHHH, STOP THAT.
EAT YOUR MEAL.
THEN WE'LL TALK.

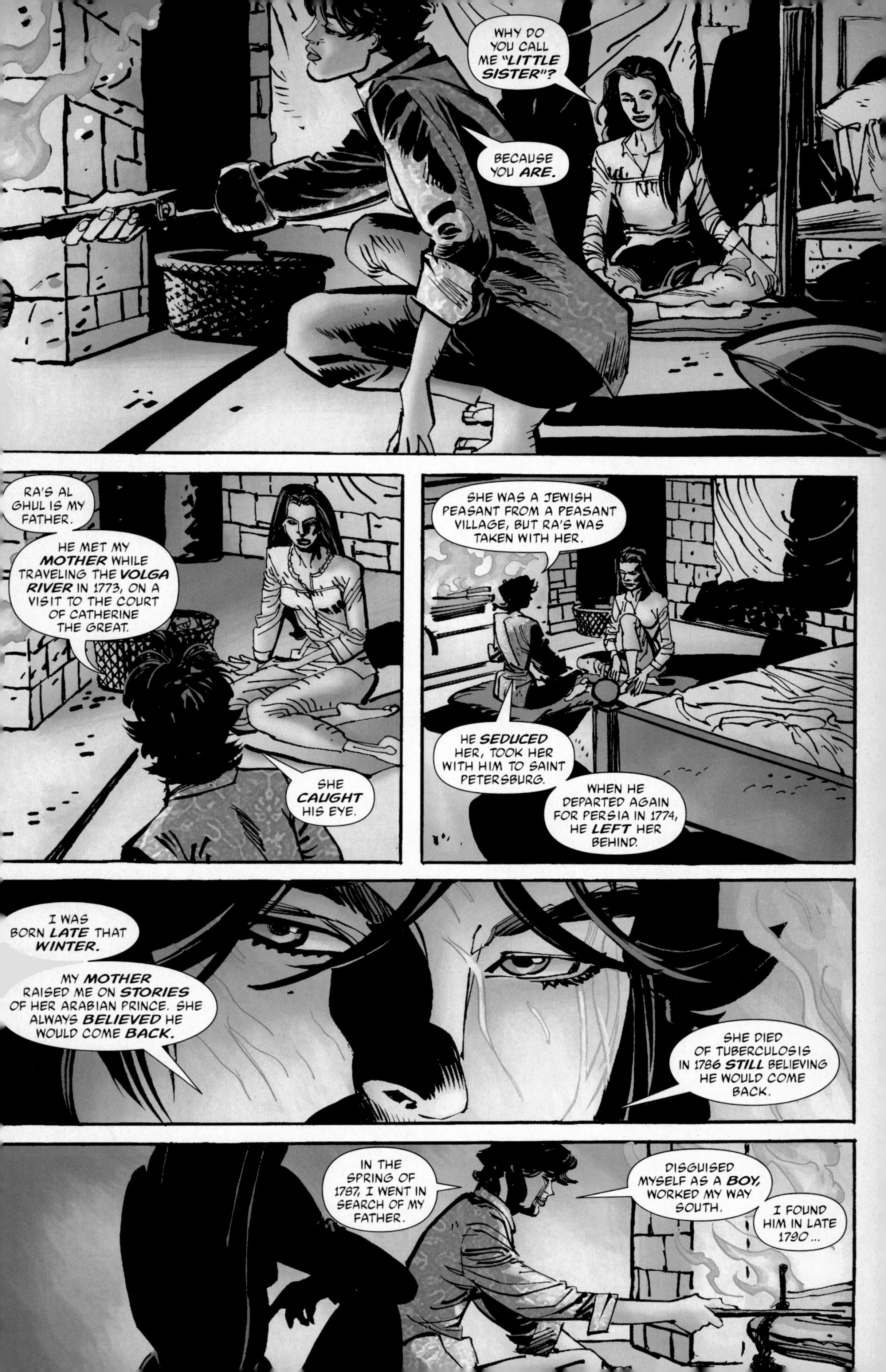

WHY DO YOU CALL ME "LITTLE SISTER"?
BECAUSE YOU ARE.
RA'S AL GHUL IS MY FATHER.
HE MET MY MOTHER WHILE TRAVELING THE VOLGA RIVER IN 1773, ON A VISIT TO THE COURT OF CATHERINE THE GREAT.
SHE CAUGHT HIS EYE.
SHE WAS A JEWISH PEASANT FROM A PEASANT VILLAGE, BUT RA'S WAS TAKEN WITH HER.
HE SEDUCED HER, TOOK HER WITH HIM TO SAINT PETERSBURG.
WHEN HE DEPARTED AGAIN FOR PERSIA IN 1774, HE LEFT HER BEHIND.
I WAS BORN LATE THAT WINTER.
MY MOTHER RAISED ME ON STORIES OF HER ARABIAN PRINCE. SHE ALWAYS BELIEVED HE WOULD COME BACK.
SHE DIED OF TUBERCULOSIS IN 1786 STILL BELIEVING HE WOULD COME BACK.
IN THE SPRING OF 1787, I WENT IN SEARCH OF MY FATHER.
DISGUISED MYSELF AS A BOY, WORKED MY WAY SOUTH.
I FOUND HIM IN LATE 1790 ...

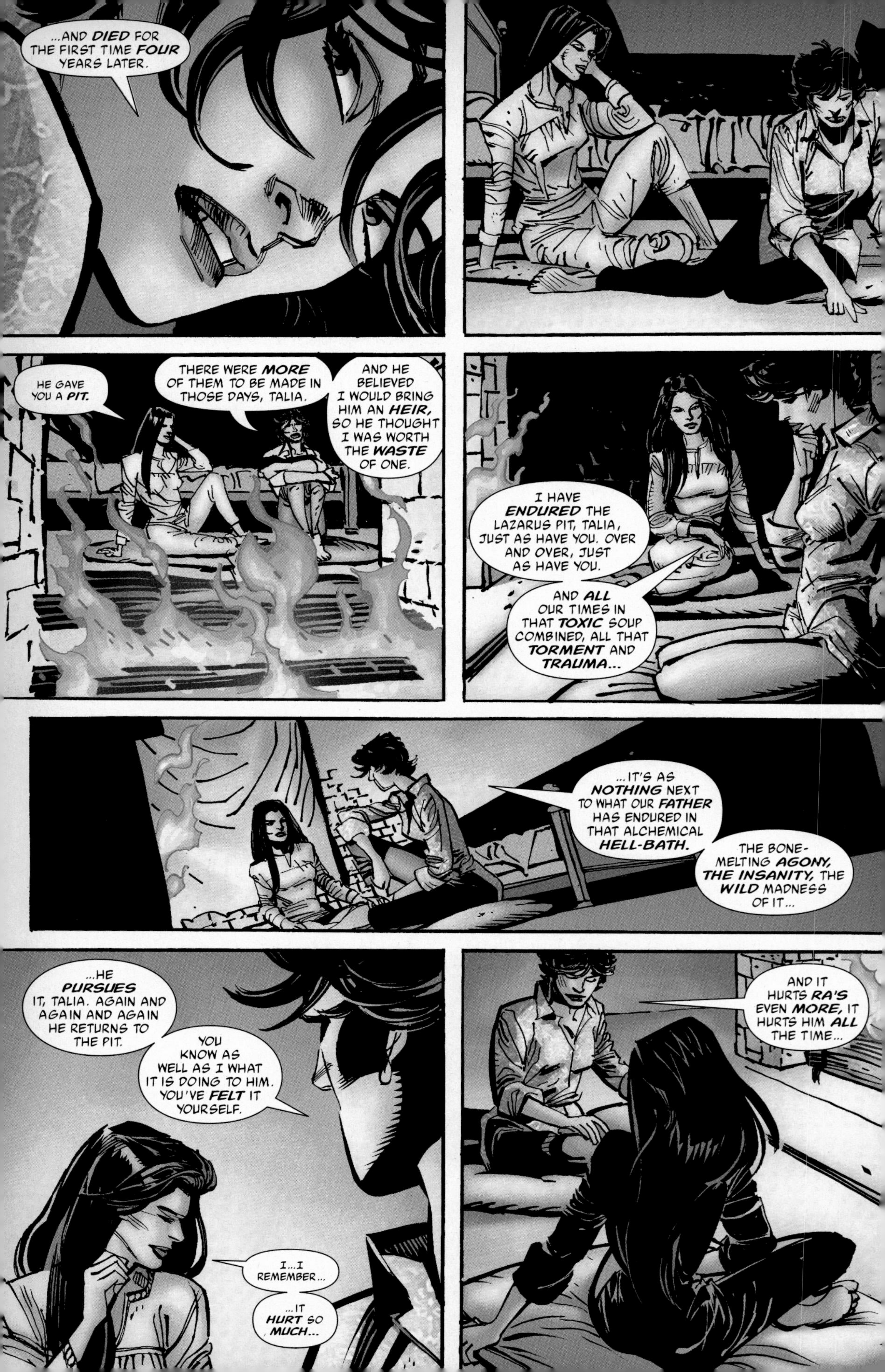

...AND DIED FOR THE FIRST TIME FOUR YEARS LATER.
HE GAVE YOU A PIT.
THERE WERE MORE OF THEM TO BE MADE IN THOSE DAYS, TALIA.
AND HE BELIEVED I WOULD BRING HIM AN HEIR, SO HE THOUGHT I WAS WORTH THE WASTE OF ONE.
I HAVE ENDURED THE LAZARUS PIT, TALIA, JUST AS HAVE YOU. OVER AND OVER, JUST AS HAVE YOU.
AND ALL OUR TIMES IN THAT TOXIC SOUP COMBINED, ALL THAT TORMENT AND TRAUMA...
...IT'S AS NOTHING NEXT TO WHAT OUR FATHER HAS ENDURED IN THAT ALCHEMICAL HELL-BATH.
THE BONE-MELTING AGONY, THE INSANITY, THE WILD MADNESS OF IT...
...HE PURSUES IT, TALIA. AGAIN AND AGAIN AND AGAIN HE RETURNS TO THE PIT.
YOU KNOW AS WELL AS I WHAT IT IS DOING TO HIM. YOU'VE FELT IT YOURSELF.
I...I REMEMBER...
...IT HURT SO MUCH...
AND IT HURTS RA'S EVEN MORE, IT HURTS HIM ALL THE TIME...

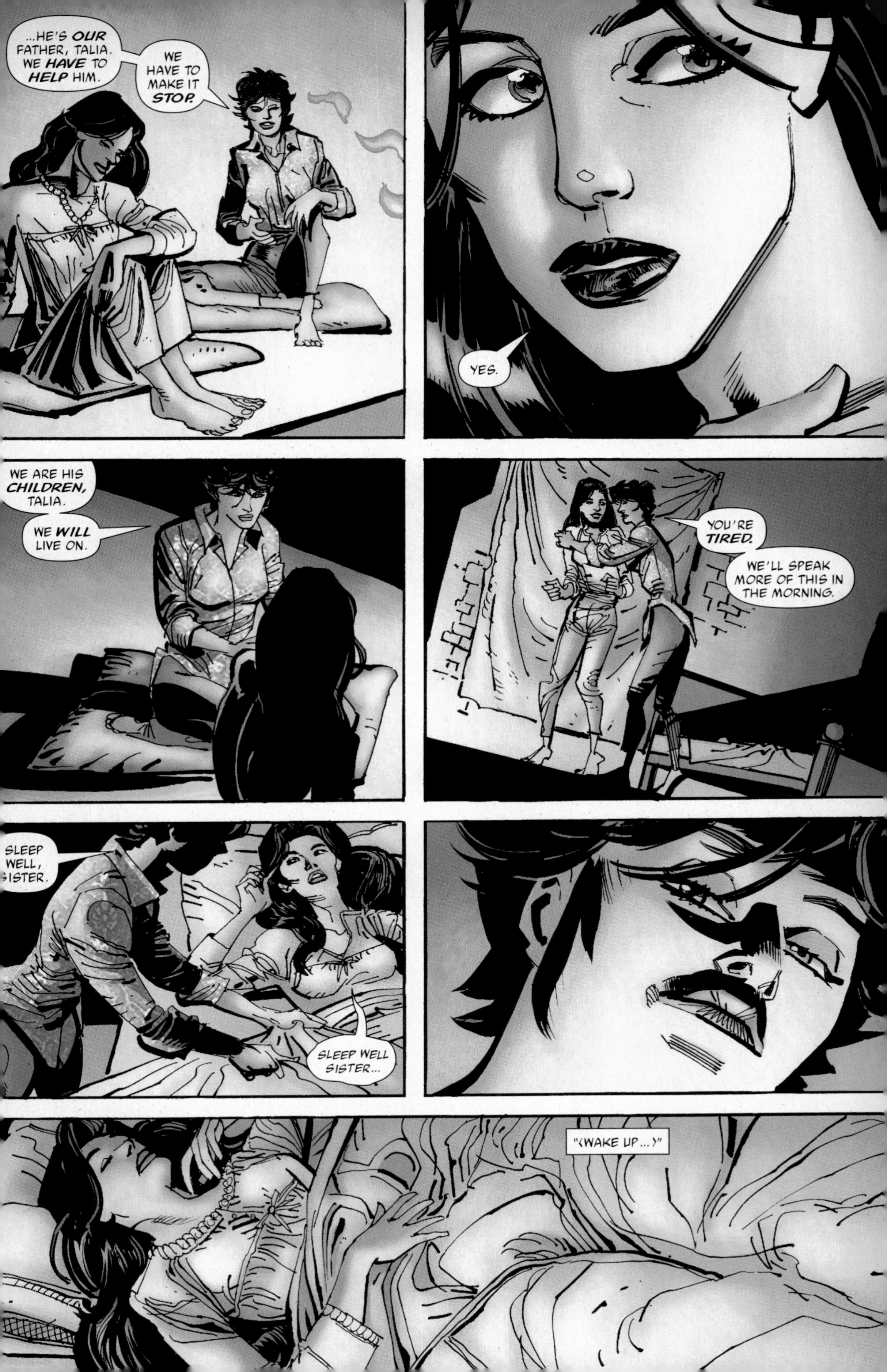

...HE'S **OUR** FATHER, TALIA. WE **HAVE** TO **HELP** HIM.
WE HAVE TO MAKE IT **STOP.**
YES.
WE ARE HIS **CHILDREN,** TALIA.
WE **WILL** LIVE ON.
YOU'RE **TIRED.**
WE'LL SPEAK MORE OF THIS IN THE MORNING.
SLEEP WELL, SISTER.
SLEEP WELL SISTER...
"‹WAKE UP...›"

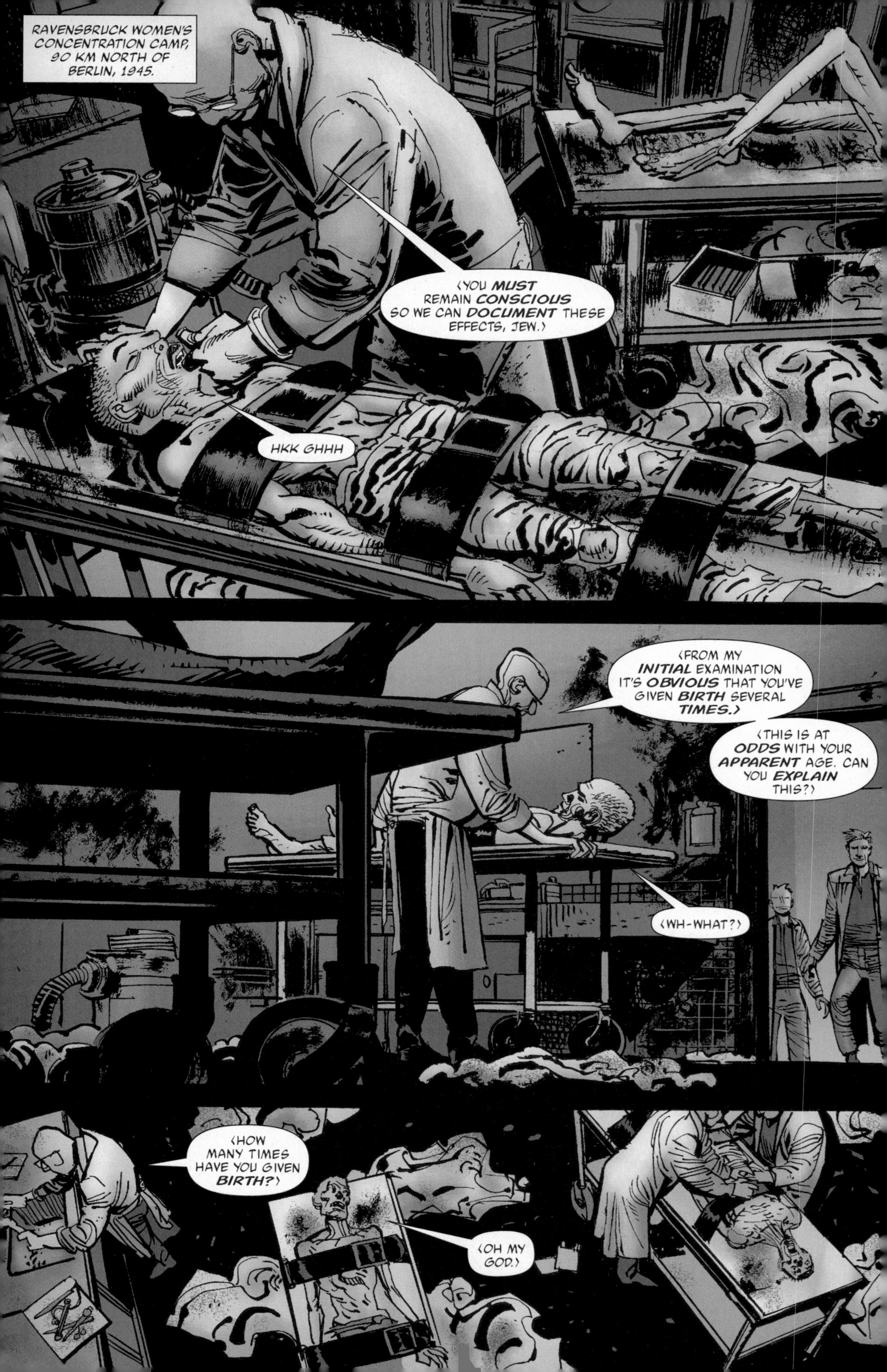
RAVENSBRUCK WOMEN'S CONCENTRATION CAMP, 90 KM NORTH OF BERLIN, 1945.
‹YOU MUST REMAIN CONSCIOUS SO WE CAN DOCUMENT THESE EFFECTS, JEW.›
HKK GHHH
‹FROM MY INITIAL EXAMINATION IT'S OBVIOUS THAT YOU'VE GIVEN BIRTH SEVERAL TIMES.›
‹THIS IS AT ODDS WITH YOUR APPARENT AGE. CAN YOU EXPLAIN THIS?›
‹WH-WHAT?›
‹HOW MANY TIMES HAVE YOU GIVEN BIRTH?›
‹OH MY GOD.›

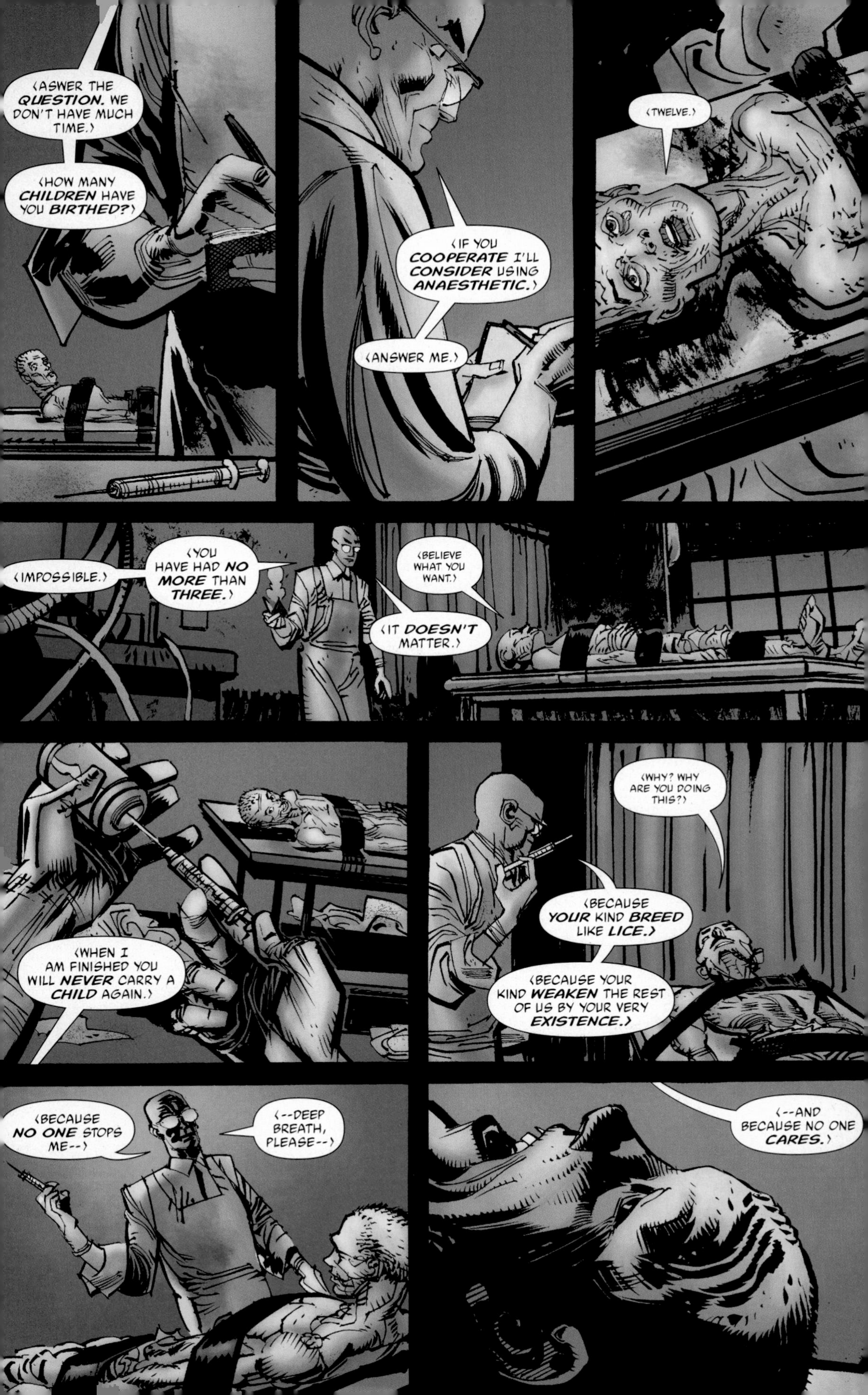
‹ASWER THE QUESTION. WE DON'T HAVE MUCH TIME.›
‹HOW MANY CHILDREN HAVE YOU BIRTHED?›
‹IF YOU COOPERATE I'LL CONSIDER USING ANAESTHETIC.›
‹ANSWER ME.›
‹TWELVE.›
‹IMPOSSIBLE.›
‹YOU HAVE HAD NO MORE THAN THREE.›
‹BELIEVE WHAT YOU WANT.›
‹IT DOESN'T MATTER.›
‹WHEN I AM FINISHED YOU WILL NEVER CARRY A CHILD AGAIN.›
‹WHY? WHY ARE YOU DOING THIS?›
‹BECAUSE YOUR KIND BREED LIKE LICE.›
‹BECAUSE YOUR KIND WEAKEN THE REST OF US BY YOUR VERY EXISTENCE.›
‹BECAUSE NO ONE STOPS ME--›
‹--DEEP BREATH, PLEASE--›
‹--AND BECAUSE NO ONE CARES.›

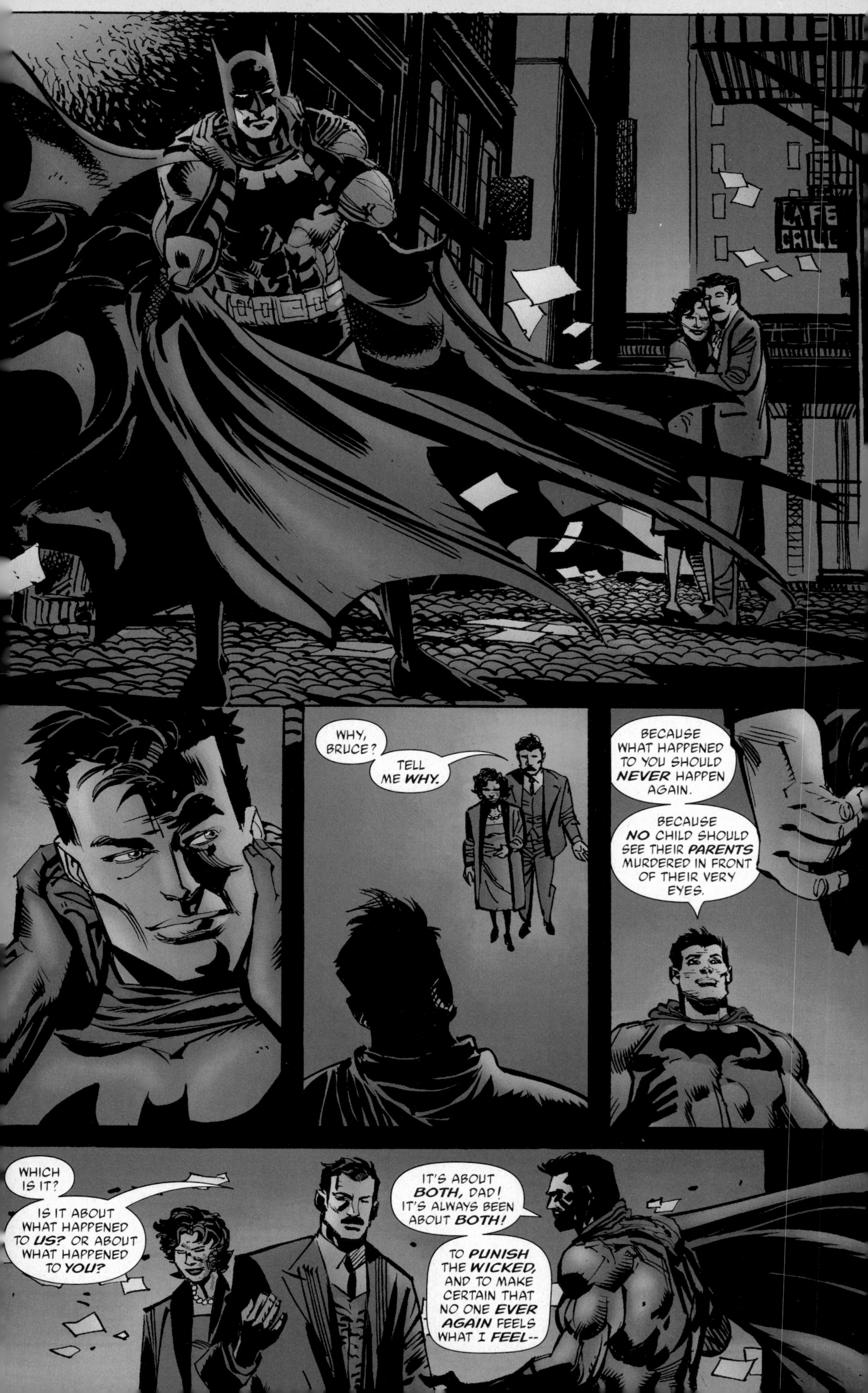
WHY, BRUCE?
TELL ME WHY.
BECAUSE WHAT HAPPENED TO YOU SHOULD NEVER HAPPEN AGAIN.
BECAUSE NO CHILD SHOULD SEE THEIR PARENTS MURDERED IN FRONT OF THEIR VERY EYES.
WHICH IS IT?
IS IT ABOUT WHAT HAPPENED TO US? OR ABOUT WHAT HAPPENED TO YOU?
IT'S ABOUT BOTH, DAD! IT'S ALWAYS BEEN ABOUT BOTH!
TO PUNISH THE WICKED, AND TO MAKE CERTAIN THAT NO ONE EVER AGAIN FEELS WHAT I FEEL--

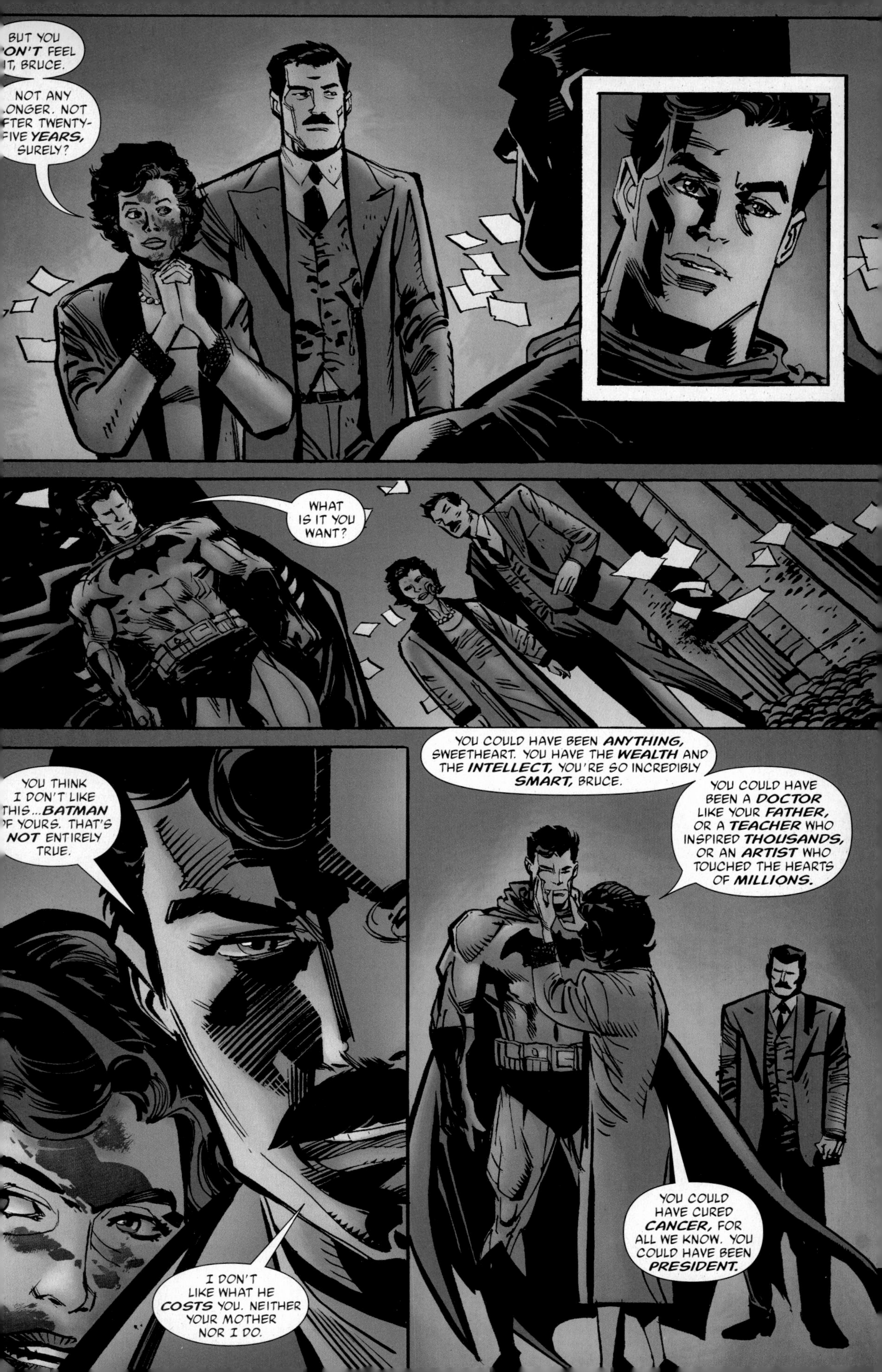

BUT YOU ON'T FEEL IT, BRUCE.
NOT ANY ONGER. NOT FTER TWENTY-FIVE YEARS, SURELY?
WHAT IS IT YOU WANT?
YOU THINK I DON'T LIKE THIS...BATMAN F YOURS. THAT'S NOT ENTIRELY TRUE.
I DON'T LIKE WHAT HE COSTS YOU. NEITHER YOUR MOTHER NOR I DO.
YOU COULD HAVE BEEN ANYTHING, SWEETHEART. YOU HAVE THE WEALTH AND THE INTELLECT, YOU'RE SO INCREDIBLY SMART, BRUCE.
YOU COULD HAVE BEEN A DOCTOR LIKE YOUR FATHER, OR A TEACHER WHO INSPIRED THOUSANDS, OR AN ARTIST WHO TOUCHED THE HEARTS OF MILLIONS.
YOU COULD HAVE CURED CANCER, FOR ALL WE KNOW. YOU COULD HAVE BEEN PRESIDENT.

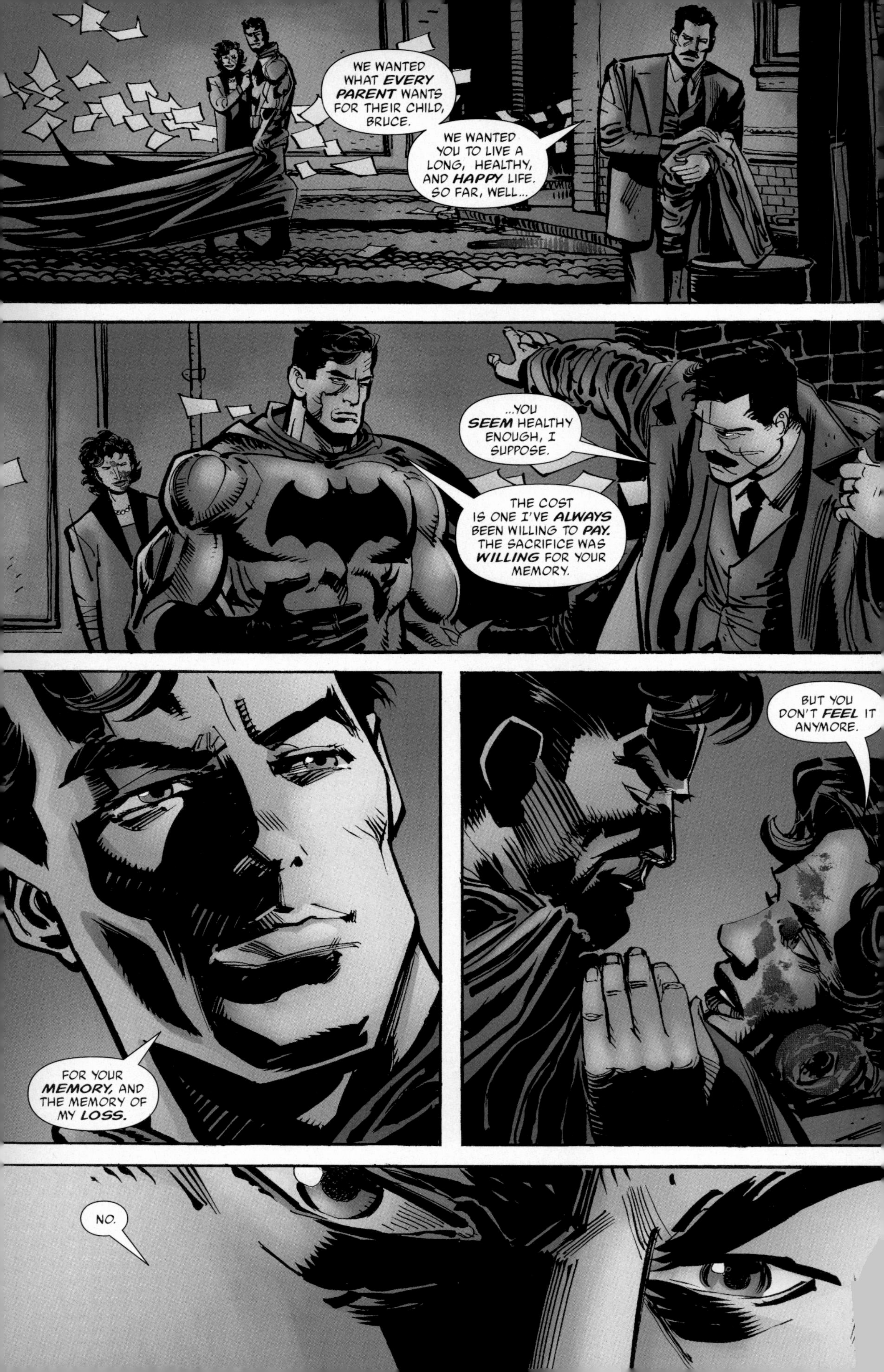

WE WANTED WHAT EVERY PARENT WANTS FOR THEIR CHILD, BRUCE.
WE WANTED YOU TO LIVE A LONG, HEALTHY, AND HAPPY LIFE. SO FAR, WELL...
...YOU SEEM HEALTHY ENOUGH, I SUPPOSE.
THE COST IS ONE I'VE ALWAYS BEEN WILLING TO PAY. THE SACRIFICE WAS WILLING FOR YOUR MEMORY.
FOR YOUR MEMORY, AND THE MEMORY OF MY LOSS.
BUT YOU DON'T FEEL IT ANYMORE.
NO.

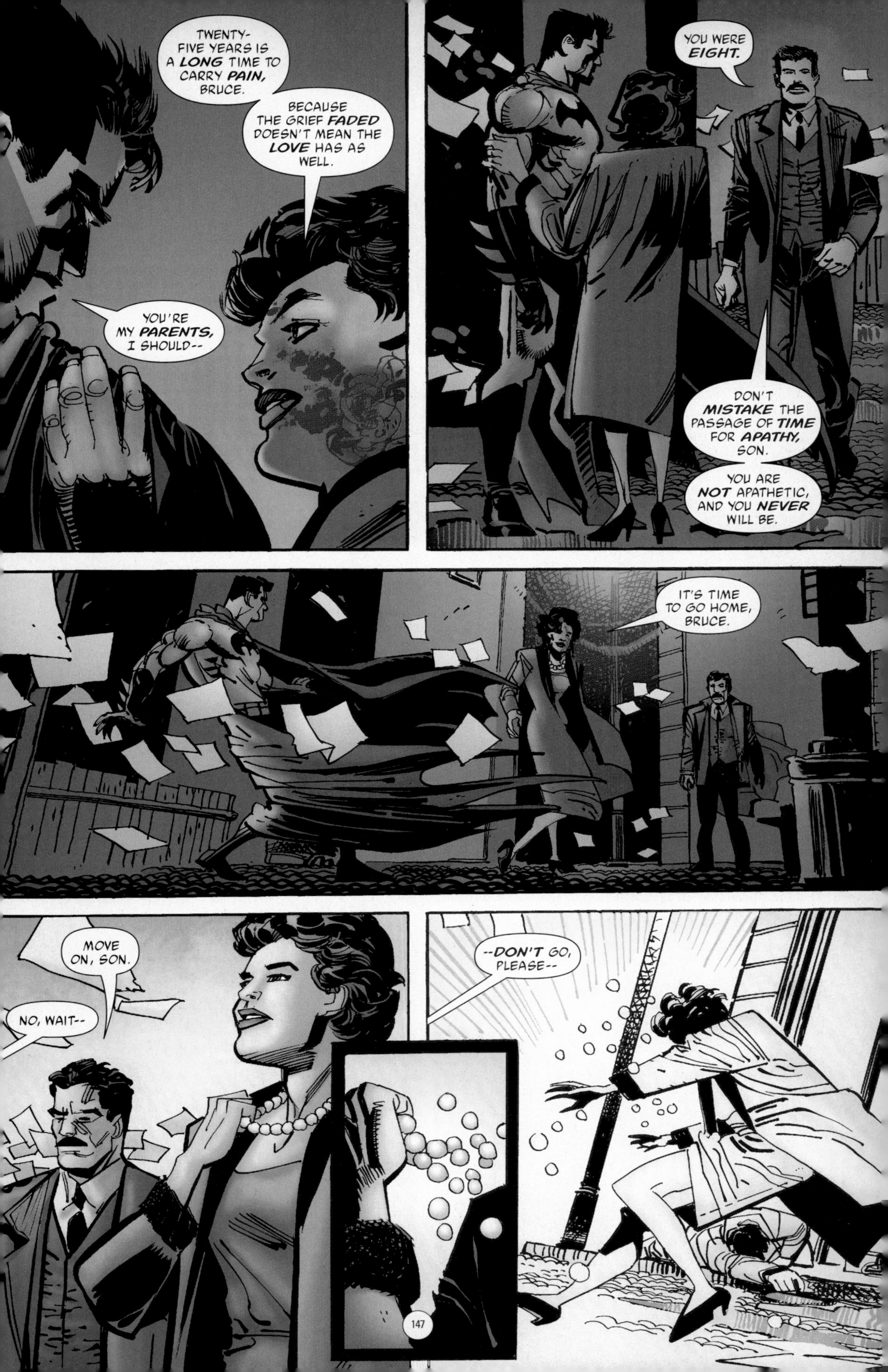
TWENTY-FIVE YEARS IS A LONG TIME TO CARRY PAIN, BRUCE.
BECAUSE THE GRIEF FADED DOESN'T MEAN THE LOVE HAS AS WELL.
YOU'RE MY PARENTS, I SHOULD--
YOU WERE EIGHT.
DON'T MISTAKE THE PASSAGE OF TIME FOR APATHY, SON.
YOU ARE NOT APATHETIC, AND YOU NEVER WILL BE.
IT'S TIME TO GO HOME, BRUCE.
MOVE ON, SON.
NO, WAIT--
--DON'T GO, PLEASE--

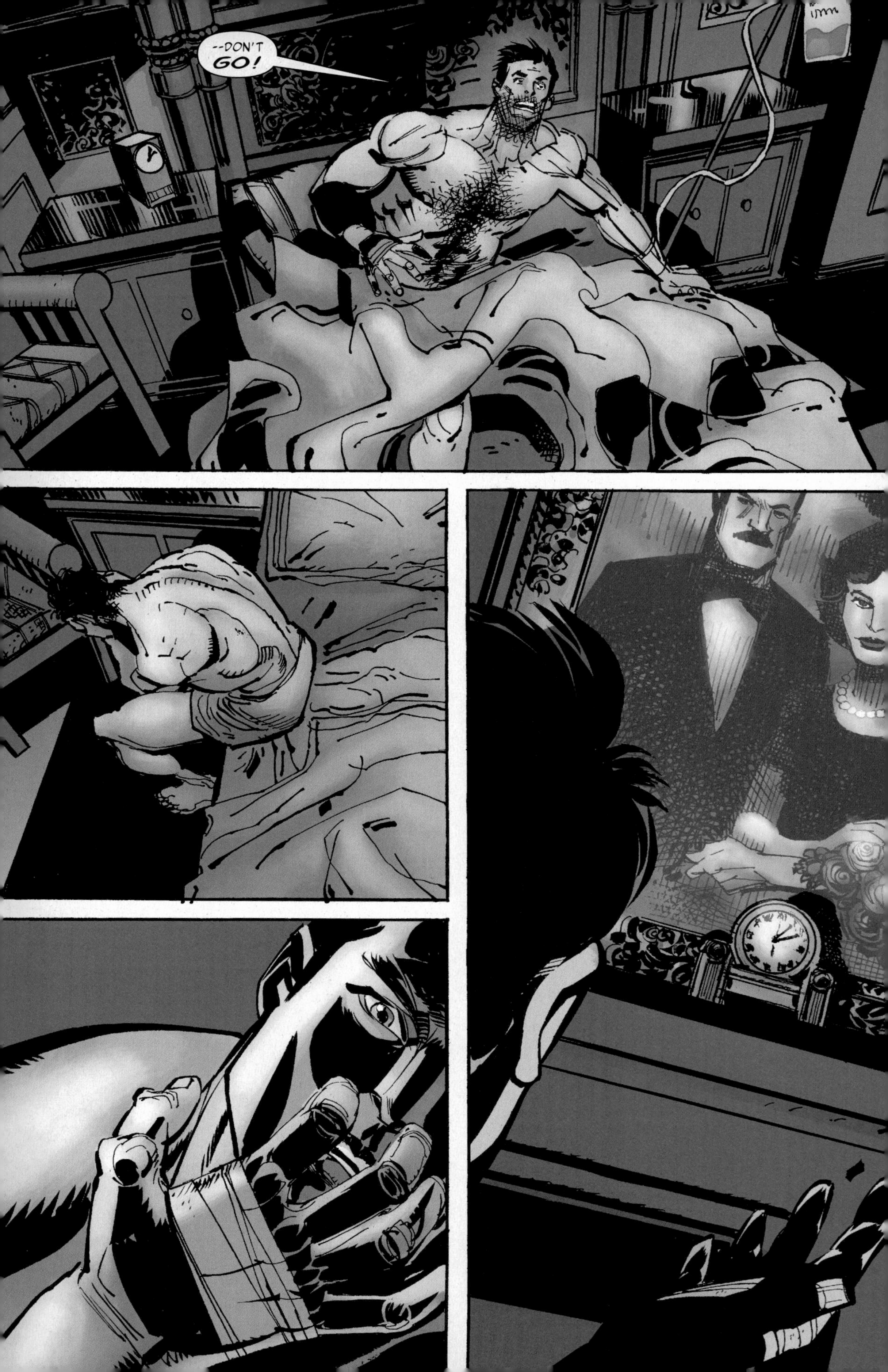
--DON'T GO!

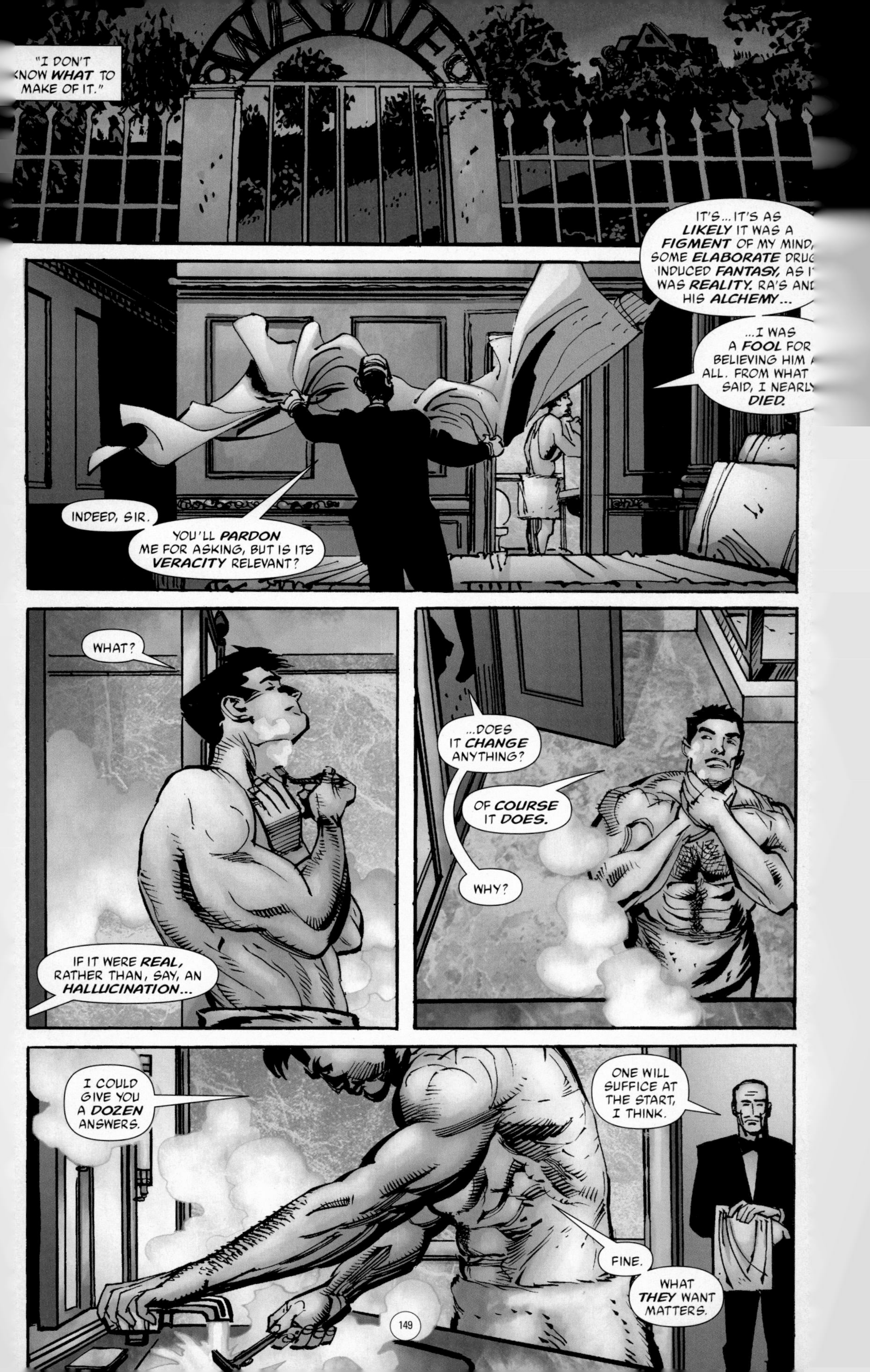
"I DON'T KNOW WHAT TO MAKE OF IT."
IT'S... IT'S AS LIKELY IT WAS A FIGMENT OF MY MIND, SOME ELABORATE DRUG INDUCED FANTASY, AS IT WAS REALITY. RA'S AND HIS ALCHEMY...
...I WAS A FOOL FOR BELIEVING HIM AT ALL. FROM WHAT HE SAID, I NEARLY DIED.
INDEED, SIR.
YOU'LL PARDON ME FOR ASKING, BUT IS ITS VERACITY RELEVANT?
WHAT?
IF IT WERE REAL, RATHER THAN, SAY, AN HALLUCINATION...
...DOES IT CHANGE ANYTHING?
OF COURSE IT DOES.
WHY?
I COULD GIVE YOU A DOZEN ANSWERS.
ONE WILL SUFFICE AT THE START, I THINK.
FINE.
WHAT THEY WANT MATTERS.

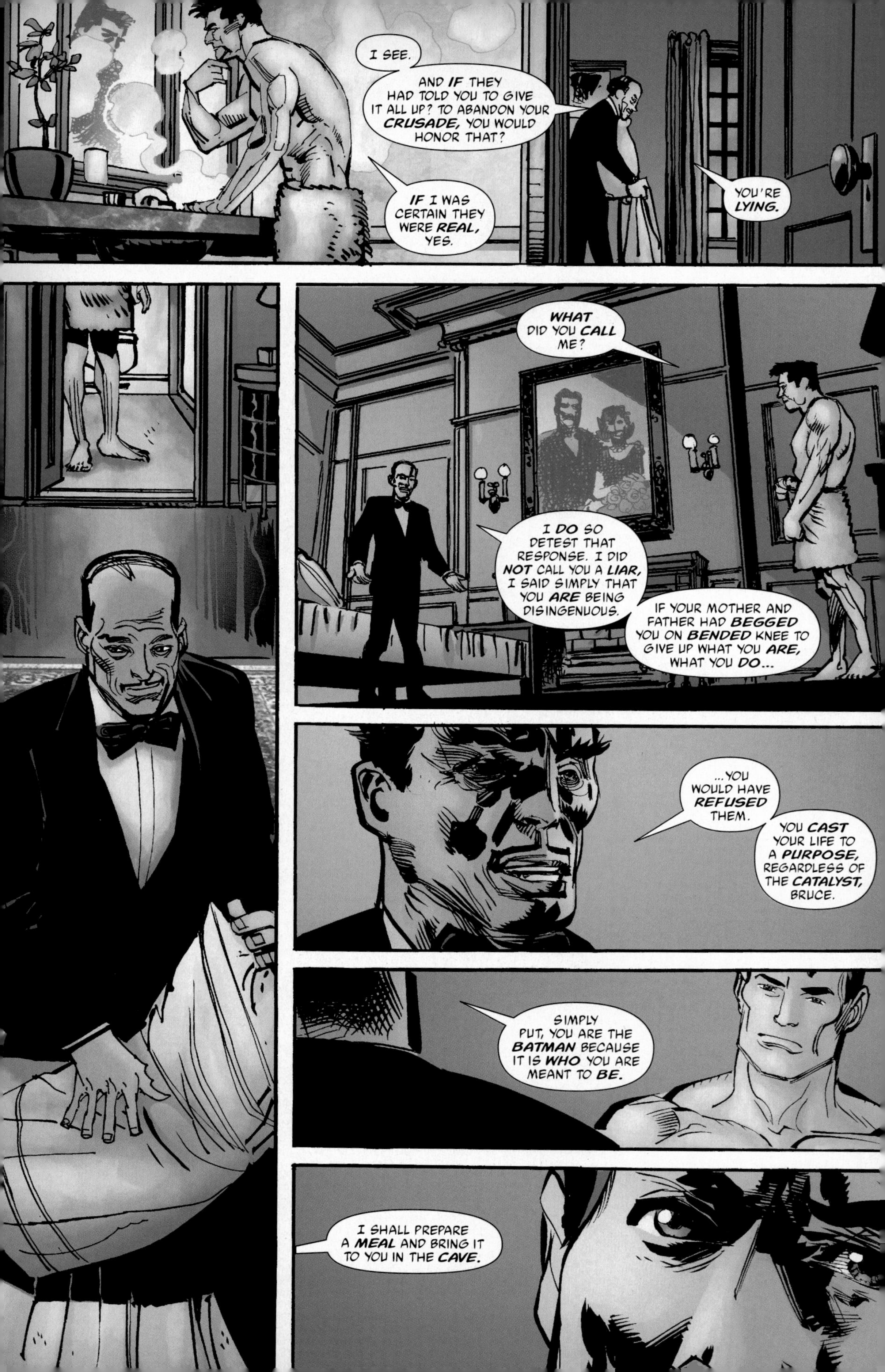

I SEE.
AND IF THEY HAD TOLD YOU TO GIVE IT ALL UP? TO ABANDON YOUR CRUSADE, YOU WOULD HONOR THAT?
IF I WAS CERTAIN THEY WERE REAL, YES.
YOU'RE LYING.
WHAT DID YOU CALL ME?
I DO SO DETEST THAT RESPONSE. I DID NOT CALL YOU A LIAR, I SAID SIMPLY THAT YOU ARE BEING DISINGENUOUS.
IF YOUR MOTHER AND FATHER HAD BEGGED YOU ON BENDED KNEE TO GIVE UP WHAT YOU ARE, WHAT YOU DO...
...YOU WOULD HAVE REFUSED THEM.
YOU CAST YOUR LIFE TO A PURPOSE, REGARDLESS OF THE CATALYST, BRUCE.
SIMPLY PUT, YOU ARE THE BATMAN BECAUSE IT IS WHO YOU ARE MEANT TO BE.
I SHALL PREPARE A MEAL AND BRING IT TO YOU IN THE CAVE.

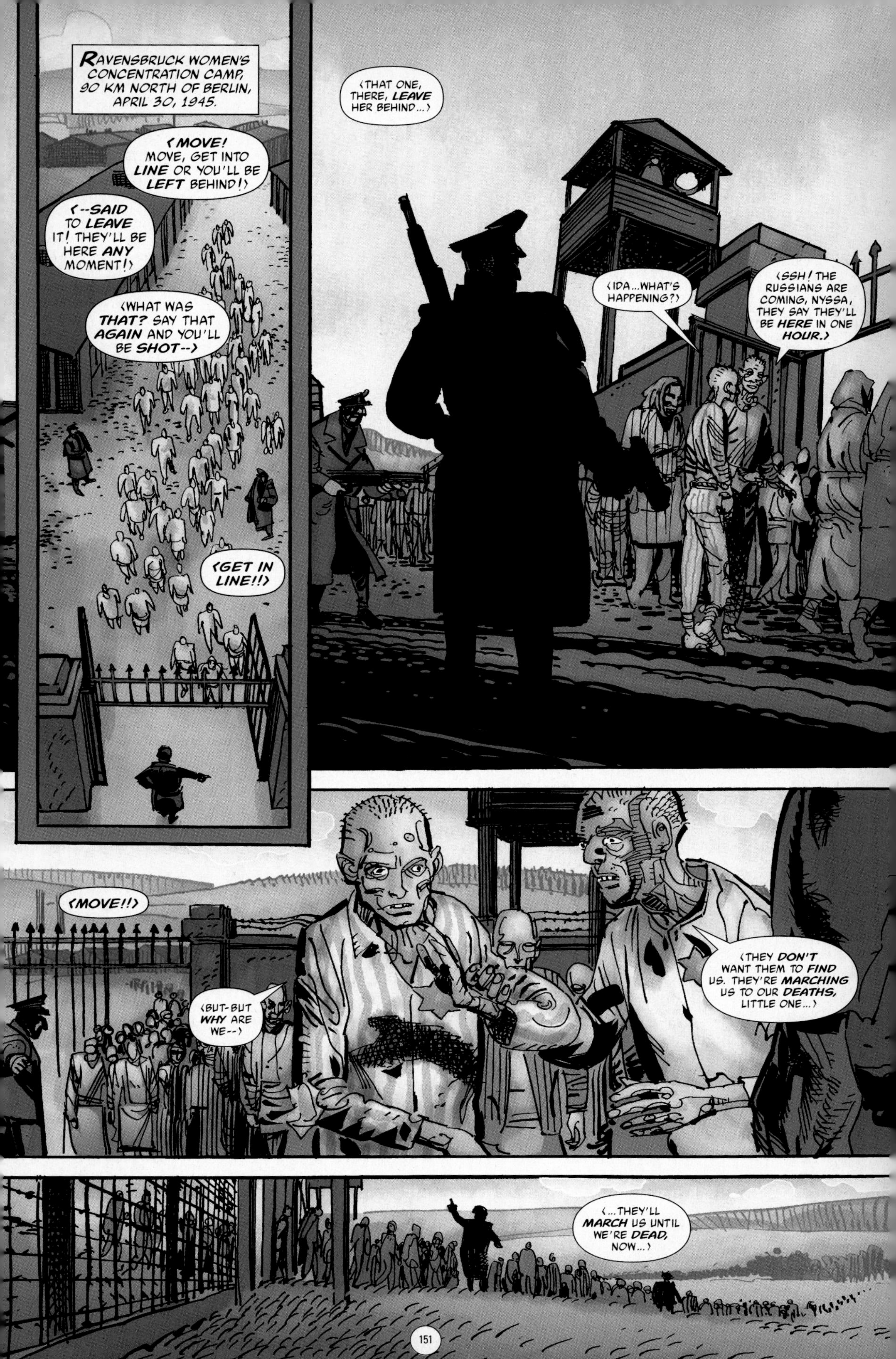

Ravensbruck Women's Concentration Camp, 90 km North of Berlin, April 30, 1945.
‹MOVE! MOVE, GET INTO LINE OR YOU'LL BE LEFT BEHIND!›
‹--SAID TO LEAVE IT! THEY'LL BE HERE ANY MOMENT!›
‹WHAT WAS THAT? SAY THAT AGAIN AND YOU'LL BE SHOT--›
‹GET IN LINE!!›
‹THAT ONE, THERE, LEAVE HER BEHIND...›
‹IDA...WHAT'S HAPPENING?›
‹SSH! THE RUSSIANS ARE COMING, NYSSA, THEY SAY THEY'LL BE HERE IN ONE HOUR.›
‹MOVE!!›
‹BUT-BUT WHY ARE WE--›
‹THEY DON'T WANT THEM TO FIND US. THEY'RE MARCHING US TO OUR DEATHS, LITTLE ONE...›
‹...THEY'LL MARCH US UNTIL WE'RE DEAD, NOW...›

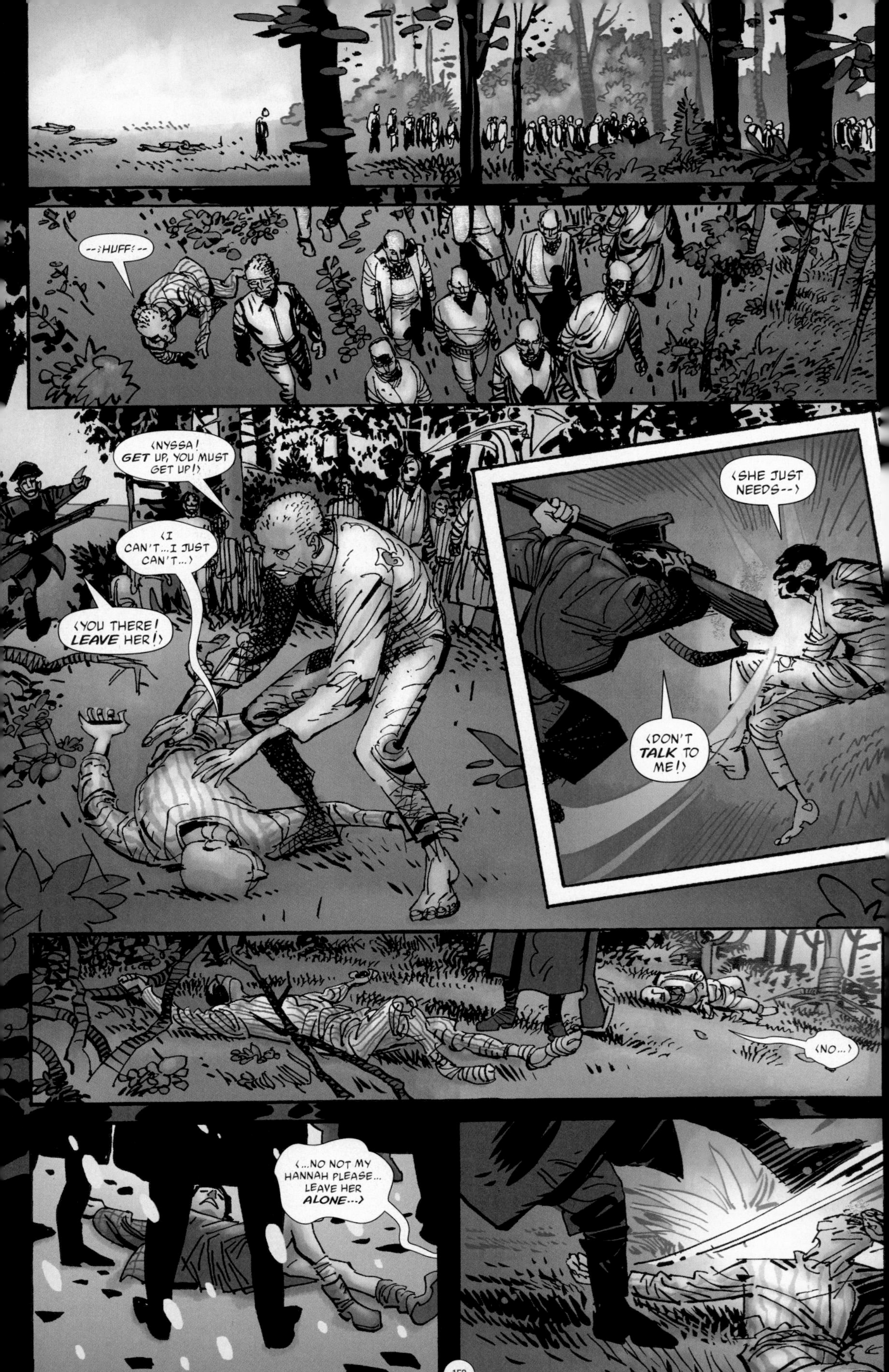
--HUFF--
‹NYSSA! GET UP, YOU MUST GET UP!›
‹I CAN'T...I JUST CAN'T...›
‹YOU THERE! LEAVE HER!›
‹SHE JUST NEEDS--›
‹DON'T TALK TO ME!›
‹NO...›
‹...NO NOT MY HANNAH PLEASE... LEAVE HER ALONE...›

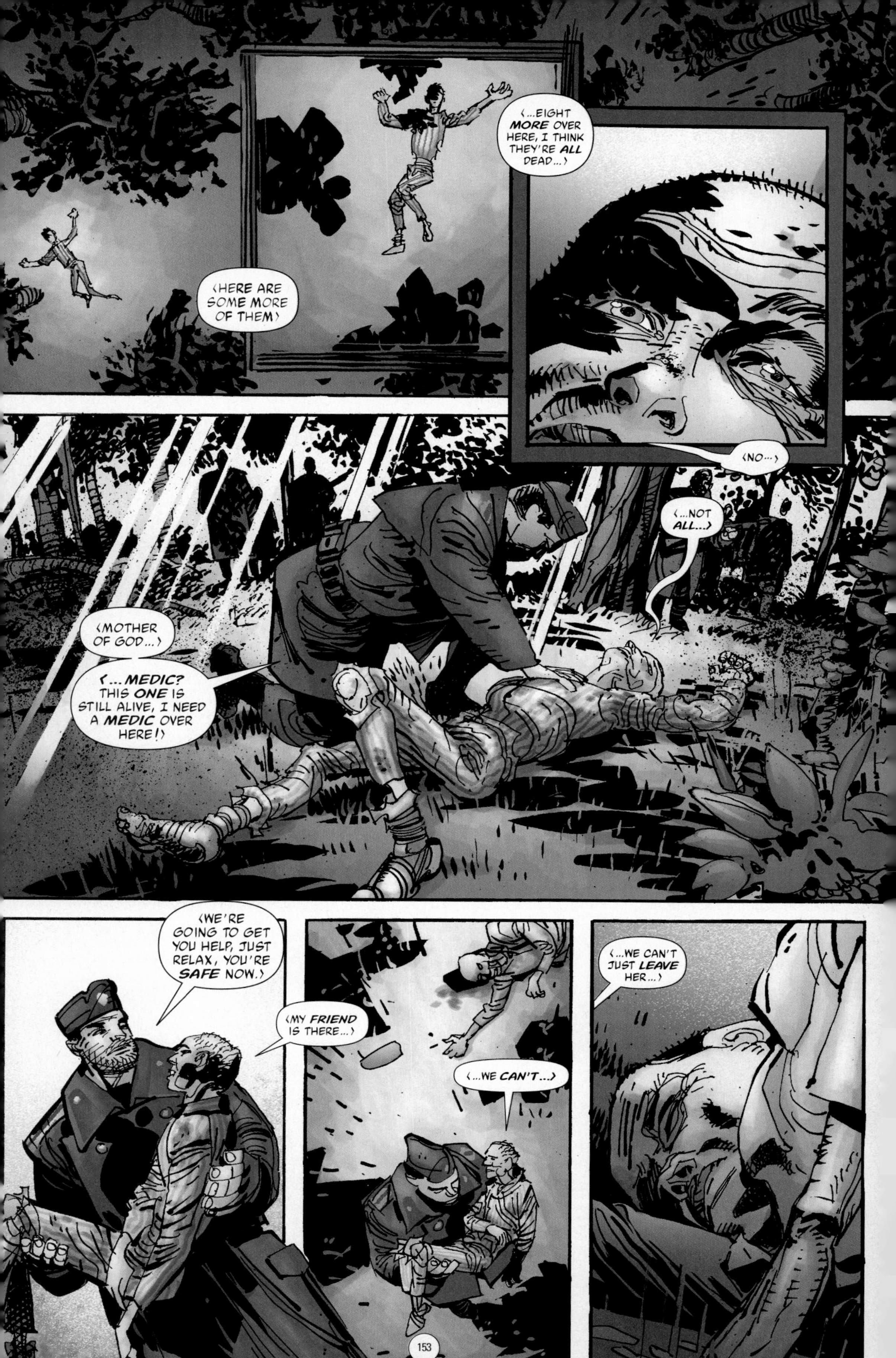
‹HERE ARE SOME MORE OF THEM›
‹...EIGHT MORE OVER HERE, I THINK THEY'RE ALL DEAD...›
‹NO...›
‹...NOT ALL...›
‹MOTHER OF GOD...›
‹...MEDIC? THIS ONE IS STILL ALIVE, I NEED A MEDIC OVER HERE!›
‹WE'RE GOING TO GET YOU HELP, JUST RELAX, YOU'RE SAFE NOW.›
‹MY FRIEND IS THERE...›
‹...WE CAN'T...›
‹...WE CAN'T JUST LEAVE HER...›

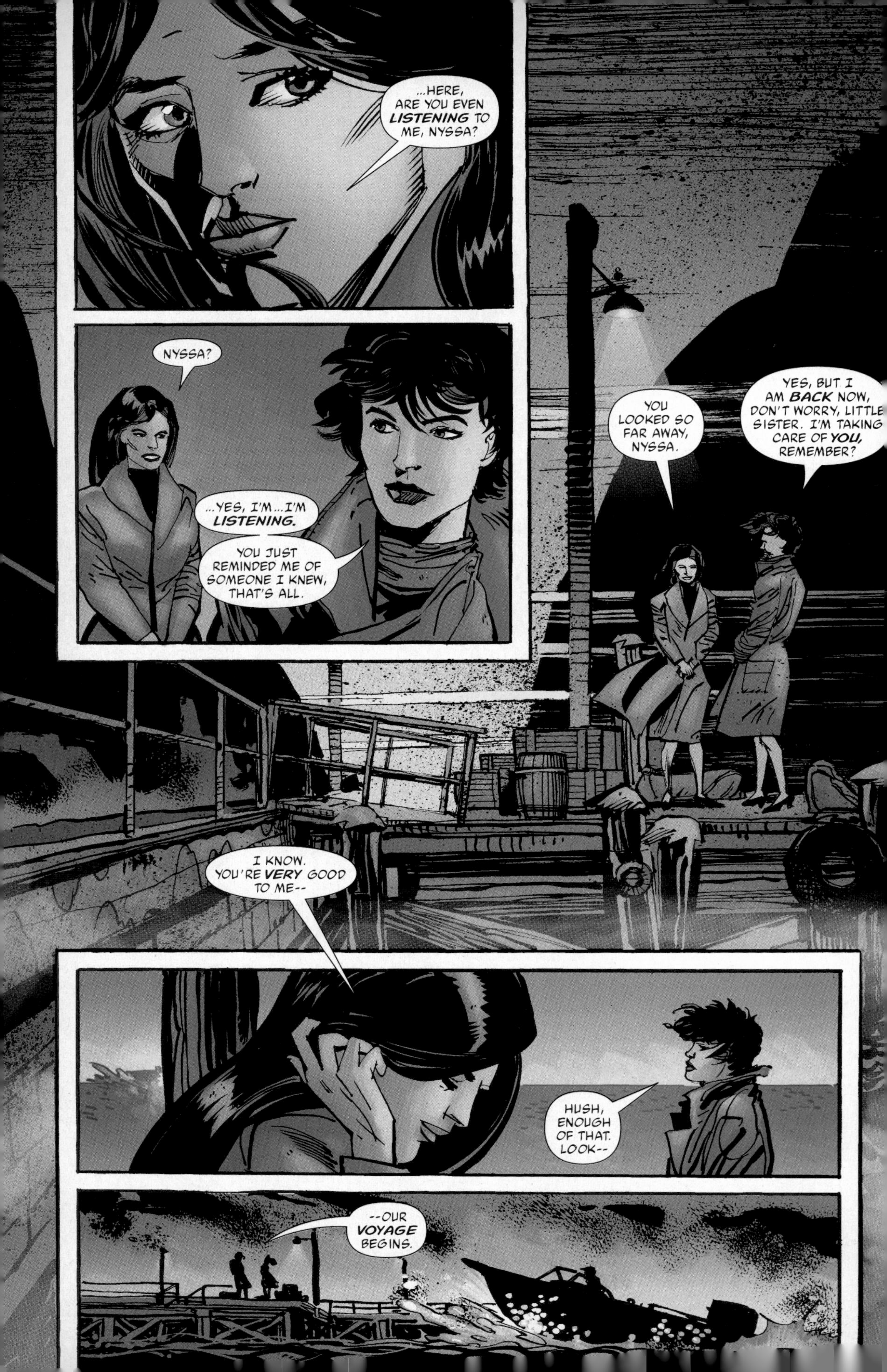
...HERE, ARE YOU EVEN LISTENING TO ME, NYSSA?
NYSSA?
...YES, I'M...I'M LISTENING.
YOU JUST REMINDED ME OF SOMEONE I KNEW, THAT'S ALL.
YOU LOOKED SO FAR AWAY, NYSSA.
YES, BUT I AM BACK NOW, DON'T WORRY, LITTLE SISTER. I'M TAKING CARE OF YOU, REMEMBER?
I KNOW. YOU'RE VERY GOOD TO ME--
HUSH, ENOUGH OF THAT. LOOK--
--OUR VOYAGE BEGINS.

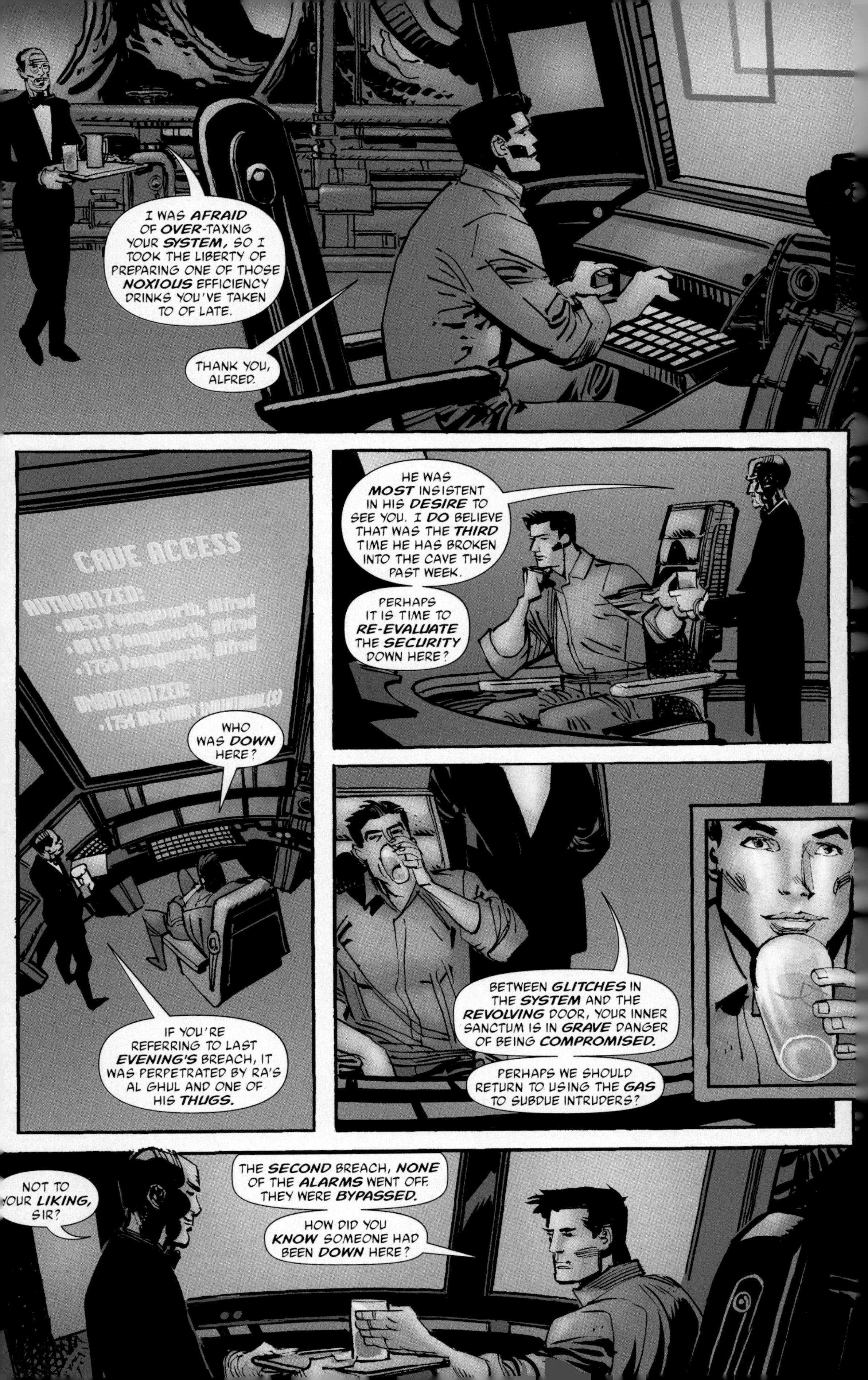
I WAS AFRAID OF OVER-TAXING YOUR SYSTEM, SO I TOOK THE LIBERTY OF PREPARING ONE OF THOSE NOXIOUS EFFICIENCY DRINKS YOU'VE TAKEN TO OF LATE.
THANK YOU, ALFRED.
CAVE ACCESS
AUTHORIZED:
•0833 Pennyworth, Alfred
•0818 Pennyworth, Alfred
•1756 Pennyworth, Alfred
UNAUTHORIZED:
•1754 UNKNOWN INDIVIDUAL(S)
WHO WAS DOWN HERE?
IF YOU'RE REFERRING TO LAST EVENING'S BREACH, IT WAS PERPETRATED BY RA'S AL GHUL AND ONE OF HIS THUGS.
HE WAS MOST INSISTENT IN HIS DESIRE TO SEE YOU. I DO BELIEVE THAT WAS THE THIRD TIME HE HAS BROKEN INTO THE CAVE THIS PAST WEEK.
PERHAPS IT IS TIME TO RE-EVALUATE THE SECURITY DOWN HERE?
BETWEEN GLITCHES IN THE SYSTEM AND THE REVOLVING DOOR, YOUR INNER SANCTUM IS IN GRAVE DANGER OF BEING COMPROMISED.
PERHAPS WE SHOULD RETURN TO USING THE GAS TO SUBDUE INTRUDERS?
NOT TO YOUR LIKING, SIR?
THE SECOND BREACH, NONE OF THE ALARMS WENT OFF. THEY WERE BYPASSED.
HOW DID YOU KNOW SOMEONE HAD BEEN DOWN HERE?

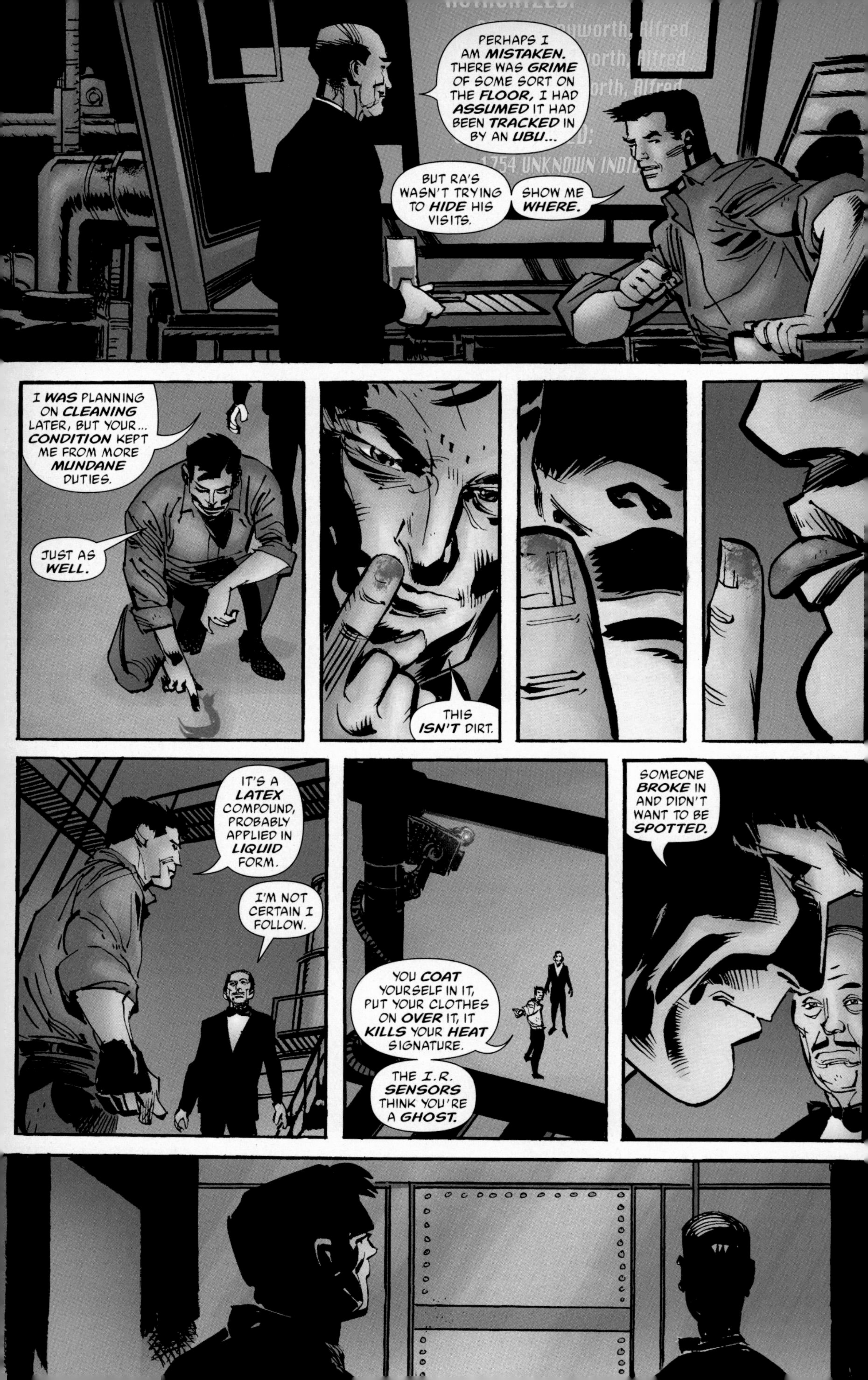
PERHAPS I AM MISTAKEN. THERE WAS GRIME OF SOME SORT ON THE FLOOR, I HAD ASSUMED IT HAD BEEN TRACKED IN BY AN UBU...
BUT RA'S WASN'T TRYING TO HIDE HIS VISITS.
SHOW ME WHERE.
I WAS PLANNING ON CLEANING LATER, BUT YOUR... CONDITION KEPT ME FROM MORE MUNDANE DUTIES.
JUST AS WELL.
THIS ISN'T DIRT.
IT'S A LATEX COMPOUND, PROBABLY APPLIED IN LIQUID FORM.
I'M NOT CERTAIN I FOLLOW.
YOU COAT YOURSELF IN IT, PUT YOUR CLOTHES ON OVER IT, IT KILLS YOUR HEAT SIGNATURE.
THE I.R. SENSORS THINK YOU'RE A GHOST.
SOMEONE BROKE IN AND DIDN'T WANT TO BE SPOTTED.

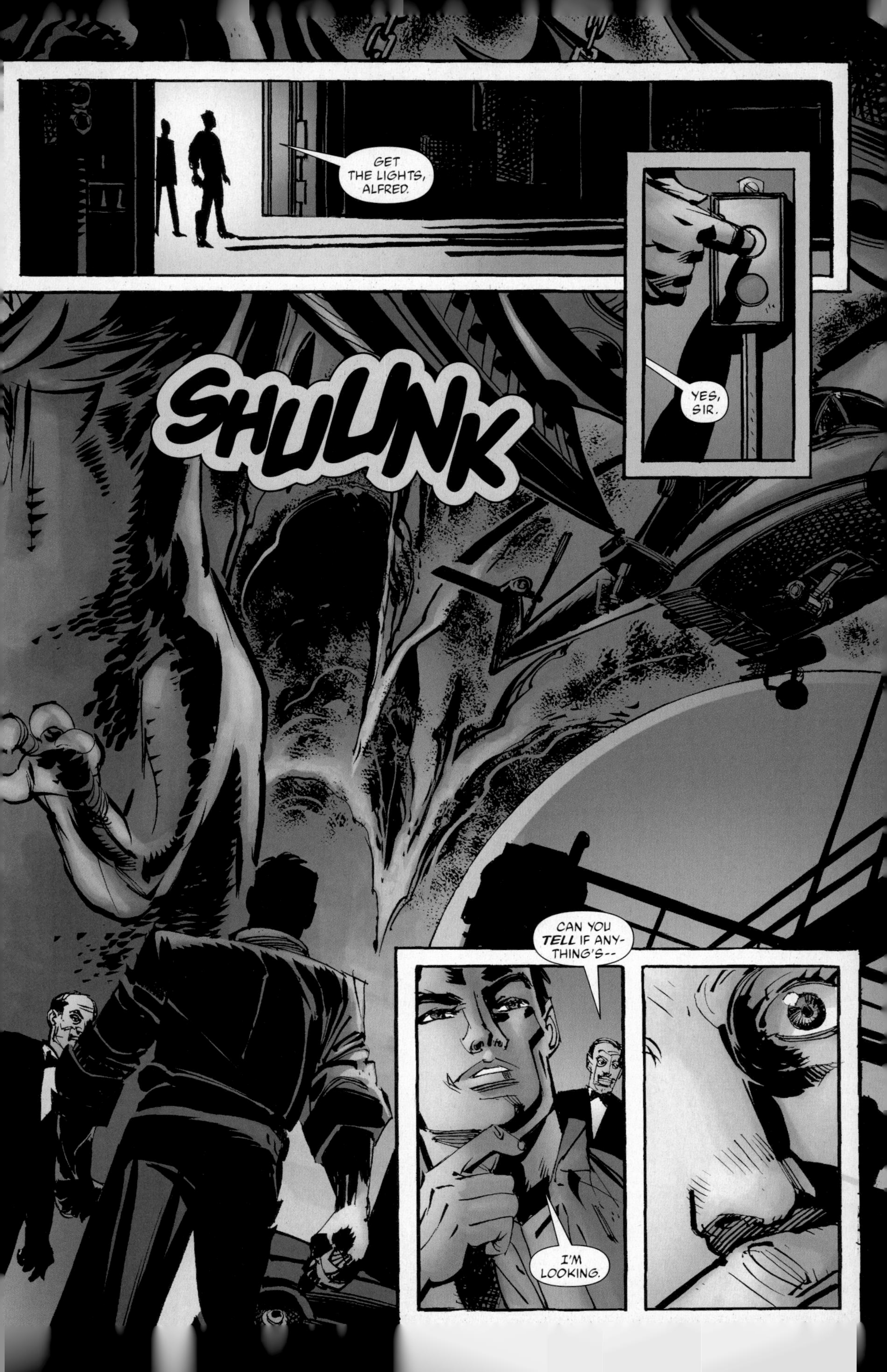
GET THE LIGHTS, ALFRED.
YES, SIR.
SHULNK
CAN YOU TELL IF ANYTHING'S--
I'M LOOKING.

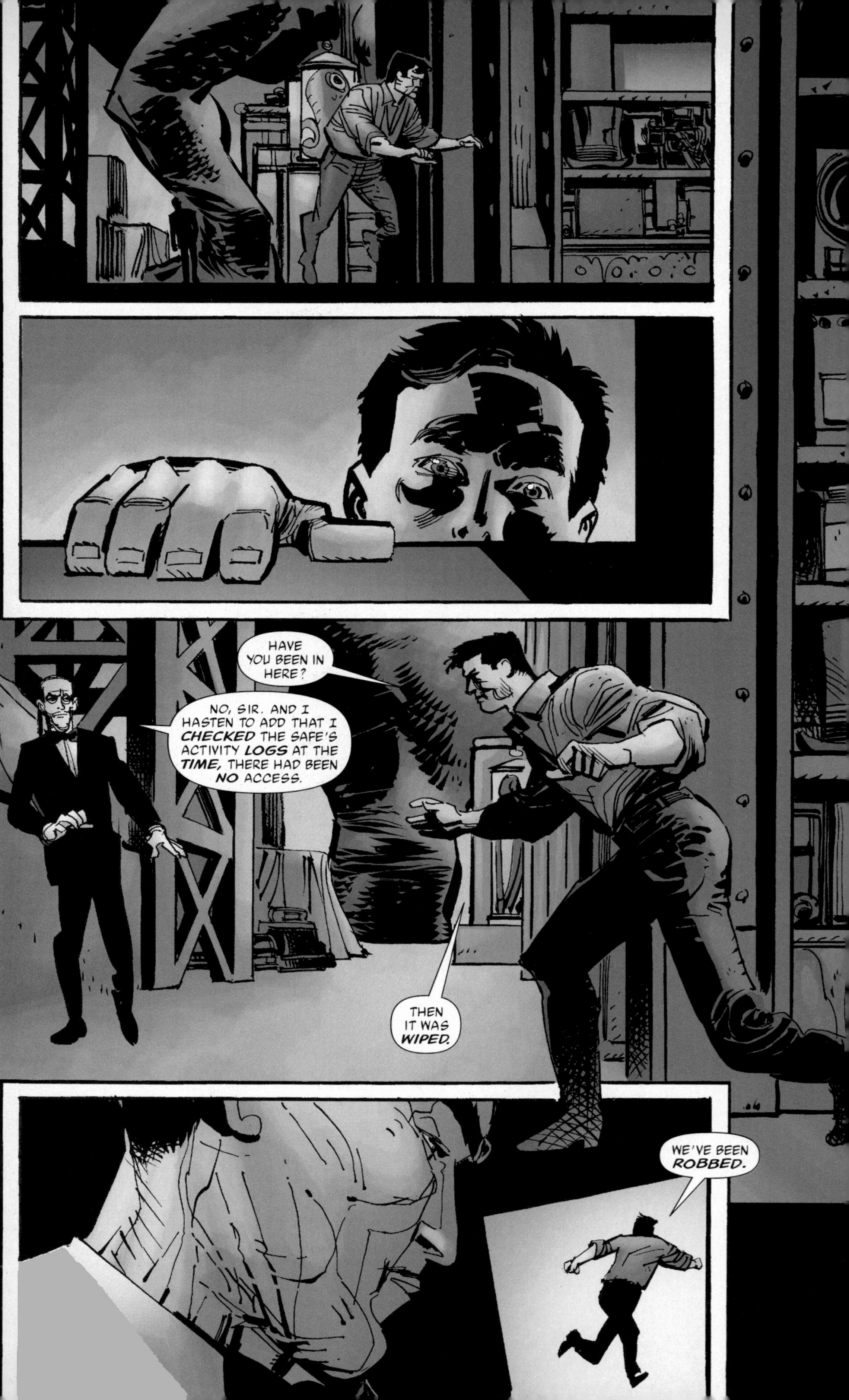
HAVE YOU BEEN IN HERE?
NO, SIR. AND I HASTEN TO ADD THAT I CHECKED THE SAFE'S ACTIVITY LOGS AT THE TIME, THERE HAD BEEN NO ACCESS.
THEN IT WAS WIPED.
WE'VE BEEN ROBBED.

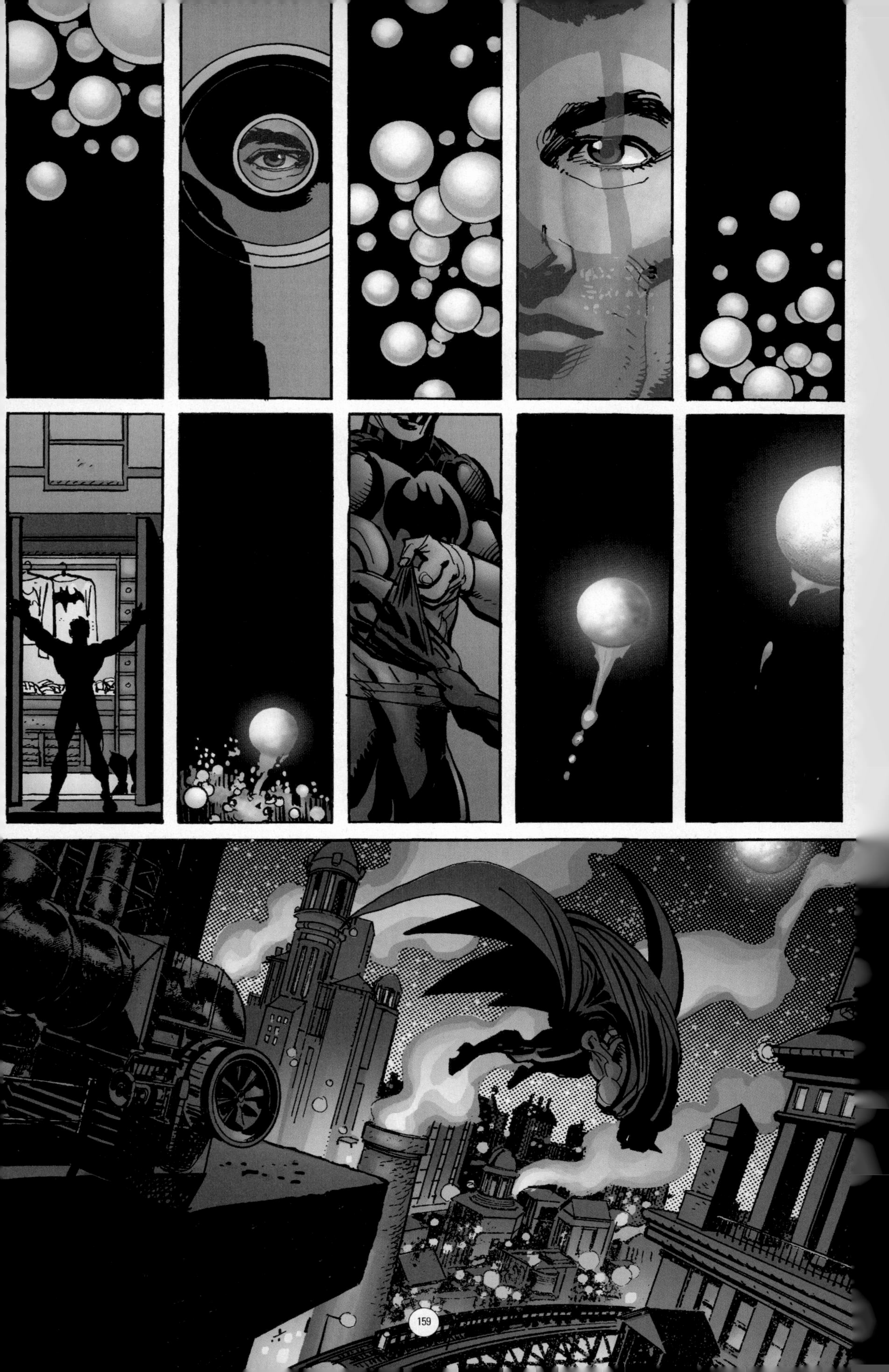

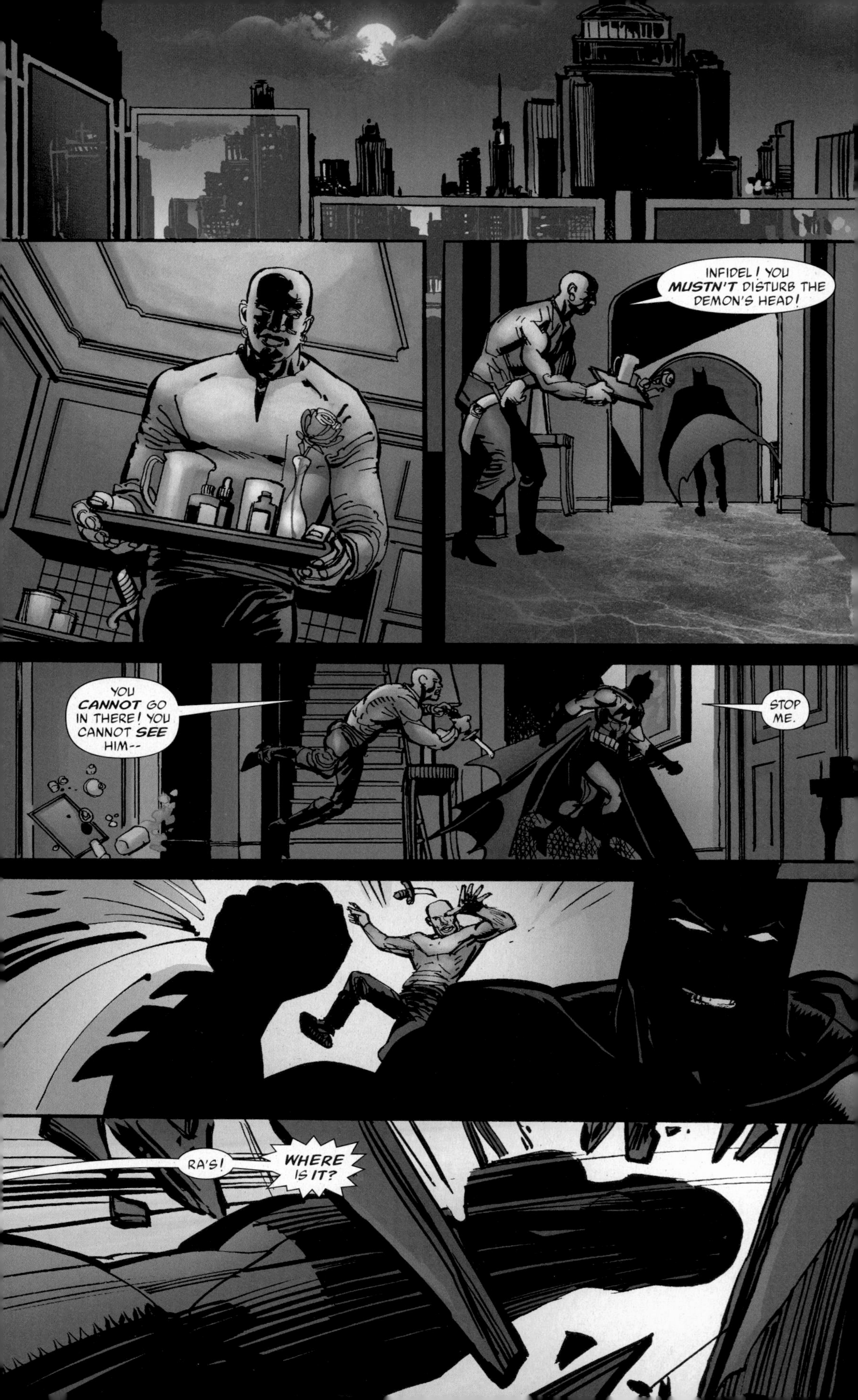
INFIDEL! YOU MUSTN'T DISTURB THE DEMON'S HEAD!
YOU CANNOT GO IN THERE! YOU CANNOT SEE HIM--
STOP ME.
RA'S!
WHERE IS IT?

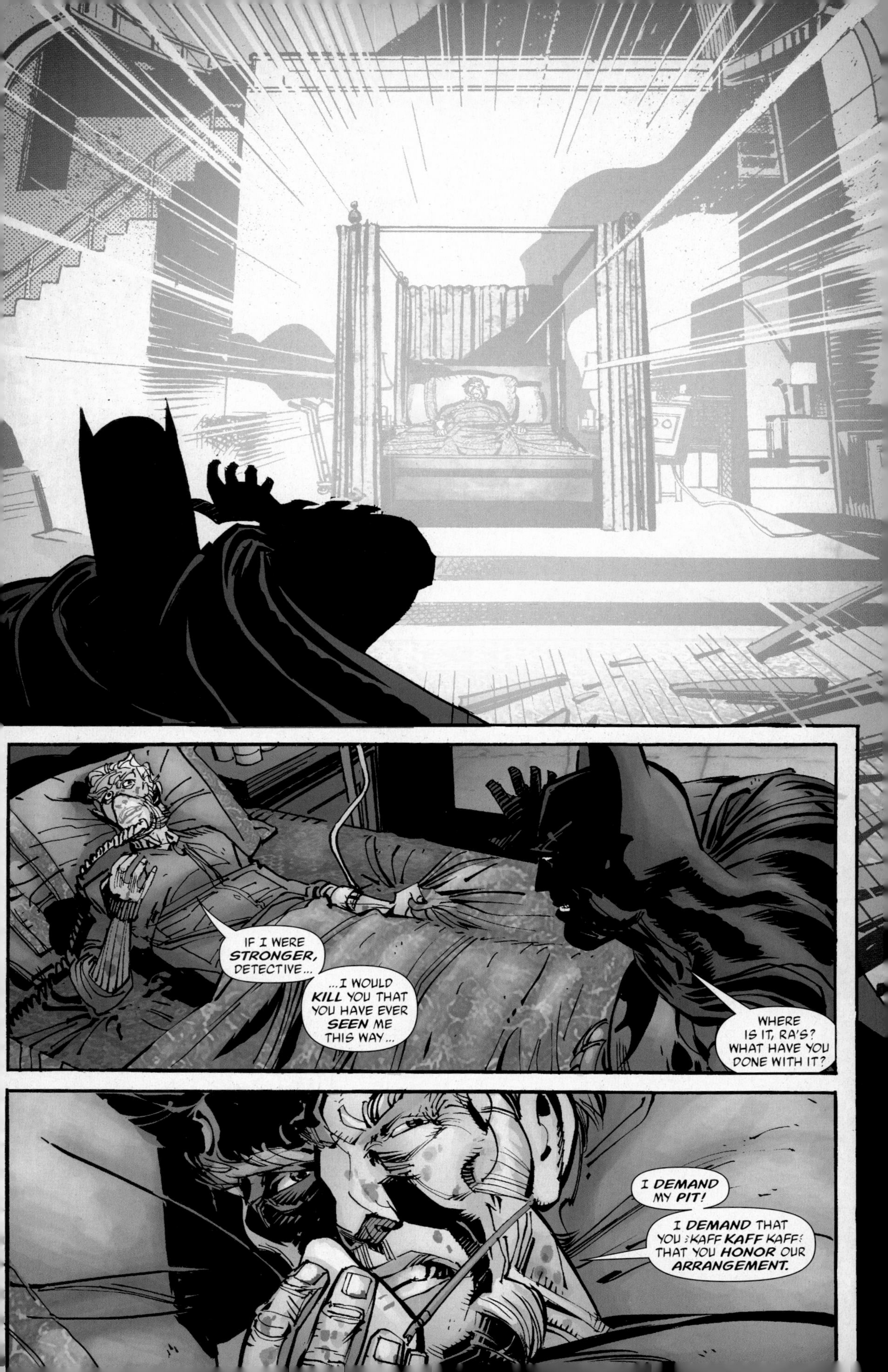
IF I WERE STRONGER, DETECTIVE...
...I WOULD KILL YOU THAT YOU HAVE EVER SEEN ME THIS WAY...
WHERE IS IT, RA'S? WHAT HAVE YOU DONE WITH IT?
I DEMAND MY PIT!
I DEMAND THAT YOU ›KAFF KAFF KAFF‹ THAT YOU HONOR OUR ARRANGEMENT.

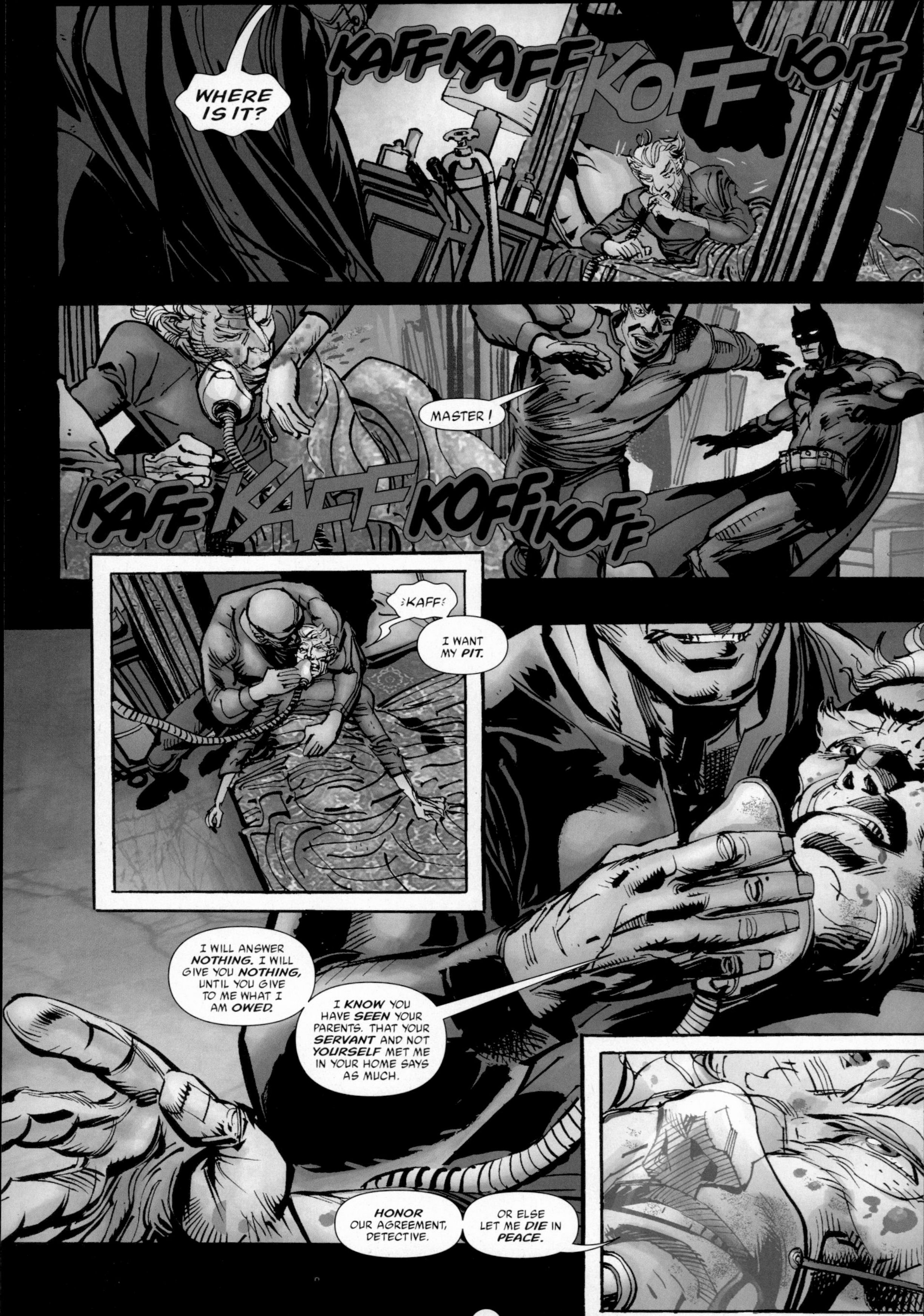

WHERE IS IT?
KAFF KAFF KOFF KOFF
MASTER!
KAFF KAFF KOFF KOFF
KAFF
I WANT MY PIT.
I WILL ANSWER NOTHING. I WILL GIVE YOU NOTHING, UNTIL YOU GIVE TO ME WHAT I AM OWED.
I KNOW YOU HAVE SEEN YOUR PARENTS. THAT YOUR SERVANT AND NOT YOURSELF MET ME IN YOUR HOME SAYS AS MUCH.
HONOR OUR AGREEMENT, DETECTIVE.
OR ELSE LET ME DIE IN PEACE.

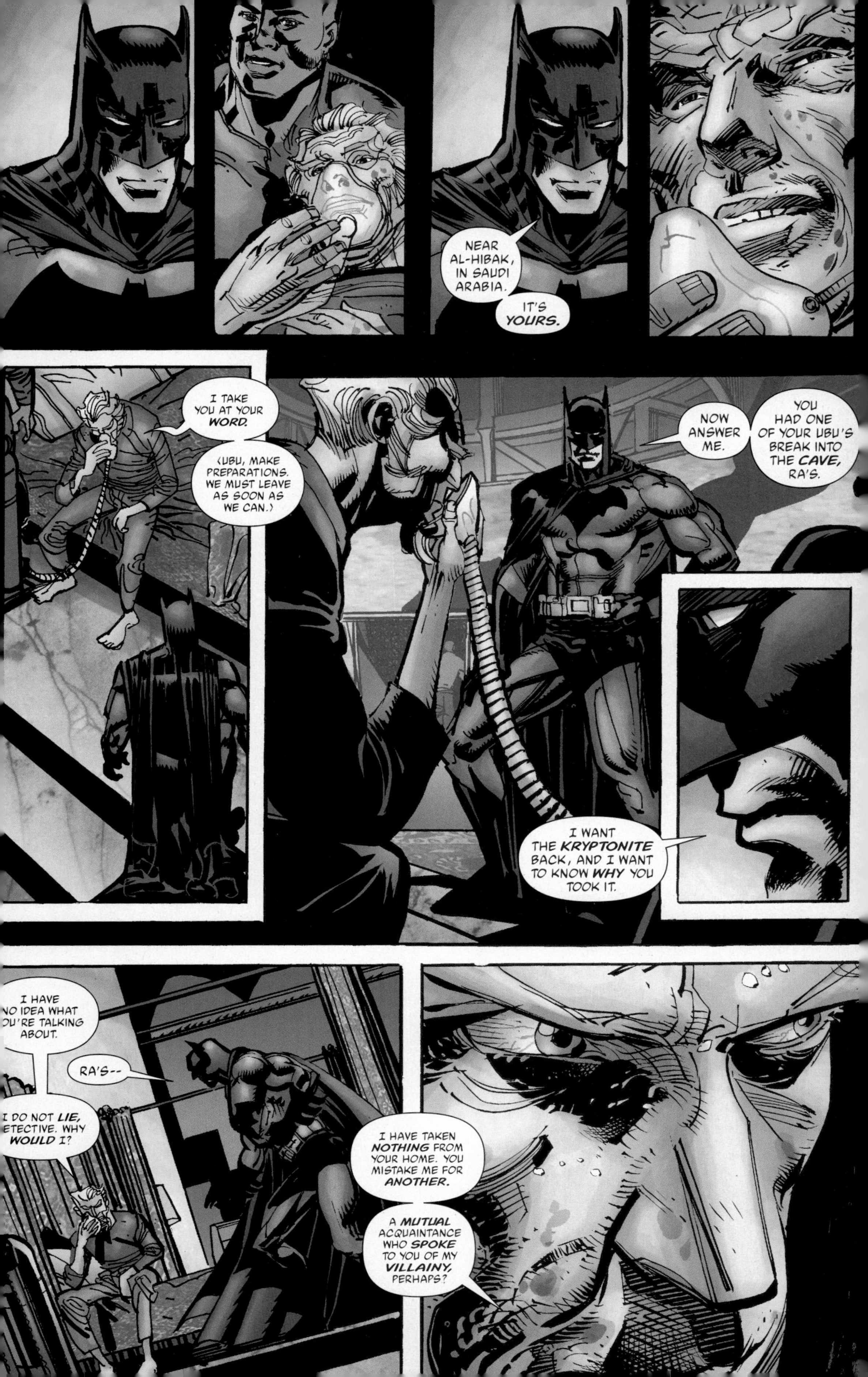
NEAR AL-HIBAK, IN SAUDI ARABIA.
IT'S YOURS.
I TAKE YOU AT YOUR WORD.
‹UBU, MAKE PREPARATIONS. WE MUST LEAVE AS SOON AS WE CAN.›
NOW ANSWER ME.
YOU HAD ONE OF YOUR UBU'S BREAK INTO THE CAVE, RA'S.
I WANT THE KRYPTONITE BACK, AND I WANT TO KNOW WHY YOU TOOK IT.
I HAVE NO IDEA WHAT OU'RE TALKING ABOUT.
RA'S--
I DO NOT LIE, ETECTIVE. WHY WOULD I?
I HAVE TAKEN NOTHING FROM YOUR HOME. YOU MISTAKE ME FOR ANOTHER.
A MUTUAL ACQUAINTANCE WHO SPOKE TO YOU OF MY VILLAINY, PERHAPS?

NYSSA.

WHO IS SHE?

HAVE YOU NOT *REALIZED?* MY *DAUGHTER,* DETECTIVE. OR, I SHOULD SAY, MY §KAFF§ *OTHER* DAUGHTER...

...WOULD YOU BELIEVE I CAN *BARELY* RECALL WHAT HER MOTHER *LOOKED* LIKE, LET ALONE THE PEASANT GIRL'S *NAME...*

THERE'S ONLY *ONE* USE FOR THAT *KRYPTONITE.*

INDEED, NYSSA MEANS TO *KILL* HIM. AS TO *WHY,* I CAN ONLY §KAFF§ *SPECULATE.* HER *GOALS* AND MY OWN *DIVERGED* CENTURIES AGO.

I SUSPECT SHE WISHES TO *CRAFT* A *UNIFYING* MOMENT. TO *SHATTER,* HOWEVER BRIEFLY, HUMANITY'S *APATHY* AND *SELFISHNESS.*

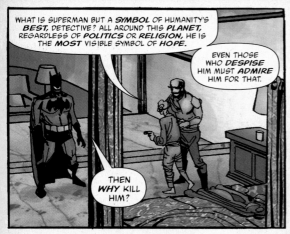

WHAT IS SUPERMAN BUT A *SYMBOL* OF HUMANITY'S *BEST,* DETECTIVE? ALL AROUND THIS *PLANET,* REGARDLESS OF *POLITICS* OR *RELIGION,* HE IS THE *MOST* VISIBLE SYMBOL OF *HOPE.*

EVEN THOSE WHO *DESPISE* HIM MUST *ADMIRE* HIM FOR THAT.

THEN *WHY* KILL HIM?

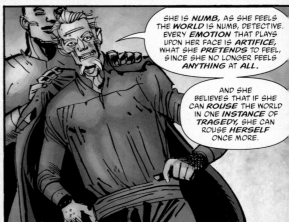

SHE IS *NUMB,* AS SHE FEELS THE *WORLD* IS NUMB, DETECTIVE. EVERY *EMOTION* THAT PLAYS UPON HER FACE IS *ARTIFICE,* WHAT SHE *PRETENDS* TO FEEL, SINCE SHE NO LONGER FEELS *ANYTHING* AT ALL.

AND SHE BELIEVES THAT IF SHE CAN *ROUSE* THE WORLD IN ONE *INSTANCE* OF *TRAGEDY,* SHE CAN ROUSE *HERSELF* ONCE MORE.

KILL SUPERMAN AND THE WORLD WEEPS.

AND IN THE *WORLD'S* TEARS, DETECTIVE, SHE *HOPES* TO FIND HER *OWN* ONCE MORE.

NEVER REALIZING THE *ONE* THING THAT COULD *TRULY* BRING THAT HOPE TO *LIFE.*

FAREWELL.

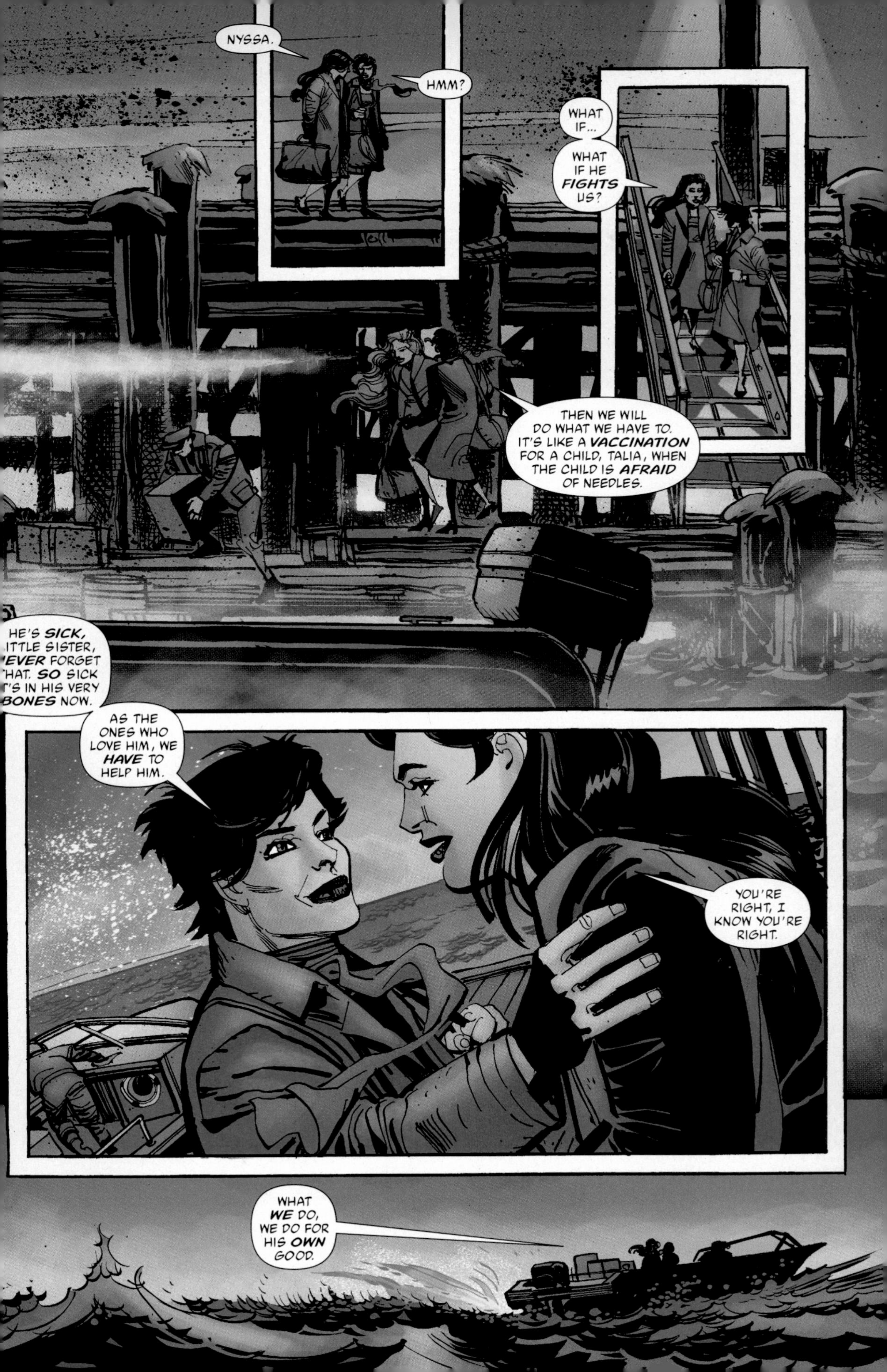
NYSSA.
HMM?
WHAT IF...
WHAT IF HE FIGHTS US?
THEN WE WILL DO WHAT WE HAVE TO. IT'S LIKE A VACCINATION FOR A CHILD, TALIA, WHEN THE CHILD IS AFRAID OF NEEDLES.
HE'S SICK, ITTLE SISTER, EVER FORGET HAT. SO SICK T'S IN HIS VERY BONES NOW.
AS THE ONES WHO LOVE HIM, WE HAVE TO HELP HIM.
YOU'RE RIGHT, I KNOW YOU'RE RIGHT.
WHAT WE DO, WE DO FOR HIS OWN GOOD.

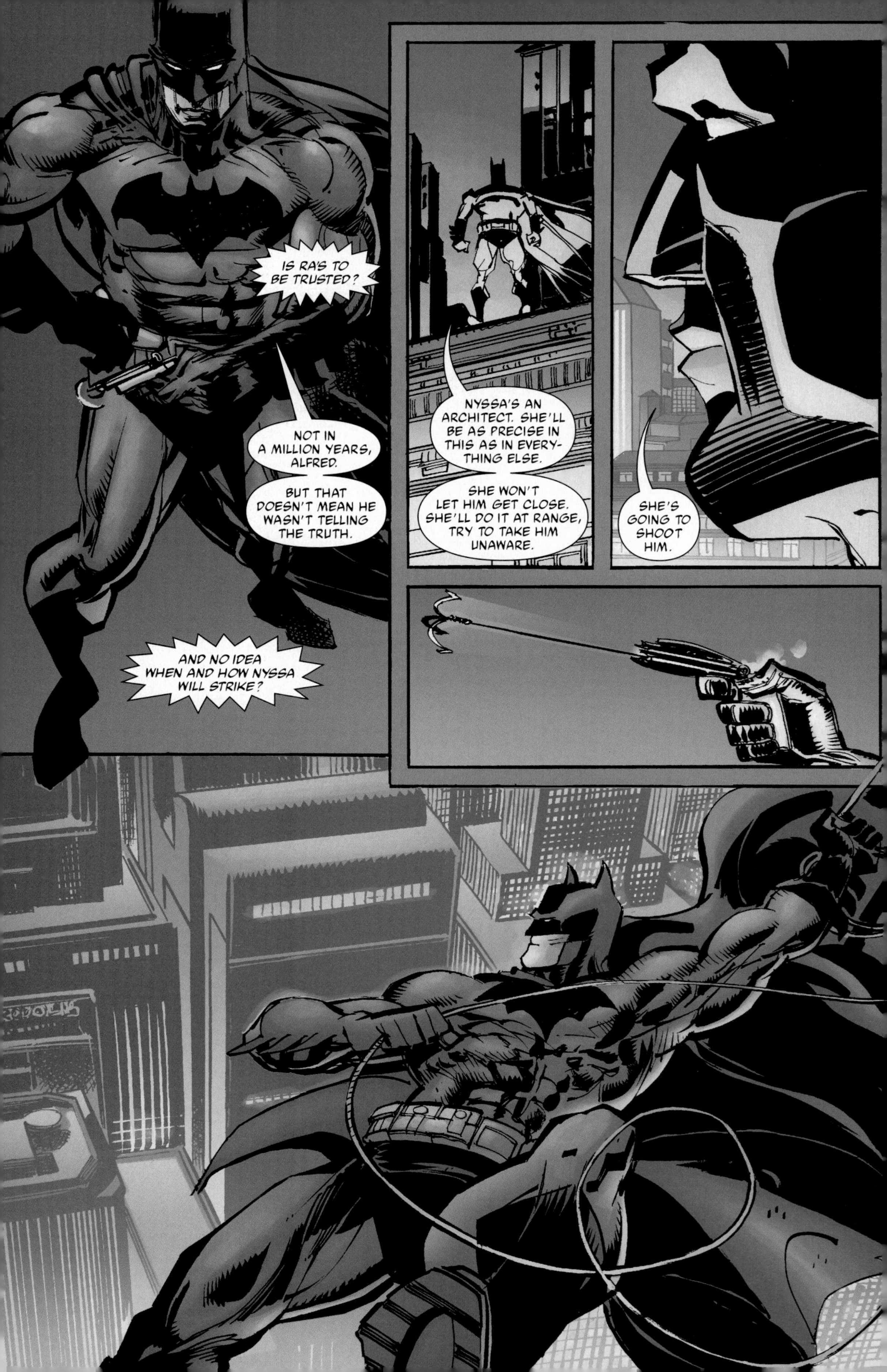
IS RA'S TO BE TRUSTED?
NOT IN A MILLION YEARS, ALFRED.
BUT THAT DOESN'T MEAN HE WASN'T TELLING THE TRUTH.
AND NO IDEA WHEN AND HOW NYSSA WILL STRIKE?
NYSSA'S AN ARCHITECT. SHE'LL BE AS PRECISE IN THIS AS IN EVERY-THING ELSE.
SHE WON'T LET HIM GET CLOSE. SHE'LL DO IT AT RANGE, TRY TO TAKE HIM UNAWARE.
SHE'S GOING TO SHOOT HIM.

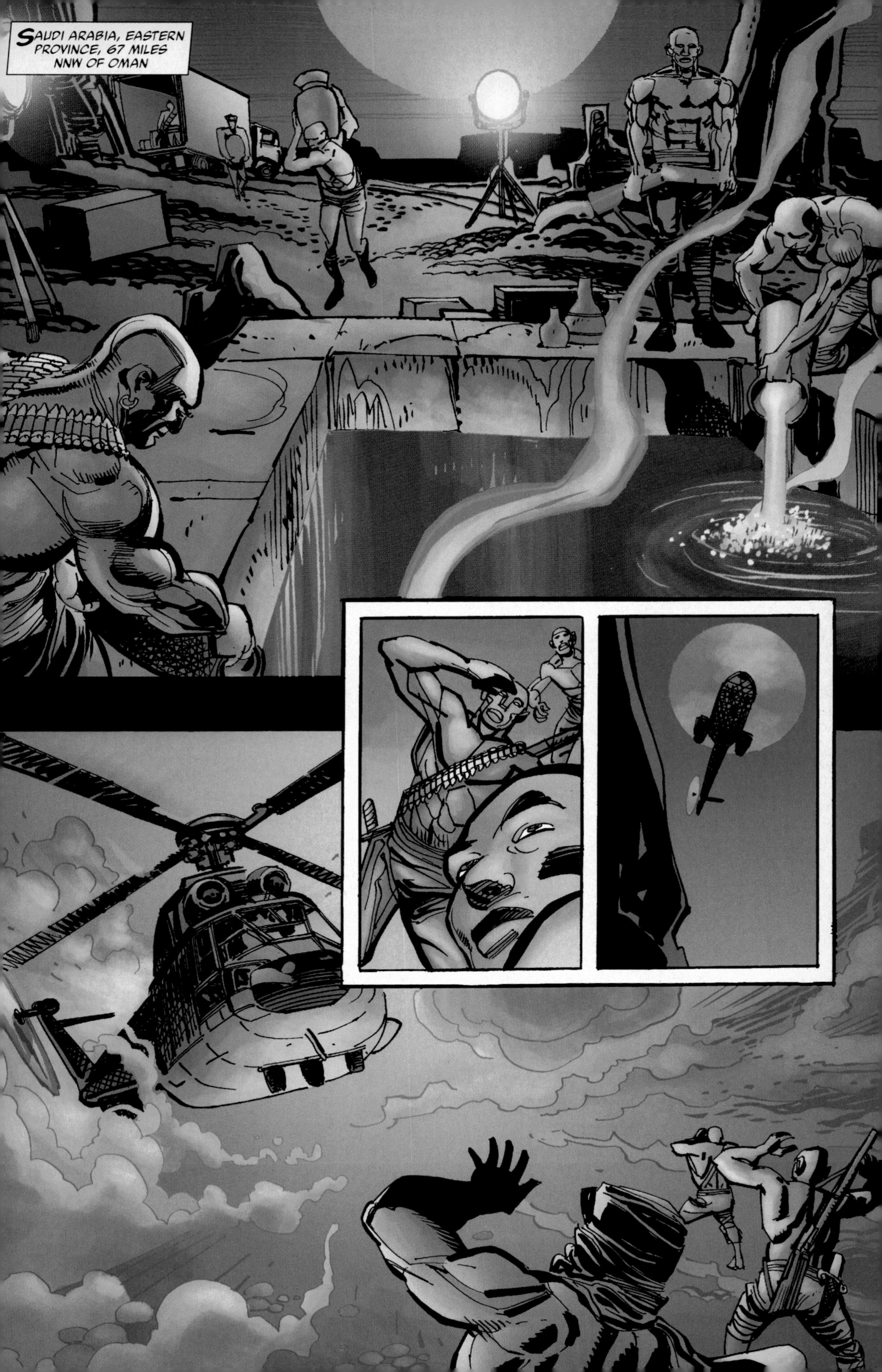
SAUDI ARABIA, EASTERN PROVINCE, 67 MILES NNW OF OMAN

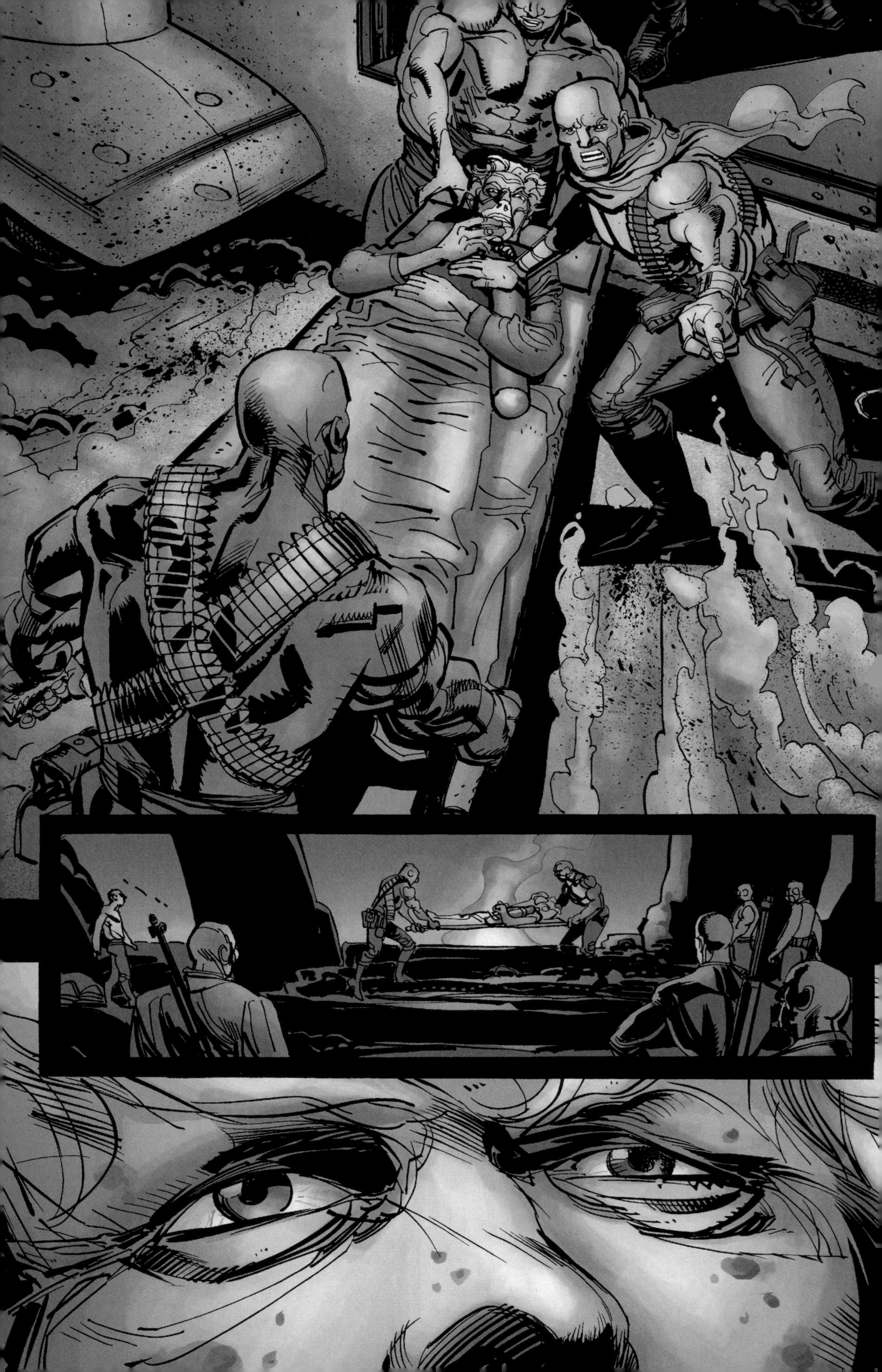

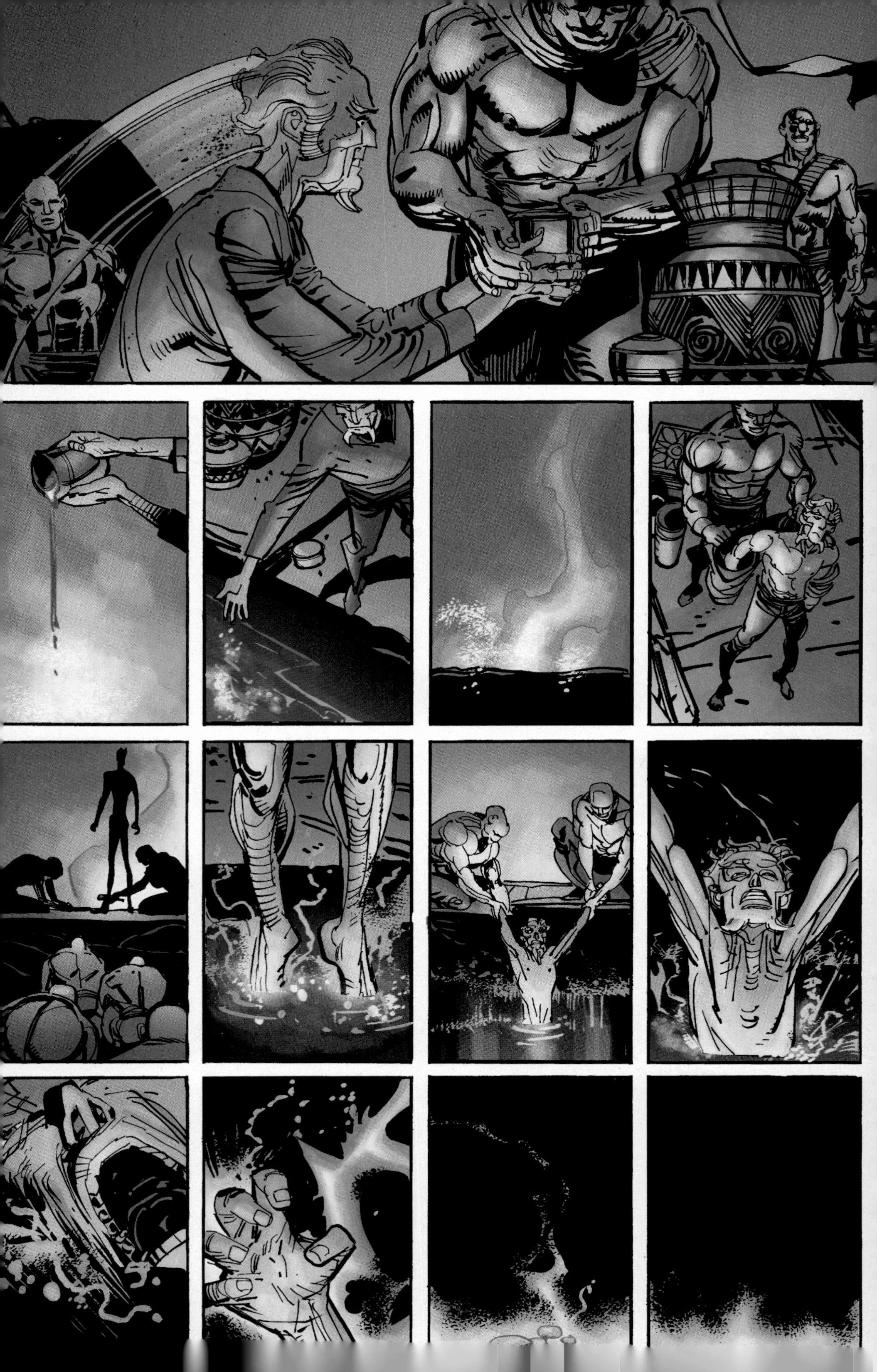

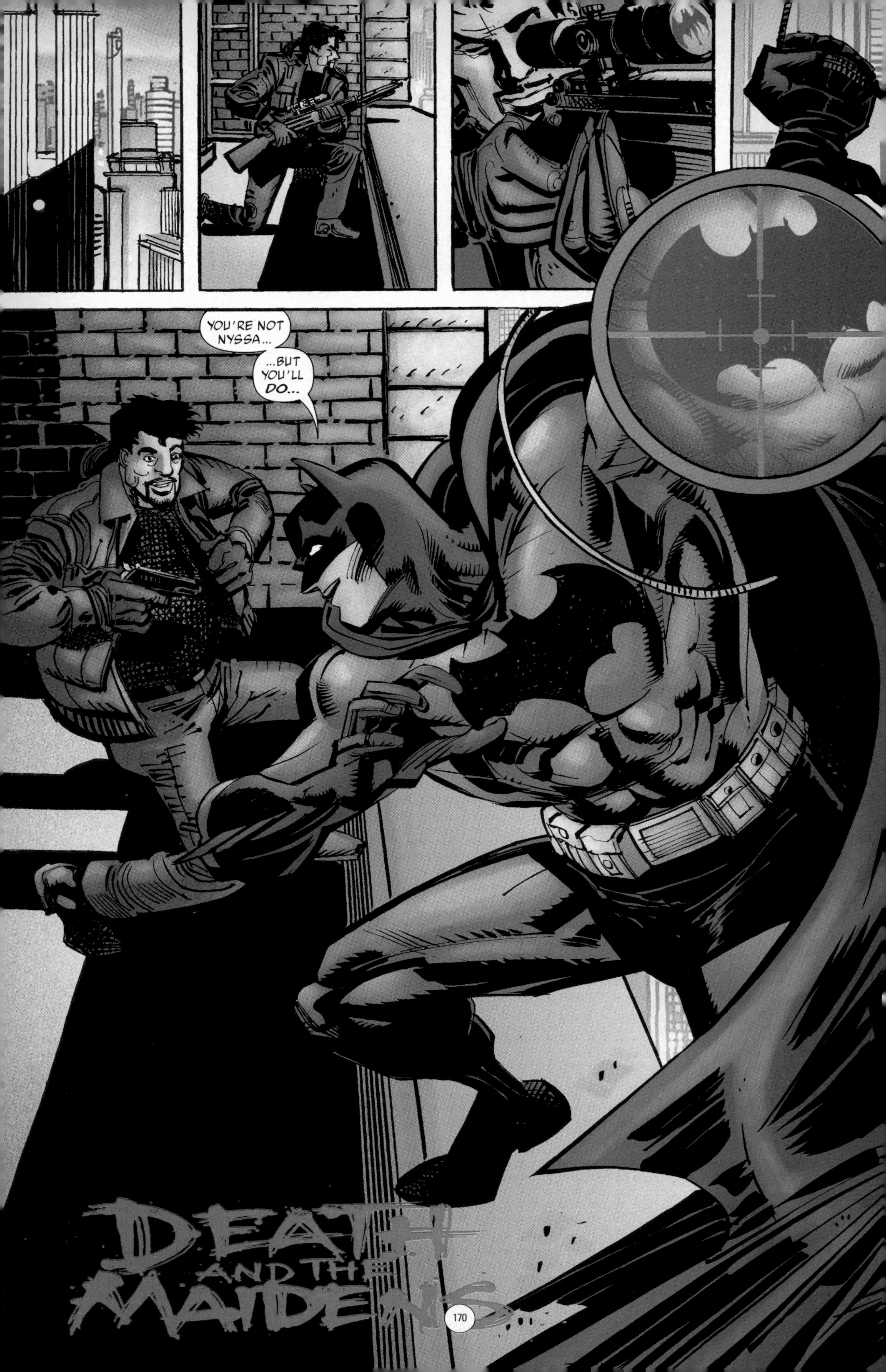

YOU'RE NOT NYSSA...
...BUT YOU'LL DO...
DEATH AND THE MAIDENS

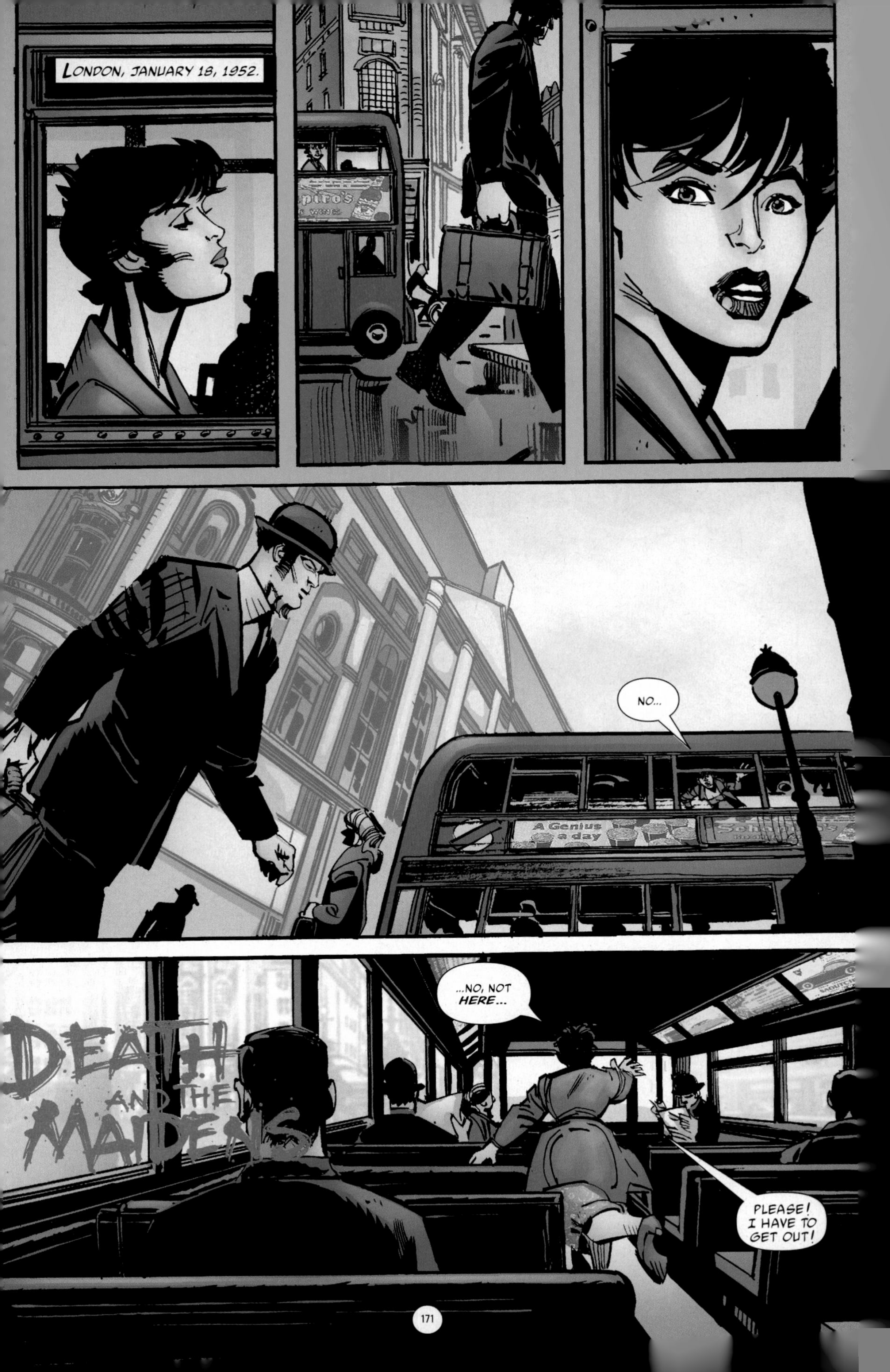
LONDON, JANUARY 18, 1952.
NO...
A Genius a day
...NO, NOT HERE...
DEATH AND THE MAIDENS
PLEASE! I HAVE TO GET OUT!

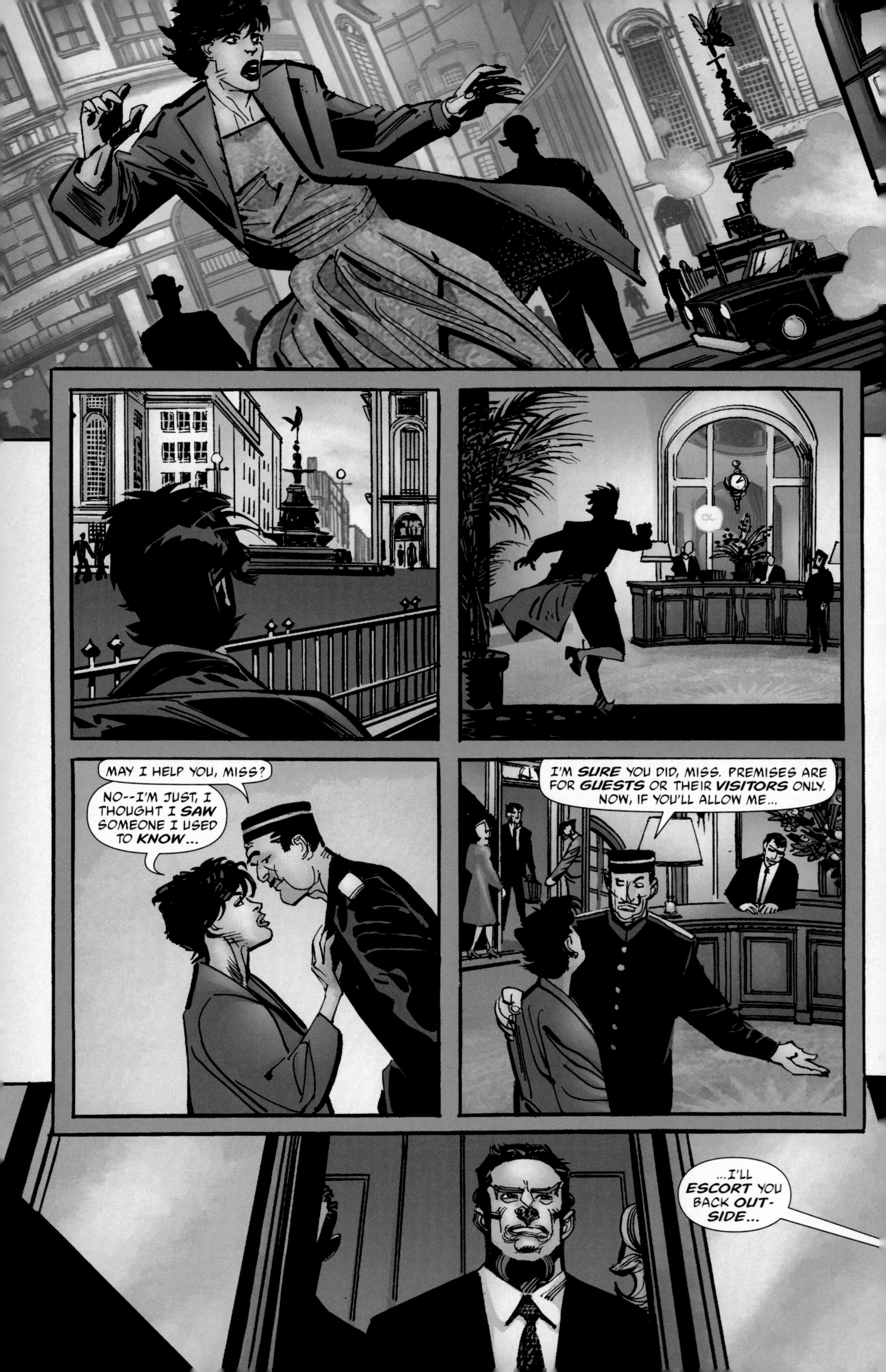
MAY I HELP YOU, MISS?
NO--I'M JUST, I THOUGHT I SAW SOMEONE I USED TO KNOW...
I'M SURE YOU DID, MISS. PREMISES ARE FOR GUESTS OR THEIR VISITORS ONLY. NOW, IF YOU'LL ALLOW ME...
...I'LL ESCORT YOU BACK OUT-SIDE...

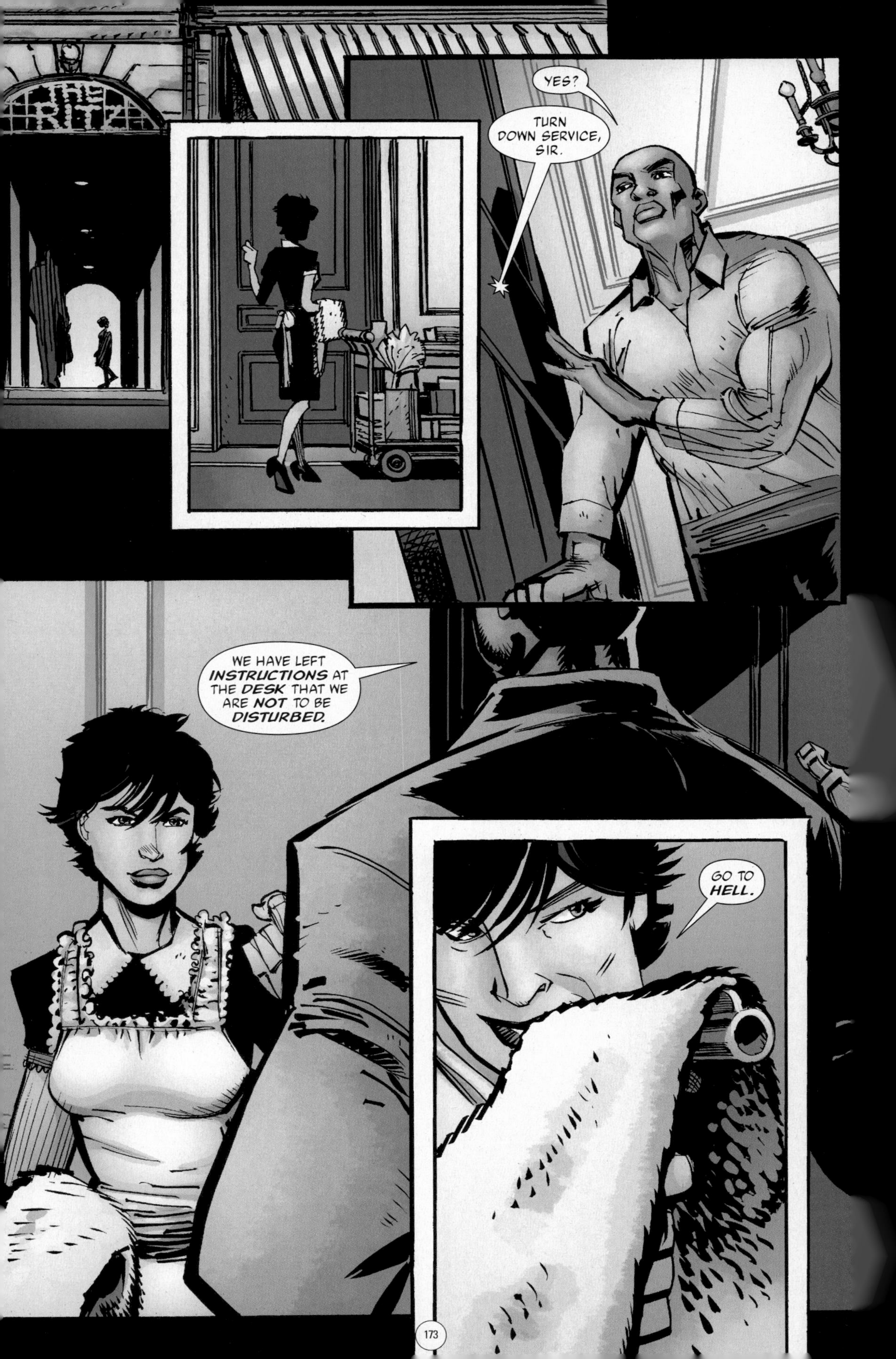
THE RITZ
YES?
TURN DOWN SERVICE, SIR.
WE HAVE LEFT INSTRUCTIONS AT THE DESK THAT WE ARE NOT TO BE DISTURBED.
GO TO HELL.

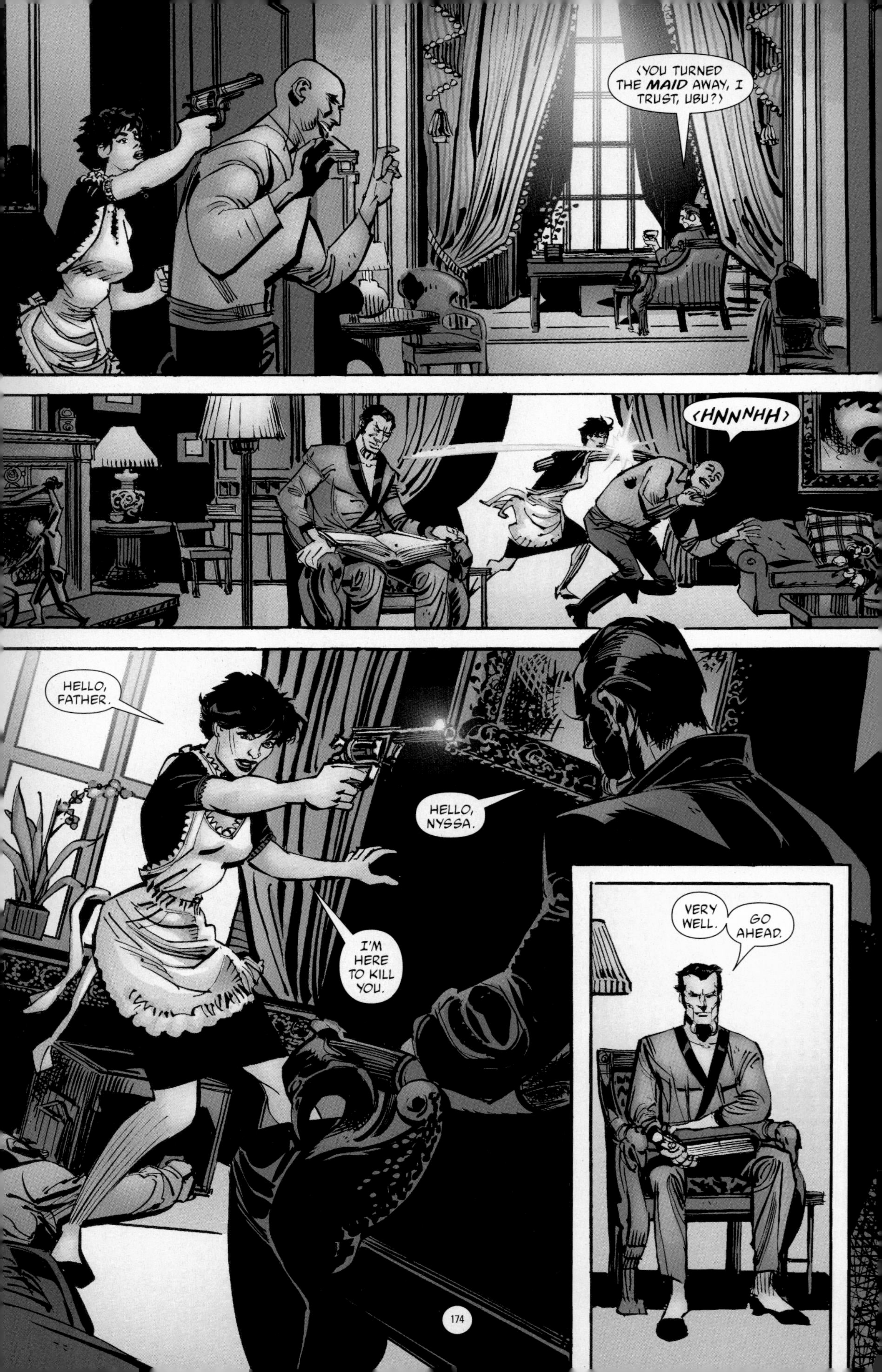
‹YOU TURNED THE MAID AWAY, I TRUST, UBU?›
‹HNNNHH›
HELLO, FATHER.
HELLO, NYSSA.
I'M HERE TO KILL YOU.
VERY WELL.
GO AHEAD.

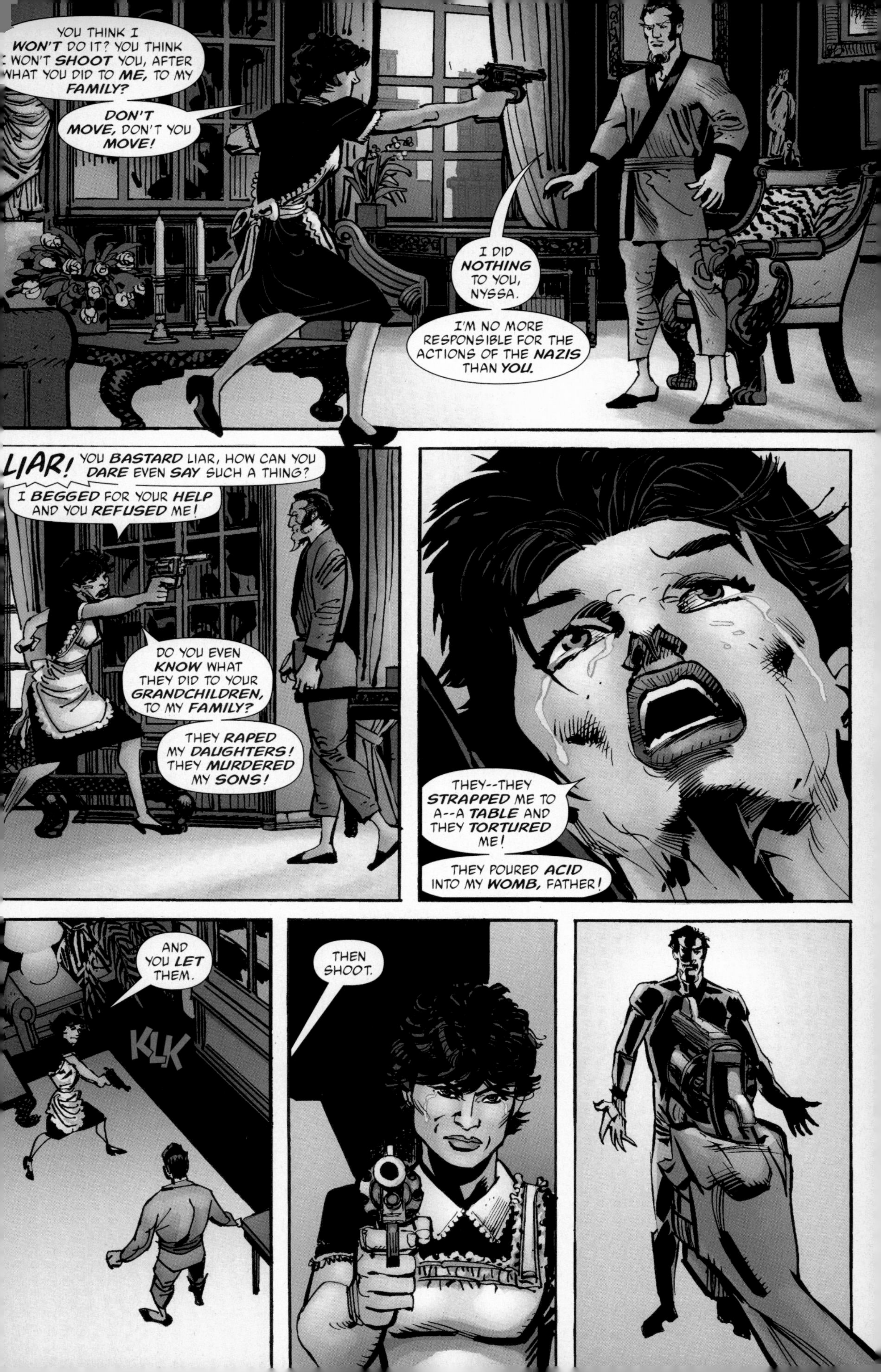
YOU THINK I WON'T DO IT? YOU THINK I WON'T SHOOT YOU, AFTER WHAT YOU DID TO ME, TO MY FAMILY?
DON'T MOVE, DON'T YOU MOVE!
I DID NOTHING TO YOU, NYSSA.
I'M NO MORE RESPONSIBLE FOR THE ACTIONS OF THE NAZIS THAN YOU.
LIAR! YOU BASTARD LIAR, HOW CAN YOU DARE EVEN SAY SUCH A THING?
I BEGGED FOR YOUR HELP AND YOU REFUSED ME!
DO YOU EVEN KNOW WHAT THEY DID TO YOUR GRANDCHILDREN, TO MY FAMILY?
THEY RAPED MY DAUGHTERS! THEY MURDERED MY SONS!
THEY--THEY STRAPPED ME TO A--A TABLE AND THEY TORTURED ME!
THEY POURED ACID INTO MY WOMB, FATHER!
AND YOU LET THEM.
KLIK
THEN SHOOT.

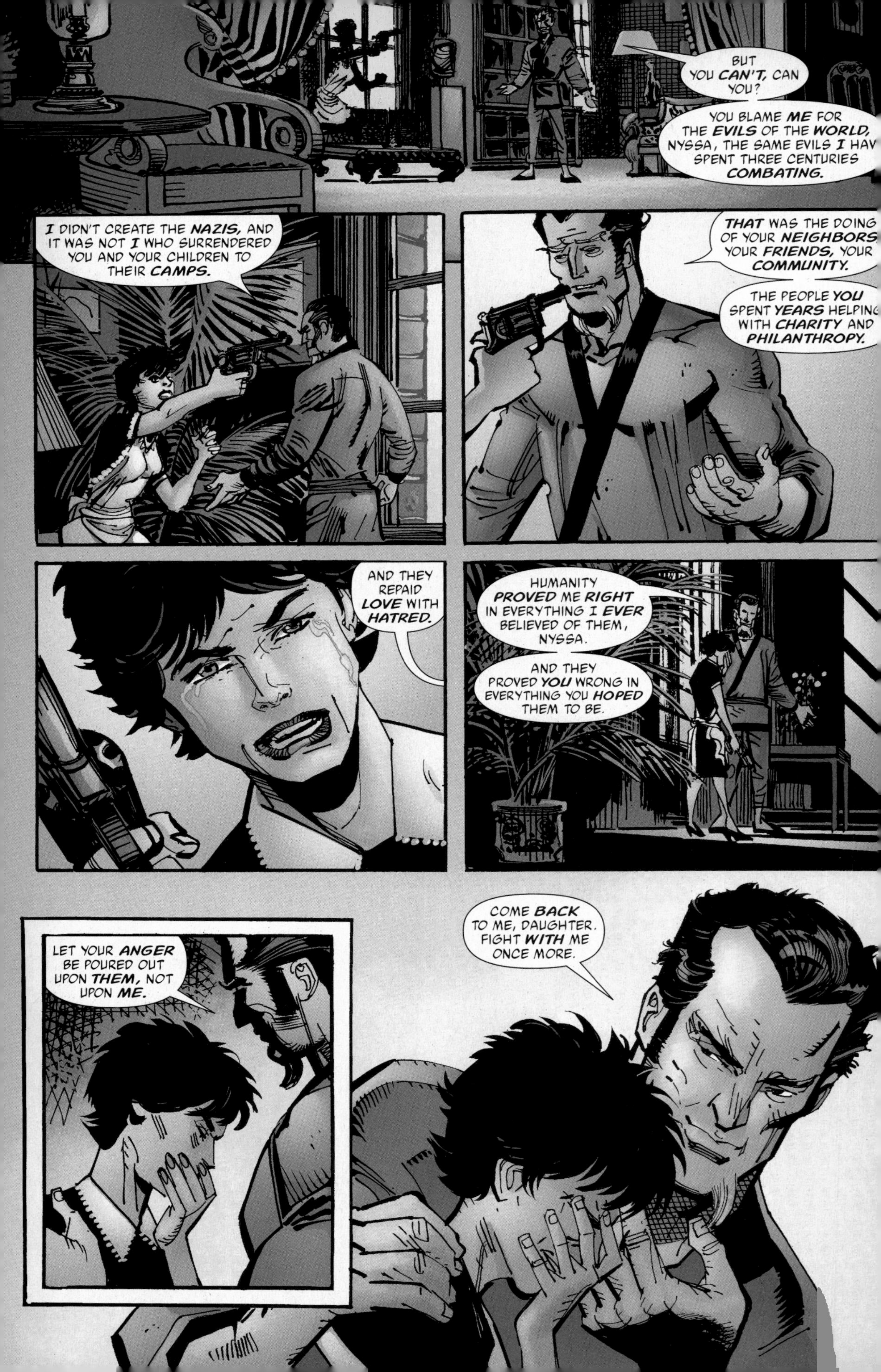

BUT YOU CAN'T, CAN YOU?
YOU BLAME ME FOR THE EVILS OF THE WORLD, NYSSA, THE SAME EVILS I HAV SPENT THREE CENTURIES COMBATING.
I DIDN'T CREATE THE NAZIS, AND IT WAS NOT I WHO SURRENDERED YOU AND YOUR CHILDREN TO THEIR CAMPS.
THAT WAS THE DOING OF YOUR NEIGHBORS YOUR FRIENDS, YOUR COMMUNITY.
THE PEOPLE YOU SPENT YEARS HELPING WITH CHARITY AND PHILANTHROPY.
AND THEY REPAID LOVE WITH HATRED.
HUMANITY PROVED ME RIGHT IN EVERYTHING I EVER BELIEVED OF THEM, NYSSA.
AND THEY PROVED YOU WRONG IN EVERYTHING YOU HOPED THEM TO BE.
LET YOUR ANGER BE POURED OUT UPON THEM, NOT UPON ME.
COME BACK TO ME, DAUGHTER. FIGHT WITH ME ONCE MORE.

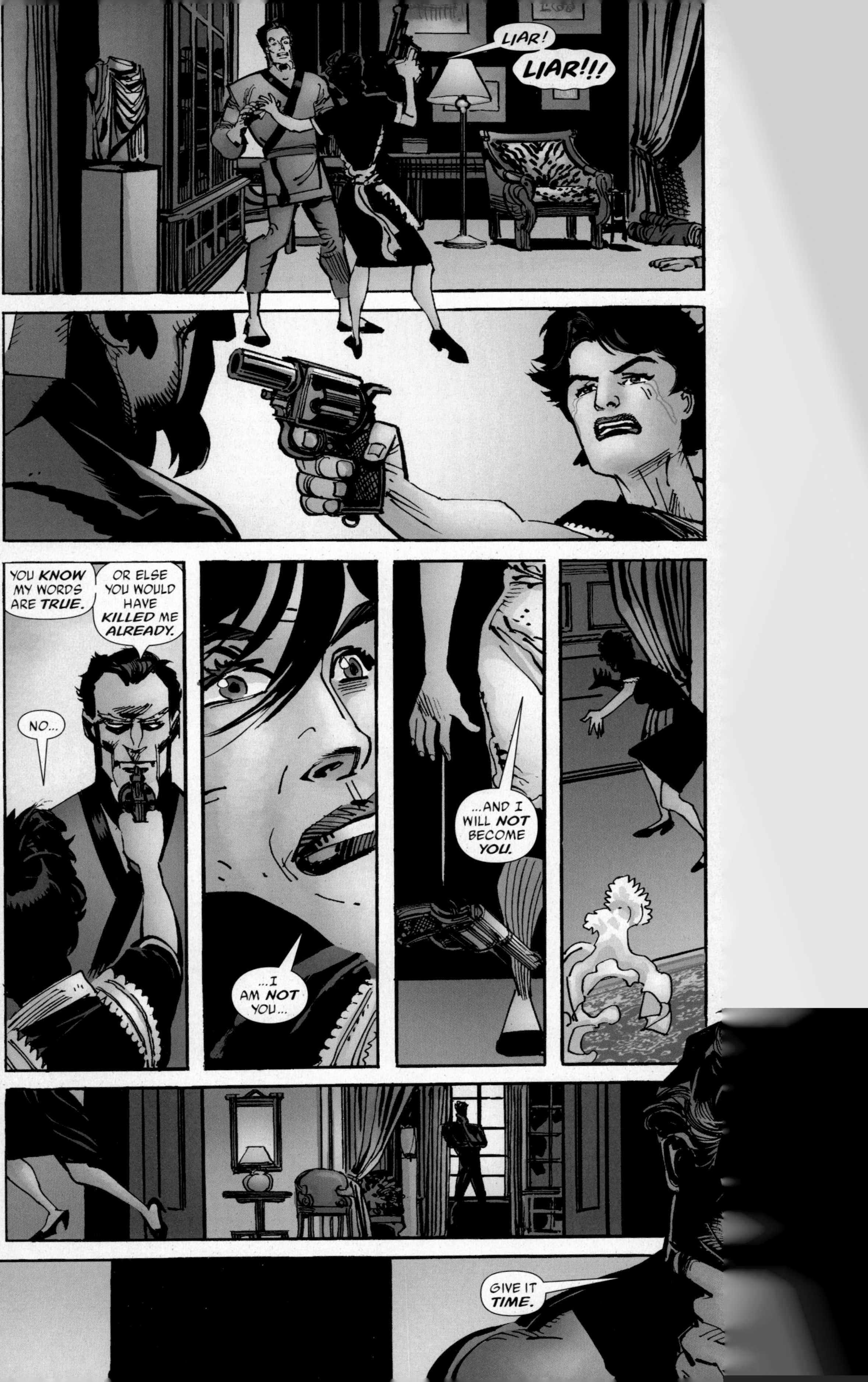
LIAR!
LIAR!!!
YOU KNOW MY WORDS ARE TRUE.
OR ELSE YOU WOULD HAVE KILLED ME ALREADY.
NO...
...I AM NOT YOU...
...AND I WILL NOT BECOME YOU.
GIVE IT TIME.

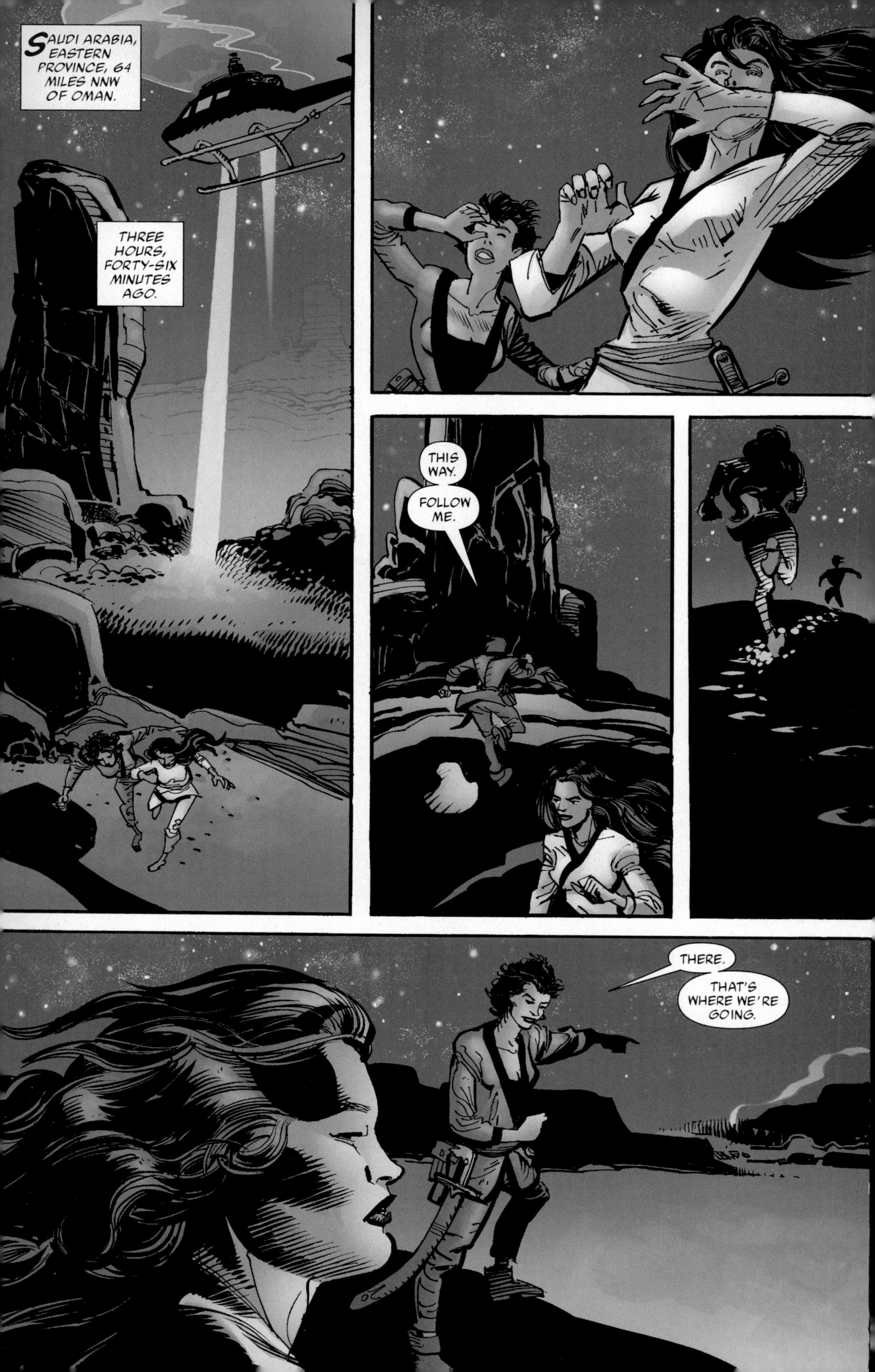
SAUDI ARABIA, EASTERN PROVINCE, 64 MILES NNW OF OMAN.
THREE HOURS, FORTY-SIX MINUTES AGO.
THIS WAY.
FOLLOW ME.
THERE.
THAT'S WHERE WE'RE GOING.

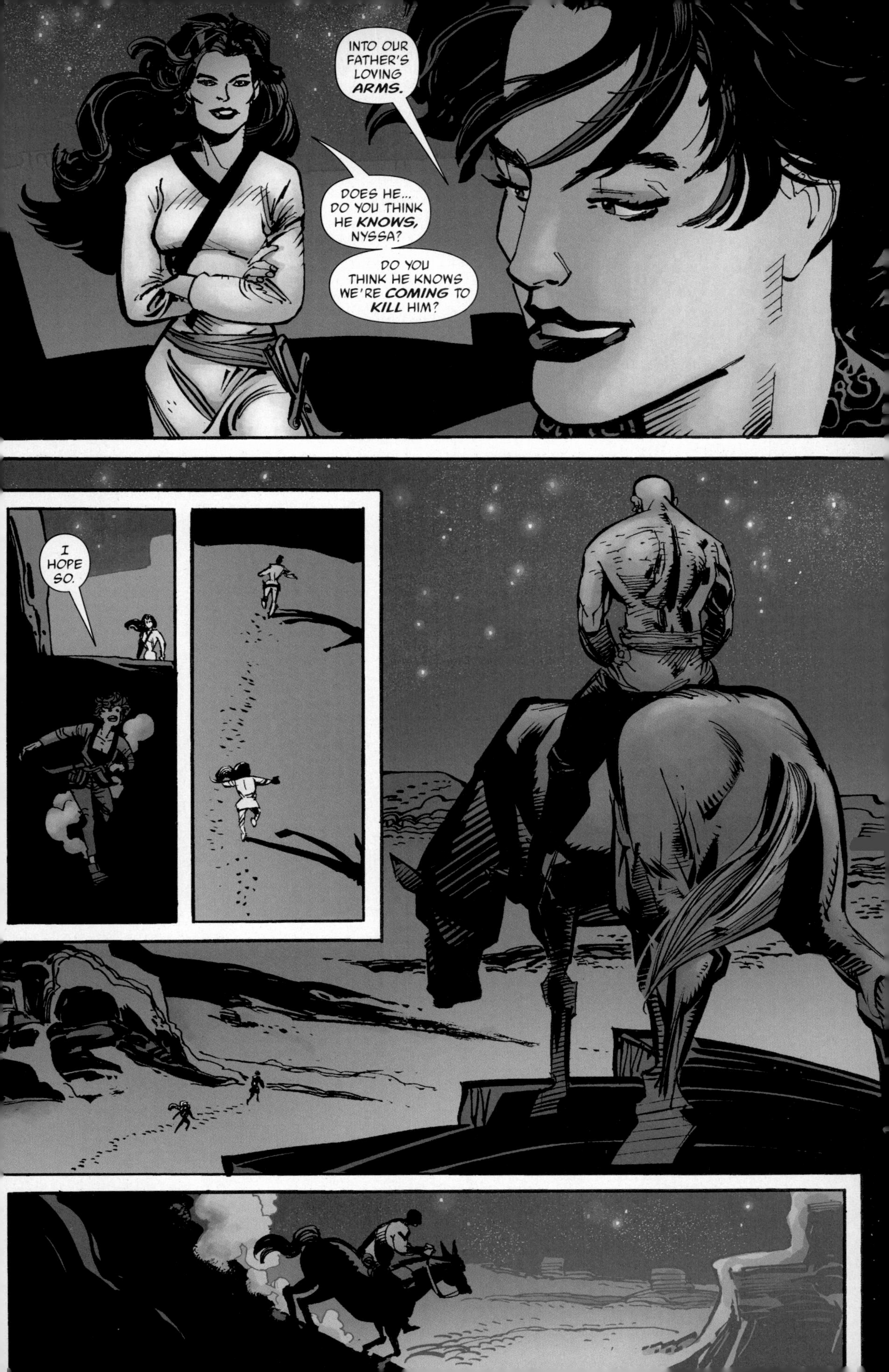
INTO OUR FATHER'S LOVING **ARMS.**
DOES HE... DO YOU THINK HE **KNOWS,** NYSSA?
DO YOU THINK HE KNOWS WE'RE **COMING** TO **KILL** HIM?
I HOPE SO.

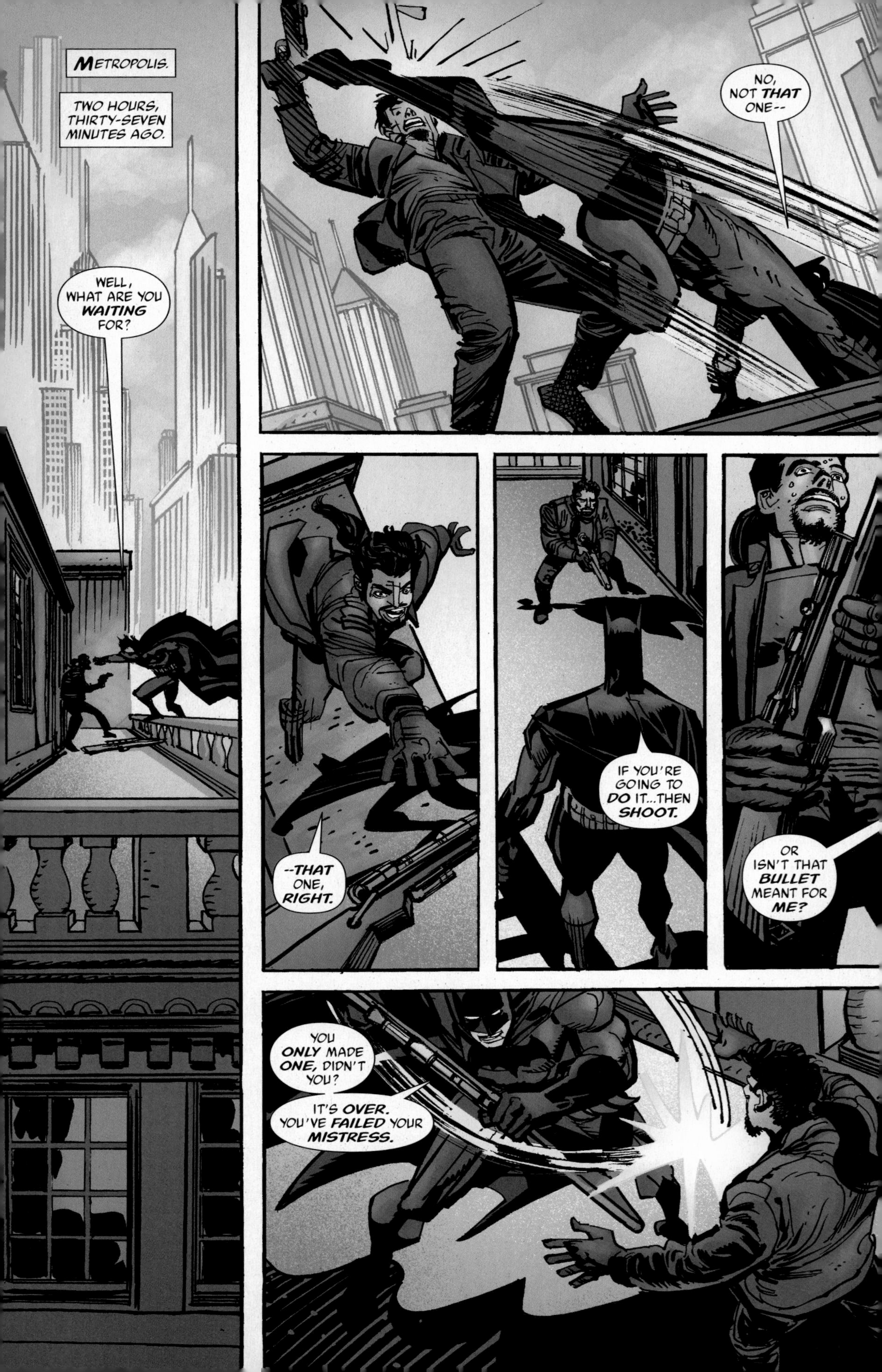
METROPOLIS.
TWO HOURS, THIRTY-SEVEN MINUTES AGO.
WELL, WHAT ARE YOU WAITING FOR?
NO, NOT THAT ONE--
--THAT ONE, RIGHT.
IF YOU'RE GOING TO DO IT...THEN SHOOT.
OR ISN'T THAT BULLET MEANT FOR ME?
YOU ONLY MADE ONE, DIDN'T YOU?
IT'S OVER. YOU'VE FAILED YOUR MISTRESS.

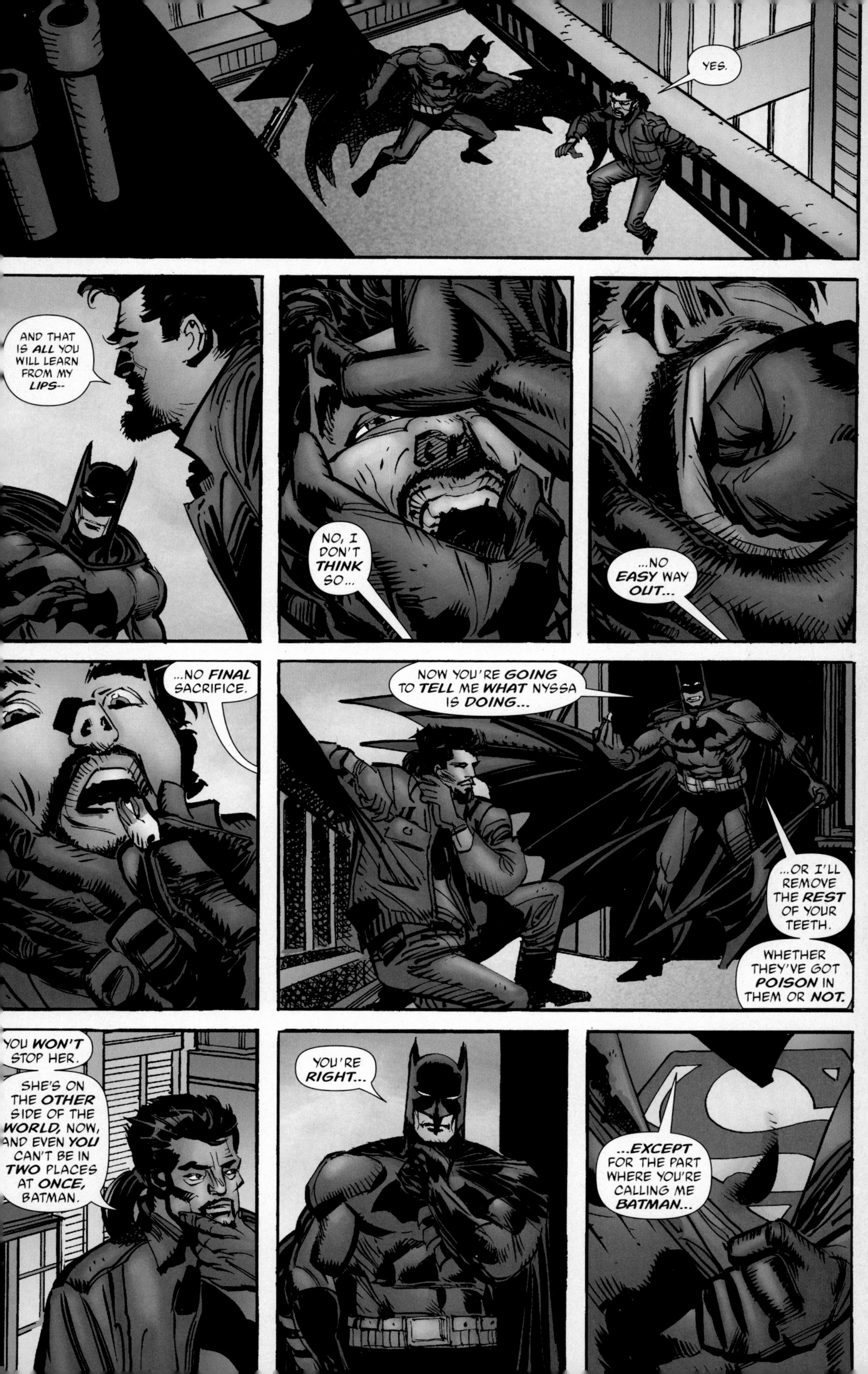
YES.
AND THAT IS ALL YOU WILL LEARN FROM MY LIPS--
NO, I DON'T THINK SO...
...NO EASY WAY OUT...
...NO FINAL SACRIFICE.
NOW YOU'RE GOING TO TELL ME WHAT NYSSA IS DOING...
...OR I'LL REMOVE THE REST OF YOUR TEETH.
WHETHER THEY'VE GOT POISON IN THEM OR NOT.
YOU WON'T STOP HER.
SHE'S ON THE OTHER SIDE OF THE WORLD, NOW, AND EVEN YOU CAN'T BE IN TWO PLACES AT ONCE, BATMAN.
YOU'RE RIGHT...
...EXCEPT FOR THE PART WHERE YOU'RE CALLING ME BATMAN...

...GOING TO **KILL** HIM. HE DOESN'T KNOW **WHERE.**

I DO.

THAT'S ALL?

HE WASN'T EXACT FORTHCOMING, AND IF I'M PRETENDING YOU, I'M **NOT** GOIN USE YOUR **TACTIC**

I'VE SURRENDERED HIM TO THE **AUTHORITIES.**

ALL RIGHT. THANKS.

I THINK **I** SHOULD THANK **YOU.**

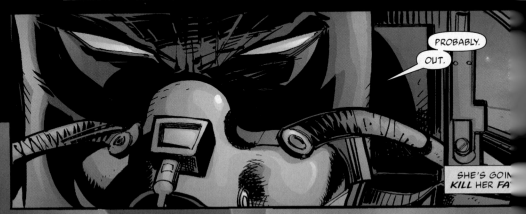

PROBABLY.

OUT.

SHE'S GOIN **KILL** HER **FA**

BECAUSE SHE DOESN'T **FEEL** IT ANYMORE.

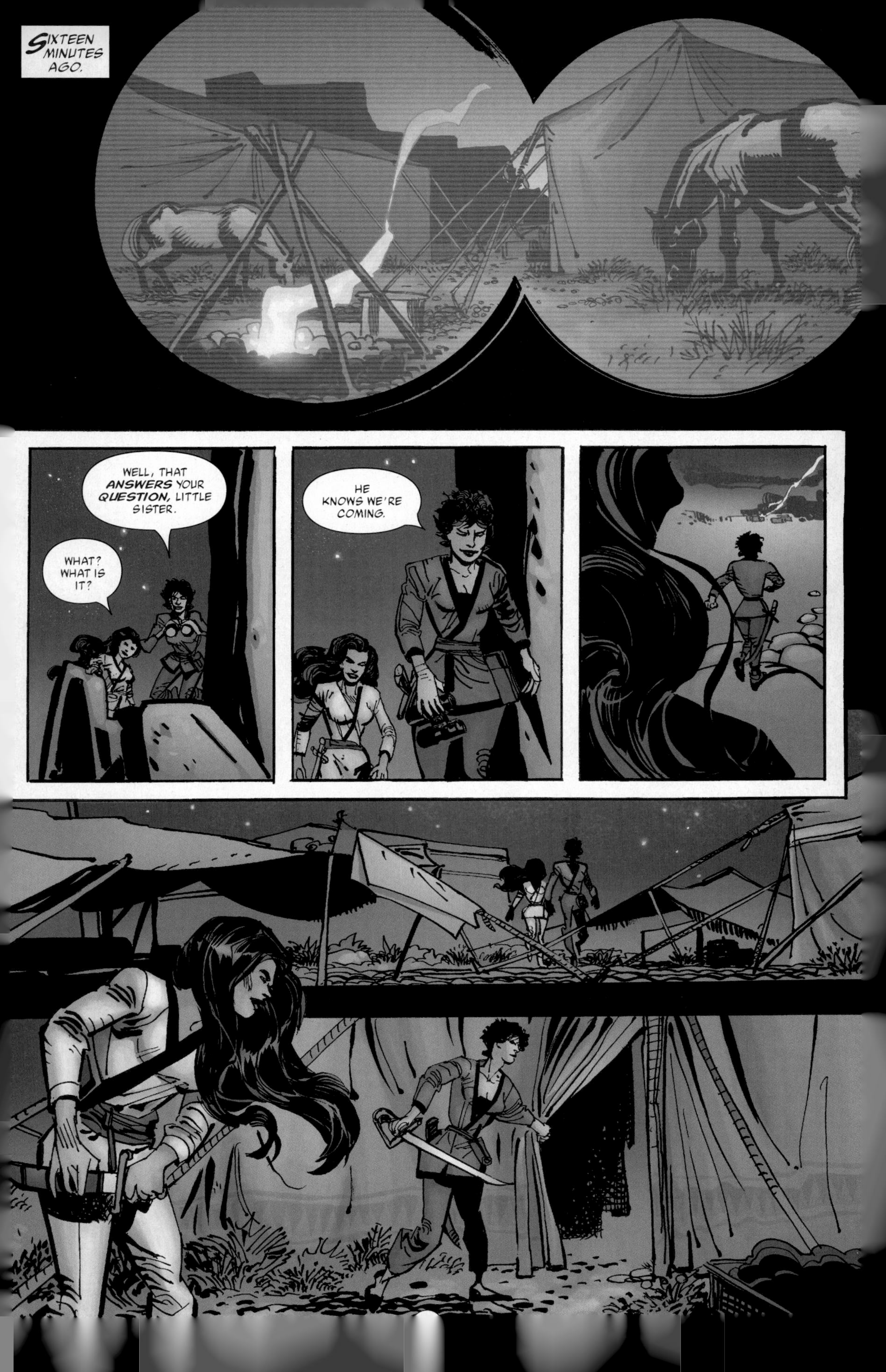

SIXTEEN MINUTES AGO.
WELL, THAT ANSWERS YOUR QUESTION, LITTLE SISTER.
WHAT? WHAT IS IT?
HE KNOWS WE'RE COMING.

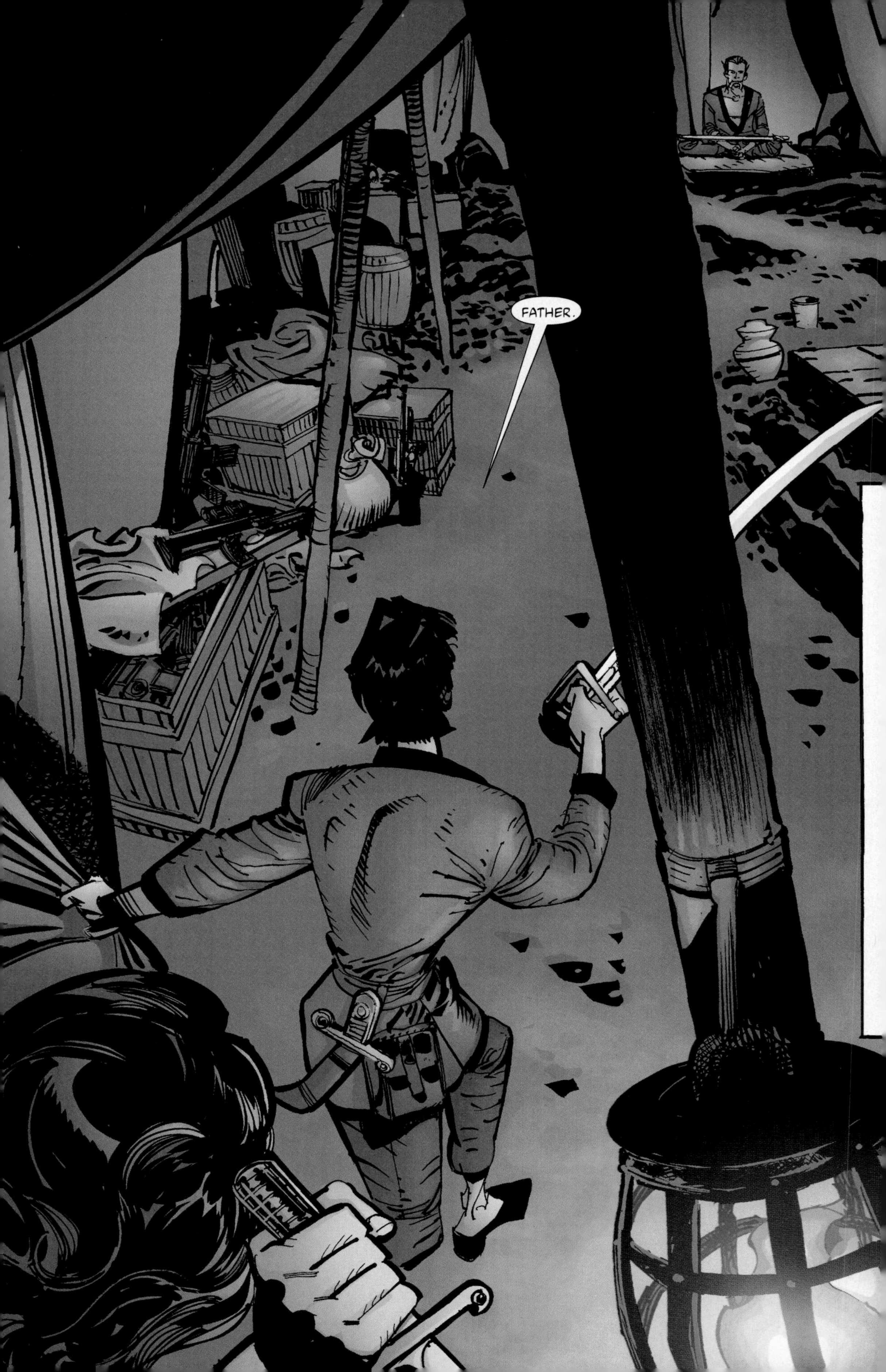
FATHER.

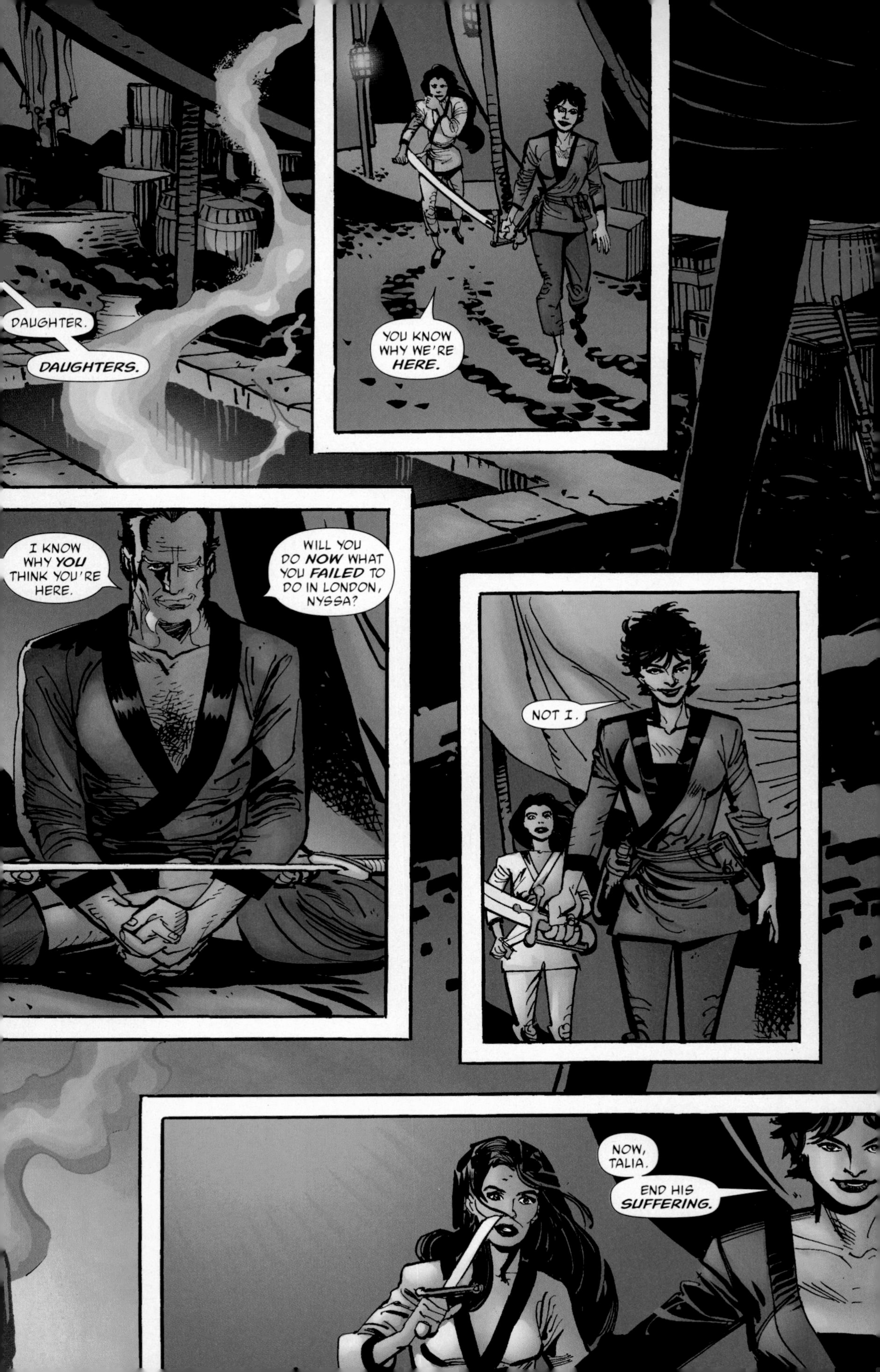
DAUGHTER.
DAUGHTERS.
YOU KNOW WHY WE'RE HERE.
I KNOW WHY YOU THINK YOU'RE HERE.
WILL YOU DO NOW WHAT YOU FAILED TO DO IN LONDON, NYSSA?
NOT I.
NOW, TALIA.
END HIS SUFFERING.

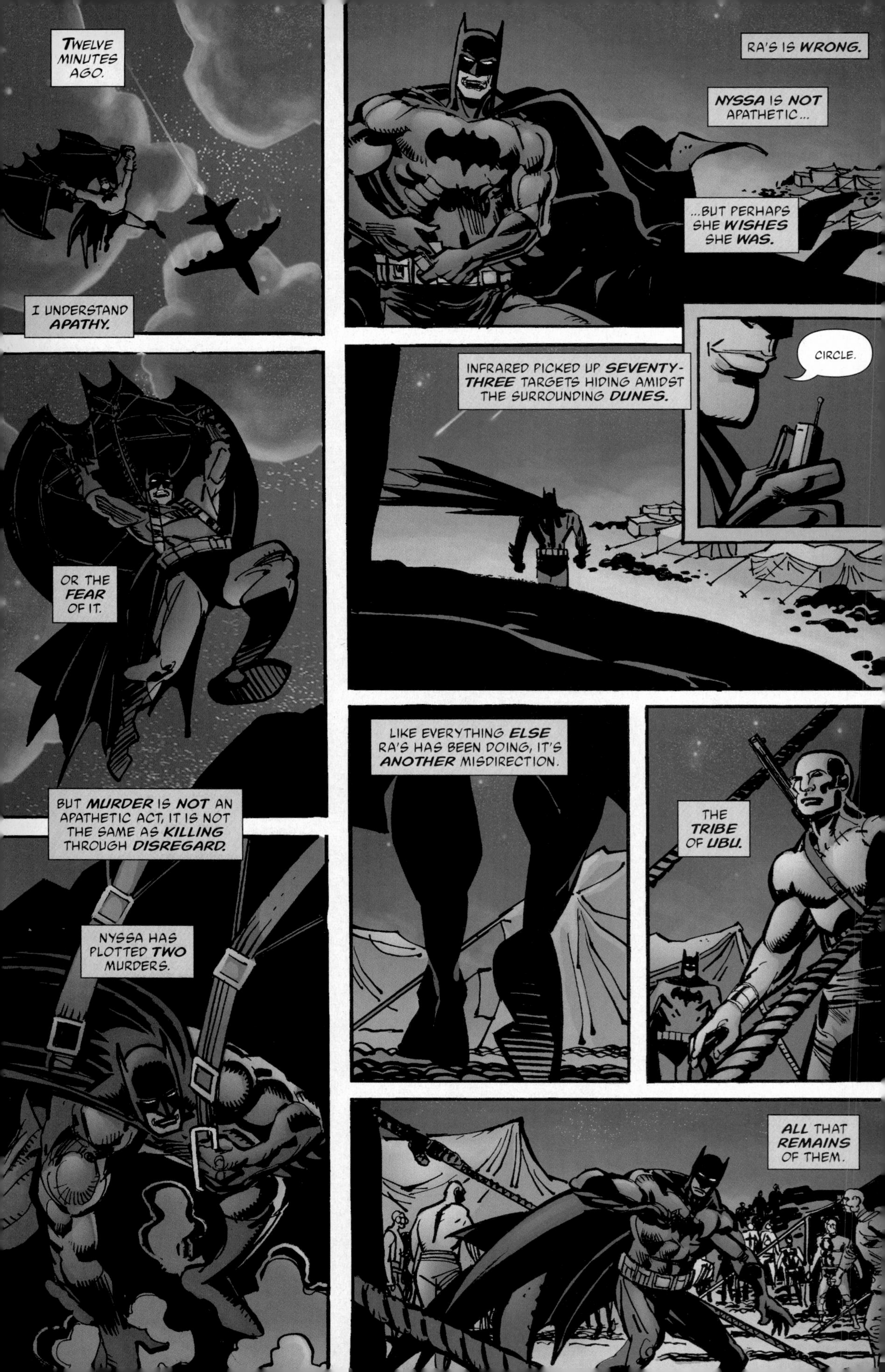
TWELVE MINUTES AGO.
I UNDERSTAND APATHY.
RA'S IS WRONG.
NYSSA IS NOT APATHETIC...
...BUT PERHAPS SHE WISHES SHE WAS.
OR THE FEAR OF IT.
INFRARED PICKED UP SEVENTY-THREE TARGETS HIDING AMIDST THE SURROUNDING DUNES.
CIRCLE.
BUT MURDER IS NOT AN APATHETIC ACT, IT IS NOT THE SAME AS KILLING THROUGH DISREGARD.
NYSSA HAS PLOTTED TWO MURDERS.
LIKE EVERYTHING ELSE RA'S HAS BEEN DOING, IT'S ANOTHER MISDIRECTION.
THE TRIBE OF UBU.
ALL THAT REMAINS OF THEM.

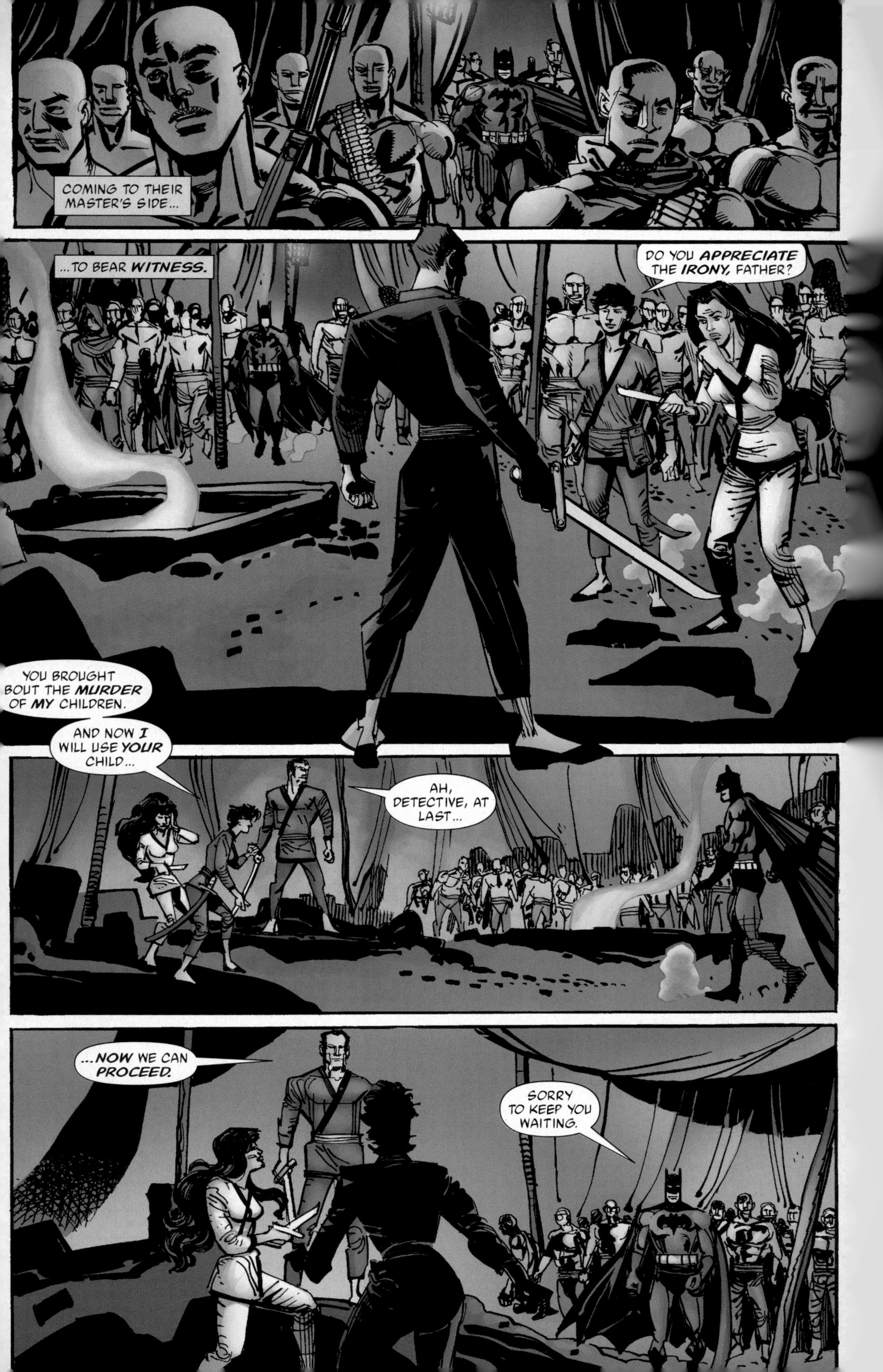
COMING TO THEIR MASTER'S SIDE...
...TO BEAR **WITNESS.**
DO YOU **APPRECIATE** THE **IRONY,** FATHER?
YOU BROUGHT BOUT THE **MURDER** OF **MY** CHILDREN.
AND NOW **I** WILL USE **YOUR** CHILD...
AH, DETECTIVE, AT LAST...
...**NOW** WE CAN **PROCEED.**
SORRY TO KEEP YOU WAITING.

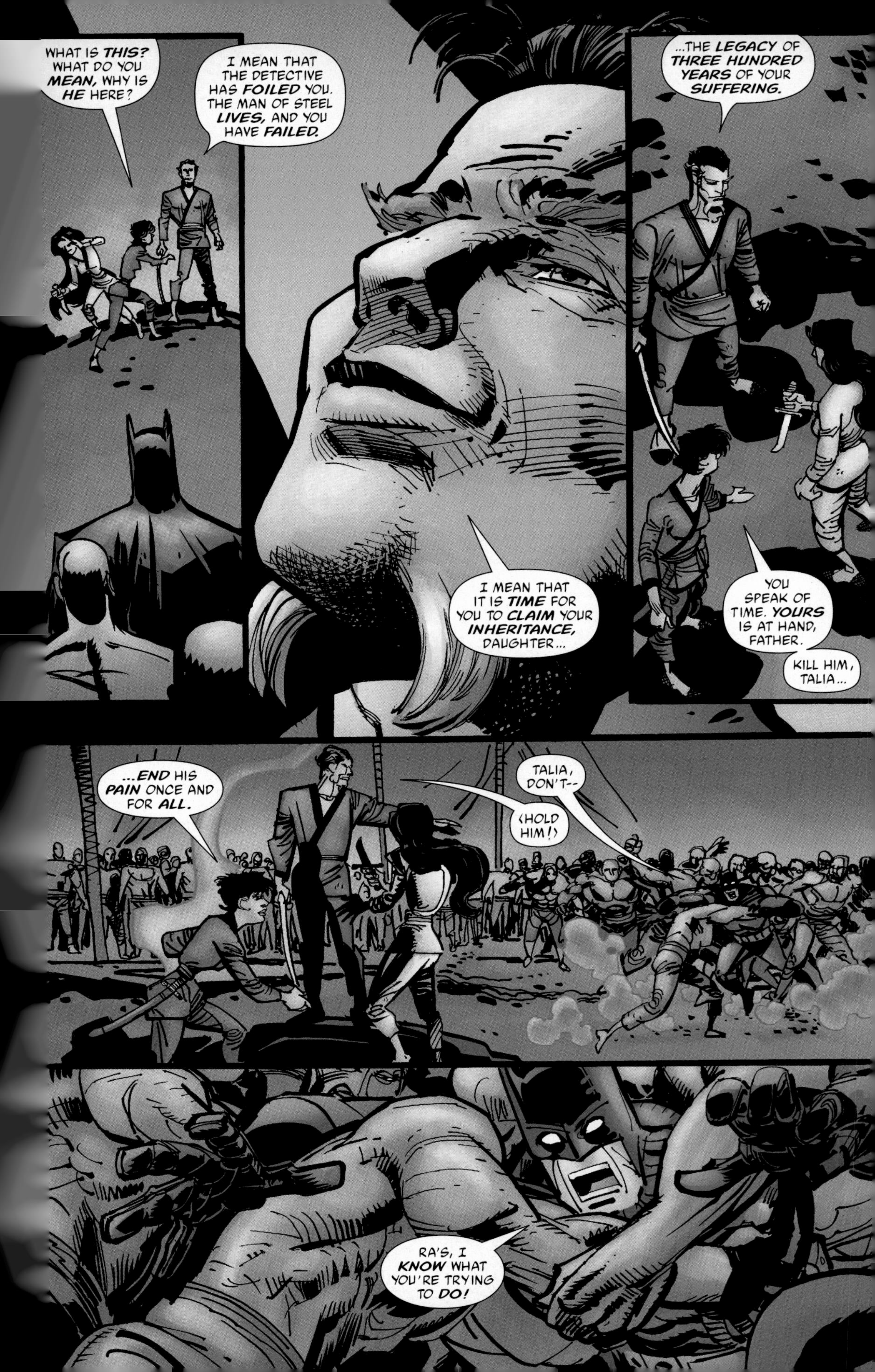

WHAT IS THIS? WHAT DO YOU MEAN, WHY IS HE HERE?
I MEAN THAT THE DETECTIVE HAS FOILED YOU. THE MAN OF STEEL LIVES, AND YOU HAVE FAILED.
I MEAN THAT IT IS TIME FOR YOU TO CLAIM YOUR INHERITANCE, DAUGHTER...
...THE LEGACY OF THREE HUNDRED YEARS OF YOUR SUFFERING.
YOU SPEAK OF TIME. YOURS IS AT HAND, FATHER.
KILL HIM, TALIA...
...END HIS PAIN ONCE AND FOR ALL.
TALIA, DON'T--
‹HOLD HIM!›
RA'S, I KNOW WHAT YOU'RE TRYING TO DO!

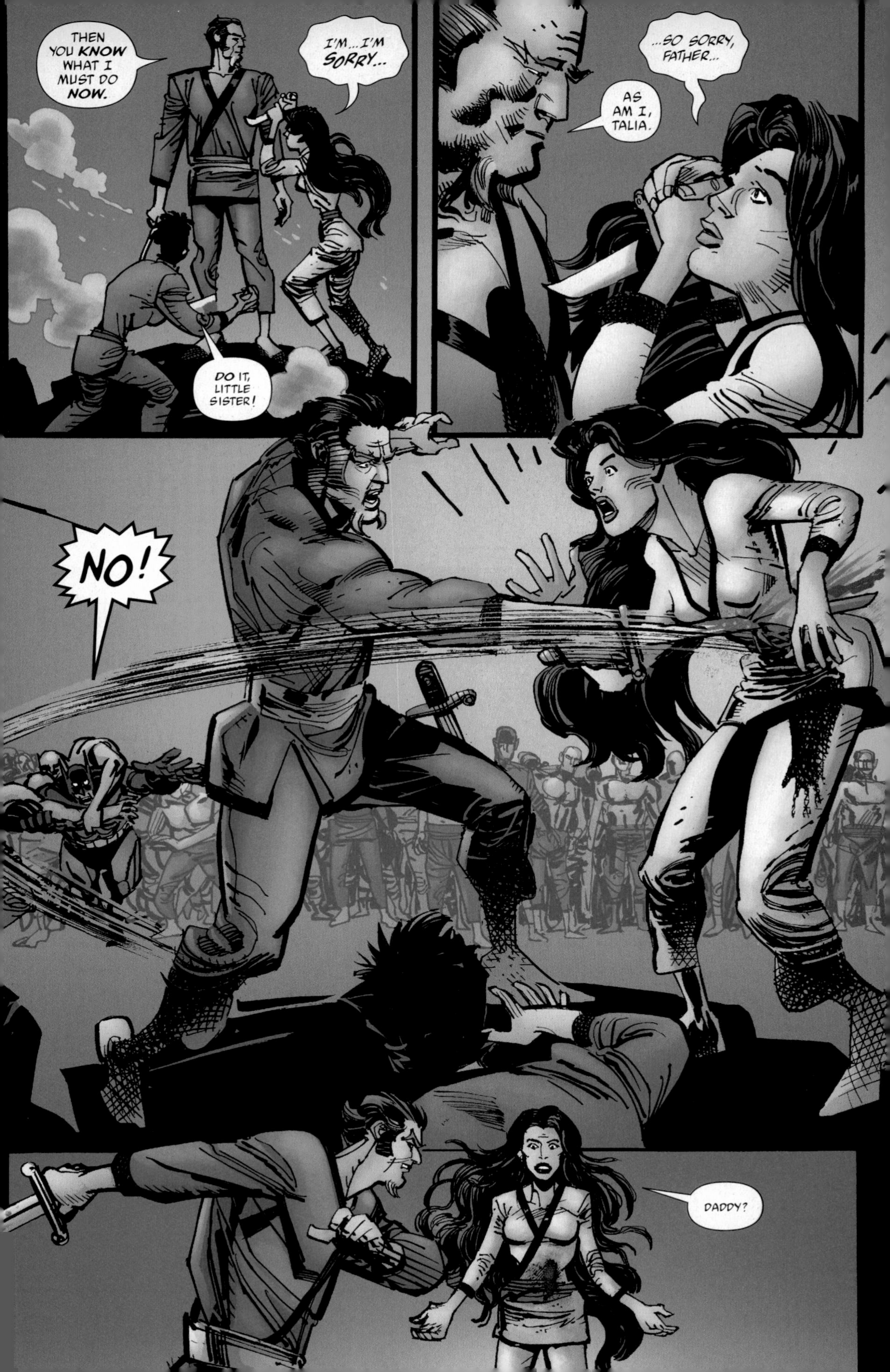
THEN YOU KNOW WHAT I MUST DO NOW.
I'M... I'M SORRY...
DO IT, LITTLE SISTER!
...SO SORRY, FATHER...
AS AM I, TALIA.
NO!
DADDY?

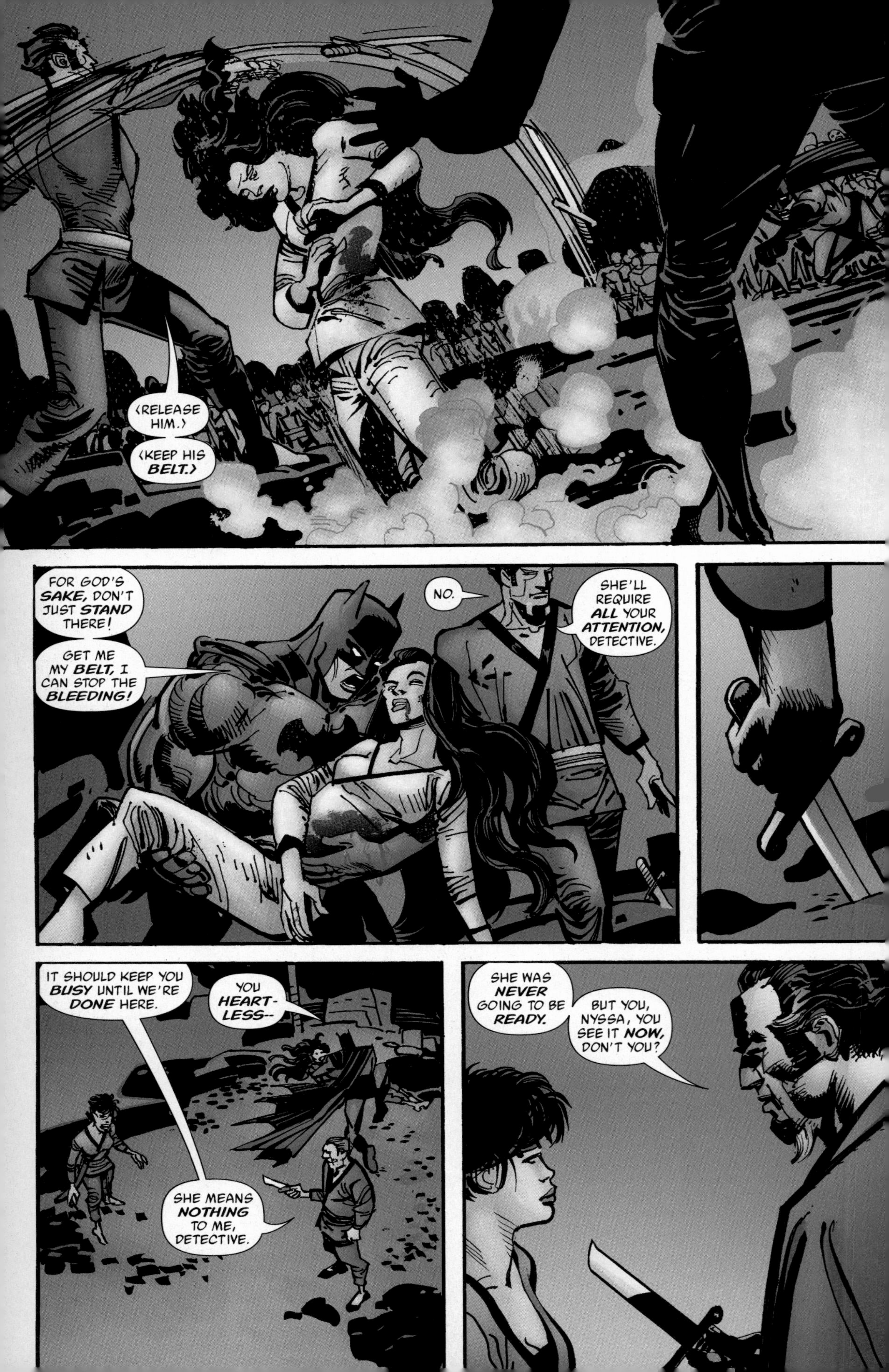

‹RELEASE HIM.›
‹KEEP HIS BELT.›
FOR GOD'S SAKE, DON'T JUST STAND THERE!
GET ME MY BELT, I CAN STOP THE BLEEDING!
NO.
SHE'LL REQUIRE ALL YOUR ATTENTION, DETECTIVE.
IT SHOULD KEEP YOU BUSY UNTIL WE'RE DONE HERE.
YOU HEARTLESS--
SHE MEANS NOTHING TO ME, DETECTIVE.
SHE WAS NEVER GOING TO BE READY.
BUT YOU, NYSSA, YOU SEE IT NOW, DON'T YOU?

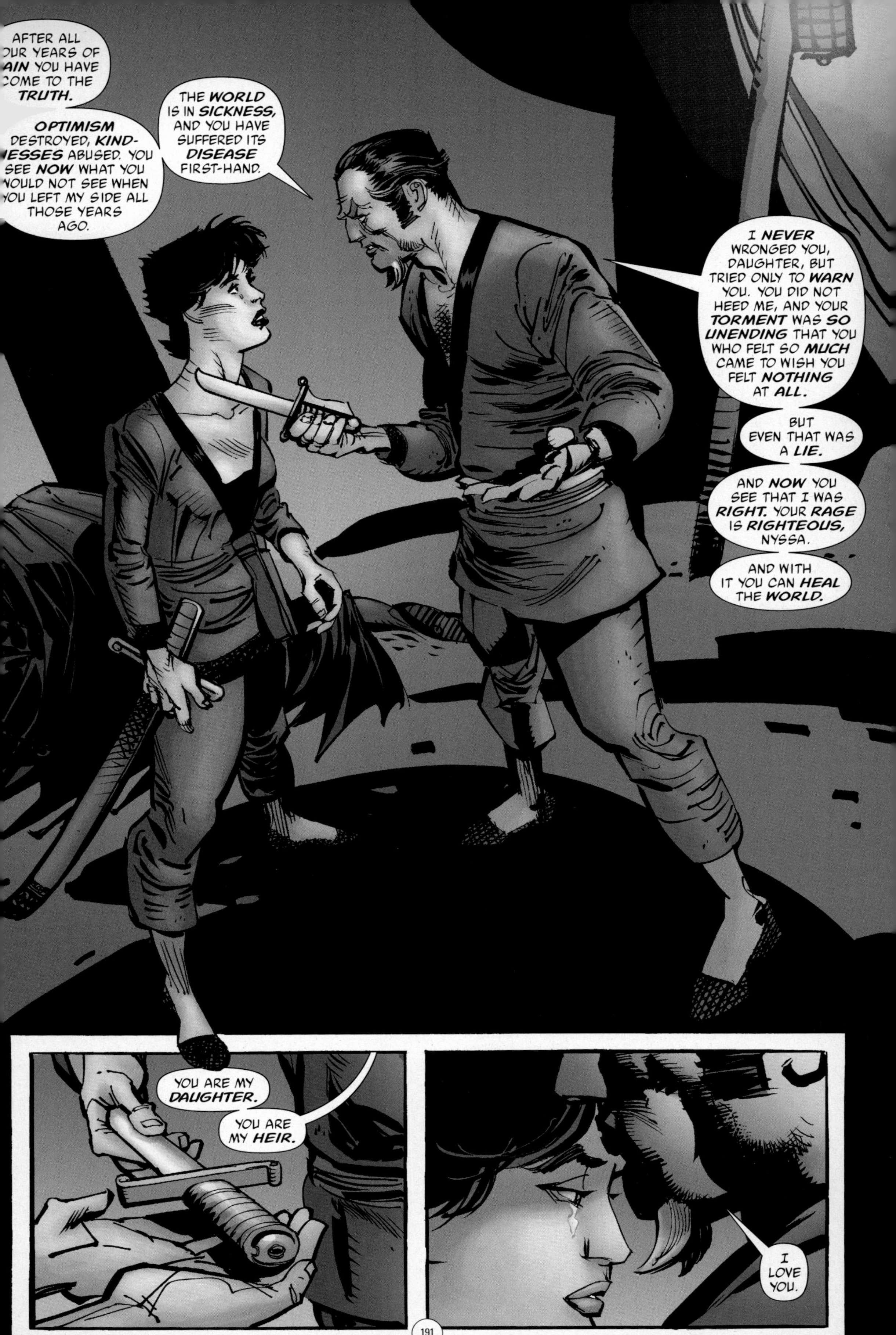
AFTER ALL OUR YEARS OF PAIN YOU HAVE COME TO THE TRUTH.
OPTIMISM DESTROYED, KINDNESSES ABUSED. YOU SEE NOW WHAT YOU WOULD NOT SEE WHEN YOU LEFT MY SIDE ALL THOSE YEARS AGO.
THE WORLD IS IN SICKNESS, AND YOU HAVE SUFFERED ITS DISEASE FIRST-HAND.
I NEVER WRONGED YOU, DAUGHTER, BUT TRIED ONLY TO WARN YOU. YOU DID NOT HEED ME, AND YOUR TORMENT WAS SO UNENDING THAT YOU WHO FELT SO MUCH CAME TO WISH YOU FELT NOTHING AT ALL.
BUT EVEN THAT WAS A LIE.
AND NOW YOU SEE THAT I WAS RIGHT. YOUR RAGE IS RIGHTEOUS, NYSSA.
AND WITH IT YOU CAN HEAL THE WORLD.
YOU ARE MY DAUGHTER.
YOU ARE MY HEIR.
I LOVE YOU.

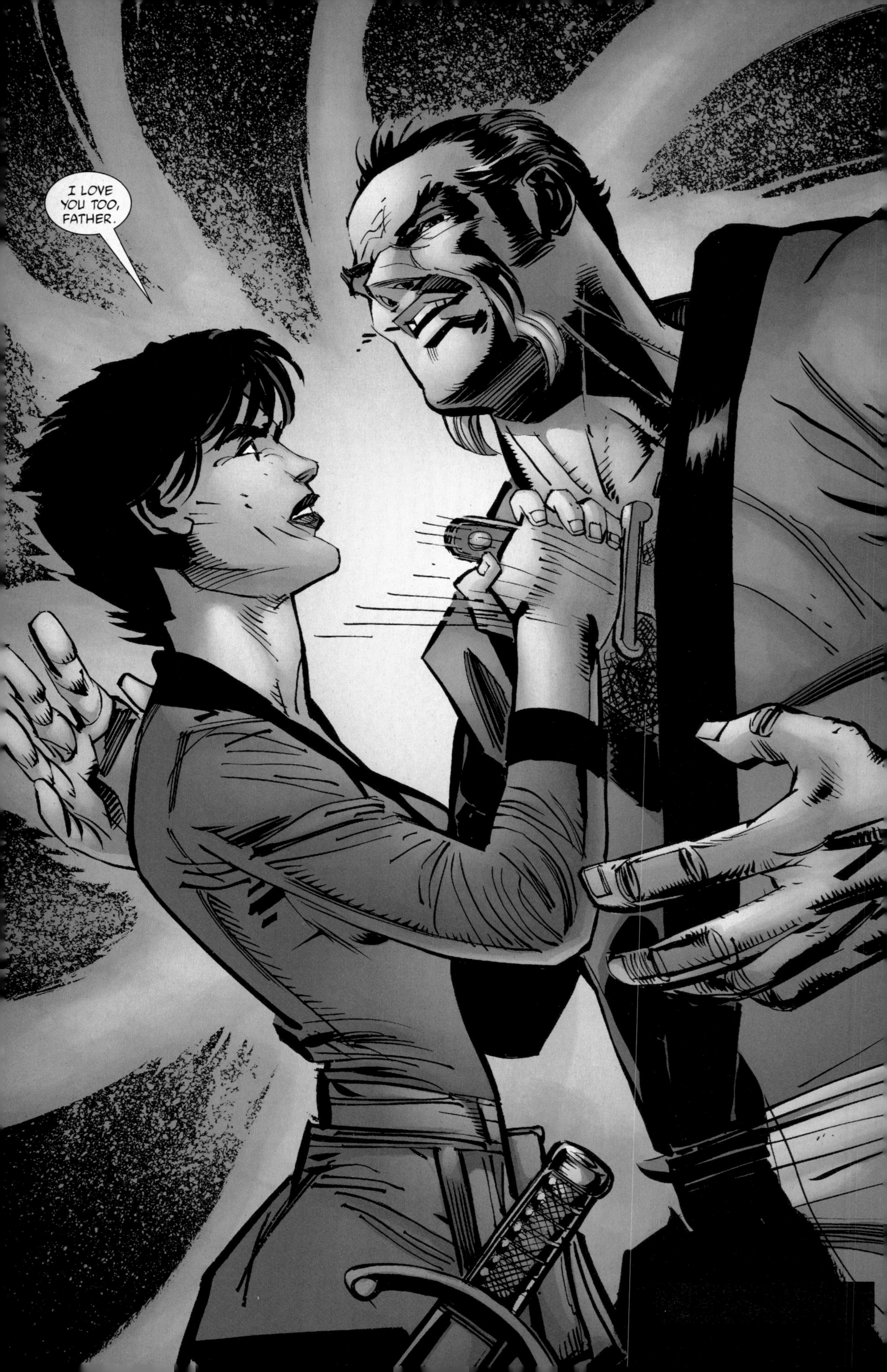
I LOVE YOU TOO, FATHER.

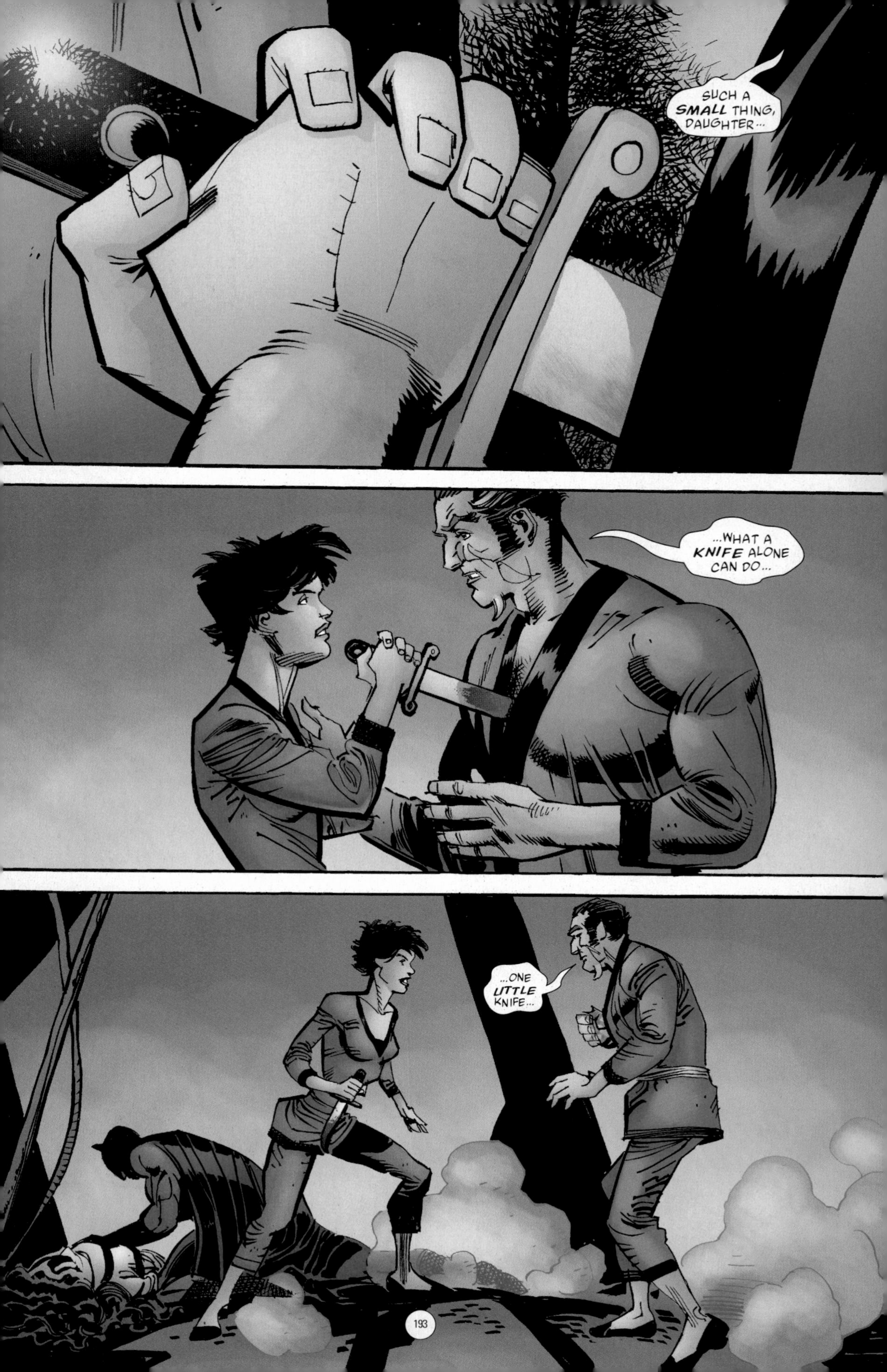
SUCH A SMALL THING, DAUGHTER...
...WHAT A KNIFE ALONE CAN DO...
...ONE LITTLE KNIFE...

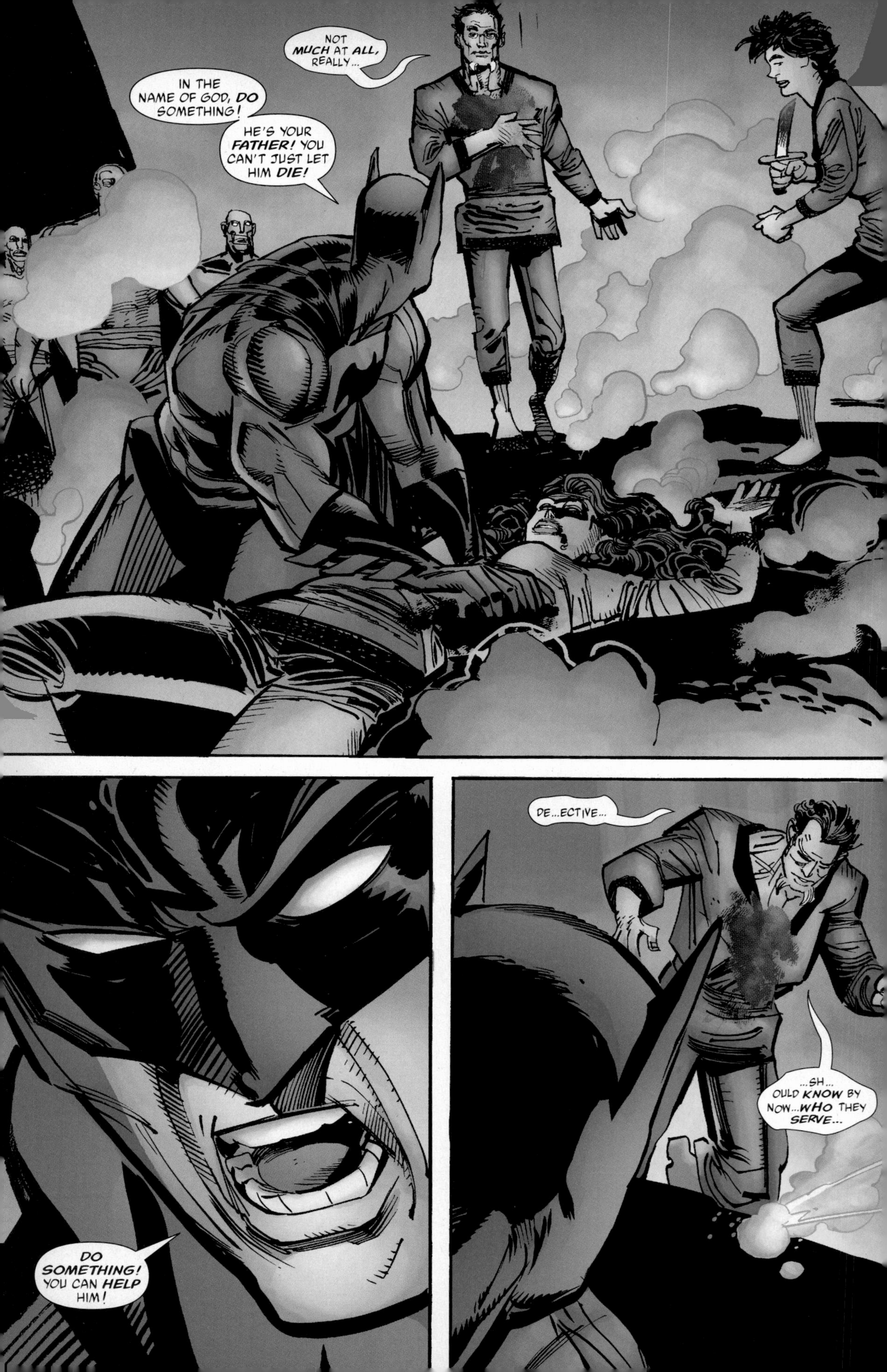
IN THE NAME OF GOD, DO SOMETHING!
HE'S YOUR FATHER! YOU CAN'T JUST LET HIM DIE!
NOT MUCH AT ALL, REALLY...
DO SOMETHING! YOU CAN HELP HIM!
DE...ECTIVE...
...SH... OULD KNOW BY NOW...WHO THEY SERVE...

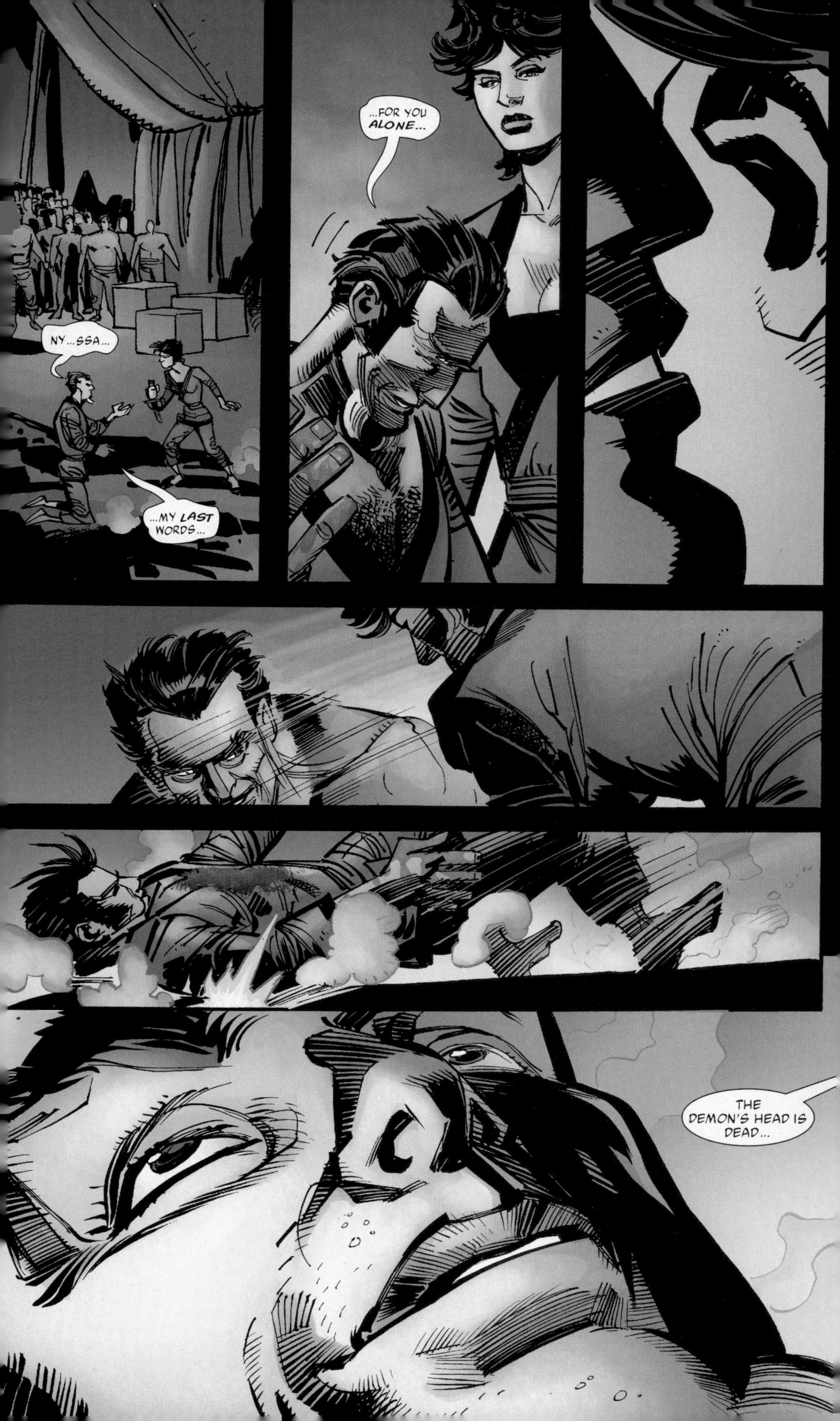
NY...SSA...
...MY LAST WORDS...
...FOR YOU ALONE...
THE DEMON'S HEAD IS DEAD...

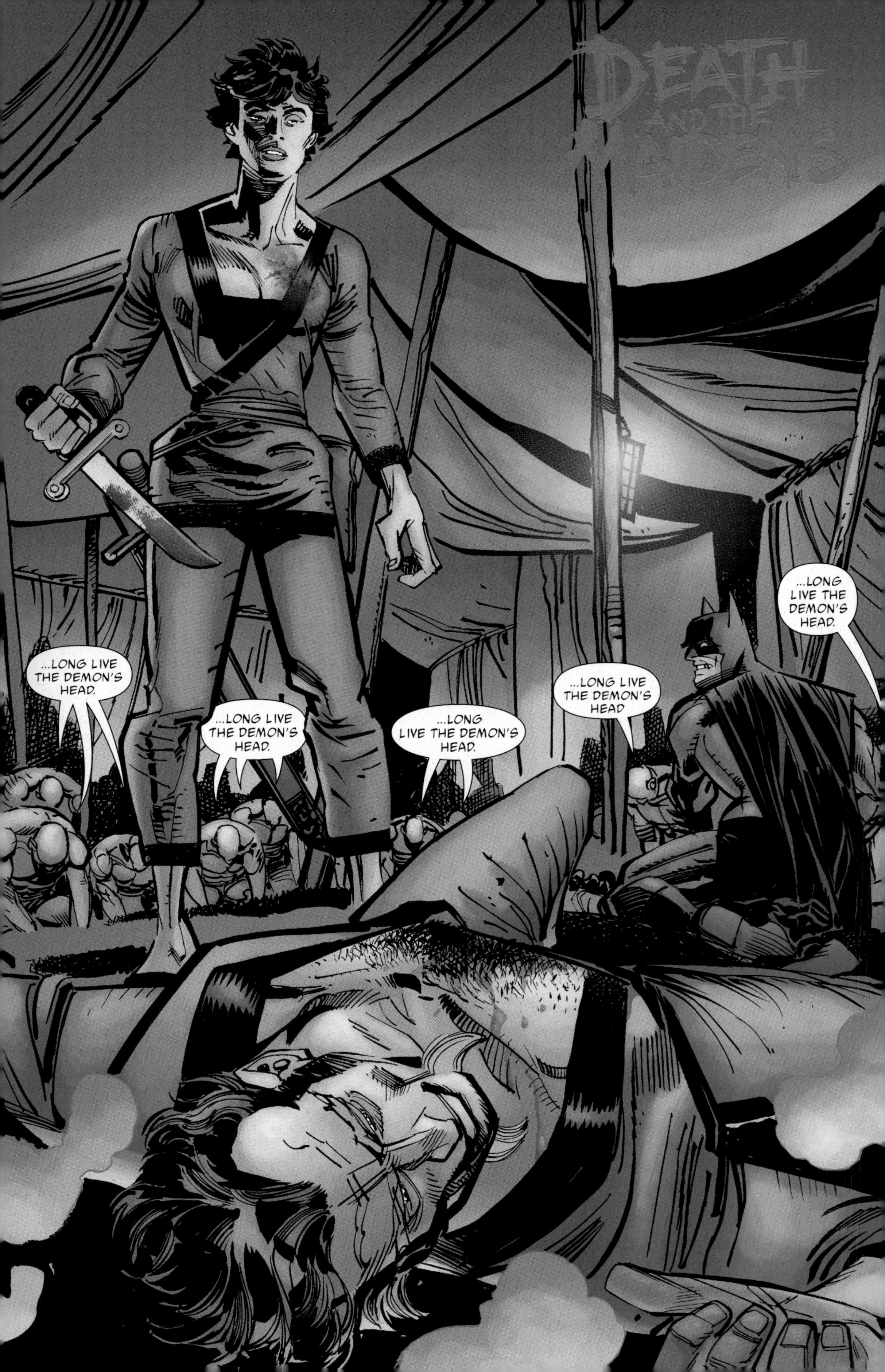
DEATH AND THE MAIDENS
...LONG LIVE THE DEMON'S HEAD.
...LONG LIVE THE DEMON'S HEAD.
...LONG LIVE THE DEMON'S HEAD.
...LONG LIVE THE DEMON'S HEAD
...LONG LIVE THE DEMON'S HEAD.

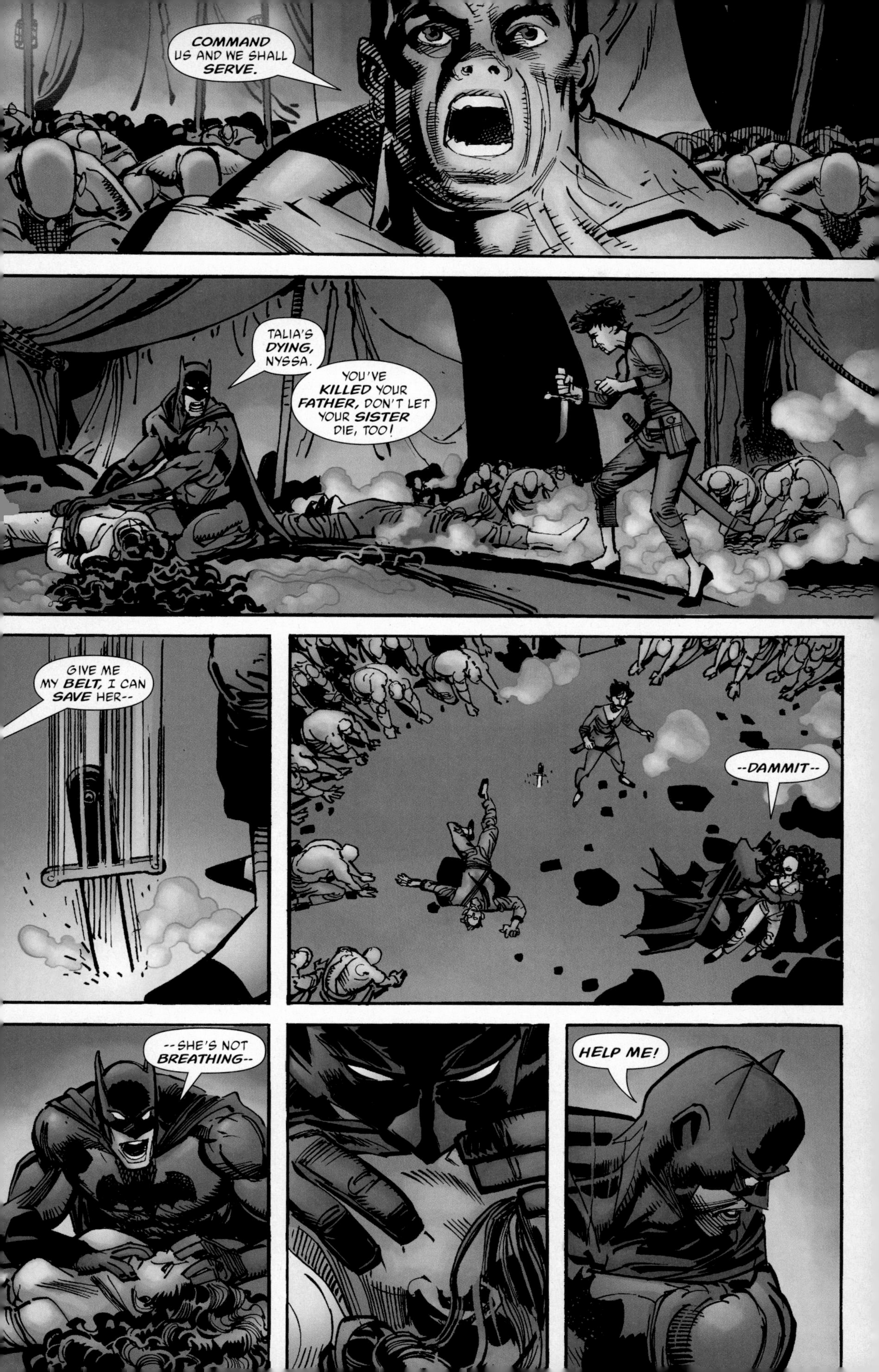
COMMAND US AND WE SHALL SERVE.
TALIA'S DYING, NYSSA.
YOU'VE KILLED YOUR FATHER, DON'T LET YOUR SISTER DIE, TOO!
GIVE ME MY BELT, I CAN SAVE HER--
--DAMMIT--
--SHE'S NOT BREATHING--
HELP ME!

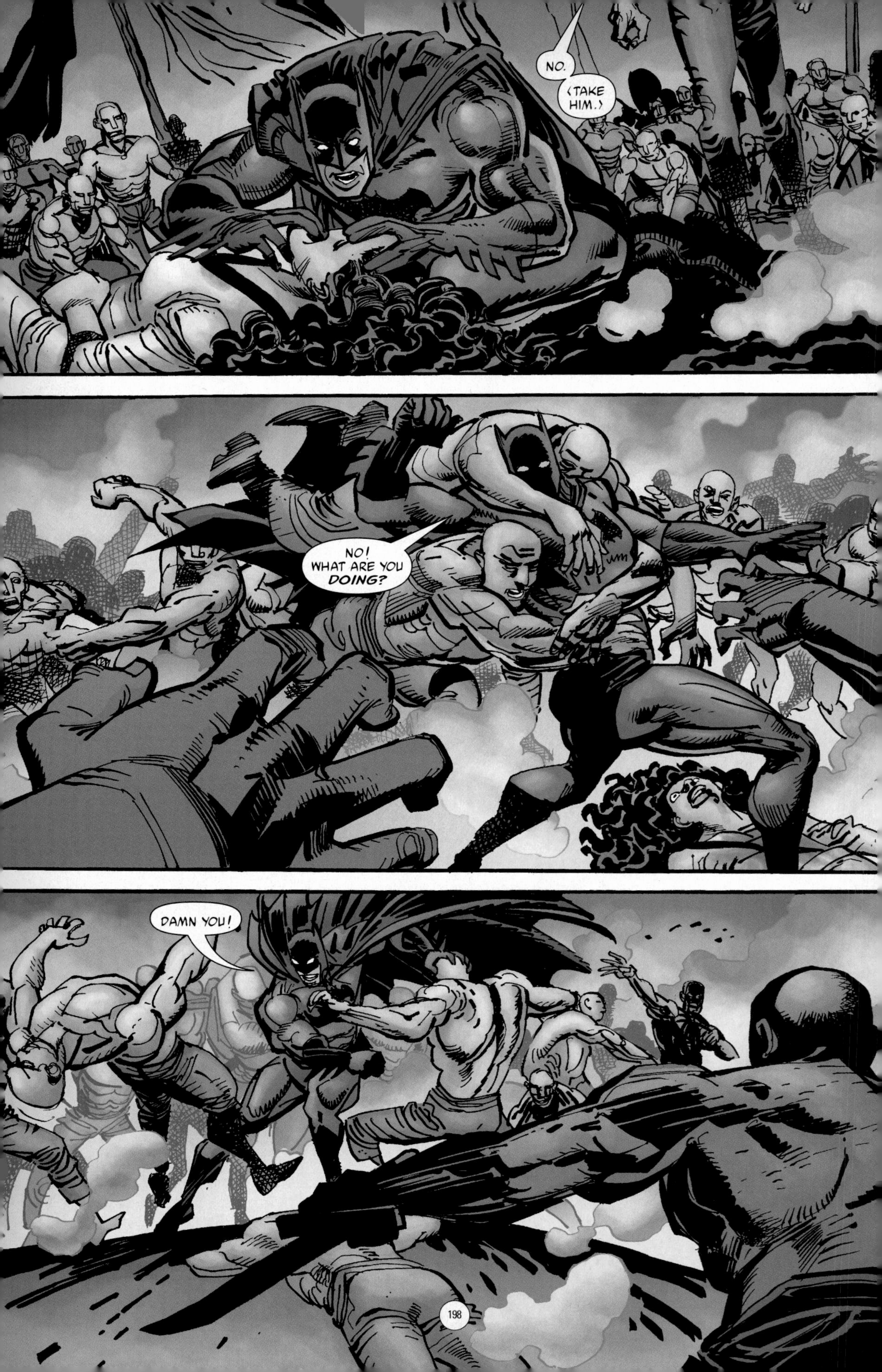
NO.
‹TAKE HIM.›
NO! WHAT ARE YOU *DOING?*
DAMN YOU!

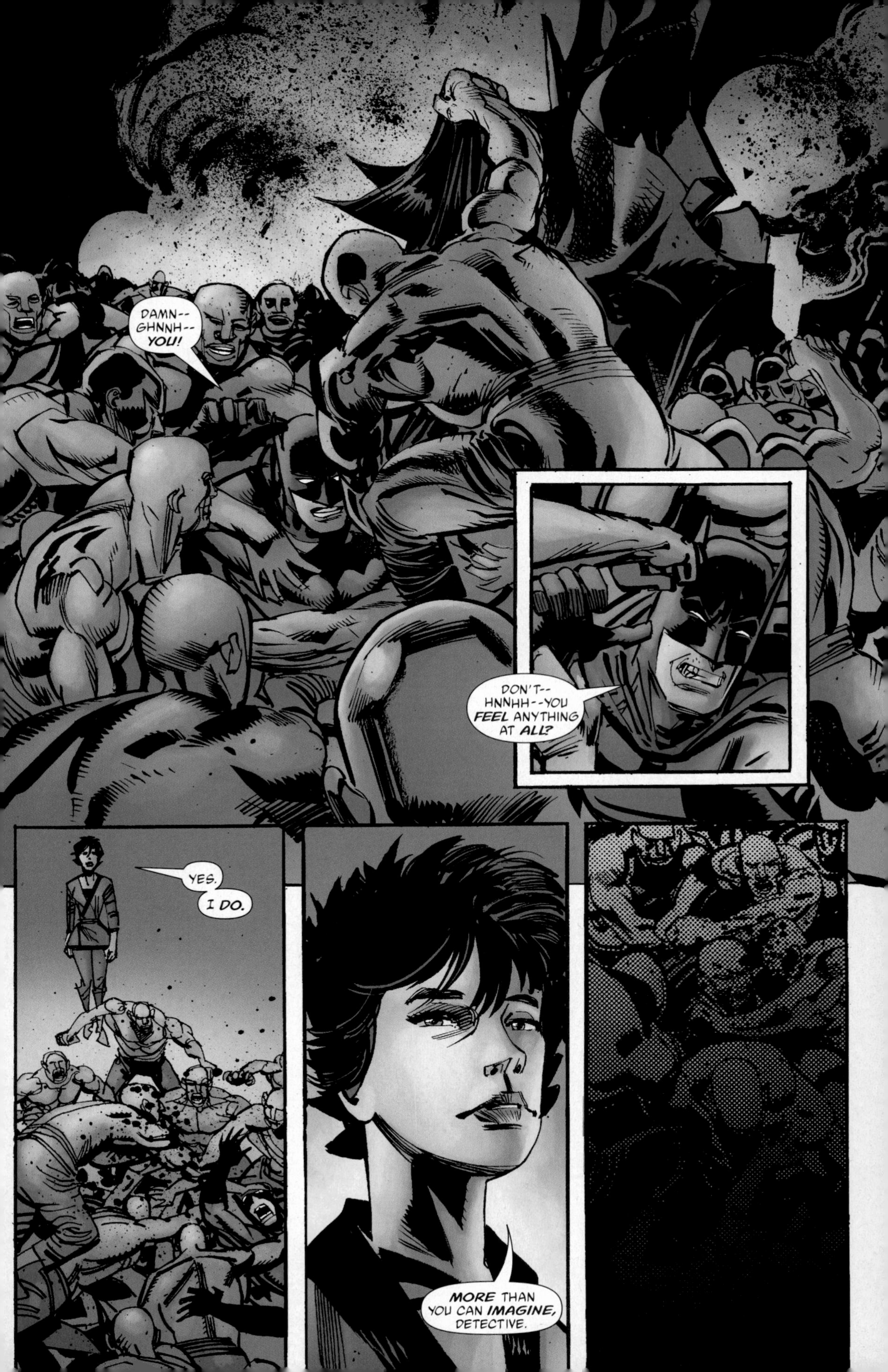
DAMN-- GHNNH-- YOU!
DON'T-- HNNHH--YOU FEEL ANYTHING AT ALL?
YES.
I DO.
MORE THAN YOU CAN IMAGINE, DETECTIVE.

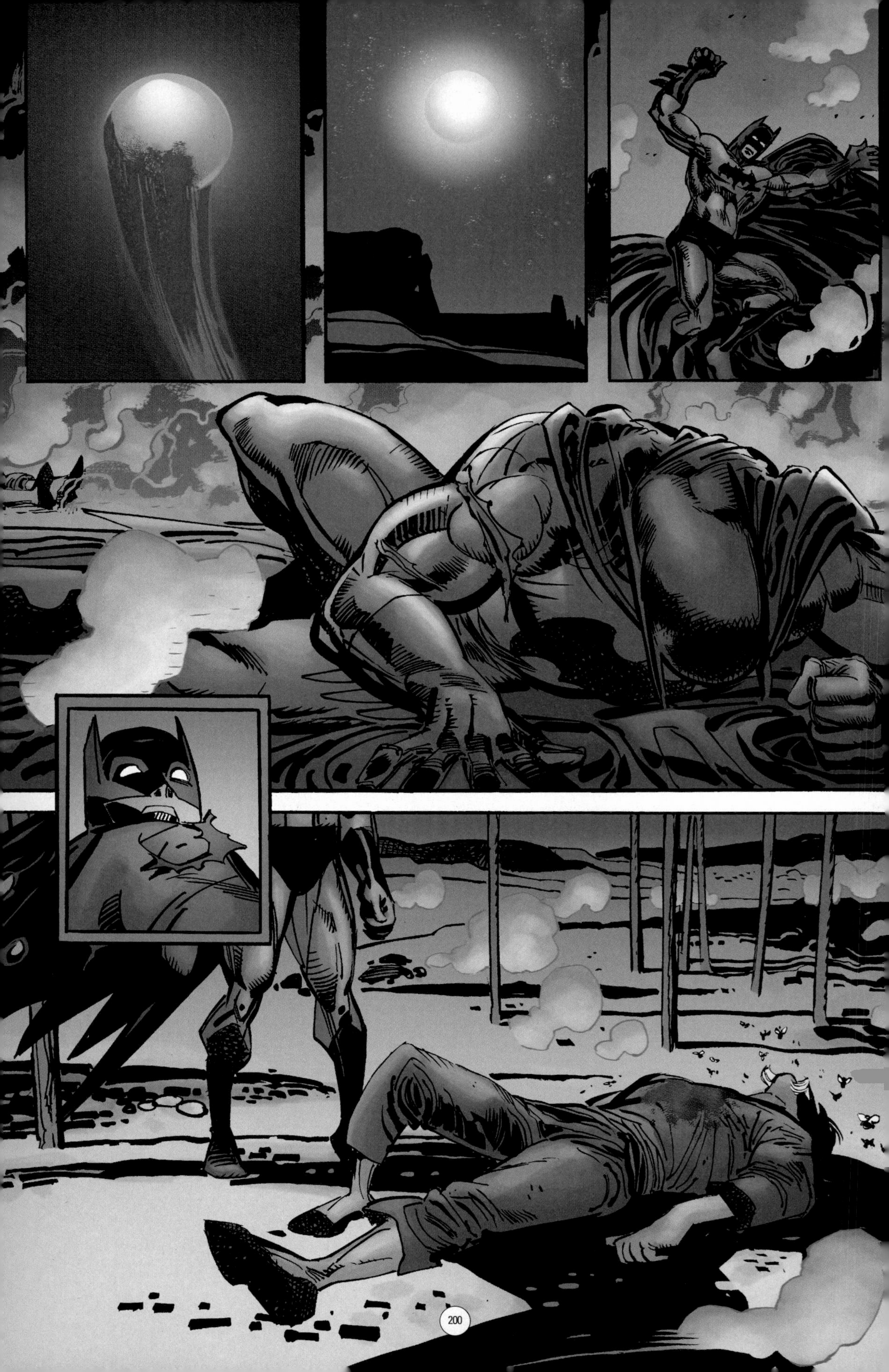

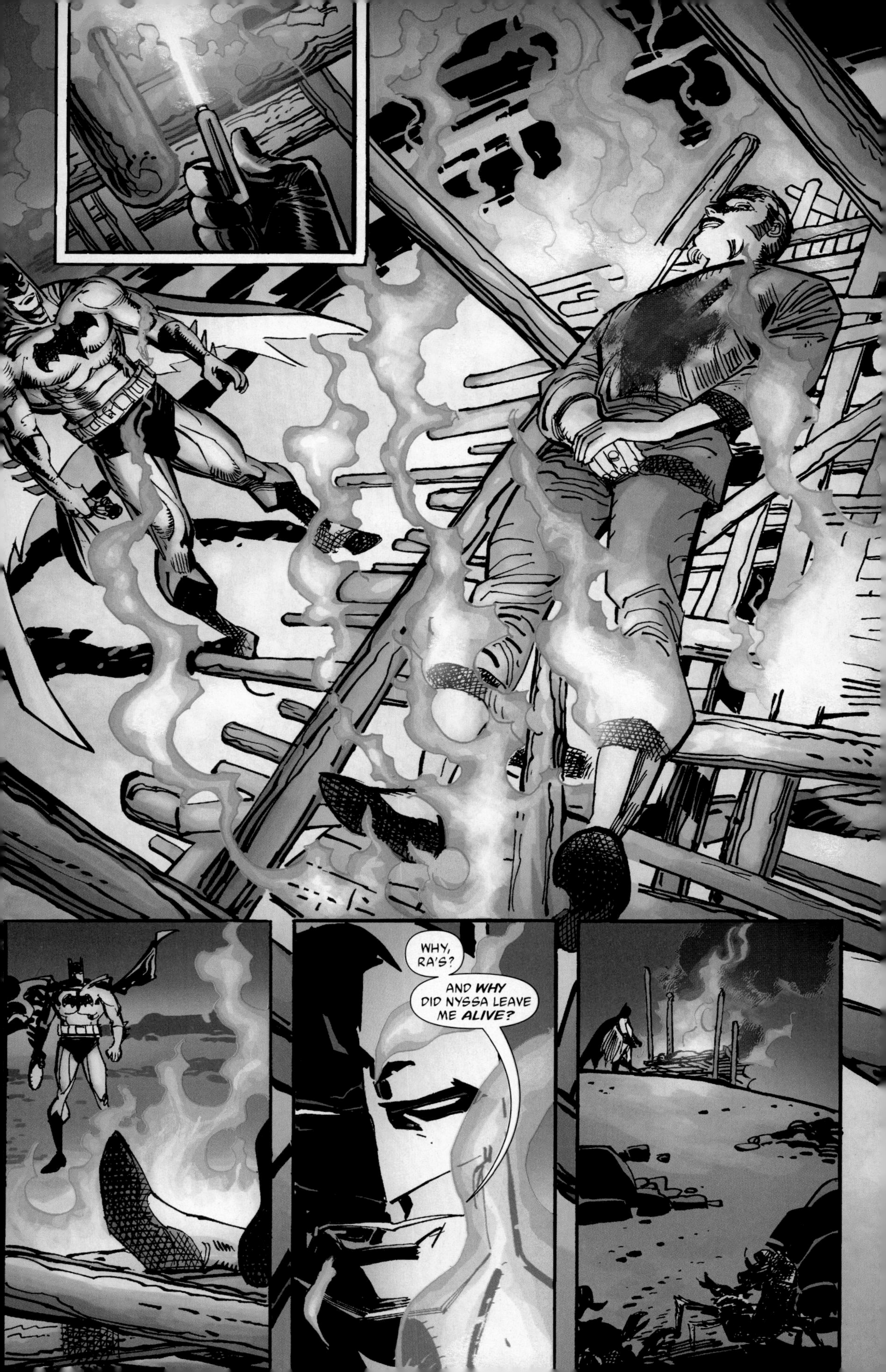
WHY, RA'S?
AND WHY DID NYSSA LEAVE ME ALIVE?

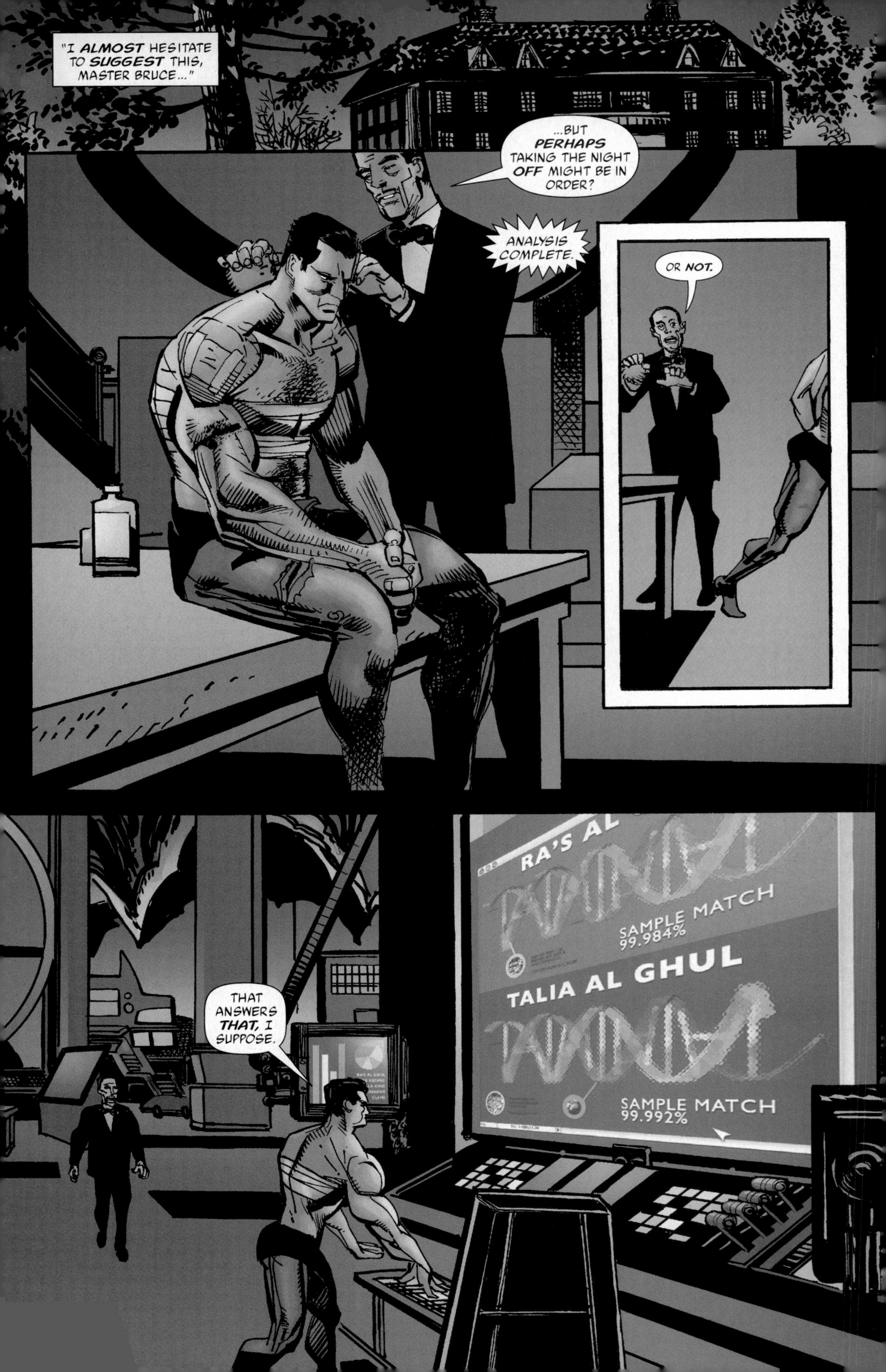
"I ALMOST HESITATE TO SUGGEST THIS, MASTER BRUCE..."
...BUT PERHAPS TAKING THE NIGHT OFF MIGHT BE IN ORDER?
ANALYSIS COMPLETE.
OR NOT.
RA'S AL
SAMPLE MATCH 99.984%
TALIA AL GHUL
SAMPLE MATCH 99.992%
THAT ANSWERS THAT, I SUPPOSE.

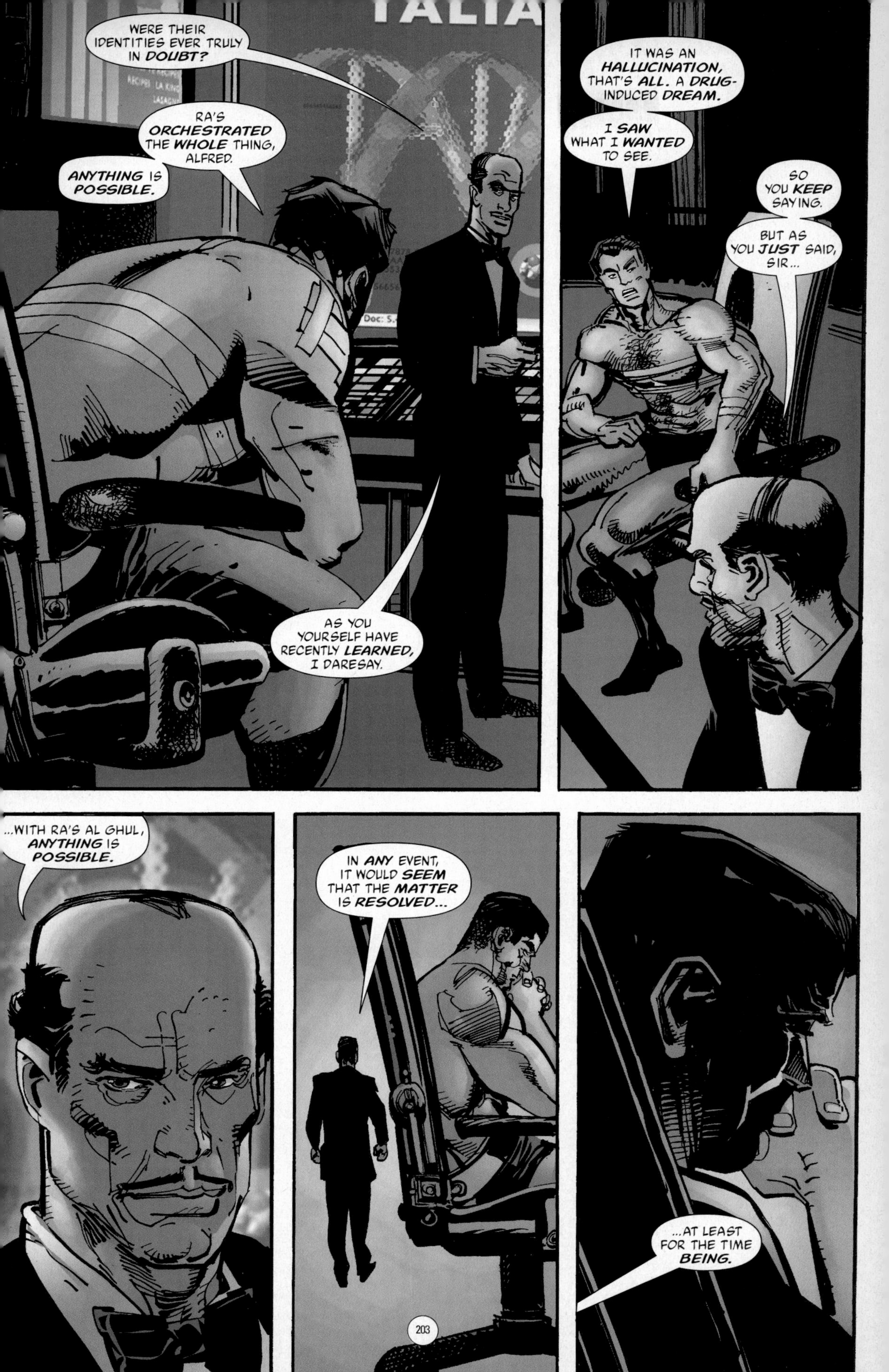
TALIA
WERE THEIR IDENTITIES EVER TRULY IN DOUBT?
RA'S ORCHESTRATED THE WHOLE THING, ALFRED.
ANYTHING IS POSSIBLE.
AS YOU YOURSELF HAVE RECENTLY LEARNED, I DARESAY.
IT WAS AN HALLUCINATION, THAT'S ALL. A DRUG-INDUCED DREAM.
I SAW WHAT I WANTED TO SEE.
SO YOU KEEP SAYING.
BUT AS YOU JUST SAID, SIR...
...WITH RA'S AL GHUL, ANYTHING IS POSSIBLE.
IN ANY EVENT, IT WOULD SEEM THAT THE MATTER IS RESOLVED...
...AT LEAST FOR THE TIME BEING.

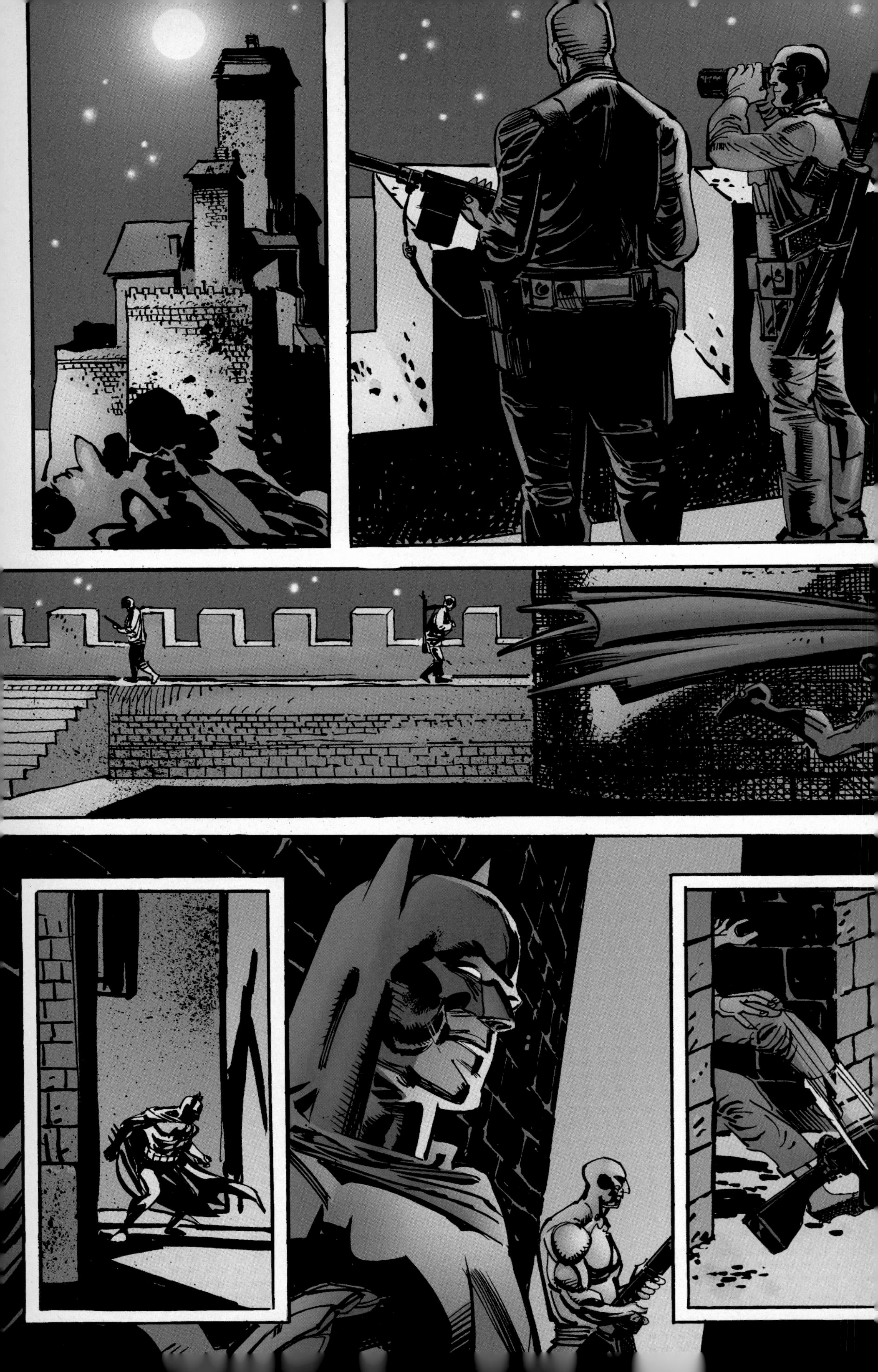

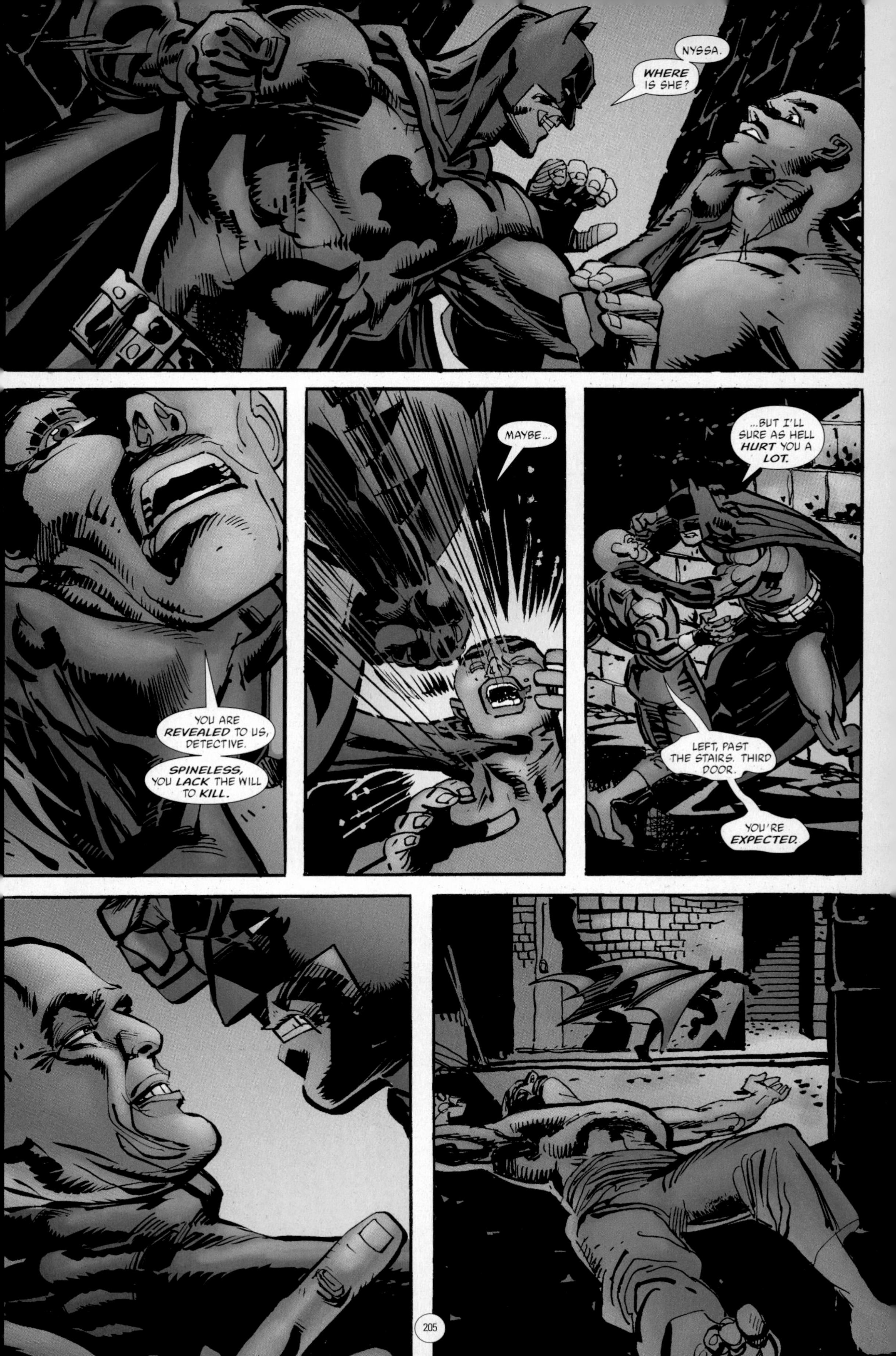
NYSSA. WHERE IS SHE?
YOU ARE REVEALED TO US, DETECTIVE.
SPINELESS, YOU LACK THE WILL TO KILL.
MAYBE...
...BUT I'LL SURE AS HELL HURT YOU A LOT.
LEFT, PAST THE STAIRS. THIRD DOOR.
YOU'RE EXPECTED.

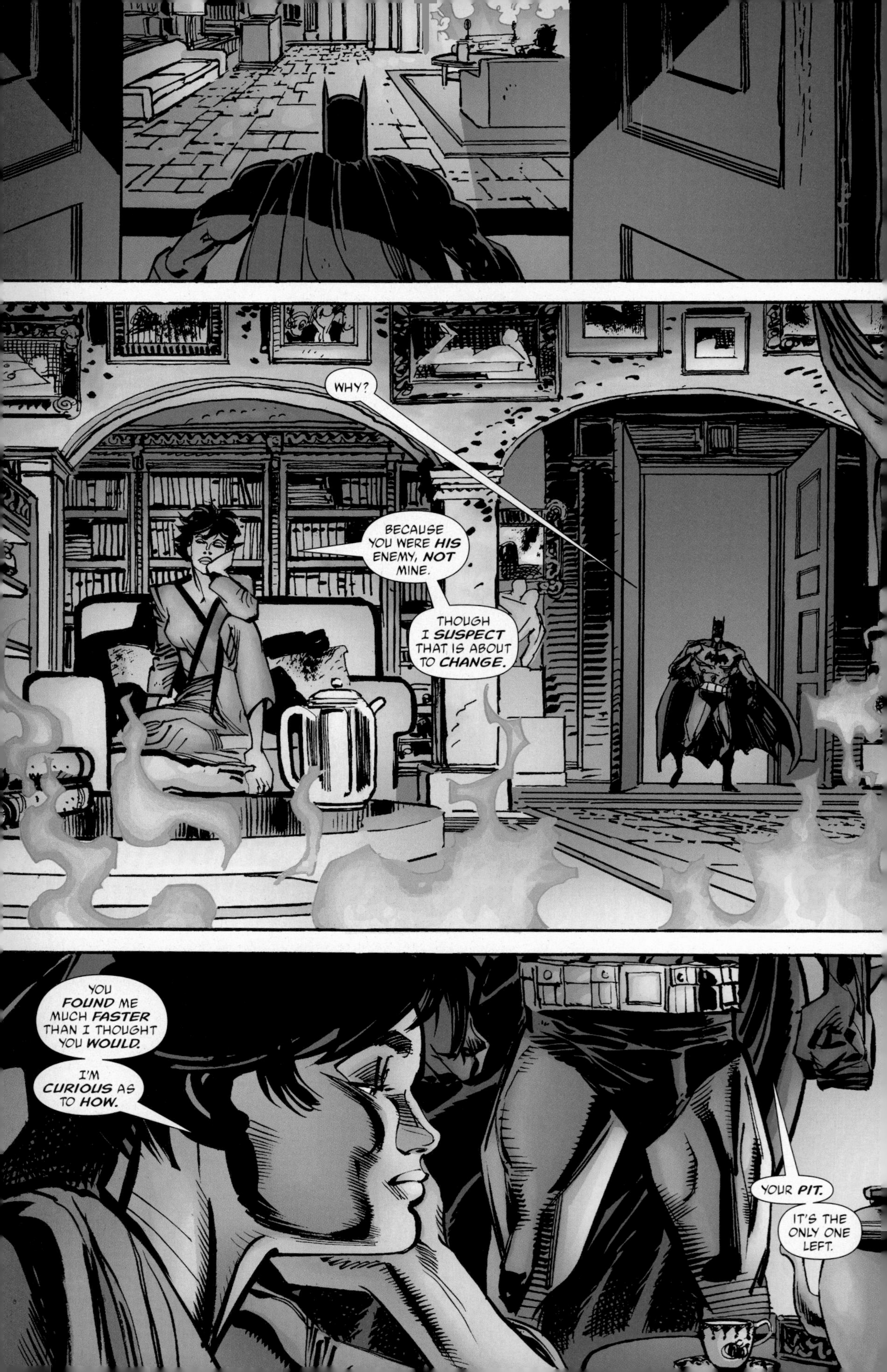
WHY?
BECAUSE YOU WERE HIS ENEMY, NOT MINE.
THOUGH I SUSPECT THAT IS ABOUT TO CHANGE.
YOU FOUND ME MUCH FASTER THAN I THOUGHT YOU WOULD.
I'M CURIOUS AS TO HOW.
YOUR PIT.
IT'S THE ONLY ONE LEFT.

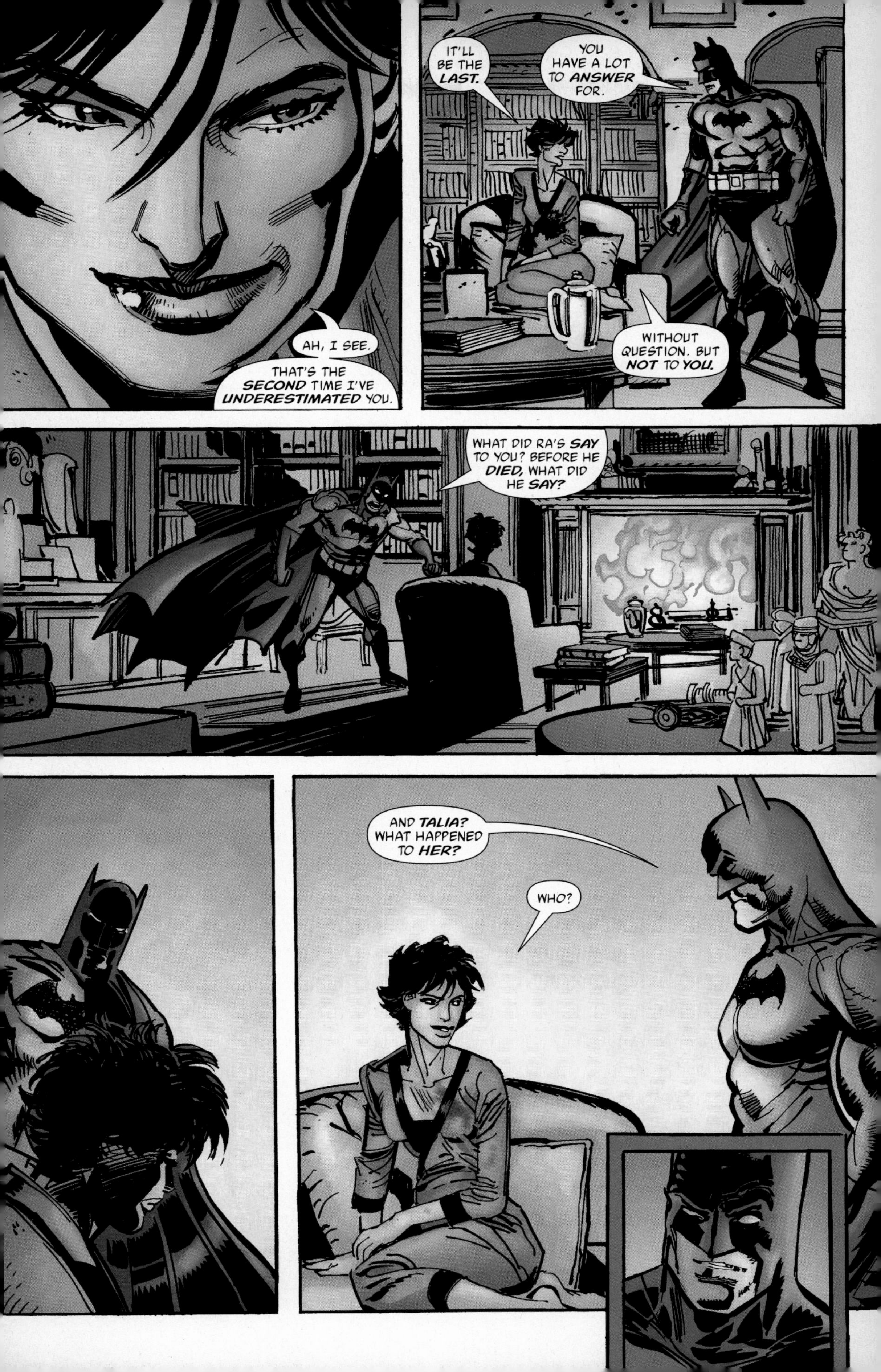
AH, I SEE.
THAT'S THE SECOND TIME I'VE UNDERESTIMATED YOU.
IT'LL BE THE LAST.
YOU HAVE A LOT TO ANSWER FOR.
WITHOUT QUESTION. BUT NOT TO YOU.
WHAT DID RA'S SAY TO YOU? BEFORE HE DIED, WHAT DID HE SAY?
AND TALIA? WHAT HAPPENED TO HER?
WHO?

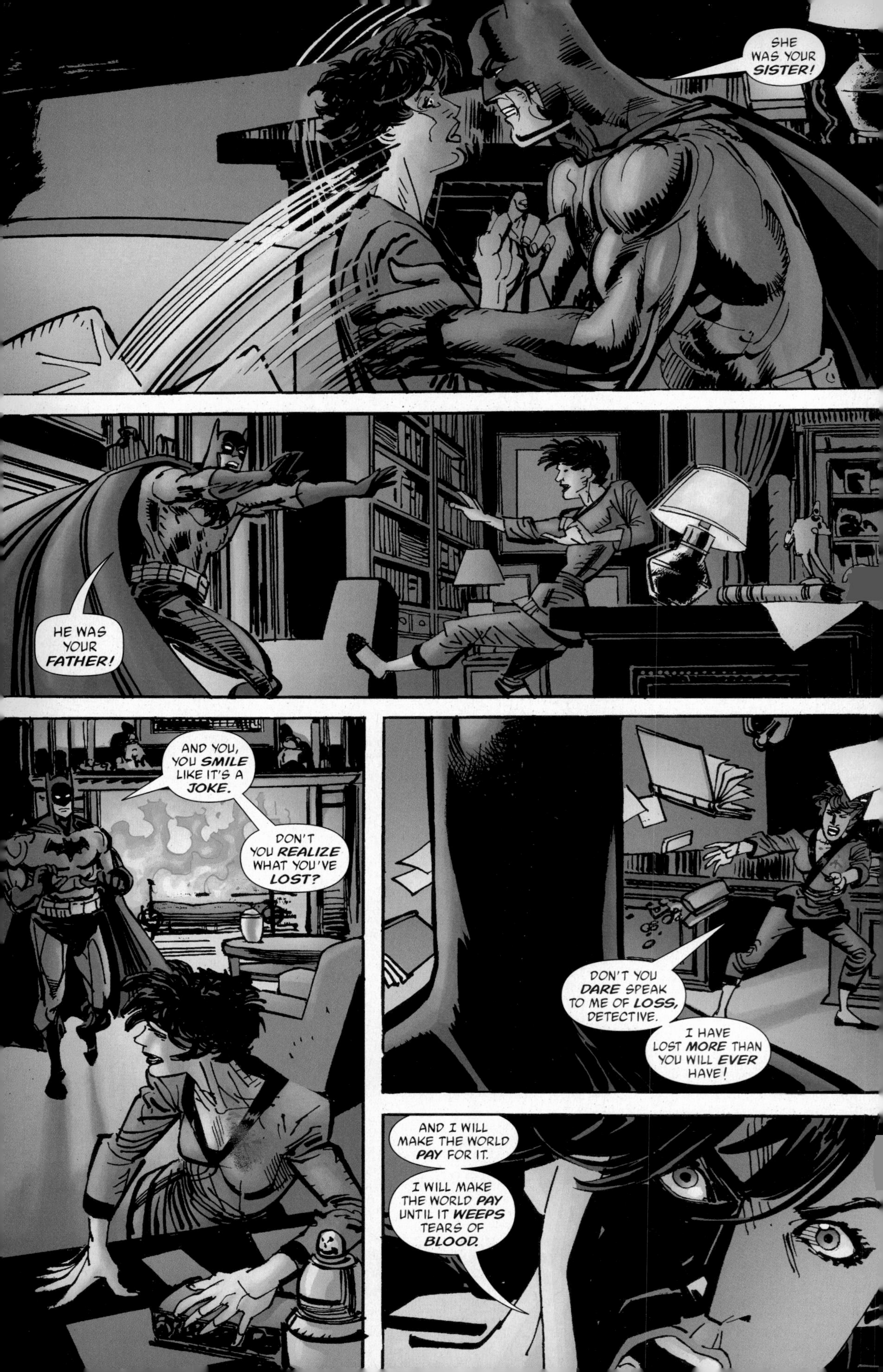
SHE WAS YOUR SISTER!
HE WAS YOUR FATHER!
AND YOU, YOU SMILE LIKE IT'S A JOKE.
DON'T YOU REALIZE WHAT YOU'VE LOST?
DON'T YOU DARE SPEAK TO ME OF LOSS, DETECTIVE.
I HAVE LOST MORE THAN YOU WILL EVER HAVE!
AND I WILL MAKE THE WORLD PAY FOR IT.
I WILL MAKE THE WORLD PAY UNTIL IT WEEPS TEARS OF BLOOD.

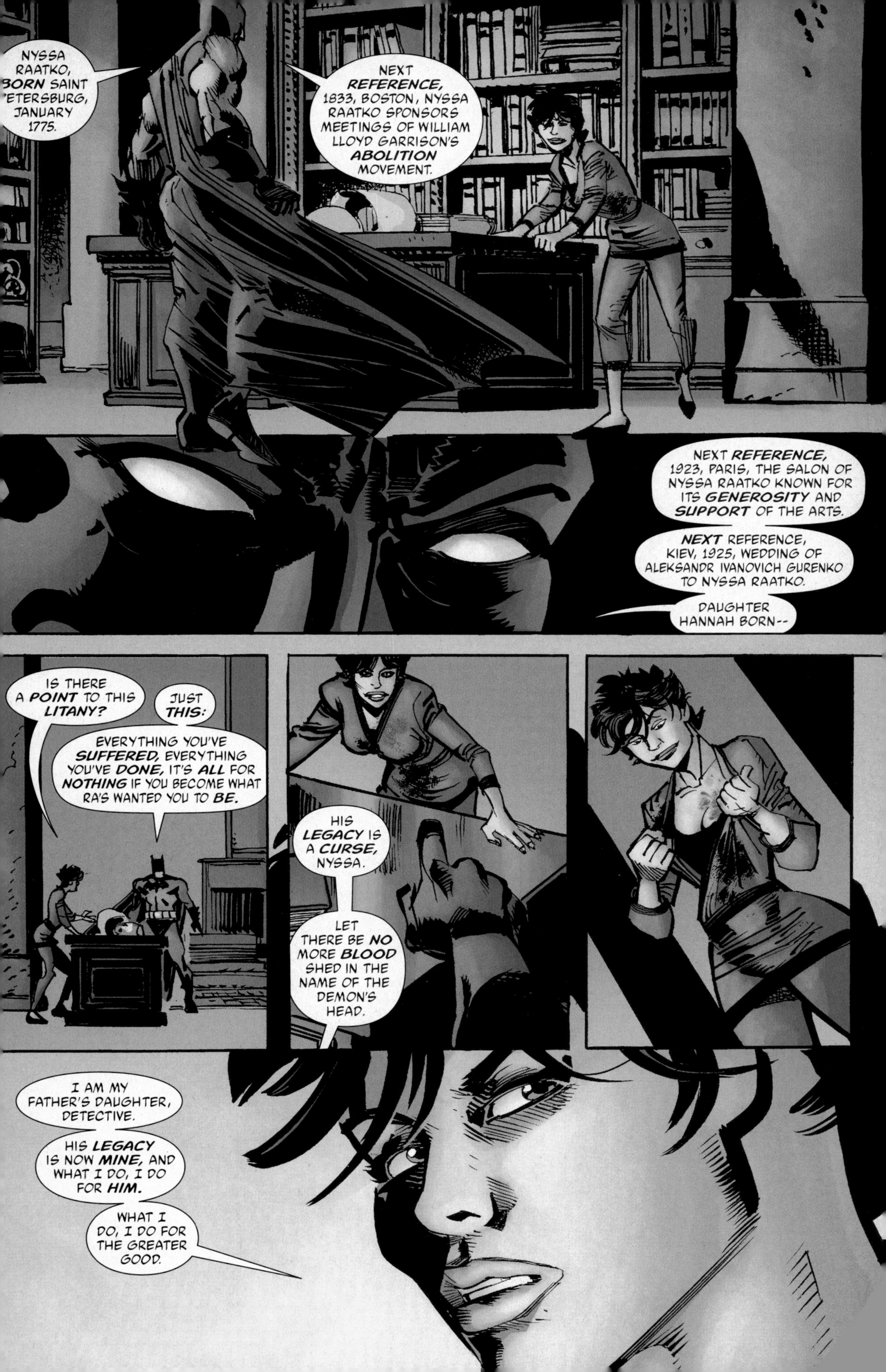
NYSSA RAATKO, BORN SAINT PETERSBURG, JANUARY 1775.
NEXT REFERENCE, 1833, BOSTON, NYSSA RAATKO SPONSORS MEETINGS OF WILLIAM LLOYD GARRISON'S ABOLITION MOVEMENT.
NEXT REFERENCE, 1923, PARIS, THE SALON OF NYSSA RAATKO KNOWN FOR ITS GENEROSITY AND SUPPORT OF THE ARTS.
NEXT REFERENCE, KIEV, 1925, WEDDING OF ALEKSANDR IVANOVICH GURENKO TO NYSSA RAATKO.
DAUGHTER HANNAH BORN--
IS THERE A POINT TO THIS LITANY?
JUST THIS:
EVERYTHING YOU'VE SUFFERED, EVERYTHING YOU'VE DONE, IT'S ALL FOR NOTHING IF YOU BECOME WHAT RA'S WANTED YOU TO BE.
HIS LEGACY IS A CURSE, NYSSA.
LET THERE BE NO MORE BLOOD SHED IN THE NAME OF THE DEMON'S HEAD.
I AM MY FATHER'S DAUGHTER, DETECTIVE.
HIS LEGACY IS NOW MINE, AND WHAT I DO, I DO FOR HIM.
WHAT I DO, I DO FOR THE GREATER GOOD.

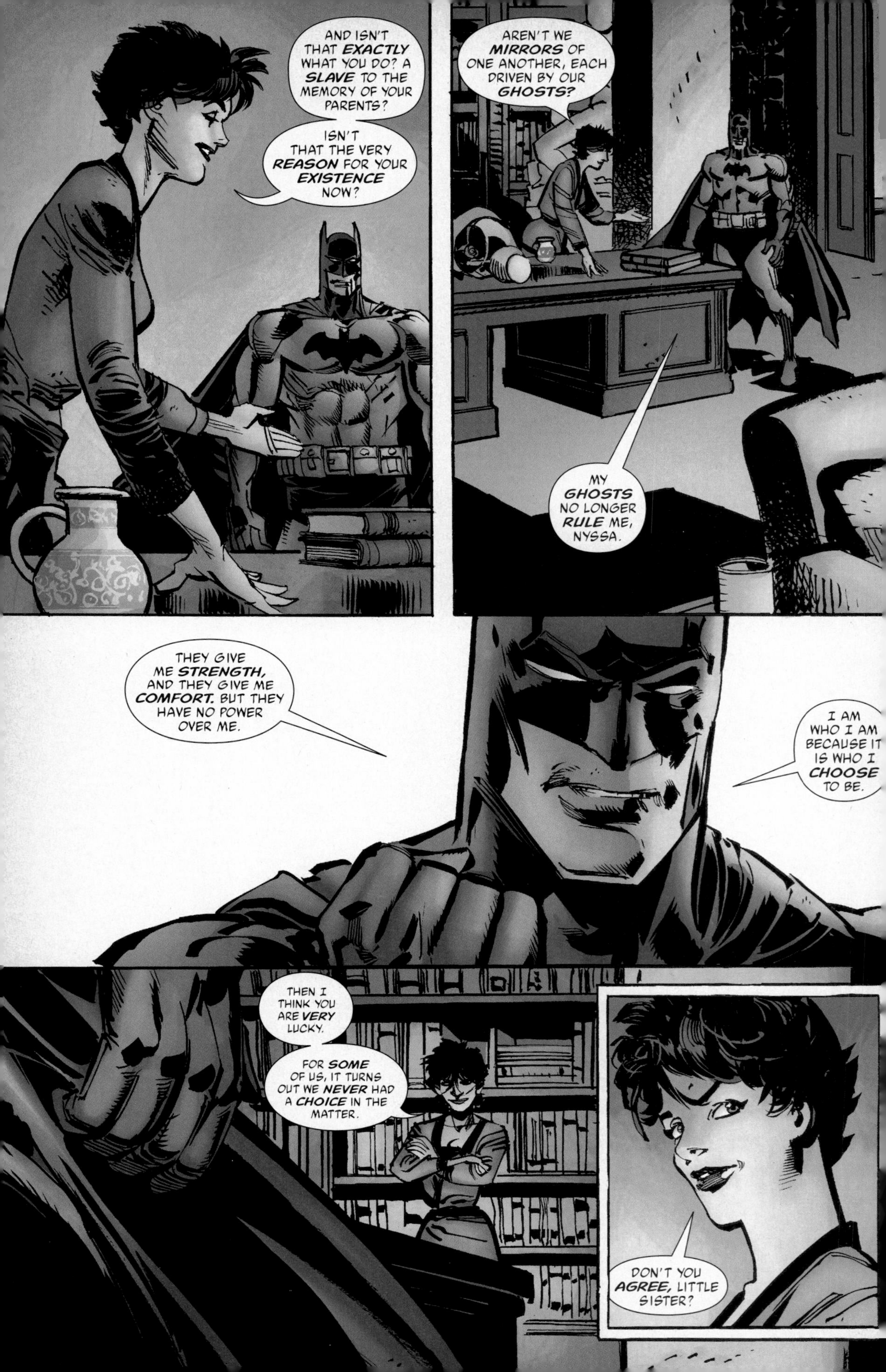
AND ISN'T THAT EXACTLY WHAT YOU DO? A SLAVE TO THE MEMORY OF YOUR PARENTS?
ISN'T THAT THE VERY REASON FOR YOUR EXISTENCE NOW?
AREN'T WE MIRRORS OF ONE ANOTHER, EACH DRIVEN BY OUR GHOSTS?
MY GHOSTS NO LONGER RULE ME, NYSSA.
THEY GIVE ME STRENGTH, AND THEY GIVE ME COMFORT. BUT THEY HAVE NO POWER OVER ME.
I AM WHO I AM BECAUSE IT IS WHO I CHOOSE TO BE.
THEN I THINK YOU ARE VERY LUCKY.
FOR SOME OF US, IT TURNS OUT WE NEVER HAD A CHOICE IN THE MATTER.
DON'T YOU AGREE, LITTLE SISTER?

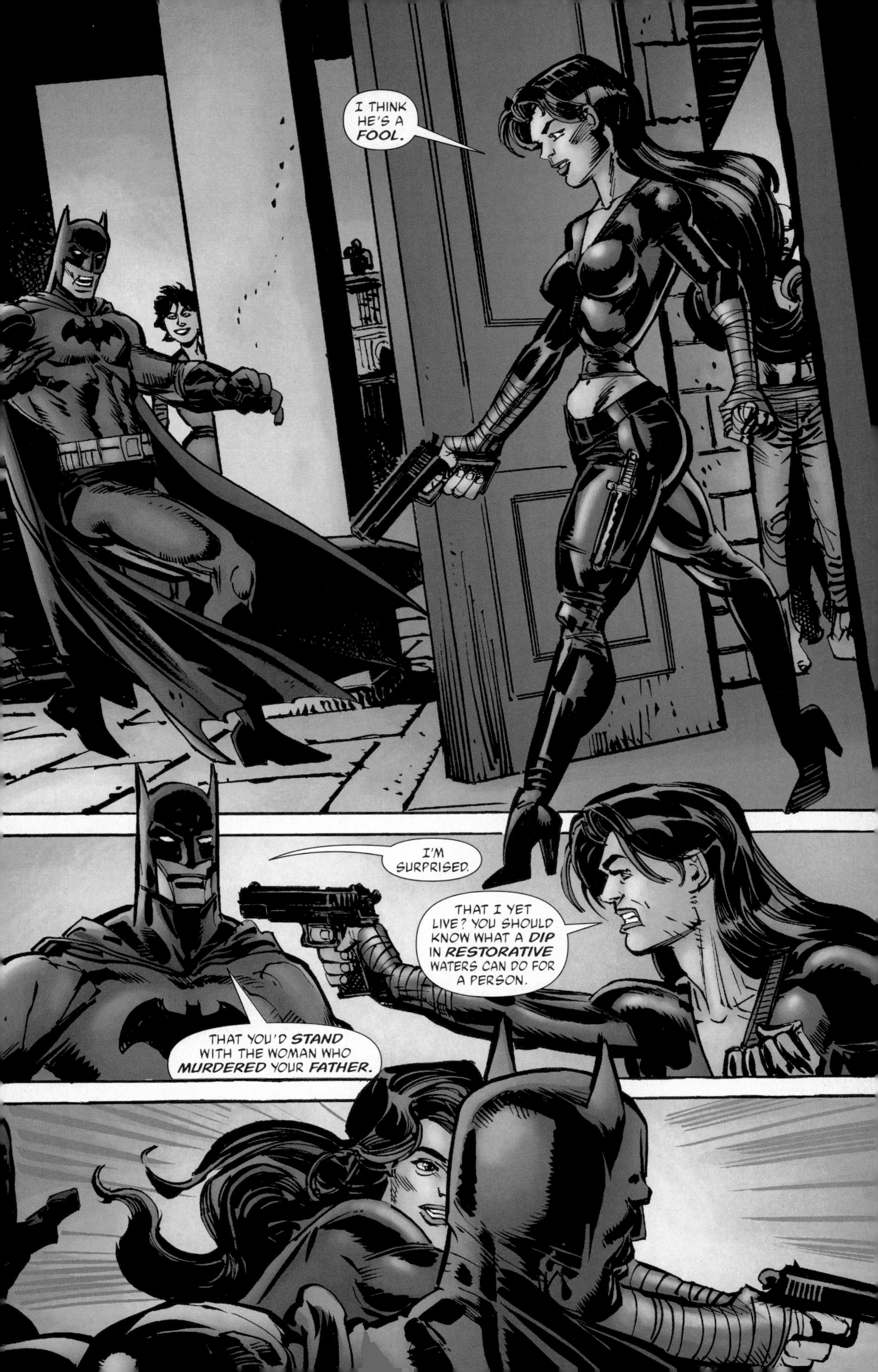
I THINK HE'S A **FOOL.**
I'M SURPRISED.
THAT I YET LIVE? YOU SHOULD KNOW WHAT A ***DIP*** IN ***RESTORATIVE*** WATERS CAN DO FOR A PERSON.
THAT YOU'D ***STAND*** WITH THE WOMAN WHO ***MURDERED*** YOUR ***FATHER.***

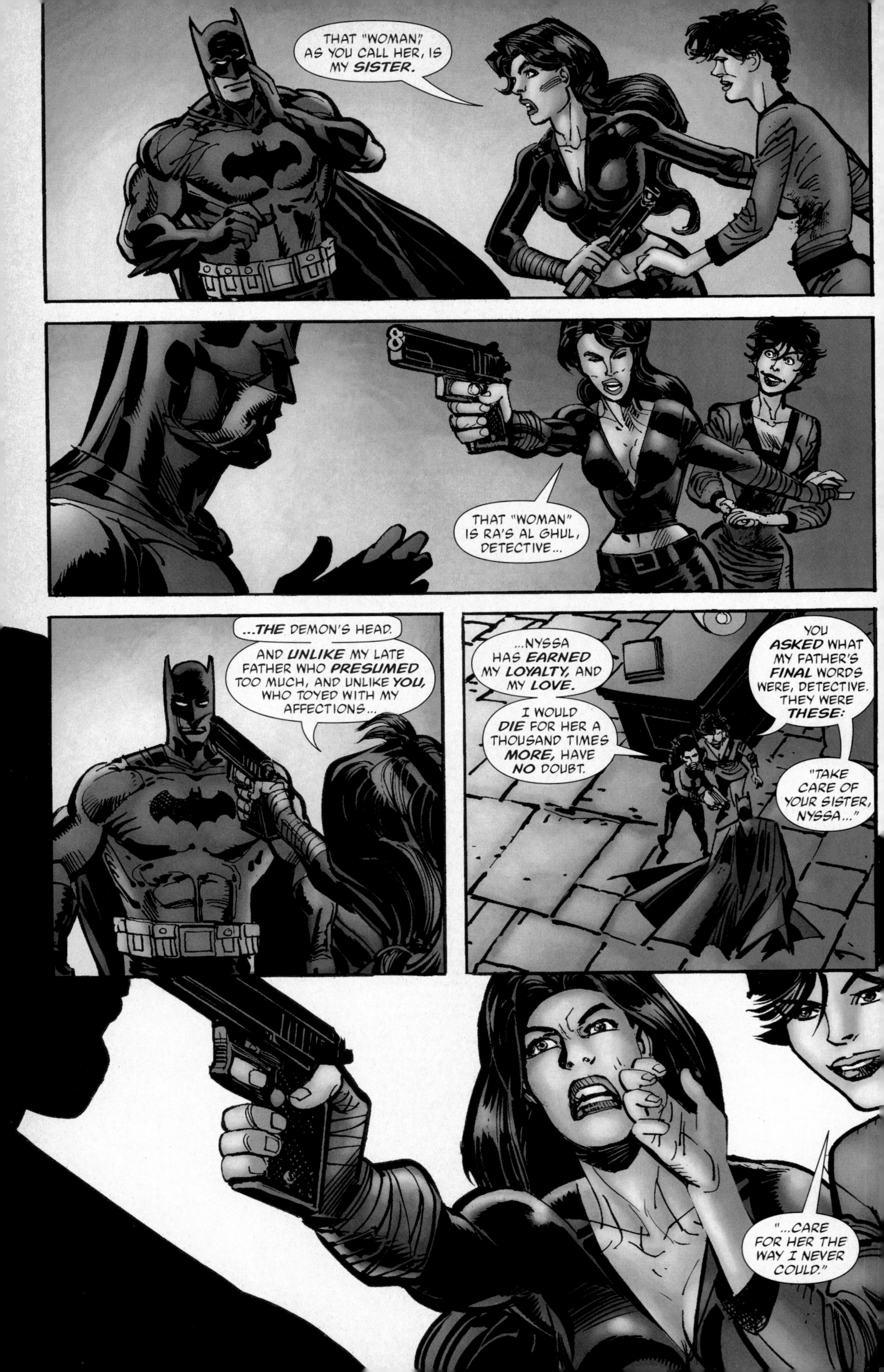

THAT "WOMAN," AS YOU CALL HER, IS MY SISTER.
THAT "WOMAN" IS RA'S AL GHUL, DETECTIVE...
...THE DEMON'S HEAD.
AND UNLIKE MY LATE FATHER WHO PRESUMED TOO MUCH, AND UNLIKE YOU, WHO TOYED WITH MY AFFECTIONS...
...NYSSA HAS EARNED MY LOYALTY, AND MY LOVE.
I WOULD DIE FOR HER A THOUSAND TIMES MORE, HAVE NO DOUBT.
YOU ASKED WHAT MY FATHER'S FINAL WORDS WERE, DETECTIVE. THEY WERE THESE:
"TAKE CARE OF YOUR SISTER, NYSSA..."
"...CARE FOR HER THE WAY I NEVER COULD."

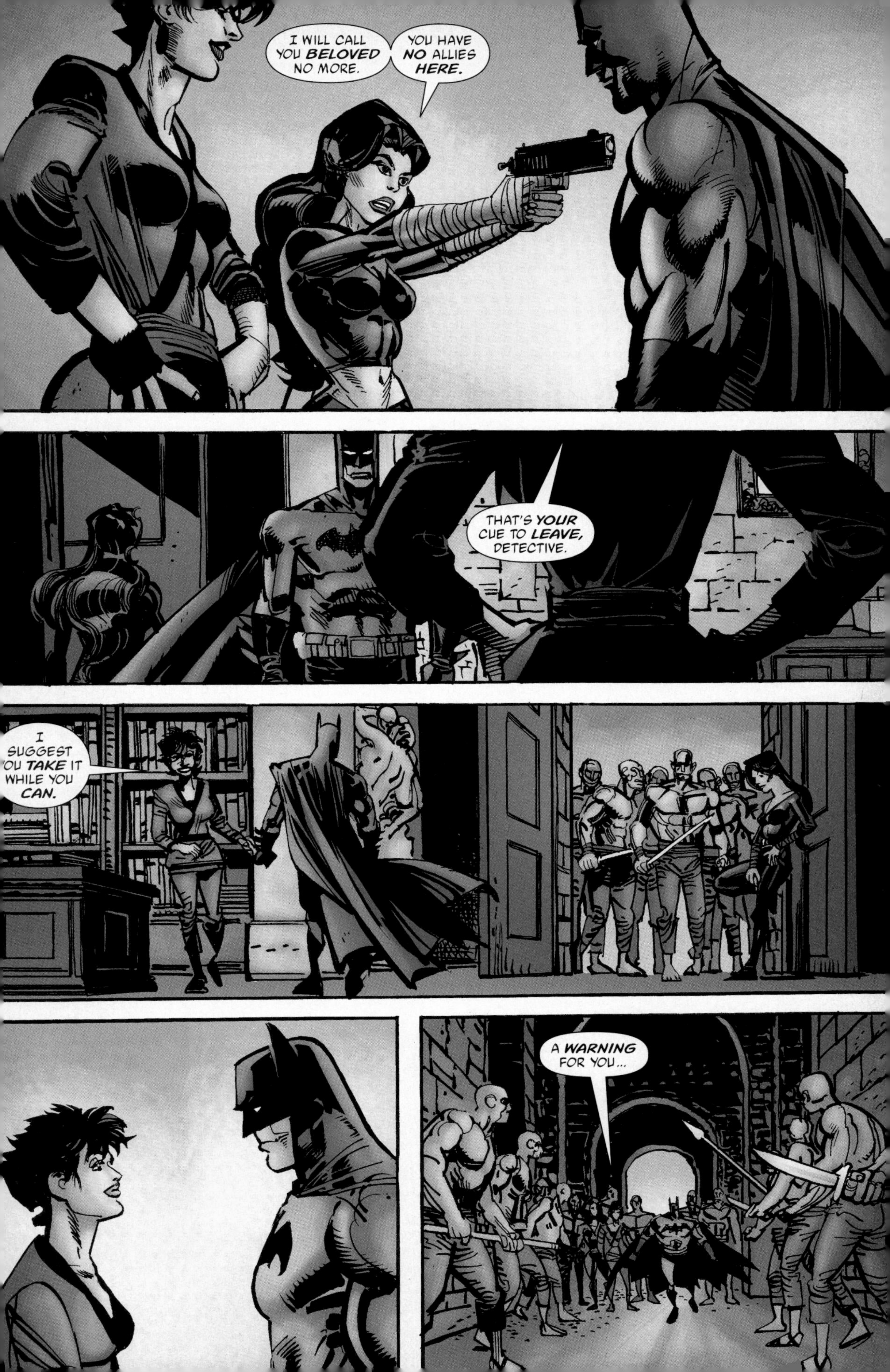

I WILL CALL YOU BELOVED NO MORE.
YOU HAVE NO ALLIES HERE.
THAT'S YOUR CUE TO LEAVE, DETECTIVE.
I SUGGEST YOU TAKE IT WHILE YOU CAN.
A WARNING FOR YOU...

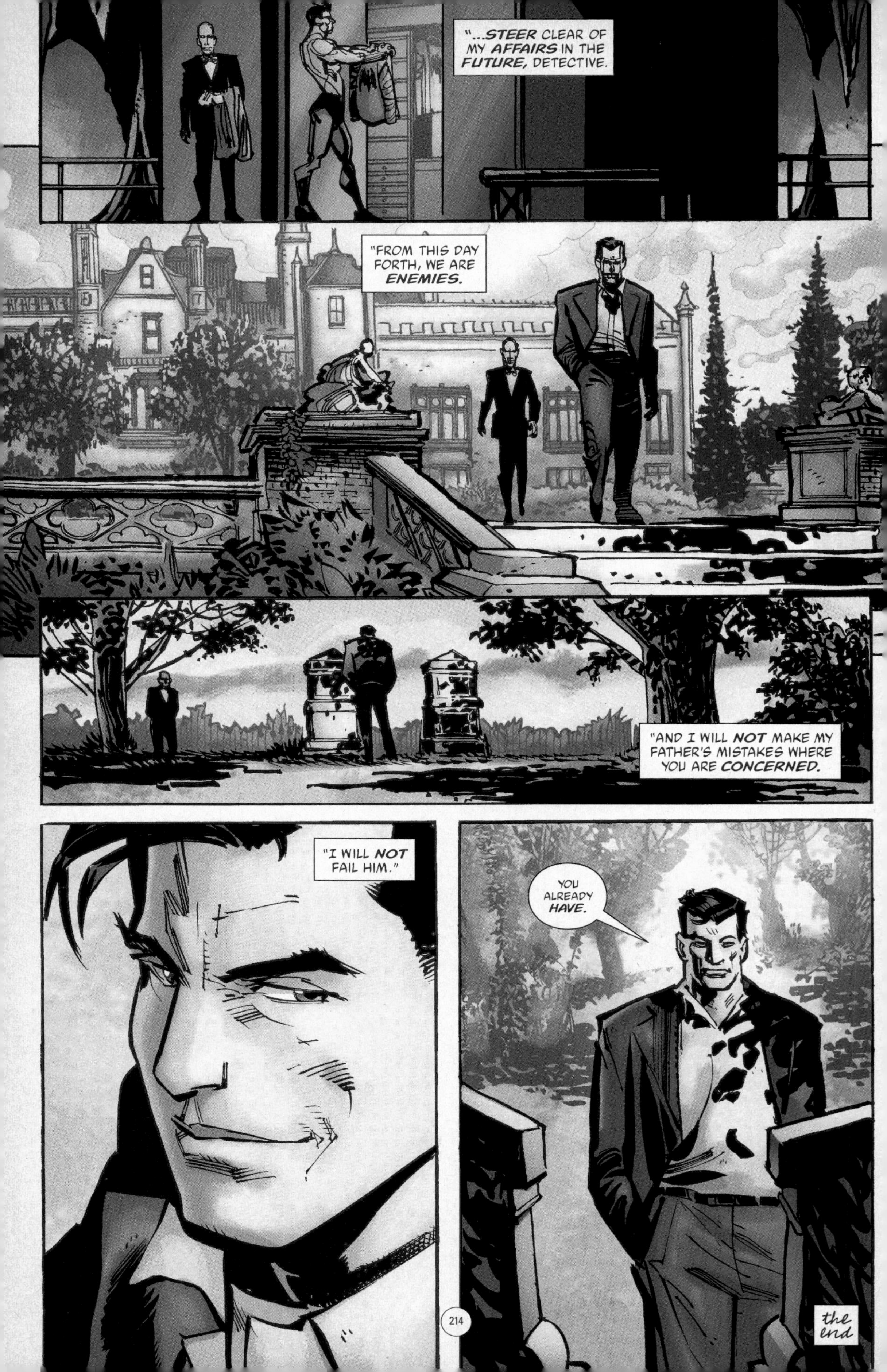
"...STEER CLEAR OF MY AFFAIRS IN THE FUTURE, DETECTIVE.
"FROM THIS DAY FORTH, WE ARE ENEMIES.
"AND I WILL NOT MAKE MY FATHER'S MISTAKES WHERE YOU ARE CONCERNED.
"I WILL NOT FAIL HIM."
YOU ALREADY HAVE.
the end

WORK-IN-PROGRESS by klaus janson

As described in the introduction, this project evolved during its production. As a result, some sequences were moved and others dropped. Additionally, as artist Klaus Janson got deeper into the work, he continued to challenge himself, redrawing already-approved pages. Here is a look at Klaus's work-in-progress.

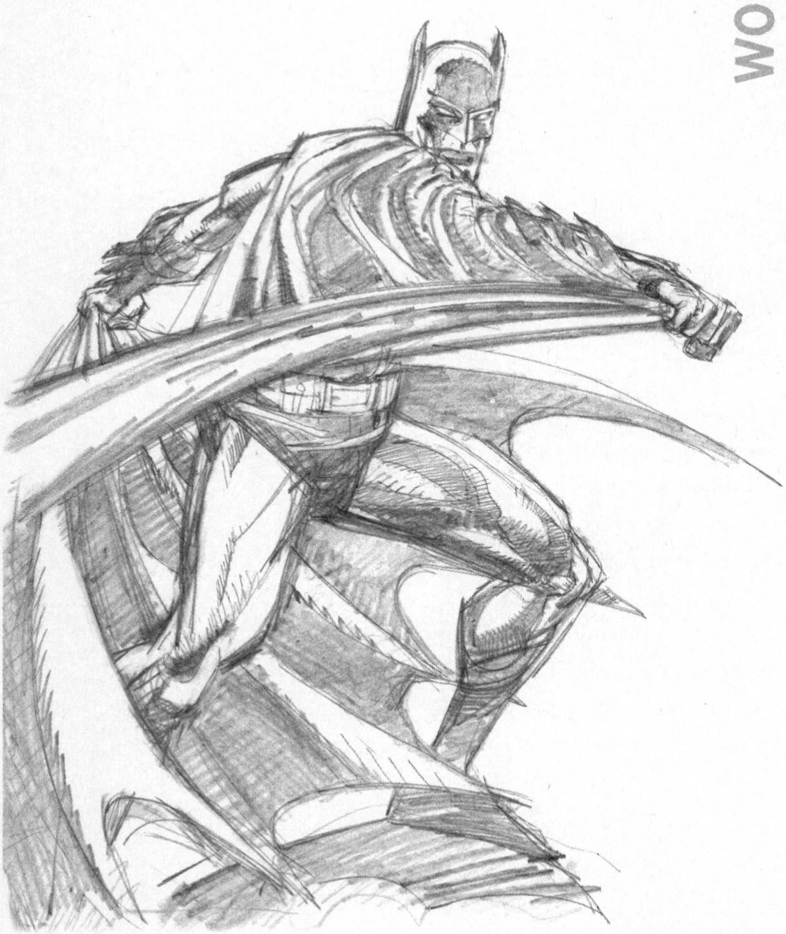

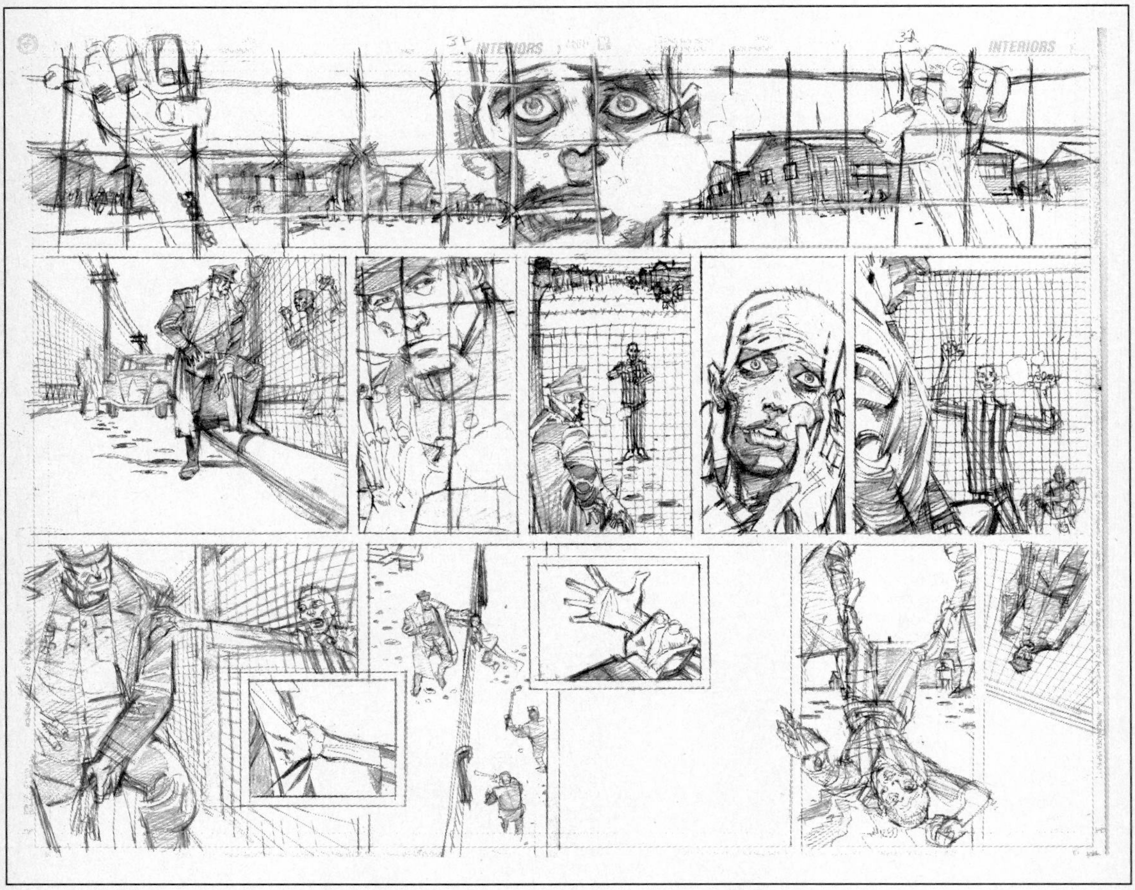
INTERIORS
INTERIORS

One of the most enjoyable aspects of any project is the give-and-take among the creative personnel. I've always believed that the best work incorporates the best ideas from the artist, writer and editor. No matter the individual discipline involved, whether it's art or writing (or music or film or dance, etc), it's important for the individual artist to stretch and challenge the comfort of the known. I remember the specifics of this particular idea very well because I knew this scene would be such a stretch. Greg Rucka, Matt Idelson and I were having one of those infamous story conferences at a diner around the corner from the offices of DC Comics. The meal was over but the story remained unfinished. The three of us stood around outside in the cold winter air determined to squeeze every bit of drama out of the relationship between Nyssa and Ra's. It was Greg who came up with the idea of Nyssa and the concentration camp. The idea that

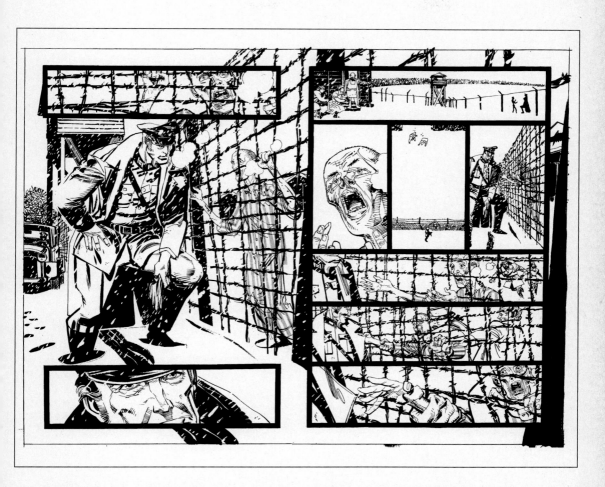

a father would abandon his daughter to a certain death certainly explained a lot of the reasons why Nyssa became who she became. I realized then that the scene would have to be artistically pivotal to the series. I approached it with much trepidation and went through several versions. In these two unfinished examples, I struggled not only to convey the horror of the scene but also with a specific storytelling problem. In the fourth panel, we are supposed to see the two guards from the background start to make their way to Nyssa. It was difficult to show them without diminishing the focus on Ra's and Nyssa. Eventually, I decided to use the version on pg. 217. I went to my class at the School of Visual Arts the next day and showed the class the two versions: the scene from pg. 217 and the scene that was eventually printed. Their reaction was so certain that I changed my mind and submitted the pages that are now part of the story.

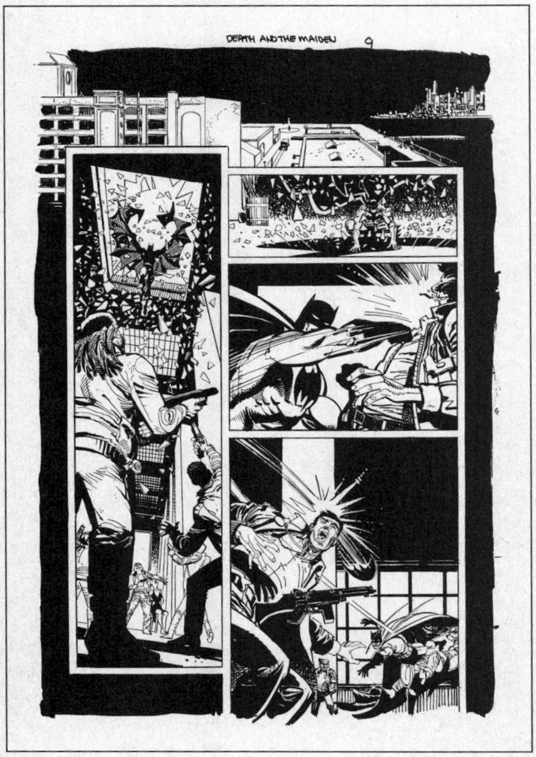
DEATH AND THE MAIDEN 9

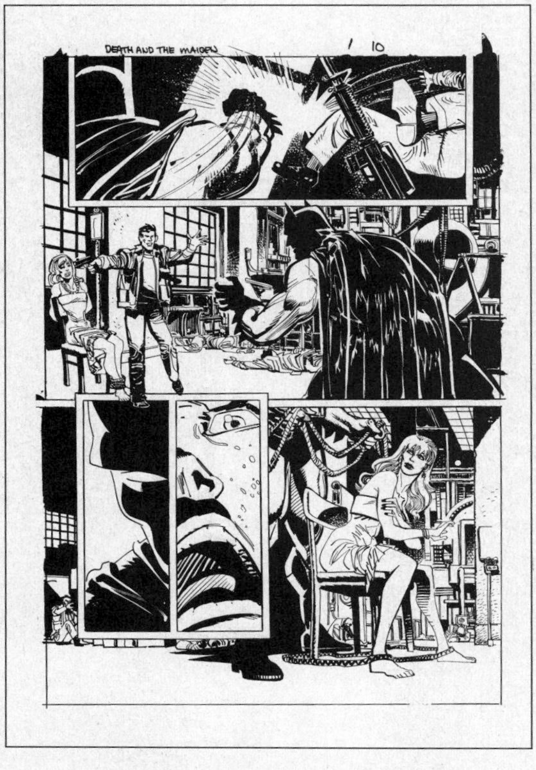
DEATH AND THE MAIDEN 1 10

The original format of *Death and the Maidens* was four books, 48 pages each. I think we all liked the symmetry of that and felt the 48-page length would allow us to pace and develop the story in a less restricted or pressured way. When it was suggested we go to the 22-page format, we were saddled with a whole different set of problems. Not the least of which was that we had about 40 pages already pencilled, inked and written when the format change was decided. That meant we had to, in some cases, literally cut and paste scenes in a new way to meet the demands of the new format. The opening scene, for instance, of Nyssa in her castle was written and drawn more than a year after the following three pages of Bruce, his parents and Batman were finished. Ultimately, the first 48-page book was reconfigured through the first five issues of the monthly series. We didn't do a "clean," wholly new issue until #6. During all that reediting, some scenes were dropped entirely. These two pages were from the first 48-page book.

BATMAN - DEATH AND THE MAIDENS
PG. 14
BATMAN - DEATH AND THE MAIDENS
PG. 15

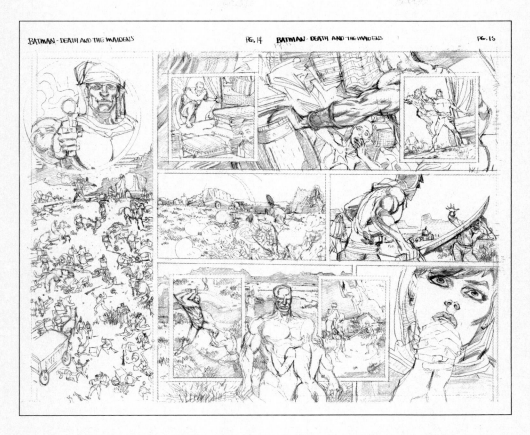

Another scene that was dropped was this four-page sequence between Ubu and a young Nyssa. I had gone through several versions of the double-page spread and finally settled on this one which I thought was pretty good. It was a fun sequence to draw. It wasn't just two people stuck in a room somewhere talking. We open with a slaughtered caravan, Ubu looking, Nyssa hiding, Ubu throwing, Nyssa begging, Ubu and Nyssa riding and coming into Ra's tent. The little bit about Ra's hiding behind a curtain watching Nyssa was a neat character bit. It was a compact and fun sequence to draw. One of the facets of this series that I really liked as an artist was the constant change of locale. It was a challenge to try and make the different locations as individualistic and different from each other as possible. The desert in this scene had its own visual identity separate and apart from the castle in the Baltics or Nyssa's apartment in Metropolis or the bar where Nyssa and Ra's meet in Paris or the synagogue in Poland. I think establishing a credible background is as important as establishing a character. This is the only scene we dropped that I regret not finishing. It would have been a cool four pages.

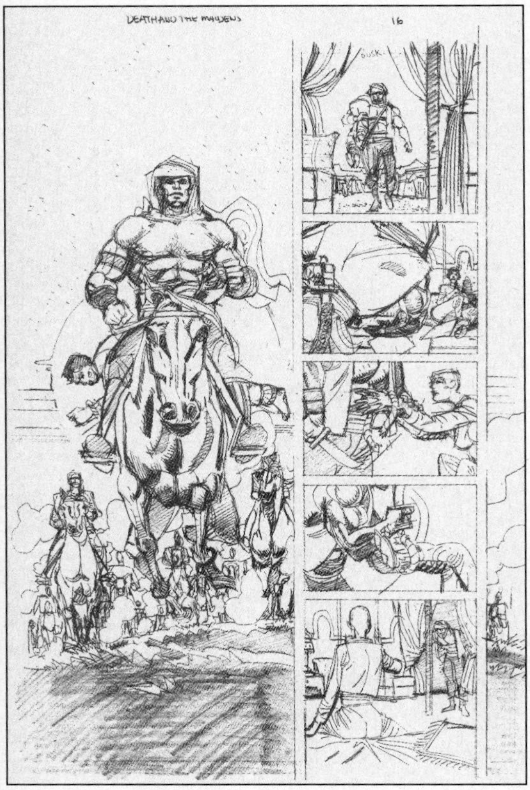
DEATH AND THE MAIDENS
16
DUSK

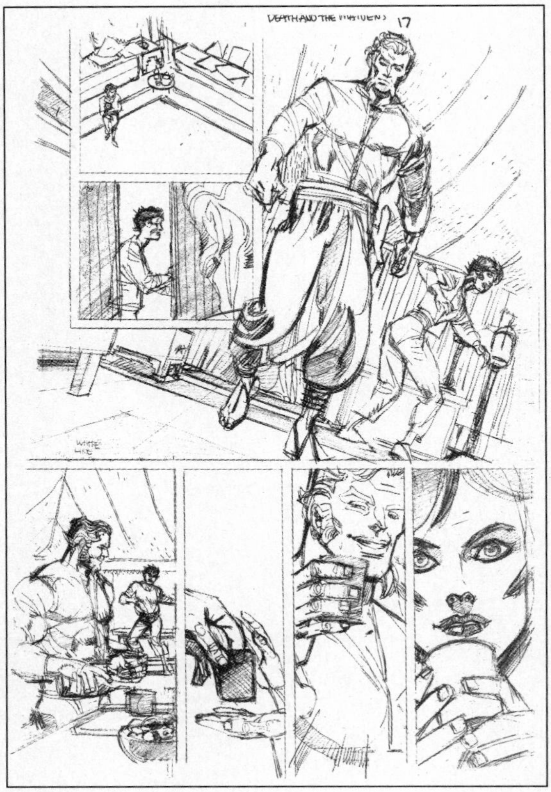
DEATH AND THE MAIDENS
17

This is the end page of the first concentration camp scene. At the time when I drew it, we were unsure if we would ever see the camp again in future issues. It was an extremely important sequence and I wanted to leave an indelible image in the head of the reader. Although we see the camp pretty clearly, I decided it was a mistake to pull the camera as far back as I did. Nyssa is being dragged in the snow by the guards to the camp doctor. I was afraid that the action was lost amidst the panoramic choice of angle. In the printed page, I focused instead on the waiting doctor. I wanted to make sure that the implication of the scene was as clear as possible.

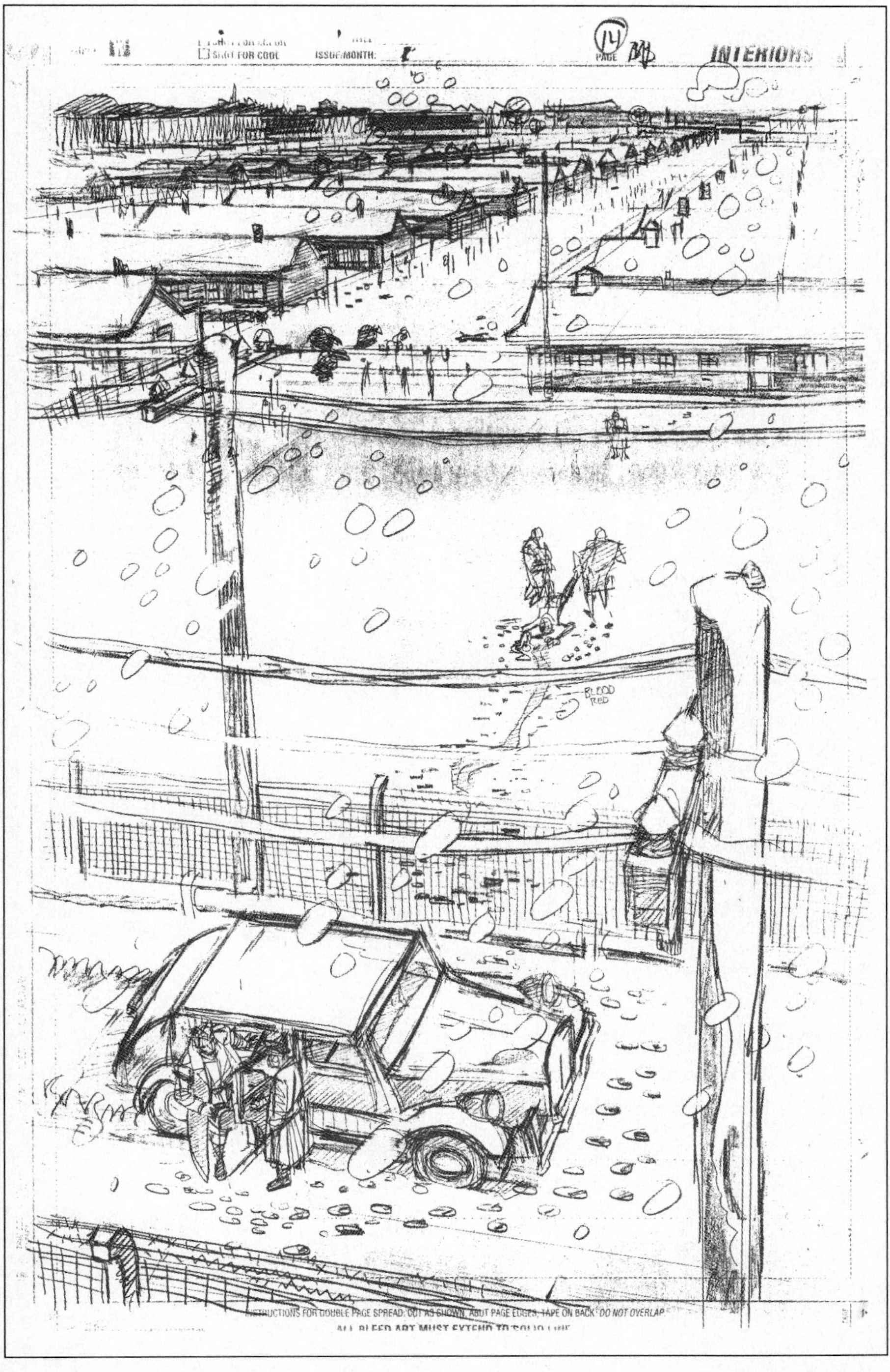
BLOOD
RED

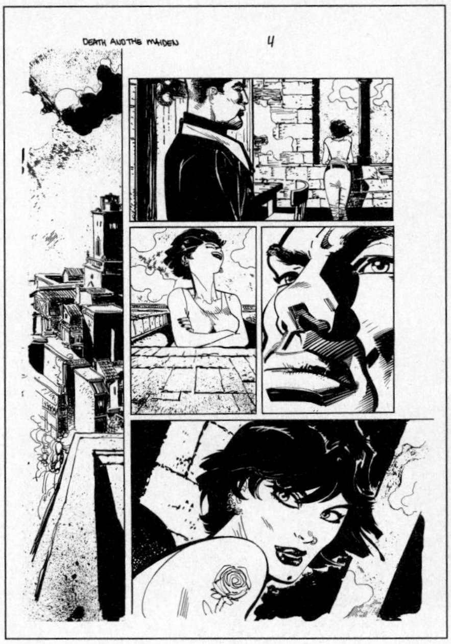
DEATH AND THE MAIDEN
4

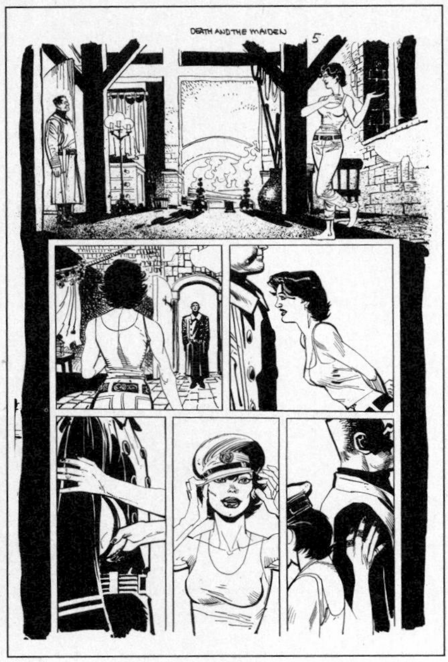
DEATH AND THE MAIDEN
5

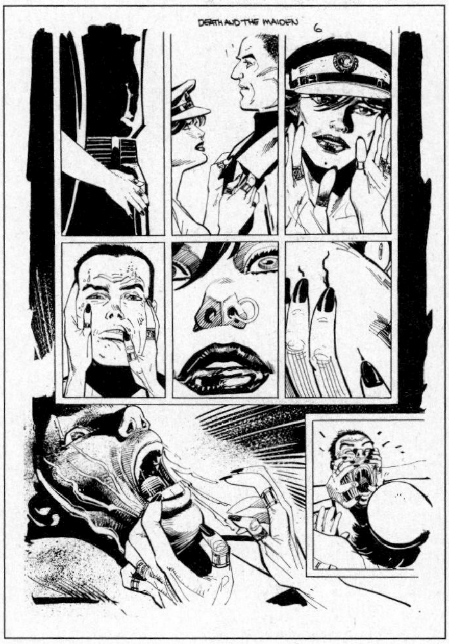
DEATH AND THE MAIDEN
6

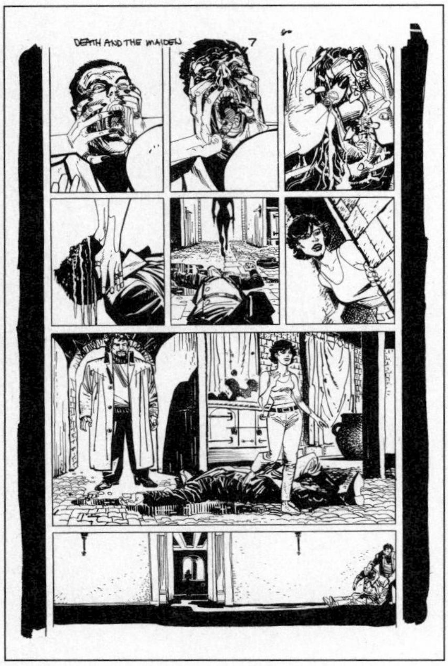
DEATH AND THE MAIDEN
7

These four pages opened the series in the original 48-page format. I think these were the very first pages I drew. We wanted to introduce the character with a memorable scene, so Greg wrote Nyssa crushing the head of the soldier who enters her room. I have to confess that at this stage, I was uncertain about Nyssa and what she was about. Greg wrote her as basically cut off from her emotions and numb from all the years of abuse she had endured. When I read the script I thought she came across as too passive. So I played the scene a bit more aggressively by having her "seduce" the soldier. I liked the idea of Nyssa taking his hat and wearing it as she kills him. I'm always attracted to characterization through purely visual means. Had we decided to use the pages, I would have redrawn most of it and certainly the head-crushing part. I didn't think it worked as well as it could have. It was an interesting idea, but I'm glad we pulled the scene.

This is a first pass at the scene where Nyssa and Talia come back from their night on the town. Nyssa has convinced Talia that she is her friend, and a bit of trust has been established between the two. Poor Talia doesn't know what she's in for. Within a page or two she is kidnapped and taken away for repeated dips in the Lazarus Pit. Sometimes I draw a page and look at it later and I can't remember what the heck I was thinking. This page is one of those: just awful on every level.

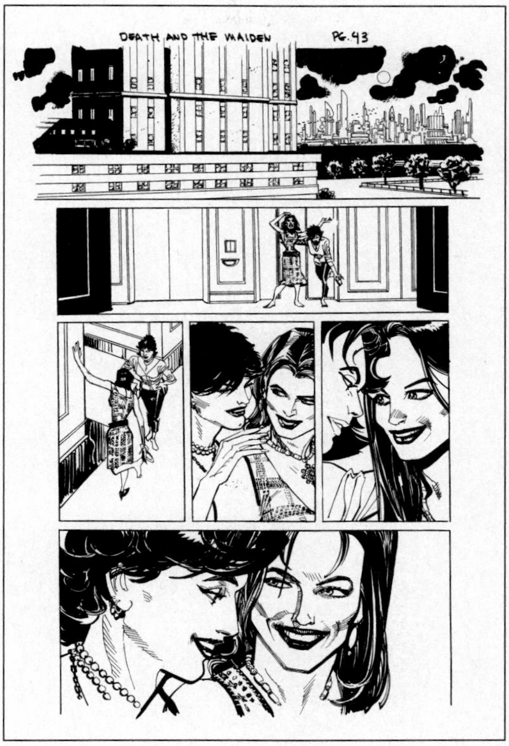
DEATH AND THE MAIDEN
PG. 43

These two pages were from issue 5. Talia emerges from the Pit and attacks Nyssa. I don't remember why we axed these two pages since this sequence still exists in the printed version with only minor alterations. Honestly, I think we just lost track with all the reediting we did, and these pages slipped through the cracks!

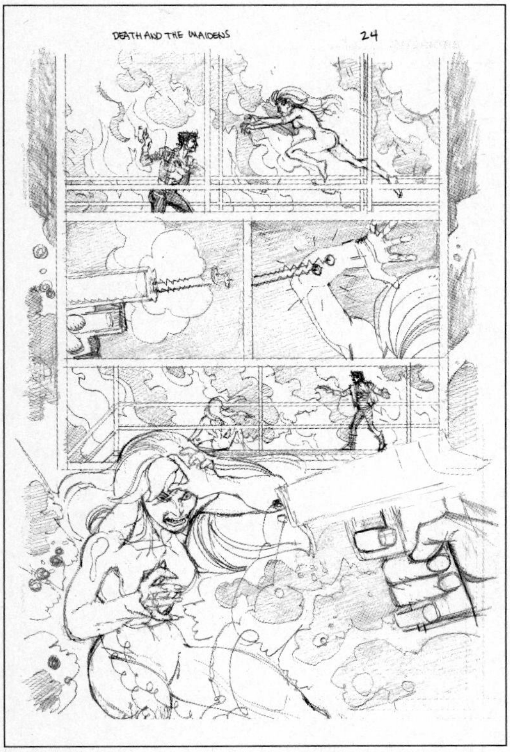
DEATH AND THE MAIDENS
24

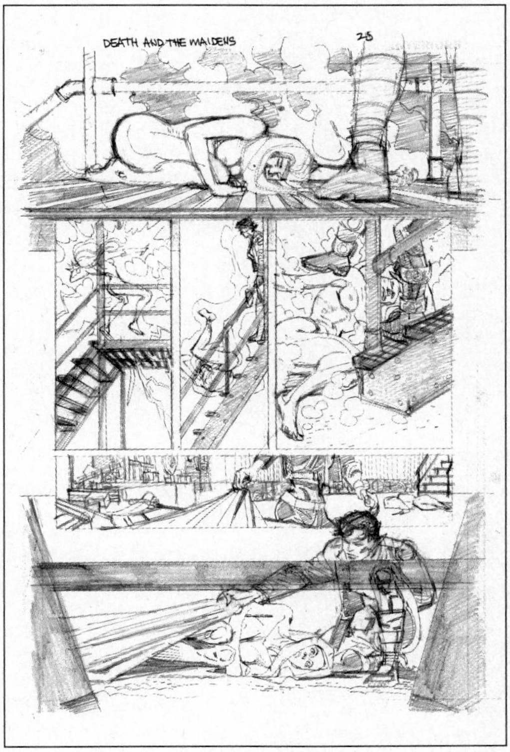
DEATH AND THE MAIDENS
25

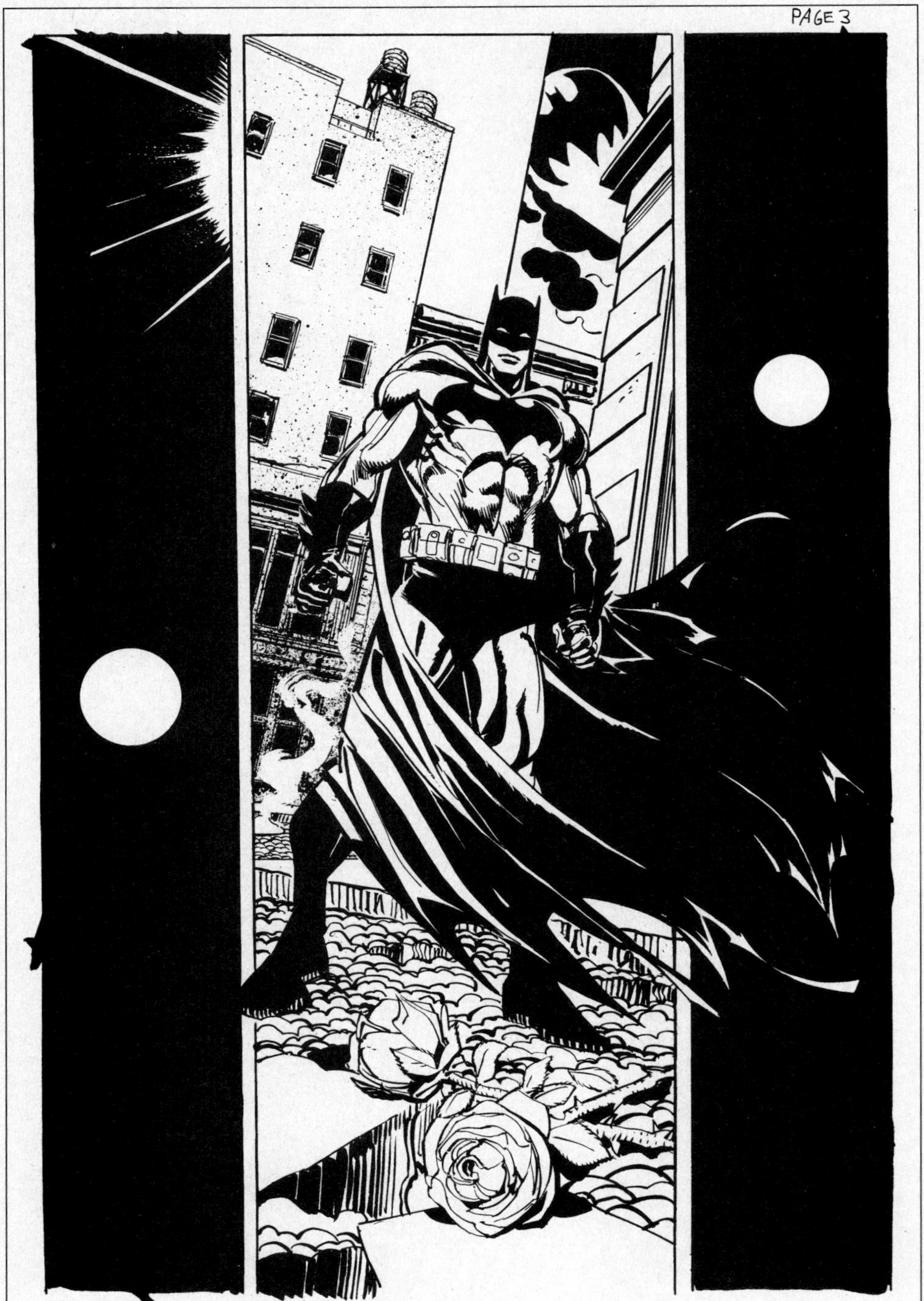
PAGE 3

The first page of the first 48-page book was originally page six of the printed version. So the first words of the series would have been "I can't remember my mother." This page was the original page three of the 48-page book. I redid it simply because I thought I could do it better. Batman seemed a bit too puny and inconsequential here, and I wanted to make him more powerful and threatening. I pushed the figure into the foreground a bit more by having him break the border in a more obvious way. I really liked the second pass much better. It came closer to the way Batman should be: scary!